White Hmong-English
Dictionary

Ernest E. Heimbach

White Hmong-English
Dictionary

SOUTHEAST ASIA PROGRAM PUBLICATIONS
Southeast Asia Program
Cornell University
Ithaca, New York
1966

Cornell Southeast Asia Program Publications
640 Stewart Avenue, Ithaca, NY 14850-3857

LANG-WHITE

© 1966, 1969, 1979 Cornell Southeast Asia Program.
Published in 1966. Ninth Printing 2003.

First published by the Cornell Southeast Asia Program in 1969 under the title,
White Meo-English Dictionary.

Printed in the United States of America

ISBN 0-87727-075-9

FOREWORD

The Southeast Asia Program takes considerable pleasure in being able to publish this <u>White Hmong-English Dictionary</u> in its Linguistic Series of data papers. Besides the value it has in its own right for students and scholars, it has an additional special value as a companion work to the <u>Yao-English Dictionary</u> of Lombard and Purnell. The two together will surely give impetus to Meo-Yao comparative studies. We are gratified to see our objectives in providing basic linguistic materials so soon being realized.

This dictionary, too, is the work of a missionary who is following a long and distinguished tradition of missionary scholarship. Mr. Heimbach has spent a number of years among the White Hmong of Northern Thailand and collected his data in the process of learning the language. The results were first compiled in a mimeographed version for use by a few friends, colleagues and other interested persons. With this publication the dictionary becomes available to a wider audience.

We are especially grateful to Dr. William A. Smalley for bringing this dictionary to our attention and his assistance in bringing it to publication. In particular we thank him for providing the Introduction. Those interested in a more detailed discussion of Hmong phonology are directed to his forthcoming <u>Linguistic Diversity and National Unity in Thailand</u>. We wish also to acknowledge our indebtedness to Mr. Don Rulison for proofreading our typescript in Mr. Heimbach's absence abroad.

Robert B. Jones, Jr.

Ithaca, New York
March 1969

v

FOREWORD TO THE REVISED EDITION

There was little demand for this dictionary in the years immediately following its first publication in 1969. The hundred-or-so copies remaining after libraries and linguists had obtained theirs seemed destined for the scrap-paper dealer when, quite suddenly in 1978, it began to sell rapidly.

The reason for the dictionary's sudden popularity was and is the presence of many thousands of Hmong refugees in Thailand and the United States who are finding it a useful aid.

In reprinting it at this time, we have made two important changes.

First, with the assent and encouragement of Mr. Heimbach, we have substituted "Hmong" for "Meo" in the title, the introductory sections, and the appendices. This has been done to conform to the wishes of Hmong, who object strongly to "Meo" as a derogatory term they themselves would never use.

Second, because the bulk of pages in the first printing made the book's binding extremely weak and subject to easy damage, we have printed the dictionary by photographically reducing two pages onto one. This makes the dictionary slightly more awkward to use, but we hope that it will prove more sturdy under regular use.

We are grateful to Mr. Heimbach for his support and encouragement in making the White Hmong-English Dictionary available again.

David K. Wyatt

Ithaca, New York
July 1979

vi

The Hmong are a vigorous mountain people whose origins were in China and who now by migration extend over the ranges of northern Vietnam, Laos, Burma, and Thailand. In Thailand they probably number in the vicinity of 48,000. Historically they are animists although in China and in Laos large numbers of them have become Christians. In Thailand there are two branches of the tribe, the White Hmong /hmoob dawb/ (Hmong Daw) and the Blue Hmong or Green Hmong /hmoob ntsaub/ (Hmong Njua). There are distinctions in dialect and in dress, but the broad features of the culture and economy are much the same. They often live in close proximity and not infrequently intermarry.

The material in this volume was gathered over the period 1954-1963 in the course of missionary activity among the White Hmong in North Thailand. This included extended residence in Hmong villages, particularly in the provinces of Petchabun and Pitsanuloke. The Hmong in Laos were visited and the language differences compared both there and in other parts of Thailand. From these comparisons and from substantial written material received from Roman Catholic missionaries in Laos, it is evident that the White Hmong spoken in Thailand and in Laos is essentially the same. Divergencies consist mostly of different words adopted from surrounding languages. While the primary material in this volume was collected in North Thailand we feel convinced that is also represents the White Hmong language as spoken in other contiguous areas.

This dictionary is by no means exhaustive, but it does contain the greatest portion of words and phraseology used in everyday speech. Much study remains to be done, particularly in specialized aspects such as the poetic language used in song, the language used in religious rites, and that used in determining and administering justice.

While we have sincerely endeavored to check and recheck this material we readily admit that mistakes may have crept in. Many definitions could also well be clarified and expanded. Before questioning variations in spelling, the reader is advised to consult Appendix 1, which describes tone changes.

Mention must be made of those without whose help this work could not have been completed. A host of Hmong friends have been our patient informants. Rev. G. Linwood Barney

and Dr. William A. Smalley in consultation with Fr. M. Bertrais
of the Catholic Mission in Laos were responsible for the working out of the phonemic analysis and the orthography.
Fr. Bertrais also provided considerable textual material for
comparison. Several missionaries of the Overseas Missionary
Fellowship have helped in the gathering and filing of
material, particularly Miss D. Jones, Miss D. Whitelock, and
Mr. D. Rulison. To all we acknowledge our deep indebtedness.

                                   Ernest E. Heimbach

March 1969

TABLE OF CONTENTS

APPENDICES

INTRODUCTION

The Hmong Daw (White Hmong) of Thailand and Laos speak
a dialect (or rather, a group of very similar dialects) which
is mutually intelligible with those spoken by the Hmong Njua
(Blue or Green Hmong). These are the principal groups of
Hmong dialects spoken in these two countries, and are a part
of the much larger group of languages and dialects known in
South China as the Miao and in Thailand as the Meo. There are
Hmong in North Vietnam as well.

The majority of the work on Hmong/Meo/Miao has been done
on the dialects in China, and by Chinese scholars. Substantive
descriptive and lexographic work on any of the Hmong dialects
spoken in Thailand or Laos is restricted to Downer (1967),
Bertrais (1964), Barney (no date), Lyman (no date), Smalley
(no date), which in turn is based on Barney and Smalley (1952
and 1953), Whitelock (1966-1968), plus less organized inves-
tigations by missionaries in North Thailand.

Hmong is almost universally agreed to be related to Yao
in the Miao-Yao language family, but there is no agreement
as to wider relationships. Haudricourt (1966) summarizes
the theories and gives a bibliography, to which Downer (1963)
should be added. Haudricourt (1966:56) himself comes to the
conclusion that

> The Miao-Yao languages seem to form a link
> between the Austroasiatic and the Tibeto-
> Burman families in the same way that the
> Karen languages do, and their phonological
> richness is useful in reconstruction.

Benedict, on the other hand, is now proposing a place for
the Miao-Yao languages in his Austro-Thai family.

A brief comparison between the present dictionary and
the mimeographed Dictionnaire Hmong-Français (Bertrais, 1964)
may be helpful. They represent substantially the same dialect,
Bertrais having worked in Laos and Heimbach in Thailand, and
the orthographies are virtually the same, for reasons which
will be mentioned below. There are, of course, some minor
differences due to the normal processes of language change,
borrowing, etc. Bertrais' dictionary is somewhat more exten-
sive in its selection of entries and its examples, while the
Heimbach dictionary is more analytical in its definitions.
There is nothing in the Bertrais dictionary to match the
Appendices of the present one.

In short, Heimbach's work is slightly more polished, that of Bertrais slightly more voluminous in examples. They are both important primary documents for White Hmong.

The orthography used in this volume (and in Bertrais, 1964) was developed in Barney and Smalley (1953) as a compromise with Bertrais so that both Roman Catholic and Protestant missions in Laos would use the same system of writing for teaching their constituents to read, for writing books, translating, etc. This fact of compromise accounts for a few details which will seem peculiar to some observers, such as <x> for /s/ and <s> for /š/.

Some other conventions in the orthography are due to an attempt to make it possible to write both Hmong Daw and Hmong Leng with the same system. Thus Hmong Daw /ã/ corresponds to Hmong Njua /ẽ/ and both are written <ee>.

Still other peculiarities resulted from practical considerations in seeking for an orthography which could be easily typed, printed, and taught. The use of consonant symbols in syllable final position to represent tones is not as unconventional in the area as it is outside the area, and works well with Hmong because of the syllable structure which has no phonemic final consonants. The extremely complex initial consonant system required considerable ingenuity in improvisation of an orthography easy for the Hmong reader to learn and use.

<ŋ- ww -on -d -x> were all added by Heimbach and/or Bertrais subsequent to Barney and Smalley (1953). They represent marginal phenomena for which varying interpretations are possible.

The orthography, then, is designed for popular use. It omits many features of stress, juncture, and intonation, which would be of value to linguistic description, but which would hardly appear in dictionary entries anyhow, although they might well be included in the examples and context citations.

We will summarize the general phonological features here, including only what is necessary for a clear understanding of the orthography used in this dictionary. A non-technical description for the non-linguist will be found following this Introduction.

The Hmong Daw syllable has three constituents: a consonant constituent, a vowel constituent and a tone constituent. Either consonant constituent or vowel con-

stituent may be composite. Phonologically there is no
final consonant, but nasalization (occurring in one kind of
composite vowel) is often realized as final [ŋ] and tone
/m/ often has an accompanying non-distinctive final [ʔ].

The inventory of the consonants, vowels, and tones is
presented in the following charts in such a way as to give
a general idea of their pronunciation. Symbols used are
those of the orthography, with additional clarification
in [ ] immediately below when required.

CONSONANTS, SIMPLE AND COMPOSITE

Labial	Lateral release	Dental	Glottalized	Dental, affricated	Retroflexed	Palatal	Palatal, affricated	Velar	Back velar	Glottal
p	pl	t	d	tx	r	c	ts	k	q	
			[ʔd]	[ts]	[ṭ]		[tš]		[ḳ]	[ʔ]
ph	plh	th	dh	txh	rh	ch	tsh	kh	qh	
	[pɫ]		[ʔth]	[tsh]	[ṭh]		[tšh]		[ḳh]	
np	npl	nt		ntx	nr	nc	nts	nk	nq	
[mb]	[mbl]	[nd]		[ndz]	[ṇḍ]	[ñj]	[ndž]	[ŋg]	[ŋ̣g]	
nph	nplh	nth		ntxh	nrh	nch	ntsh	nkh	nqh	
[mph]	[mpɫ]			[ntsh]	[ṇṭh]	[ñch]	[ntšh]	[ŋkh]	[ŋ̣kh]	
m	nl	n				ny		g		
	[ml]					[ñ]		[ŋ]		
hm	hnl	hn				hny				
[M]	[Mml]	[N]				[Ñ]				
f	hl	x			s	xy				h
	[ɫ]	[s]			[š]	[x̣]				
v	l				z	y				
					[ž]					

Initial glottal stop is not marked. Absence of such
a glottal stop is indicated by <'>.

VOWELS, SIMPLE AND COMPOSITE

Front	Central		Back	
	non-nasal	nasal	non-nasal	nasal
i	w [ɨ]	ww [ɨ̃ŋ]	u	oo [õŋ]
e	a	ee [ʌ̃ŋ]	o [ɔ]	on [ɔ̃]
ai [ay]	aw [ə̞ɨ]		au [ɔw]	
ia			ua [uə]	

/ww/ and /on/ are extra-systematic and rare.

TONES

b	j	v	s	g	m	/	d
[⌐]	[ˎ]	[ˏ]	[⊣]	[_|]	[↲]	[_|ˀ]	[ˏ]

Tone values are given as in isolation. Tone symbols are written in final position in the orthographic syllable. /g/ is characterized by breathiness, /m/ by glottal constriction as well as pitch. [m d] are probably the same phoneme, but the evidence is not clear; see Appendix 1. Two words in the dictionary are listed with an <x> 'tone,' but this is an intonational feature better handled in some other way.

BIBLIOGRAPHY

Barney, G. Linwood
    n.d.   Unpublished Hmong Njua fieldwork, Xieng Khouang, Laos, 1950-1954.

Berney, G. Linwood, and William A. Smalley
    1952   <u>Report of Second Conference on Problems in Meo (Miao) Phonemic Structure and Orthography</u>. (mimeo).

    1953   <u>Third Report on Meo (Miao): Orthography and Grammar</u>. (mimeo).

Benedict, Paul K.
    n.d.   Austro-Thai (to be published by the Human
            Relations Area Files, New Haven, Connecticut).

Bertrais-Charrier, M.
    1964   Dictionnaire Hmong-Français. (mimeo). Vientiane:
            Mission Catholique.

Downer, G. B.
    1963   "Chinese, Thai and Miao-Yao," in Shorto (Ed.)
            1963: 133-139.

    1967   "Tone Change and Tone-Shift in White Miao,"
            Bulletin of the School of Oriental and
            African Studies. 30.3:589-599.

Haudricourt, André-G.
    1947-50 "Introduction à la phonologie historique des
            langues miao-yao," Bulletin de l'Ecôle Français
            d'Extrême Orient. 44.2:555-76.

    1966   "The Limits and Connections of Austroasiatic in
            the Northeast," in Zide 1966:44-56.

Lewis, Paul
    1968   Akha-English Dictionary. Ithaca, New York:
            Cornell University, Southeast Asia Program.

Lombard, Sylvia J. (compiler) and Herbert C. Purnell (Ed.)
    1968   Yao-English Dictionary. Ithaca, New York:
            Cornell University, Southeast Asia Program.

Lyman, Thomas A.
    n.d.   Unpublished Hmong Njua (Blue/Green Meo) research,
            Nan Province, Thailand.

Savina, F. M.
    1916   Dictionnaire Miao-tseu-français, Bulletin de
            l'Ecôle Française d'Extrême-Orient 16.

    1926   Dictionnaire Français-man, Bulletin de l'Ecôle
            Française d'Extrême-Orient 26.

Shorto, H. L. (Ed.)
    1963   Linguistic Comparison in South East Asia and
            the Pacific. London: University of London,
            School of Oriental and African Studies.

Smalley, William A.
     1962   Manual of Articulatory Phonetics. Tarrytown,
              N. Y.: Practical Anthropology.

     n.d.   Linguistic Diversity and National Unity in
              Thailand (forthcoming). Contains a chapter on
              Hmong (Meo).

Whitelock, Doris A.
     1966-1968 White Meo Language Lessons. Chiang Mai,
              Thailand: Overseas Missionary Fellowship (mimeo).

Zide, Norman H. (Ed.)
     1966   Studies in Comparative Austroasiatic Linguistics.
              The Hague: Mouton and Co.

The letters of the English alphabet have been used throughout, but in many cases symbolizing a sound different from that represented in English or other European languages. This must be carefully kept in mind.

There are also cases where one symbol may be used for sounds which are not exactly the same. These never confuse Hmong readers but must be carefully noted by those learning the language. For example, the 't' of 'tuaj' is unaspirated and voiceless similar to the 't' in the English word steak, whereas the 't' in 'ntawm' is voiced like the 'd' in English condemn because it is influenced by the 'n' which immediately precedes it.

The basic syllable pattern is CV, i.e., one consonant followed by one vowel. However, in place of the C there may be a cluster of one to three consonants pronounced as a unit. In place of the V there may also be a cluster of two vowels.

The only consonant sound which occurs at the close of a syllable is [ng]. Since this occurs only with nasalized vowels it is recognized as belonging to these nasalized vowels, which are written with a double letter. Thus 'ee' and 'oo' are always said with an [ng] ending.

Each syllable has a basic tone. This is symbolized by one of several consonant letters written at the close of the syllable. Since no syllable requires a consonant symbol to represent a spoken consonant in final position, this lends no confusion. See the tone chart below.

Whereas the Hmong language is for the most part isolating in structure, (i.e. each syllable usually carries meaning on its own), in actual speech some syllables are said in closer connection than others. We have therefore joined these together into words.

We include here an approximate description of the sounds used in Hmong speech in terms of the nearest similar sound in English. It is impossible to be altogether exact, but this section is meant for the benefit of those who would find it difficult to understand technical description.

Note that 'n' is used to represent nazalization and 'h' to represent aspiration (a puff of air).

xvii

CONSONANTS

Hmong Symbol	English Equivalent or Description
p	unaspirated 'p' (without a puff of air) as in English speak. Cf. the 'p' in French, Thai, etc.
ph	'p' with a puff of air, as in part
np	English 'm' blending into a 'b'
nph	English 'm' blending into Hmong 'ph'
pl	like the 'pl' in explode
plh	like the 'pl' in play
npl	English 'm' blending into the English 'bl'
nplh	English 'm' blending into English initial 'pl'
t	unaspirated 't' (without a puff of air) as in steak. Cf. the 't' in French, Thai, etc.
th	't' with a puff of air, as in talk
nt	English 'n' blending into English initial 'd'
nth	English 'n' blending into English initial 't'
tx	like the 'ds' in adds but without the vocal cords vibrating
txh	like the 'ts' in cats
ntx	English 'n' blending into the Hmong 'tx'
ntxh	English 'n' blending into the Hmong 'txh'
d	like the 'd' in dream but with a glottal stop before it. That is, complete stop of the air flow in the throat before beginning the sound.
dh	the Hmong sound 'd' said with a puff of air after it
r	similar to the Hmong 't' but made with the tip of the tongue curved back until it hits the top of the mouth

Hmong Symbol	English Equivalent or Description
rh	the Hmong 'r' said with a puff of air following
nr	'n' blending into the Hmong 'r'
nrh	'n' blending into the Hmong 'rh'
c	made by closing off the air with a hump of the tongue behind ridge back of the upper teeth. Similar to the 'ty' in put you
ch	the Hmong sound 'c' with a puff of air
nc	'n' blending into the Hmong sound 'c'
nch	'n' blending into the Hmong sound 'c' following by a puff of air
ts	like the 'j' in jot but without the vocal cords vibrating
tsh	similar to the 'ch' in chop
nts	'n' blending into the Hmong sound 'ts' Similar to the 'nj' in unjust
ntsh	similar to the 'nch' in inch
k	unaspirated (without a puff of air) as in skill. Cf. the 'k' in French, Thai, etc.
kh	'k' with a puff of air as in kite
nk	'n' blending into a 'g' as in finger
nkh	'n' blending into a 'k'
q, qh, nq, nqh	these are the counterparts of 'k' etc., but made way back in the mouth behind the position where the English 'k' is made
n, f, h	as in English
s	as 'sh' in English (e.g., shoe)
v, m, l, y	as in English
x	like the 's' in see or sip

Hmong Symbol	English Equivalent or Description
z	like the 'z' in <u>azure</u>
xy	the Hmong 'x' (as described above) blending into a 'y'
ny	Similar to the 'ni' in <u>menial</u> or <u>Virginia</u>
hny	'h' blending into the Meo sound 'ny'
hl	'h' blending into an 'l' but without the vocal cords vibrating. Similar to the Welsh 'll'
nl	'm' blending into an 'l' as the 'ml' in <u>seemly</u>
hn	'h' and 'n' said as a unit
hm	'h' and 'm' said as a unit
hnl	the Hmong 'nl' preceded by an 'h' and said as one unit
g	the 'ng' of <u>sing</u> but used as an initial consonant. This particular phoneme is found in only a very few Hmong words.

VOWELS

Hmong Symbol	English Equivalent or Description
a	roughly equivalent to the 'a' in the New England (or British) pronunciation of <u>father</u>
ai	a vowel cluster composed of the Hmong 'a' and 'i' somewhat similar to the vowel in <u>try</u> but not as a long a glide
au	a vowel cluster composed of the Hmong 'a' and 'u' something between the 'ou' of <u>ouch</u> and the 'ow' of <u>throw</u>
aw	somewhat similar to the Oxford English <u>Oh</u>
e	similar to the 'e' in <u>they</u>
ee	nasalized vowel varying from the 'ing' of <u>ring</u> toward the 'ung' of <u>rung</u> depending upon the preceding consonant

Hmong Symbol	English Equivalent or Description
i	similar to the 'e' in we
ia	a vowel cluster composed of the Hmong 'i' and 'a' somewhat similar to the combined vowels 'ee' and 'a' in see a man
o	somewhat similar to the 'aw' in law or the 'o' in lost
oo	nasalized vowel something between the 'o' of do followed by 'ng' and the 'o' of lost followed by 'ng'
u	somewhat similar to the 'o' in do or the 'ou' in through
ua	a vowel cluster composed of the Hmong 'u' and 'a' somewhat similar to the combined vowels in to a as heard in rapid speech
w	There is no English equivalent of this vowel. It is something between the Hmong 'i' and the 'u' made mid way back in the mouth with the tongue close to the palate.
ww	No English equivalent. It is like the Hmong 'w' with 'ng' following it. This vowel only appears in a very few words. e.g. loj hwwv' Very large. 'zoo hwwv' Very good.
-n	representing nasalization on one vowel without the 'ng' quality of 'ee' and 'oo.' Thus, 'hon' sounds like the 'aw' of law preceded by 'h' and said "through the nose." e.g. 'ua li no hons' Like this. 'yuav kuv qhia nej hons' Must I teach you?

almost all Hmong vowels are preceded by a glottal
stop when said in isolation, i.e., as a syllable
without a consonant beginning. By this we
mean the throat is closed before the sound is
initiated as in the English Oh oh! However,
there are some words without consonant beginning
where the glottal stop is absent. This is
significant, and we indicate the absence of
initial glottal stop by the apostrophe.

xxi

Hmong Symbol	English Equivalent or Description

e.g.	koj tias yog kuv,	You said it was I,
	yog koj 'auj!	but it was you!
	mus ho tuaj 'ov	Come again.
	nws tuaj noj 'auv	He came to eat!
	txujkum dim 'oj	How will we escape?
	ua lawm 'os	(I) did it.

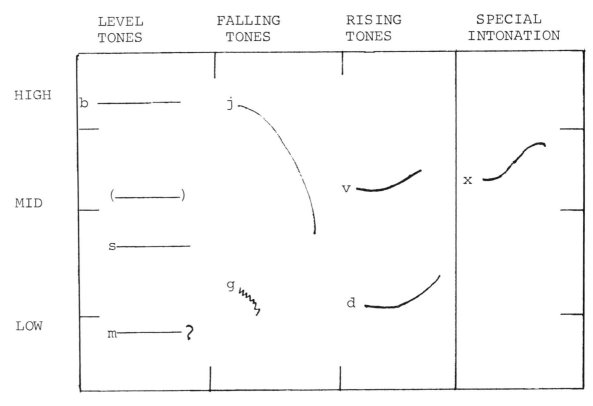

CHART OF WHITE HMONG TONAL PATTERN

Tone Chart: Explanatory Notes

1. Since no syllable ends in a final consonant, the tone
    (except the mid tone) is indicated by an English consonant
    letter written at the end of each syllable and corre-
    sponding to the chart above. Where no special tone
    mark is written, the word has a mid tone. Relative
    pitch, length and contour of the tones is indicated
    on the chart.

2. The tone chart is drawn to indicate the tones as heard
    in isolation. That is, as heard on separate unconnected

xxii

syllables. In the normal flow of speech these tones tend to vary somewhat in pitch and quality depending both upon patterns of stress and upon the influence of other contiguous tones. This should be carefully noted.

3. Note that tone '-m' ends in a glottal stop and is said with some constriction of the throat. Tone '-g' is characterized by considerable breathiness.

4. Special intonation pattern '-x' indicates a particular tone contour given some words to indicate wonder or surprise. It appears most often in final particles. See Appendix 1, for illustrations. Note that it is not a tone phoneme in the same category as the other tones here indicated but is symbolized in the same way as these other tones for convenience.

5. Tone '-d' appears only on a certain class of words. Historically it probably was a conditioned variant of tone '-m' and in all the illustrations we have thus far, the '-d' tone appears on words which elsewhere have the tone '-m.' The majority of these words are nouns but illustrations also include verbs and post verbal particles. Tone '-d' is most noticeable on words indicating time or location, such as:

> thaud, tamsid, ib sid, ntawd, nrad, nraud, ped, saud, tid, tod

There are one or two words which almost always appear with tone '-d' and very seldom with tone '-m', and therefore, we treat '-d' as a completely separate tone (See Appendix 1).

ORDER OF ENTRIES

All syllables, and words of more than one syllable,
are listed under the initial in English alphabetical order.
Consonant clusters are treated as units, so that all entries
beginning with 'tx' appear before any entries beginning
with 'txh,' etc.

Within each vowel category, listed in English alphabetical order, the syllables are grouped by tones with the
mid tone put first. Thus:

The order of the vowels is:		The order of tones is:
a	ia	___( )
ai	o	___b
au	on	___d
aw	oo	___g
e	u	___j
ee	ua	___m
i	w	___s
	ww	___v

After each noun, the appropriate classifier is given
in parentheses.

ABBREVIATIONS

(C)	from Chinese
cf.	confer, compare
clf.	classifier
colloq.	colloquial
contr.	contrast
cont'd.	continued
def.	definition
e.g.	for example
i.e.	that is
n.	noun
ptcl.	particle
(p.v.int.)	post verbal intensifier (see Appendix 8)
(T)	from Thai
(t.c.)	tone change This is a tone change from the word to which you are referred; or this word is subject to tone change. (See Appendix 1)
v.	verb

a

ab Exclamatory initial particle.
    Ab! us cas kuv tsis nloog? Why didn't I listen?

1. as Exclamatory initial particle.
       As! kuv pom Zab! Aha! I see Mr. Zab.

2. as Exclamatory final particle.
       Kuv tsis paub as! I don't know!

av Earth, ground, mud.
    av zom zom Sticky mud.
    lo lo av Muddy, dirty.
    roj av Kerosene.
    hmoov av Dust, powdery soil.
    av noo noo Damp, moist ground.
    av xuav Loose ground.
    pob av luaj Anthill.
    pob av muas yis tib Anthill.
    nyob saum plua tshauv av On the ashes and the ground.

1. aib A species of bird (tus).

2. aib

    aib yab! An exclamation of disgust or impatience.

aim A word used in cursing (lus dev).

ais Initial exclamatory particle.
     Ais, koj yuav hais li cas? Well then, what do you say?
     (Often used in running conversation in much the
      same way as "Well... Then...")

aiv To oppress, yoke, seal with a curse (cf. 'khaum').
     Dab tuaj aiv yus. The spirits come to trouble one.

aub Dog (tus) (as used in some places; cf. 'dev' which
     is more common).

'aub Final exclamatory particle.
      Yuav tau luag dua 'aub! You will have more company!

auj Exclamatory initial particle.
     Auj, tsis zoo lauj Oh, it is ruined!
     Auj, tsis pom lauj Oh, it has disappeared!

'auj Final emphatic particle.
      Koj yuav quaj 'auj! You will weep!
      Txhob ua li ko 'auj Stop it!

1. auv
    Faj suab auv auv It's foggy, misty.

2. auv txiv mam auv (lub) The pumelo (T).

'auv Final emphatic particle.
      Nws tuaj noj 'auv! He will come to eat!
      Cav mus thiab 'auv! He went after all!

1. aws Particle used in conversation as an acknowledgement
        of having heard what was said. (As we would say
        ...Yes...Yes..., etc.) Agreement.

2. aws Mob aws Newcastle disease in poultry.

3. aws To mark out, identify as one's own.
        "Qab teb peb xub ncaws, nkauj nyab peb xub aws."
        (cf. 'ncaws').

e

eb Initial exclamatory particle.
    Kuv hais tias, "Eb! muaj tus kevcai dabtsi?" I said,
    "Eh! What's going on?"

1. es Particle used to indicate pause in a flow of speech.

2. es Mes es (tus) Goat (but not used as commonly as
       'mias ias' cf. 'tshis').

ev To carry on the back (as a child, a basket, etc.)
    (cf. 'ris').

eeb A saddle.
     Eeb nees Horse saddle.

i The former, the one just seen or dealt with, previously.
   tus i That one before (just seen).
   zaum i The former occasion.
   thaum i Previously, the former time.

1. ib Numeral one.
   ib tug One person.
   ib ntsis A moment.
   ib chim A little while.
   ib tsam Several hours.
   ib txhij All together.
   ib txhia Some, a portion.
   ib sim Continuously.
   ib sim neej A lifetime.
   ib txhis tsis kawg Forever.
   (a) ib sim tom los Forever, continually.
   (b) ib los ib txhis Forever, continually.
   ib sij ua To do together.

2. ib A cock's comb (lub).
   ib qaib Cock's comb.
   ib qaib ntsau A cock's comb that is spread out a bit.

3. ib To make excuse, seek to escape obligation.
   Lawv ib. They deliberately refuse to accept the charge
             or face the issue.

4. ib To lean against, to lean (cf. 'pheeb').

5. ib Idiom for "as soon as."
   Ib noj mov txawm mob plab. As soon as I had eaten I
                               had a tummy ache.

ia
   liaj ia Lands, teritory.
   liaj ia tebchaws Fields and lands.

1. iab Bitter.

2. iab oo To haze (cf. 'faj suab').

3. iab p.v. int. joined with 'ntsa.'
   (a) ci ntsa iab Bright and glittering.
   (b) ci qos iab Bright and glittering.
   hauv ntuj ntsa iab The horizon just becoming bright,
                       early dawn.

1. iam A kind of small parrot (tus).

2. iam
   (a) menyuam mos liab A new baby, very young child.
   (b) menyuam iam liab A new baby, very young child.

ias mias ias (tus) A goat (This term is used in imitation
                     of the goat's cry. It is sometimes said 'mes es.'
                     cf. tshis for the actual name).

1. iav piam iav A kind of grass or short vegetation.
        hav iav A grassy valley.

2. iav tsom iav (daim) A mirror.

o To swell, be inflamed.

1. ob The numeral two.

2. ob ob cag Others.
       kwvtij ob cag peb txhais All others, brethren and
                                 outsiders.
       tej moos ob cag People of other cities.

oj Exclamatory initial particle.
    Oj, ua li cas? Oh, how is that?
    Oj, lawv tauj sub Oh, they have come haven't they?

'oj Final question particle.
     Txaus tsawg leej ris 'oj? Enough for how many to carry?
     Txujkum dim 'oj? How will (he) escape?

os The duck (tus).

'os Final emphatic particle.
     Tuaj 'os. You've come.
     Pom 'os. I see it.
     Ua lawm 'os (I) have done it.

'ov Final emphatic particle.
     Nej saib 'ov! You watch!
     Mus ho tuaj 'ov Come again.

oo iab oo Haze (cf.'faj suab').

<u>u</u>

u siab Not happy in heart, dissatisfied (cf. 'dhuav siab').
ntshai u koj siab mentsis I'm afraid you won't be
   very happy about it.

1. ub Extreme limit.
thaum ub Long ago, way back when.
pem ub Way up there (up the hill, up north).
(a) tim ub Way over there across the valley.
(b) puag tim ub Way over there across the valley.

2. ub no (unrestricted p.v. int. cf. APPENDIX p. 468).
(a) ua ub ua no To do this and that.
(b) ua li ub ua li no To do this and that.
hais li ub hais li no To say this and that.

us The camel (tus) (T).
tus tsiaj us The camel.

uv To bear with, be patient under provocation.
uv taus To be able to bear with it.
ua tiag uv To make a real effort to bear it.

1. ua To make, to do (in certain contexts 'to be').
ua teb To make fields, to do field work.
ua zoo zoo To do well.
Nws ua txiv He is the father.
ua dab To do spirit rites.
ua neeb To do spirit rites.
(a) ua ub ua no To do this and that.
(b) us li ub ua li no To do this and that.
Ua li lawm That's the way it is. (or) Is that so?
Ua li koj hais Just as you say.
ua si To play.
(Used with certain p.v.int. cf. APPENDIX 8).
ua ntias To cast aside.
ua nkauj To come to young womanhood.
ua hlo To do right away.
ua quj qees To do perserveringly.
ua luaj (p.v. int.) greatly, very.
   mob ua luaj Hurts terribly.
ua zom zaws To do all together, many engaged in it.

2. ua (a) Ua li cas Why? How? (cf. 'cas').
(b) Ua cas Why? How? (cf. 'cas').

3. ua ua li no In this way, in that case.

uab The crow (tus).
uab lag A kind of black wild bird.

uaj Exclamatory particle indicating pain.

1. uas Which, that which.
tus uas The one which.
thaum uas The time which, when.

2. uas Sometimes used as a particle to express pause in a
      flow of speech.
no uas ...er, that is,....

3. uas Completive particle used to express indignation.
koj tsis teb dabtsi uas! So you won't answer!!

uav
   mob uav mob ruas Leprosy (cf. 'ruas').

<u>w</u>

1. w To scatter by overhand throw.
w noob To scatter seed (by overhand throw).

2. w The quail (tus).
noog w The quail.

wb We two, (first person dual pronoun).

C

ca (t.c.) (cf. 'cav').

1. cab To lead, take along (forcibly, or with a rope as an animal).
   cab nees To lead a horse.
   cab tibneeg los tsev Bring him home (against his inclination).

2. cab Intestinal or abdominal worms (tus).
   mob plab cab To have intestinal worms.

1. cag Roots.
   cag ntoo Tree roots.
   nkoj cag Uprooted tree.

2. cag Others.
   ob cag Others.
   kwvtij ob cag peb txhais All others, brethren and outsiders.

caj Pertaining to certain parts of the body.
   caj pas Throat.
   caj dab Neck.
   caj tw Buttocks (cf. ntsag) (animal or human).
   caj npab The arm (upper).
   (a) caj ntswm The bridge of the nose.
   (b) txiv caj ntswm The bridge of the nose.
   caj qaum The backbone.
   caj qwb The depression at the back of the neck.
   ua tuv txias tom caj qwb Like a louse biting the back of my neck (talking behind my back).
   hais nraum caj qwb Talking behind one's back.

1. cam To argue, disagree (contr. cav).
   sib cam To argue together.
   cam thawj To disobey, not listen to authority.
   txhob cam txhob chaj Don't be stubborn and bullheaded.

2. cam Log cam A chopping block (lub).

1. cas Why? How? (in combination with other words).
   (a) Ua li cas ua? How is it done or made?
   Ua li cas? Why? How?
   (b) Ua cas Why? How?
   ua li cas ua? How is it done or made?
   Ua li cas yuav mus? Why go?
   Yuav ua li cas mus? How shall we go?
   Ua li cas nws tsis los? Why hasn't he come?
   Mob ua li cas tuaj? How did the illness start?
   Ua li cas kuj yog Whichever way is all right with me.

2. cas A kind of venereal disease.
   (a) mob yeeg To have venereal disease with pussy discharge.
   (b) mob cas To have venereal disease with pussy discharge.

1. cav To argue hotly (contr. 'cam').
   sib cav To argue hotly together.

2. cav hemcav (lub) A boat or ship (self-propelled).

3. cav A free log (cf. 'ca') (t.c.)
   cav taws A log of firewood.
   hauv qab ca Under the log.
   chaws qab ca Went under the log.
   cav cos The beam of the foot-mill for pounding rice.

4. cav High language for going to a king, etc.
   cav txog Huabtais Took it to the ruler, committed to the ruler.

5. cav Initial particle indicating surprise (cf. 'ua ciav').
   Cav tuag thiab 'auv'! (You mean) he died?
   Cav mus thiab 'auv'! He went??

cai Law, rule, custom.
   kevcai Rules, laws (txoj).
   tsis paub cai Doesn't know the laws or customs.
   tsis muaj cai There is no law to back (him) up.
   tsa cai 'the case stands' (terms used in litigation).
   qhau cai 'the case falls'
   ua cuav cai To falsely accuse, raise a case on no grounds.

1. caij To ride.
   caij nees To ride a horse.
   caij tsheb mus To go by vehicle.

2. caij An age, epoch, season (lub).
   lub caij ntuj Season of the year.
   lub caij ntuj no The cold season.
   lub caij ntuj los nag The rainy season.
   lub caij ntuj qhua The dry season.
   tav caij sawvdaws mus teb los At the time when everyone comes home from the fields.

1. cais To separate from.
   cais tseg To banish.
   cais mis To wean.
   cais npho To separate, each go his own way.

2. cais Shortened and easier way of saying "ua li cas"
   Koj cais yuav ua li? Why do you do that?

caiv Prohibition, rule, special observance, taboo.
  hnub caiv A day of special observance.
  Tsis caiv? You have no taboo? (today)
    (common reply to an invitation to enter a house)

cau khaus cau "itchy hands," of a person who must always
    be up to some mischief or evil.

caub Rob caub To seek revenge, to avenge (cf. 'pauj').

1. caug The knees.
  (a) qhau hauvcaug To kneel.
  (b) txhos caug To kneel.
  kim caug To kneel on one knee.

2. caug (numeral for tens, t.c. from 'caum,' cf 'caum').

cauj Early-bearing (of crops, animals, etc.) (contr. 'taj').
  pobkws cauj Early corn.
  hniav cauj Early tooth.
  npua cauj A pig that bears young twice a year.

1 caum To chase, run after to catch, to catch.
  caum tau lawm Caught (him).

2. caum Numeral for tens from 30 onward (but cf.'caug') (t.c.)
  peb caug Thirty.
  xya caum Seventy.
  rau caum Sixty.
  tsib caug Fifty.

3. caum
  noj peb caug (t.c.) To 'eat the 30th' i.e. to eat
    the New Year feast.

1. caus A knot (lub) (a solid knot, not a slip-knot. cf.
    'rhaus').
  lub pob caus A knot.

2. caus A knot in a tree (lub).

1. caw
  dej caw Another way of saying 'cawv' Whisky.

2. caw
  caw tai To call the 'tai' spirit.

cawj A kind of tree (tus).

cawm To save, to rescue (C).
  cawmseej (tus) Savior (C).
  cawm dim To save, to effect release.

1. caws Crouched, shrivelled, tightened like a spring.
  caws ceg Knees bent up.
  caws tes 'Withered' hand.
  caws vos All crouched together.
  (a) tibneeg caws caws A hunchback.
  (b) tibneeg khoov khoov A hunchback.

2. caws
  Caws pliav A scar.

3. caws
  (a) caws qia To leap.
  (b) caws qia ntsos To leap.
  (c) dhia caws qia To leap.

4. caws To truss up (as tying a pig's four legs together).

5. caws
  tus quam yej caws Trigger for a type of deadfall trap.

6. caws
  (a) muab txiav nreej To sever two parts of a
      split log.
  (b) muab caws nreej To sever two parts of a split log.

cawv Whisky (clf. 'txaum' for "batches").
  qaug cawv Drunk.
  vwm cawv Crazy drunk.
  cawv nplaum Sweet, partially fermented glutinous rice
    eaten as a delicacy. Non-intoxicating.

ce To lift from a running source into a vessel (cf. 'hais').
  ce dej To dip water (from a stream).

ceb Dirty (of the face).
  ceb muag Dirty face (cf. 'txab,' 'vuab tsuab').

1. ceg Leg, limb, branch (clf. 'txhais' of 'sab' for legs).
  ib txhais ceg One leg.
  ceg ntoo Tree branch or limb.
  ceg hiavtxwv A branch (leg) of the sea.
  plaub ceg ntuj The four branches of the heavens
    every direction (cf.'xwm fab puaj meem').
  ceg tawv Lame leg.
  ua ceg tawv mus To hop along.

2. ceg Clf. for lengths or sections of a journey, etc.

3. ceg sib ceg (cf. 'cem').

cej A kind of grain.

1. cem To scold, to curse, revile.
   sib ceg To scold one another, curse each other.
   cem txhom To scold fiercely.
   cem tawg ntho To scold loudly.
   cem qees Kept scolding.
   loj xov cem huvsi To scold the whole bunch for one man's fault.
   (a) ua ib tog cem All ganging up together to scold a person.
   (b) ua ib nqag cem All ganging up together to scold a person.

2. cem
   cem quav Constipation.

3. cem
   phua cem phij To split (boards) off the side of a log rather than through the middle.

4. cem One's self (C).
   Kuv cemcev ua I did it myself.

1. ces Leg (but cf. 'ceg').
   ces nees Leg of a horse.
   ces npua Leg of a pig.
   ces nyuj Leg of a cow.
   (these are sometimes also said 'ceg').

2. ces Initial particle used at the beginning of sentences to carry forward the action. Similar to "And..."

3. ces Shorter and easier way of saying 'ua li cas' (cf. 'cas' also cf. 'cais'.)
   Koj ces yuav ua li? Why do you do that?

1. cev Body, trunk, main frame (lub).
   kuv lub cev My body.
   cev ntoo Tree trunk.
   daws cev To give birth.
   nchuav cev To abort, miscarry.
   khuv cev Scanty menstruation.
   yawg cev To menstruate (cf. 'coj khaubncaws').

2. cev Clf. for suits of clothing.

3. cev To lift or raise something to a higher level.
   cev tes ua To raise the hand to do something.
   cev rau nws Hand it up to him.

4. cev One's self (C).
   cemcev ua To do myself.

1. ceeb
   ceeblaj Trouble, troublesome.
   kev ceeblaj Trouble.

2. ceeb To be tense, frightened, startled.
   ceebfaj To be alert, watch with care (as for robbers).
   ceebtoom To warn.
   ceeb nkaus Startled, muscular spasm, tenseness (cf. 'huam tshom').

3. ceeb
   lem ceeb Lengthwise rafter of a house.

4. ceeb
   ceebthawj Weight, heaviness (in referring to little children. contr. 'hnyav' which is not polite in this context).

5. ceeb
   hais lus tseem ceeb To speak what is important.

6. ceeb A headband (txoj).
   sivceeb ('thooj' for sets) The Hmong woman's variegated headband.

7. ceeb
   ceeb tsheej The Hmong abode of the dead.

ceej A kind of animal whose offal can be gathered and used for medicine (tus).

1. ceem To temper metal.

2. ceem
   muaj ceem Has strength.

1. ceev Tight (C).

2. ceev Tense (as of a tense situation).
   tebchaws ceev ceev The country is tense (with danger).

3. ceev Swiftly (of running, of vehicles in motion).

4. ceev Forcibly.
   hais ceev Speak forcibly (contr. 'hais xoob').
   hais ceev nrooj Speak with conviction, earnestly.

5. ceev
   yomceev Important (C).

6. ceev
   ceev ceev nchi nchi Flatulent, feeling of abdominal tightness without having eaten.

7. ceev Be concerned about (in a limited context).
   nyias ceev nyias li Let each look after his own interests.

2. cia To allow, permit (cf.'kheev').
   Cia nws ua nws li. Let him do as he likes.
   Cia nws mus. Let him go.
   Cia li lawm. Let it go at that.
   tshwj cia Put aside for disposal.
   Cia nws tuaj. Let him come.
   (cf. 'Kheev nws tuaj' If only he would come.)

ciab Wax made by insects.
   (a) ciab mem A sticky kind of insect wax used as an adhesive on the tip of the crossbow to hold the arrow in position.
   (b) kua ciab A sticky kind of insect wax used as an adhesive on the tip of the crossbow to hold the arrow in position.

1. ciaj Alive, living.
   (a) ciaj siav Alive.
   (b) ua ciaj Alive.
   neeg ciaj A living person.
   tsis ciaj ncaig Won't sustain fire, won't produce living coals.
   Plaub qaib tsis ciaj ncaig. You don't get live coals from chicken feathers. (i.e. "It will come to nothing.")

2. ciaj Tongs, pliers (rab).
   Muab rab ciaj tais. Hold it with the pliers.

3. ciaj ciaj ib nceeg vaj To establish a dynasty or kingdom.

4. ciaj A boundary (cf.'kaij kiam').
   (a) kiaj kiam Boundary.
   (b) ciaj ciam Boundary.
   (Note: 'kiaj kiam' is used more commonly but 'ciaj ciam' is also understood.)

ciam A boundary, a division (tus).
   tus ciam A boundary line.
   ciam teb A field boundary.
   sib puas ciam To have a common boundary.
   ua ciam teb To divide off fields.
   (a) ciaj ciam Boundary.
   (b) kiaj kiam Boundary.
   (Note: 'kiaj kiam' is used more commonly.)

1. ciav ciav dej A water line (tus), trough (Made of bamboo or palm lengths set on posts and put end to end to bring water from a stream).

2. ciav nas ciav The Zebra Squirrel (tus).

8. ceev To store up.
   lub tsev ceev nyiaj A bank (cf. 'cia').

1. ci Bright, brilliant (contr. 'cig').
   ci vus A great brightness in one place (cf. 'vog').
   ci nplas An expanse of brightness.
   ci vog ci vog Flashing (cf. lightning).
   (a) ci ntsa iab Bright and glittering.
   (b) ci qos iab Bright and glittering.

2. ci To toast (over or beside a fire, not in a vessel) (cf. 'txhiab').

3. ci cilu Kilogram (T).

4. ci txujci, tus txuj tus ci (cf. 'txuj' Definition No. 2).

1. cib thwvcib (lub) A brick.

2. cib ciblaug (lub) An open basket for carrying earth, refuse, etc.

3. cib sabcib (lub) A basket-type rice strainer.

cig Alight, to be alight (contr. 'ci').
   hluavtaws cig Light of a fire.
   faivfuaj cig The flashlight is lighted.
   cig plaws To flame up.

cij siab cij Impatient, quick-tempered (C).

1. cim To remember, memorize (C) (cf. 'nco').
   cim tau To remember.
   cimxeeb The memory, power of memory (C).

2. cim A mark, seal, stamp (lub).
   ntaus ib lub cim To make a mark of identification.

3 cim Clf. for seasons of or 'turns' of work.
   daim teb ua ib cim xwb Field only worked one season.
   ntov ib cim ntoo Fell trees one season.

1. cia To put aside, put down, put away, store.
   Muab cia. Put it aside.

3. ciav To persecute.
   Txhob muab kuv ciav Don't persecute me.

4. ciav Used with 'ua' (or as a single syllable) to
      express something unexpected. "How is it?"
      cf. 'ua cas'.

   Ua ciav koj tuaj? How is it that you have come?
   Ciav tsis pom lix? How is it that I can't see it?
   (also cf. 'cav' In some contexts the meaning is
      close to 'txawmsis' Just then, so.)

1. co To shake, to sway, to quake, to move to and fro.
   co tes To shake the hand, to beckon with the hand.
      (cf.'Ntxuaj teb').

2. co People of the Yao 'tribe.

3. co
   poj co (lub) The common earring worn by Hmong women.

1. cob To teach to behave, to train (a child or animal).
   Lawv tsis cob menyuam. They don't train their children
      to obey.

2. cob Sticklac, black lac resin used as a base for shellac
      and varnish. Used by the Hmong to cement handles
      to knife blades.

3. cob
   cob siav npua Said in offering whisky to a spirit
      as representing the life of a pig to be killed
      and offered. (contr. 'txais').

1. cog To plant, insert.
   cog nplej To plant rice.
   cog hniav To 'fit' false teeth.

2. cog To promise, swear (as used in Laos).
   cog lus To promise, swear.
   ntawv cog lus Written covenant, agreement.

3. cog (t.c.) (cf. 'cos').

1. coj To lead, guide, bring along (as persons).
   Kuv yuav coj kuv tus tub tuaj. I'll bring my son.

2. coj To wear (as jewelry on the neck, arms, etc.).
   coj rawv To wear or hold tightly.

3. coj To join (as a group or an organization).

4. coj To bear as a message.
   coj lus To bear a message (cf.'xa lus').
   coj xov To bear news or tidings.

5. coj
   coj khaubncaws To menstruate (cf.'yawg khaubncaws').

1. com
   com cum To make fields in another area in preparation
      to move there another year.

2. com
   com viab Crooked, deceitful (cf. 'lim hiam').
   neeg com viab A deceitful person, one who goes back
      on agreements, etc. (cf.'khib').
   siab com viab A deceitful heart.
   neeg zoo phij sam siab com viab Hypocrites (good
      skin with a deceitful crooked heart).

1. cos Treadmill for de-husking rice. (lub)
   qhov cos The bowl of the rice treadmill.
   tuav cos To work the treadmill.
   ncej cog The posts of the treadmill.
   cav cos The beam of the treadmill.
   dauj cog The pestle of the treadmill.
   taw cos The foot end of the treadmill.
   nqos cos The crossbeam of the treadmill.
   dej cog Rice pounding mill run by water.
   tus niam hauvpaus cos The woman in charge of pounding
      the rice for a funeral feast.

2. cos A bud.
   cos paj Flower bud.

3. cos A birthmark (lub) (except on the face, cf. 'tias').

4. cos A wart.
   mob cos Warts.

5. cos The firing cap of a cartridge.
   cos ntawv A firing cap.

1. cov A class, group, kind, bunch (cf. 'yam').
   cov tibneeg People.
   cov no This kind.
   cov ntoo Trees, forest.
   ib co neeg One class of people.

2. cov To pour into.
   cov dej To pour water into.

3. cov Elephant's trunk, proboscis.
   covtxwv Elephant's trunk, proboscis.

4. cov Of words difficult to say or enunciate.
   lus cov Difficult words, twisted language.

1. cua The wind (clf. 'tw' or 'nthwv' for gusts).
   cua tshuab The wind blows.
   cua ntab saud lawm The wind sweeps over above.
   cua moj lwg A great wind (poetical).
   nag xob nag cua A storm, tempest.
   cua moj lwg xib kaw A great wind (poetical).
   khauv zeeg cua A whirlwind.
   hav cua The air, the atmosphere.
   cua daj cua dub Bad wind, storm.

2. cua
   cua nab The earthworm (tus).

3. cua To bite hard on something.

1. cuab A family (C).
   (a) ib cuab tibneeg One family.
   (b) ib cuab neeg One family.
   tuam cuab (C) everyone.
   ua twb cuab To live together as a single family,
      several families living together.
   faib cuab To divide house, separate households.
   neeg kib cuab One who stays close to home and cares
      for his own business.

2. cuab
   (a) cuabyeej (lub) All the goods of the household,
      household equipment and utensils, (hence)
      inheritance.
   (b) cuabtam All the goods of the household, household
      equipment and utensils, (hence) inheritance.
   (c) cuabtiv All the goods of the household, household
      equipment and utensils, (hence) inheritance.
   (a) cuabyeej toomtxeem The household goods, the
      inheritance.
   (b) cuabyeej cuabtam The household goods, the
      inheritance.
   nyias ceev nyias li cuabyeej Let each attend to his
      own affairs (household).
   (a) cuabyeej Tools, equipment, utensils.
   (b) cuabxwm Tools, equipment, utensils.
   (a) lub cuab lub yig Tools, equipment, utensils.
   (b) lub cuabtam Tools, equipment, utensils.
   ib lub cuabtiv cuabtam One household and all the
      goods pertaining to it.
   koom txais ib lub cuabtam To receive one joint
      inheritance.
   tshob cuabtam To disrupt and scatter the family
      and household.
   tshawb cuabtam To pillage, destroy and breakup
      the household.

1 coob Many, numerous, crowded.
   tibneeg coob coob A multitude, a crowd.
   neeg coob nphoo ntxoj nphoo ntxuas A very large
      crowd, a huge multitude.

2. coob A species of bird (tus).

cooj A roost, coop for chickens or fowl (lub).
   lub cooj qaib Chicken roost.
   qaib ncawg cooj Chickens come to roost.

1. cub A fire, fire confined to one place (cf.'hluavtaws').
   cub hluavtaws Furnace, large fire.
   qhov cub The cooking fireplace in Hmong home.
   cub tawg Large fire.

2. cub To steam.
   cub mov To steam rice in a steamer.

3. cub
   txiaj cub, txiaj npliv Two kinds of Indo-Chinese
      coins used by the Hmong for decoration.

cug To collect in a vessel.
   cug dej To collect water in a vessel (bucket, etc.)
      from a running source.
   cug nyiaj To collect money (in a box, bag, etc.)

1. cuj
   loj cuj Shackle, ankle ring.

2. cuj
   xabcuj A tripod (lub) (C).

1. cum clf. for a group, a side.
   ob cum Two sides, two groups, two clans.

2. cum To make fields in another area in prepara-
      tion to move there later.

3. cum
   (a) thob fab The foundation beams of a house.
   (b) tim cum The foundation beams of a house.

1. cus Of a person who talks a lot and talks loudly,
      virile, active; a 'spirited' animal or person.

2. cus Of an animal that cries loud and often.

3. cuab To trap, snare, entrap, ensnare.
   cuab noog To trap birds.
   tawb cuab ntses A woven fish trap.
   cuab nas A rat trap, to trap rats.

4. cuab To make a trap or snare.
   cuab ntxiab To make trap with a lithe springy sapling
       (cf. 'ntxiab').

5. cuab To call animals or birds, of animals and birds
       calling their young.
   cuab yaj To call sheep.
   cuab npua To call pigs.
   qaib cuab menyuam Hen clucks to call her chicks.

6. cuab To lay hold of, conform to.
   cuab lub hauvpaus To lay hold of the root of things,
       grasp the essence or principle.

7. cuab The guava.
   txiv cuab thoj The guava (lub).

8. cuab
   cuab xeeb puj teem (C) In confusion and uncertainty.
   us tus cuab xeeb puj teem Of one who doesn't know
       what to do. Especially in cases of dispute
       where the decision seems unacceptable and the
       person is confused about the outcome.

9. cuab
   tus cuab tsav The 'master' of the spirit rites at
       a funeral, responsible for sending food to the
       deceased together with the life-value of the
       animals sacrificed.

1. cuag To reach to, extend to.
   cuag nkaus To reach to.
   muab tsis cuag Can't reach (to grasp).
   cev tsis cuag Can't reach (to hand to).
   zoo tsis cuag Not as good as (not reaching to standard.)

2. cuag To meet with.
   sib cuag To meet together.
   Peb yuav rov sib cuag We will meet again.

1. cuaj The number nine.

2. cuaj
   cuajkhaum Greedy, selfish (cf. 'qia dub').

1. cuam The gibbon (tus).

2. cuam To press together in a frame or rack or between
       two strips of wood, etc.
   cuam nplooj To fit leaves into bamboo lengths for
       use in roofing.
   cuam nqeeb To so fix grass into lengths for thatch.

3. cuam clf. for lengths of thatch or roofing leaves.
   ib cuam nplooj A length of roofing leaves.

4. cuam To throw underhanded.
   cuam tseg To throw away (underhanded).

5. cuam To clasp under the arm.
   cuam rawv To clasp tightly under the arm.

6. cuam To make a big fire, pile up for a fire.
   cuam taws To make a big fire.
   cuam taws muab hlawv Pile up wood and set fire to it.

7. cuam
   cuamtawv nees To carry frame which fits over the
       pack saddle on a horse.

8. cuam
   cuamtxwv npua (tus) A half-grown castrated pig.

9. cuam
   pabcuam To help, assist.

10. cuam
    tebchaws cuam cuam kawb A country of hills and
        valleys close together.

11. cuam
    cuam koob (rooj) A type of trap to catch rodents,
        etc. (cf. 'rooj').

12. cuam
    muab cuam cuab To put in a stock, to entrap.

13. cuam
    txham cuam Of animals getting water in the windpipe.

14. cuam muas Doesn't meet properly, e.g. in cutting a
        tree one cut slanted and the other straight.

15. cuam 'phijcuam' Cf. 'phij'

cuas
    yawg cuas Father of my son's wife (or) father of
        my daughter's husband.
    poj cuag (t.c.) Mother of my son's wife (or) mother
        of my daughter's husband.

cha (t.c.) (cf. 'chav').

1. chab
   khawv chab Songs (cf. 'kwv txhiaj').

2. chab
   sib chab sib chua To grab back and forth as in
       fighting for something.

3. chab
   sib chab sib chaws To go over and under repeatedly.

chaj
   txhob cam txhob chaj Don't be bullheaded. Don't
       be stubborn in purposely refusing to obey.

1. chav A room.
   chav tsev A room.
   chav tsev pw A bedroom.

2. chav clf. for rooms.
   rau chav tsev Six rooms.
   ib cha tsev One room (t.c.)

3. chav A kind of snare for catching small animals or
       birds
   clf. 'rooj' (cf. 'rooj').
   cuab chav To make such a snare or trap.

1. chais To shave.
   chais taubhau To shave the head.
   chais hwjtxwv To shave the beard.

2. chais To slice off (as vegetables for cooking).

chaub To crawl on the belly.
   chaub laug To crawl on one's belly (as of soldiers
       sneaking up on an enemy).
   chaub laug mus To go by crawling as described above.

1. chaw Place, region (lub).
   chaw pw Sleeping place, bed.
   ib lub chaw One place.
   qhovtxhiachaw Things, articles.
   chaw chim Cause for hatred or enmity.
   tebchaws (t.c.) Country, state (clf. 'lub').

2. chaw Clf. for lengths of cloth.
   (also cf. 'chaws').

1. cuav Counterfeit, false.
   txiaj ntawv cuav Counterfeit paper money.
   xibhwb cuav False teachers.
   ua cuav cai To falsely accuse.

2. cuav To visit around
   cuav zos To visit around the village (cf. 'yos').

3. cuav
   cuav qaub Of no account, useless.
   lus cuav qaub Lying, untrustworthy language.

cw A lobster or prawn (tus).

cwg Lub yis cwg kua muag (cf. 'yis').

1. cwj A sharp pointed stick (tus).
   Nws txiav cwj los nrig He cut a stick to use as
       a cane.
   cwj nrig (tus) A rod, a stick.
   rab cwj A crutch or stick used by a lame man.

2. cwj
   cwjmen (tus) A pen for writing.
   twb cwjmem To lower the pen to write.
   tshem cwjmem To lift the pen.

3. cwj
   cwj tsiag The trigger of a trap.

4. cwj
   cwjpwm (tus) Example, manner of, custom, practice,
       manner of walk.

23

1. chawj
chawj rov qab los To seek to reconcile, to go and bring someone back after a quarrel.

2. chawj
chib chawj puaj liam To do poorly, do sloppily (C)
cf. 'ua dab ua tuag' (or) 'ua xya chawj yim liam'

1. chaws To pass through an opening.
chaws qab ca To go under the log.
sib chab sib chaws To go over and under repeatedly.
Nws chaws nplho mus hauv tsev. He 'ducked' into the house. Entered the house quickly.

2. chaws
rab chaws las The metal rod used in making holes in wood after heating in a fire.

3. chaws
tebchaws Country, state (lub) cf. 'chaw' (t.c.)

4. chaws
ib chaws ntaub A length of cloth, one weaving of cloth (t.c. from 'chaw,' cf. 'chaw').

cheb To sweep.
cheb tsev To sweep up the house.
cheb pov tseg To sweep up and discard.

chev To curl up in a coil.
chev ua ib kauj To curl it up in a coil.
tus nab chev ua ib kauj The snake curled up.
dab tshos chev A ladies jacket collar with embroidered pattern in coils.

cheeb Meo man's name.

1. cheej A unit of measurement, the width of a fist (cf. 'taus') (used in measuring for neck rings, etc.)

2. cheej
cheej tswb (C) Wild pigs which go about in a group.

3. cheej
huam cheej The last spasm before death.

1. cheem To politely seek to retain a visitor when he starts to leave.
khuam cheem To entangle, to delay, to retain, keep from leaving.

2. cheem To seek to stop others who are quarreling or fighting. (cf. 'ntuas')

24

3. cheem To take advantage of an opportunity.
Cheem tseem nruab hnub peb yuav mus. We will go while it is still day.

1. chib A period of time (lub).
ib lub chib so One period of rest (i.e. one week).

2. chib To slander, despise.
hais lub chib To slander, speak disparagingly.

3. chib
ua chib chawj puaj liam To do poorly, do sloppily.
(C) cf. 'ua dab ua tuag' (or) 'ua xya chawj yim liam'

1. chij A flag (tus) (C).

2. chij
vimchij Because (cf.'yibvim').
vimchij li no For this reason, for this cause.

1. chim To hate, be angry at, be incensed (also cf. 'chis').
chim siab To be angry, be incensed.
chim kuv siab heev Made me very angry.
kev chim siab Anger, hatred.
chim rawv Firmly holding to anger.
chim quj qees To gradually give rise to anger.

2. chim
tshawjchim Enemy (tus).
ua niag tuam tshawjchim To be great enemies.

3. chim A short period of time, an hour or two.
(cf. APPENDIX p. 492).
ib chim A little while.

4. chim
mob tsam chim Exhaustion and pain as after hard exercise.

chis To be angry (cf. 'chim').
lub siab chis qos tshwv Mildly angry, dark face.

1. chiv To begin, originate, start.
chivkeeb To begin, beginning.
Chivkeeb mob li cas? How did the ailment begin?
chivthawj Beginning, the beginning, the first.
chiv ua To begin to do.
chiv kiag hais Began to say (cf. 'pib hais').

2. chiv Manure, fertilizer (cov).
cov chiv Manure.
quav chiv Manure, fertilizer of excrement.

3. chiv
    lub siab ntxhi chiv To say something over in the
        heart, something you would say to the person
        if you could see them.

chiab
    majmam mus chuj chiab To absentmindedly or
        unconsciously walk very slowly.

1. chob To pierce, be pierced (not intentionally)
        contr. 'nkaug'
    ntoo chob A splinter, to be pierced by a splinter.
    (a) xyoob chob To be pierced by a piece of bamboo.
    (b) xyoob tshum To be pierced by a piece of bamboo.
    chob rau ib tug ntoo To put it on a pointed stick.
    chob nrees Has been pierced for some time.

2. chob Offended, 'pierced' in heart, grieved.
    chob siab Offended, grieved, inwardly hurt because
        of some offense.

3. chob
    phijchob (txoj) Tough leather thong for tying
        baskets to a pack saddle.

1. choj A bridge (tus) (C).
    tuam choj To erect a bridge.
    choj qev A rattan suspension brdige.
    taug choj mus To go over the bridge.
    tus choj A bridge, also used of the pole which is
        set up against a tree to form a platform upon
        which to stand in felling the tree.
    tus tab choj The small wooden support set to hold
        the 'choj' (above) from falling sidewise
        while felling a tree.

2. choj
    (a) choj txhwj (rab) A hoe, a mattock.
    (b) pav txhwij (rab) A hoe, a mattock.

3. choj
    peev choj Rice noodles.

chom To bend backward (of fingers, trees, etc.)
    xya tes chom chom li To stretch the fingers and
        bend them backward.

chov An evil omen.
    (a) ua chov An evil omen, to be an evil sign.
    (b) ua npog An evil omen, to be an evil sign.
    (c) ua xu An evil omen, to be an evil sign.

chuj
    majmam mus chuj chiab To absentmindedly or unconsciously
        walk very slowly.

chum
    pejchum Aluminum.

1. chua To forcibly snatch something away from another person.
    sib chab sib chua To grab or snatch back and forth
        as in fighting over some article.

2. chua
    chua moo (Thai) An hour, one hour.

1. chwv To rub against something with part of the body
        (contr. 'tshiav')
    npua chwv chwv ntoo The pig scrapes against the tree.
    sib chwv Very close together, rubbing against one
        another (cf. 'sib ti').

2. chwv
    chwv chwv thawj Won't talk, refuses to answer.

D

1. da To immerse, submerge (cf. 'raus,' 'tsaug').
   da dej To immerse (oneself) in water, take a bath.

2. da To roll over (cf. 'phov,' 'nti').
   da mus da los To roll back and forth on the ground (as a person with delirium or spasm or in sleep).

1. dab A spirit, a demon (tus) cf. 'neeb'
   ua dab To do spirit rites.
   laig dab To set aside food for the spirits, offer food to the spirits.
   txi dab To offer to the spirits.
   dab nyeg 'Tame' household spirits.
   dab qus 'Wild' jungle spirits.
   pej kum dab qus Wild jungle spirits, all others than the 'dab nyeg.'

The 'tame' or household spirits are these:
   ntuj dab (or) ncej dab The greatest of the household spirits. The one who rules and protects the whole family. Once in three years an adult female pig that has had young is sacrificed for this spirit. This spirit is said to reside in the 'ncej' or main supporting house pillar nearest the fire.
   dab txwvkoob (or) dab neeb These spirits of the ancestors are also said to reside in the pillars of the house.
   dab xwmkab (tus) The spirits of wealth and possessions. These are represented by a paper on the wall of the uphill side. These spirits also protect the household. At new year one large male pig is killed and offered to the 'xwmkab.'
   dab roog The spirit of the door. This spirit looks after the domestic animals and fowl. This spirit is particularly cared for by the woman of the house. A small gourd or similar articles dedicated to this spirit are kept in the bedroom. The spirit guards the door on the downhill side of the house (qhov rooj tag) which is always the door for spirit rites and that by which spirits enter. One young female pig a year is offered to the 'dab roog.'
   dab cub (or) dab qhovcub The spirit of the fire-place or of the cooking fire. Sometimes incense is offered to this spirit but chickens or animals are never sacrificed for it.
   dab qhovtxos Spirit of the fireplace under the cauldron for boiling pig food. This spirit is also sometimes offered incense but never chicken or animal sacrifice.

The 'wild' spirits, or spirits of the jungle, etc. often have special names.
   dab ntxwg nyoog (sometimes said 'ntxwg nyug') The spirit 'king.' The greatest of the spirits.
   nyuj vaj The 'cow king.' Another powerful spirit but most persons say it is not as powerful as 'ntxwg nyoog.'
   dab ntxaug A powerful spirit greatly feared. It has certain places of abode and if troubled it may cause the death of whole families. Plagues or epidemics are often blamed on this spirit.
   dab theeb kawg Name of another certain spirit.
   poj ntxoog A female jungle spirit greatly feared. She rides a tiger and her father was supposed to have been a tiger. To deceive her and protect against her the Hmong sometimes put twisted rings on their necks, ankles, etc.
   dab nruab ntug Spirit of the heavens.

   fiv dab (or) fiv rau dab A promise made to the spirits if they will help (as in sickness, etc.) (cf. 'fiv yeem').
   dab qhuas The spirit worshipping apparatus in the home.
   teev dab The whole system of offerings, etc. for entreating the help of the spirits, entreaty or worship of spirits.
   dab tai The name of a spirit who is supposed to have helped the Hmong when they crossed the water coming from China. This spirit is served by men only. (cf. 'nyuj' also see 'nyuj vaj' above).
   ua nyuj dab

   txheev dab (C) To invite the spirits, call the spirits to come.
   raug dab To meet some misfortune at the hands of a bad spirit.
   dab yob tsov los tom The spirits have sent a tiger to come and bite someone.
   coj dab neem (cf. 'neem').

2. dab A trough, a hollowed out length of log, etc. (lub).
   dab npua A trough for pig food.
   dab dej A trough for holding water.
   dab nees A horse feeding trough.
   dab zaub A trough for putting vegetable greens in.

3. dab
   dab ntub Drowsiness, sleepiness.
   qaug dab ntub Very drowsy, very sleepy, dopey with sleep.
   ncaws dab ntub To doze, to nod the head in sleep, bend over in sleep.
   ua dab ntub To sleep well (also 'ua dab loog').

4. dab
    dab ros Funny.
    tuaj dab ros Funny, laughable, to laugh.
    lus tuaj dab ros A joke, funny saying.

5. dab
    dab tuag Poor, shoddy, careless.
    dab tuag li Shoddily, carelessly, ragged, etc.
    ua dab ua tuag To do carelessly, do poorly and
        without concern.

6. dab
    dabtsi What? anything.
    yog dabtsi? What is it?
    Koj hais dabtsi? What did you say?
    Tsis muaj dabtsi. (I) have nothing. Haven't anything.
    Koj muaj dabtsi? What do you have?
    Koj muaj dabtsi tsis muaj? Have you anything or not?
    Koj ua dabtsi? What are you doing?

7. dab
    dab tshos Embroidered patch on the back of a Hmong
        woman's collar. Many kinds of 'dab tshos'
        cf. 'tsho.'

8. dab
    (a) dab neeg Folklore, tradition, story, legend.
    (b) lus dab neeg Folklore, tradition, story, legend.

9. dab
    dab tub nkeeg Fever and chills, malaria.
    ua dab tub nkeeg To have fever and chills, have malaria.

10. dab
    caj dab The neck.

11. dab
    dab teg The wrist.

12. dab
    dab taws The ankle.

13. dab Used in combination for referring to certain
    relatives. (see APPENDIX 10).
    dab laug Mother's brothers.
    yawm dab Wife's brothers.
    yaum dab Male cousins of a different surname as
        called by a woman.

1. dag To lie, to cheat, falsehood.
    (a) hais dag To lie, speak falsehood.
    (b) hais lus dag To lie, speak falsehood.
    txhobtxwm dag xwb Intentionally deceived (him),
        that's all.

2. dag To be idle.
    nyob dag To be idle, hand around doing nothing.

1. daj Yellow.
    daj daj li Quite yellow.
    daj rhuv Very bright yellow.
    daj vog Speckled yellow.
    daj lis Slightly yellow.
    daj tawv A species of large tree with yellow
        bark and sap.
    taub dag (t.c.) (lub) A pumpkin.

2. daj A double arm's length, a measurement of length.
    rau daj Six lengths from fingertip to fingertip
        with arms spread.
    ib dag (t.c.) One such double arm's length.
    ib txhais dag Half such a measurement, i.e. one arm's
        length from the center of the chest to the end
        of the outstretched arm and fingers.

dam To be broken in two, broken off.
    dam ceg The (tree) branch has broken off (this
        word is used most often in scolding or
        cursing, thus-).
    koj yuav dam ces You will break your leg.
        cf. the more ordinary word 'lov.'

1. dav A hawk (tus) a hawk-like bird.
    ib tug dav One hawk.
    tus dav noj twm A buzzard (buffalo-eating bird).
    dav hlau (tus) An airplane (iron hawk) cf. 'nkoj cua.'

2. dav Wide, broad, expansive.
    qhov dav Width.
    siab dav Generous, gracious, kind.
    kev dav Wide road.

3. dav Lonely, cheerless (of a house, etc.)
    lub tsev dav dav li A cheerless house, lonely house
        with few inhabitants. contr. 'sov.'

dai To hang, to hang up.
    dai ntawm phab ntsa To hang it on the wall.
    dai tuag To die by hanging.
    dai vias Hanging up (swinging from one point).
    muab ntsia dai vias To hang up, crucify, hang on
        nails.
    hnub dai npoo ncuv Sunset, sun hanging on the horizon.
    muab dai To put the corpse on the shelf against
        the wall at a funeral ceremony.
    nyiaj dai Decorative silver ornaments hung on the
        apparel.

1. daig To be caught, hooked up on, clogged, stopped up.
   daig ntoo Caught in the tree.
   daig kub Caught by the horns.

2. daig t.c. from 'daim,' cf. 'daim.'

daim Clf. for sheets, pages, flat expanses of surface.
   daim ntawv Sheet of paper.
   ib daig ntawv One sheet of paper (t.c.)
   daim teb A field.
   ib daig teb One field (t.c.)

dais A bear (tus) (Many species and varieties indicated
       by qualifying words.)
   dais dev The honey bear.
   dais nees The black bear.

daiv Large species of bumble bee. A large insect with
   red head and black bee-shaped body. It makes
   no honey but the grubs are eaten and considered
   a delicacy. The nests are found on the ground
   or under logs. The 'daiv' has a powerful
   and dangerous sting. (cf. 'muv').

daub A species of bird.
   puj daub A species of bird.

daug To hatch.
   qe daug The egg hatched, eggs hatch (contr. 'qauj').

dauj Mallet, pounder (tus).
   dauj cog The pounding end of a foot rice-mill,
       the pestle end.
   dauj ncuav (tus) The mallet used in making pounded
       glutinous rice cakes.

daum To hop up a vertical surface.
   daum ntoo To hop up a tree (as a bird, etc.)

1. daus To scoop up, dip out (cf. 'hais').
   Daus los rau peb noj. Scoop some out for us to eat.

2. daus
   daus xib daus npu Snow (n.)
   los daus xib daus npu To snow, snow falling.

3. daus
   laub zeb daus cf. 'laub.'

dauv To lower, to drop (in certain contexts), to droop.
   dauv tes To drop the arms to one's side.
   dauv muag To drop the eyes, look at the ground
       as when shy or ashamed.
   dauv tw qaib cf. 'nplej' and 'pobkws.'

daw Salty, tasting of salt (contr. 'tsuag').
   daw daw ntsev Very salty.

1. dawb White, clean.
   dawb dawb li Very white.
   dawb dawb tshiab tshiab White and new.
   dawb paug Perfectly white.
   (a) dawb tib paug Very white, perfectly white.
   (b) dawb qos paug Very white, perfectly white.
   dawb rhwb Very white, extremely white.
   dawb vog Speckled white, mottled white.
   dawb lias Not very white, off white.

2. dawb Morally clean and upright.
   siab dawb dawb A clean heart, morally pure heart.

3. dawb Free, freely, without charge.
   pub dawb dawb li To give without charge, to give free.

4. dawb Unoccupied, idle.
   nyob dawb nyob do To be idle, to live without
       doing any work.

5. dawb
   xovdawb (cf. 'xov').

6. dawb
   ua neeb muag dawb A certain form of spirit exorcism
       calling upon a greater spirit to deliver from
       a lesser spirit.

7. dawb Finished.
   (a) dawb lawm Finished.
   (b) hle lawm Finished.
   (c) khauv lawm Finished.
   (d) tag lawm Finished.

dawg
   sib dawg cuam To quarrel, scold each other.

1. dawj To gouge out, to forcibly pry or scoop out.
   muab lub pobzeb dawj los Dig out the stone, take
       the stone away.
   dawj qhovmuag To gouge out the eye.
   dawj qhovrooj To pry open the door.

2. dawj Final completive particle used in derision.
   niag neeg dawj The big fool.

1. dawm To stumble, to cause to stumble.
   Nws dawm ntawm kev lawm He stumbled on the way.

2. dawm A mountain pass, high valley, wind gap on top
     of a ridge, low place between two peaks. (lub)
   dawm saj A gap, a pass (as above).

3. dawm A crotch (lub).
   dawm ntoo Crotch in a tree.
   dawm pobzeb A crotch in a stone.
   dawm hmab Crotch in a vine.
   dawm tes Crotch between the thumb and the rest
     of the hand.

1. daws To untie, release, unfetter, set free.
   daws txoj hlua Untie the rope.
   daws tus nees mus Let the horse go free.

2. daws To forgive, to release from obligation.
   daws lub txim To forgive sin, release from guilt.

3. daws To name, to give a name.
   daws npe To name, give a name (cf. 'tis,' 'hu').

4. daws To give birth (human).
   daws cev To give birth, bear a child (cf. 'tu').

5. daws
   (a) mus daws duam To walk with big steps.
   (b) mus duj duam To walk with big steps.

6. daws p.v.int. in combination with 'txhaws'
   tawm txhaws daws Many emerging all at once,
     tumbling out.

1. de To pluck, to pinch.
   de zaub To pinch off leafy vegetables.
   de nrho To pinch sharply, pinch so as to hurt.

2. de qaug doj qaug de Unsteady, reeling from side to side.

deb Distant, distance.
   deb deb li Far away, very distant.
   qhov deb Distance.
   nyob nrug deb Separated far off.
   deb li cas? How far?

deg t.c. from 'dej' cf. 'dej'

dej Water (clf. 'tus' for streams and watercourses).
   tus dej The stream, the river.
   lub hav dej A gulley or river valley.
   tus menyuam dej The small stream.
   dej tsaws tsag Rapids, waterfall.
   (a) lub qhov dej A water spring.
   (b) qhov dej txhawv A water spring.
   qhov dej saus Place where water sinks or disap-
     pears into the ground.
   hauv dej Upstream, river or stream source (lub),
     in the water.
   nram qab dej Downstream
   dej dag Yellow muddy water, high water.
   dej dag nyab Flood, flooding water.
   dej hlob High water.
   dej ntas Small waves of water (contr. 'twv').
   ua luam dej To swim.
   tus niag dej A large river.
   lub hauv dej The source of a river or stream.
   dej tsaws ntxhee Swift and turbulent water.
   dej txiag Cold water.
   dej ntshiab Clear fresh water.
   dej huv Pure water, clean and drinkable.
   dej sov Warm water.
   dej kub Hot water.
   dej sia Boiled water.
   (a) dej sov so Lukewarm water.
   (b) dej ntem ntawv Lukewarm water.
   muab dej nchuav Pour away the water, throw water away.
   hliv dej To pour water.
   dej vuab Water flows around an obstruction.
   (a) tav dej A dam, to dam water.
   (b) tauv dej A dam, to dam water.
   (c) xov dej A dam, to dam water.
   dej xiv Water murmurs before it boils.
   cug dej los Water seeps in.
   dej cog A rice pounding mill run by water power.
   nruab deg On the sea, in the midst of the water.
   nkoj deg A boat (cf. 'hemcav').
   kwj deg A gulley (wet only after a rain).
   (a) pliag deg A small clam, also the piece of shell,
     etc. on which opium is rolled in preparation
     for smoking.
   (b) piag deg A small clam, also the piece of shell,
     etc. on which opium is rolled in preparation
     for smoking.

1. dev Dog (tus) (cf. 'aub').
   dev hnyo A long haired dog.
   dev kuas A kind of varicolored dog.
   dev tawb Dog scratching.
   dev tsem Dog barking. (The sound of barking is
     described as 'nkhoob nkhoob').
   txhaub dev To send a dog after someone or something,
     to 'sic' a dog.

dim To release, to be released, escape, be freed, be saved.
    dim lawm Released, saved.
    tso dim To set free, to release.
    dim pa To release air pressure.
    dim plaws Freed suddenly, escaped.
    dim plhuav khoom haujlwm Escape from work, freed from work and responsibility.

dis Gruel.
    Kua dis Rice gruel.

diab A species of bird (tus).

diaj To push and pull back and forth, make something move backward and forward.
    diaj zeb To push and pull the handle turning a millstone, to grind at the stone mill.
    Txhob diaj diaj qhovrooj. Don't keep pushing and pulling the door.

diam p.v.int. conveying the idea "really" or, "as many as that," "as much as that."
    Ua tau diam. (He) can really do it (well)!
    Qab diam mog. Really tasty!
    Tsib tug diam Five! (as many as that!)

dias dias taubhau Headache, head hurts.

1. diav Spoon, spoon-like (rab).
    ib rab diav One spoon.
    diav nyiaj Silver spoon.
    diav hmuv Fork (lit. 'spear spoon').

2. diav Clf. for spoonfuls.
    ib dia mov One spoonful of rice (t.c.)
    rau diav tshuaj Six spoonfuls of medicine.

1. do To stir, to mix (as powder into liquid, etc.) cf. 'tov'
    do tshuaj To mix up medicine.

2. do Bald, smoothe and vacant.
    do do hau Bald headed.
    qhovmuag do Expressionless roving eyes of a sick person.

dob To pull up by the roots.
    dob nroj To pull weeds.
    dob plaub To pull out a hair, pluck hair.

dog Used in combination with 'dig.'
    ua dog ua dig To do sloppily, to do carelessly.

2. dev Pertaining to dogs.
    hais lus dev To speak filthy language, 'dog' language.
    tibneeg dev A filthy and immoral person, a 'dog.'
    dev thawj tswv A dog that knows not its master, one that wanders about seeking food from one and all. Also used fig. of persons in serious scolding and cursing.

3. dev
    dev mub (tus) The flea, fleas.

4. dev
    dais dev (tus) The honey bear.

1. deev Illicit sexual relations.
    deev hluas nkauj Extra-marital relations with a young woman.
    deev hluas nraug Extra-marital relations with a young man.
    (These terms are also used loosely of visiting among young people since sex relations might or might not follow.)

2. deev To comfort.
    deev siab To comfort, encourage the heart (cf. 'nplij').

di Lip, lips.
    di ncauj The lips.

1. dib Cucumber, cucumber-like melon (lub).
    dib pag (lub) A type of melon tasting something like a cucumber.

2. dib To entice, to bait.
    qaib dib A chicken used to draw others into a trap.

1. dig Blind, to be blind.
    dig muag Blind, blinded eyes.
    neeg dig muag A blind person (tus).

2. dig To pick, probe, dig at.
    dig av To shovel up earth.
    dig ntxeev hlo To flick over, to turn something over (as with a finger or a stick).
    dig kiav txhab To pick off a scab.
    dig hniav To pick the teeth.
    dig pobntseg To pick or probe in the ear.

3. dig Used in combination with 'dog.'
    ua dog ua dig To do sloppily, to do carelessly.

doj
    qaug doj qaug de Unsteady, reeling from side to side.

1. dos Measure of width representing the distance between
        thumb and extended middle finger.

2. dos Small onion, leek (lub).

1. dov To roll along, roll something along (contr. 'ntog').
        dov toj To roll down the hill.

2. dov In combination with 'nplaig' pertaining to diffi-
        culty of speech.
        dov dov nplaig Difficult to say.
        hais lus dov nplaig To utter words hard to enunciate.

1. doog Tanned, sunburned, pertaining to sunburn.

2. doog Of blood congealed in the tissues.
        doog ntshav A blood bruise under the skin "black
        and blue."
        ntshav doog lawm Of blood confined in the tissues
        as in strangulation.

3. doog Dark red color.
        liab doog doog Very dark red, color of congealed
        blood.

doom
    muv doom Large species of edible bee (tus).

1. du Smooth, level.
        (a) du du li Very smooth.
        (b) du lug Very smooth.

2. du Clear of all extraneous matter as a clean table or
        clear ground.

1. dub Black
        dub dub li Very black.
        (a) dub txig Perfectly black.
        (b) dub nciab Perfectly black.
        siab dub txig A 'black' heart, evil heart, unmerciful.
        dub lias Not very black.

2. dub Selfish.
        qia dub Selfish.

3. dub A bad wind, storm.
        cua daj cua dub A bad wind, storm.

duj
        (a) mus duj duam To walk with big steps.
        (b) mus daws duam To walk with big steps.

1. dua Again, another, to repeat, used to indicate similar
        action on another occasion past or present.
        ua dua To do again.
        ua dua lawm To have done before.
        yuav ua dua Will do again.
        tsis tau ua dua Haven't done before.
        dua ib zaug A second time.
        ua dua ib zaug To do a second time.
        yug dua tshiab To be born again.
        tsis tau hnov dua Have not heard before.
        dua ib hnub Another day.

2. dua To pass on, to go (cf. 'mus').
        dua tim lawv lawm Gone on over to them across the
        valley.
        Dua twg lawm? Where has (he, it) gone?
        Dua hauv dej lawm Gone into the water.
        sijhawm dua lawm Too late, the time has passed.

3. dua To surpass, more than, better than.
        zoo dua Better than.
        loj dua Bigger than.
        dua ntais 'Much better.'
        loj dua ntais Much bigger.
        loj dua ntais huvsi Much bigger than all others.
        ntseeg dua To really believe.
        hlob dua tej Greater than others.

4. dua To tear, to rip (intentionally) (contr. 'ntuag').
        Torn by something.
        Muab dua pov tseg. Tear it up and get rid of it.
        (a) pos khawb Torn by a thorn.
        (b) pos dua Torn by a thorn.
        dua rhe lawm Torn up, completely torn apart.

5. dua Whether or not, makes no difference (cf. 'xijpeem').
        Hlub kuj tsis dua, tsis hlub kuj tsis dua. It makes
        no difference whether he looks after me or not.
        Tsis dua ntawm koj It's up to you. Do as you will.

6. dua
        ncab dua ntsag Obstinate.

1. duab Shadow (tus).
        tus duab The shadow.
        (a) duab ntxoov Shadow, shade.
        (b) ntxoov duab Shadow, shade.

2. duab Ray, light or sunbeam.
        duab tshav ntuj A sunbeam, ray of sunlight.

duaj Peach (lub).
        txiv duaj Peach.

duam Big steps.
  (a) mus duj duam To walk with big steps.
  (b) mus daws duam To walk with big steps.

1. duas The notch made in a tree when it is being
     felled (lub).
    duas ntoo Notch made in a tree for felling.

2. duas yuaj xyoob Bamboo sheath, the thin tough sheath
     around a joint of bamboo.

1. duav A shovel, spatula, paddle (rab).
    rab duav do mov Small wooden paddle used to stir
     cooked rice.
    duav phuaj An oar (rab).

2. duav The region of the lower back or waist (lub).
    mob duav Pain in the back.
    nruab duav The region of the waist (lub).
    ncab duav To stretch oneself, stretch the
     body erect.
    tiag duav A pad tied at the back of the waist for
     carrying water buckets, etc.
    duav siv A Hmong man's sash (txoj).

3. duav
    (a) duav pus The shoulder blades.
    (b) nplooj pus The shoulder blades.

4. duav Term used in putting on a roof.
    duav ruv tsev To put on the roofing leaves, etc.
     over the ridge pole.

dwb A man's given name, a name given to men.

---

dhas To shell, separate the kernels from the cob.
    dhas pobkws To shell corn, separate Indian corn
     kernels from the cob.

dhau Through, to pass through, beyond.
    mus dhau lawm Has gone through, beyond the mark.
    dhau ib hnub After one day, having passed through
     one day.
    lig dhau lawm Too late, late beyond the mark.
    dhau plaws Through, has gone or come through.
    loj dhau Too big, big beyond the measure.
    Tus mob dhau tug li tiag. The epidemic keeps on
     spreading. (The sickness passes on from one
     to another).

dhawv p.v.int. used with 'dhev' cf. 'dhev.'
    quaj nqus ntswg dhawv dhev To cry bitterly.

dhev p.v.int.
    (a) quaj dhuj dhev To cry a little bit.
    (b) quaj dhev To cry a little bit.
    luag nrov dhev To laugh loudly.
    nrov dhev Loud.
    sib xyaws dhev To be mixed up together (cf. mixed
     rice and vegetables).

dhees To limp, of a limping gait.
    mus ib dhees ib dhees To limp along, of an unsteady
     gait due to injury, pain, etc.

dheev p.v.int. indicating suddenness.
    tsim dheev los To wake up suddenly.
    (a) nco dheev To suddenly remember.
    (b) nco dhuj dheev To suddenly remember.
    (a) ras dheev To be startled, suddenly surprised.
    (b) ras pes dheev To be startled, suddenly surprised.
    nco dheev tsos Suddenly remembered something.
    siab ras dheev To suddenly awake to something.
    Also used with the following verbs:
    saib, pom, hnov, xav, paub, txhais

1. dhia To jump, skip, gallop.
    dhia ib plhaw To make one leap, leap up, one jump.
    dhia ib caws qia sawv ntsug With one leap (he) stood up.
    dhia ib tsaug nrov ntwg mus Noisily ran away in a
     crowd together.
    (a) dhia paj paws To jump, to leap.
    (b) dhia ntsos To jump, to leap.

2. dhia To throb, to beat (used of heartbeat).

dhos To fit together, to fit (cf. 'txuas').
sib dhos Fitting close together (although not
    actually connected), as in a wood joint,
    boards fitting, etc.
dhos kuv siab According to my wish, agrees with
    my heart's desire (cf. 'raug,' 'hum').

dhuj P.v.int. Used in connection with other p.v.
    intensives.
quaj dhuj dhev To cry a little bit.
nco dhuj dheev To suddenly remember.

dhuas To eat ravenously (of animals).
npua dhuas dhuas The pig is eating ravenously.

dhuav Indicating action carried to the place of being
    tired of it, thoroughly and beyond measure.
caij tsheb dhuav lawm Tire of riding in cars.
so dhuav Rested to full satisfaction.
(a) dhuav siab Don't like it.
(b) siab tsis nyiam Don't like it.

F

fa An adulteress (tus).
nkauj fa (tus) An adulteress, one who runs away
    from her husband and prefers another.

1. fab Weedy, overgrown (cf. 'ntxhos').
    hav fab (lub) A weedy overgrown valley.
    kev fab fab li An overgrown trail.

2. fab A division, a section, clf. for sections, divisions.
    hais ob fab lus Double-tongued, speaking in two
        different ways.
    plaub fab Having four sections, the 'four points' of
        the compass, four corners of the earth.
    xwmfab (C) Square, four sided.

3. fab To turn over (as a page, etc.) (C) cf. 'ntxeev.'

4. fab
    fab thiaj To fall backward.

5. fab
    tsis liab fab Don't like.

6. fab To be upset, distressed, confused.
    siab fab Heart upset, confused, mind not clear.

7. fab
    phob fab All the work of moving, making new fields,
        building a new house, etc.

8. fab
    mob fab Of a fit or coma after eating something
        that doesn't agree.

9. fab
    (a) thob fab The foundation beams of a house.
    (b) tim cum The foundation beams of a house.

10. fab (fab fo)
    ntxuav yias fab fo To clean the pan out all around.

1. faj To be on the alert, careful, wary of, watchful.
    ceebfaj Careful, watchful, on the alert.
    faj mob faj tuag. To be wary of sickness and death.

2. faj fajsuab Haze.

3. faj (a) loj faj Prison, jail.
    (b) tsev loj faj Prison, jail (lub).

4. faj
   (a) mob faj   Carbuncle.
   (b) mob npuag faj   Carbuncle.

5. faj   lawj faj   Sulphur.

6. faj   nees faj kav   A yellow horse (C).

7. faj
   (a) tamfaj   Probably (C).
   (b) kwvlam   Probably.

8. faj   fajtim   Emperor (C)   (cf. 'huabtais')

9. faj   fajkhum, hmab fajkhum (txoj) A kind of jungle vine that lives on trees and gradually strangles them. It creaks noisily as soon as it is cut and it therefore is used metaphorically of liars.
   Koj taug ceg fajkhum You're telling tall tales, lying.
   (You are following the branches of the 'fajkhum'
   NOTE: This is also sometimes spelled 'fajkhaum')

10. faj   Clf. for one of a couplet.
    ib faj   One of a pair, half of a rhyme.

11. faj   mob muas faj   Sickness with pain all over, no fever.

12. faj   fajlem (C) (see below)
    ntawv fajlem   Book of astrology, book used to foretell lucky and unlucky years, sickness and calamity etc., especially Chinese books so used but also of any book or document used in foretelling.

1. fam   Of things blinding the eyes.
   fam fam qhovmuag (so bright it...) blinds the eyes.

2. fam   fam tawb   Needlework basket (lub).

3. fam
   (a) tus niam txam fam   The woman responsible for cooking rice at a funeral.
   (b) tus niam fam txam   The woman responsible for cooking rice at a funeral.

1. fav   To turn around (C).
   fav xeeb   To turn against, rebel, change heart (C) (cf. 'ntxeev siab').

2. fav   saib tsis fav   To see indistinctly.

faib   To divide, divide off, divide into parts.
   faib ua ob co   Divide into two parts.
   Faib ib tug rau kuv.   Give (divide off) one to me.
   Muab faib rau sawvdaws noj.   Divide it up for everyone to eat.

faij   lub tsib faij   A type of small bottle.

faiv
   faiv fuaj (lub)   A flashlight (T).
   nta faiv fuaj   To light a flashlight.
   faiv fuaj cig   The flashlight is on.
   txo faiv fuaj   To put out the flashlight.
   roj faiv fuaj   Flashlight batteries (lub).

faus   To turn over the earth, to cultivate, to turn the weeds and sod over and expose the fresh earth (cf. 'voob').
   faus teb   To cultivate the fields, prepare fields for planting.

fawb   To search for something amid a mass of other things, e.g. amid trash or leaves on the ground or in a stack of grain, etc. (cf. 'tshawb').

fem   ua fem feeb   To talk in one's sleep.

fee   To turn away from.
   fee rau nws   Turned from him, turned face from him.
   fee plhu   To turn the face, turn the cheek.

1. feeb   To distinguish, discern, divide (C).
   feeb meej   To distinguish clearly, discern clearly.
   feeb tsis meej   Can't distinguish clearly, confused.
   siab feeb pes tsia   Confused.
   (a) tsis feeb tsis fwm   Confused, not clearheaded, drunken.
   (b) cis feeb cis fwm   Confused, not clearheaded, drunken.

2. feeb   Fainted, unconscious (C).
   feeb lawm   Fainted, unconscious.

3. feeb   ua fem feeb   To talk in one's sleep.

1. feem   A part, a portion (C).
   kuv li feem   My portion.
   pub kuv ib feem   To give me a portion.

2. feem feem lawm To disappear.
   ua feem lawm To disappear.

fi To send, to send something to someone (cf. 'xa').
   fi xov To send a message (cf. 'xa xov').
   tus fi xov A messenger.
   fi mus rau lawv Send it to them.

1. fim To be acquainted with a person, to have met.
   tsis tau sib fim (we) haven't yet met, not acquainted with (him or her).

2. fim Must, certainly, concerning certainty.
   Kuv fim yuav ua. I certainly must do it. I certainly will do it.
   Tsis ntev fim yuav txog. We certainly will be there before long.
   Kuv tsis fim hais li cas. I wasn't certain what to say. I didn't care to say anything. (For lack of evidence, would do no good, etc.)
   Kuv tsis fim ua li cas. I wasn't certain what to do. Didn't know what to do.

3. fim To ignore.
   tsis fim kuv Ignores me.

4. fim To interfere in the affairs of others (cf. 'txuam').

fiv To make a request for aid with the promise of future pay.
   (a) fiv rau dab To request of the spirits with promise of suitable sacrifice at a future date.
   (b) fiv dab To request of the spirits with promise of suitable sacrifice at a future date.
   fiv yeem Promise of offering to the spirits later. (cf. 'txi dab,' contr. 'pauj yeem').

fiab One one-hundredth of an ounce, unit of weight.

fiav To push something and set it in motion swinging like a pendulum or swing (cf. 'yoj').

fo ntxuav yias fab fo Clean the pan out all around.

fob To compress with the hands.
   fob mov To compress and pack cooked rice together with the hands as done by the Lao to make it more solid and easier to handle in eating.

fos To be covered up out of sight.
   fos ntais Covered up and out of sight.
   Koj yuav fos. You will die. (be buried) (an expression used in cursing).

1. foob To seal something shut (C), sew up the seam of a jacket.
   foob lub qhovntxa To seal the grave or tomb.

2. foob
   foobxab (lub) A windbox used as a bellows to pump air for the fire in forging metal (cf. 'lwj') (C)

3. foob
   sab foob To have a cold (C) (cf. 'khaub thuas').

4. foob
   foob pob (lub) A bomb (C) (sometimes pronounced 'hoob pob').
   foob pob tawg The bomb exploded.

fooj To accuse (T).

1. foom To fix (as a judgment), seal the fate whether for good or for evil. (cf. 'tsawm') (C).
   Ob leeg sib foom. The two set a curse on each other.

2. foom A curse (lub).

fuab fuabtais Alternate spelling for 'huabtais' cf. 'huabtais'

fuaj faiv fuaj (lub) A flashlight (T) cf. 'faiv.'

1. fwm Clf. for sets, suits, etc. e.g. A set of horse harness.

2. fwm cis feeb cis fwm cf. 'feeb.'

fwv fwv khawv (lub) A natural gateway or pass through the jungle or landscape where any wild game will be forced to pass by reason of the natural configuration.

G

gig The sound of tigers fighting.
   Tsov tom gig gog gig gog. The tigers are fighting
     and making a noise of growling 'gig gog.'

gog The sound of tigers fighting.
   Tsov tom gig gog gig gog. The tigers are fighting
     and making a noise of growling 'gig gog.'

gus A goose (tus).

H

ha   t.c. from 'hav,' (cf. 'hav').

hab Stupid, dazed, confused.
   hab lawm Stupid, dazed, dazed, confused.
   Nws nyob ib tug hab nuv tseg. He was confused, dazed.
     (because of amazement and apprehension)
     'hab nuv tseg' (cf. 'yoob zog tseg' and
     'ruaj zog tseg').

1. haj Yet, still.
   Nws haj hais dua. He still said more. He said again.
     He spoke further saying...

2. haj yam Still more, more so, comparative degree.
   (a) haj yam zoo dua Still better than (cf. 'keem').
   (b) keem zoo dua Still better than.
   (c) haj yam keem zoo Still better than.
   Nws tseem haj yam yuav... Much more likely will
     he...

3. haj tseem Still in process of doing.
   haj tseem noj mov Is still eating.
   haj tseem ua Still doing.

4. haj tsheej haj Industrious, energetic (C).

1. ham To weld, to solder.
   ham thawj To solder, to solder together.
   ham hlau To weld iron or steel.

2. ham
   ham cia To keep a person confined, to lock someone
     up in one place.

1. hav A valley, a broad expanse, (lub) t.c.
   hav dej A river valley (lub).
   hav zoov The jungle.
   hav fab An overgrown grassy valley.
   hav cua The atmosphere.
   hav huab An expanse of clouds.
   hav pos A valley of thorns, a large area of thorn
     bushes.
   txhoj hav A shallow valley.
   (a) lub kwj ha A valley.
   (b) lub hav A valley.
   lub hav zawj An enclosed valley.
   lub vos hav A broad level valley.

2. hav An introductory exclamatory particle.
   Hav, lwm hnub? What, in a day or so?

1. hais To speak, to say.
   hais lus To speak words, to speak.
   hais tias... Spoke saying...
   hais nkauj Speak songs, i.e. to sing.
     (more commonly, to sing is 'hu nkauj').
   hais kwv txhiaj To serenade, to sing ballads
     (cf. 'kwv txhiaj').
   hais quj qees To speak slowly and steadily.
   hais nrawm nrawm li To speak very quickly.
   hais lus sis To speak with an accent, speak not
     clearly.
   (a) hais dag To lie, to deceive.
   (b) hais nkaub To lie, to deceive.
   hais tshawv tshawv To speak roughly, raucously,
     impolitely.
   hais lus mos mos To speak kindly, courteously.
   hais qees To keep on speaking even when told to stop.
   hais tsuag las To speak unconvincingly, speak
     without force or conviction.
   hais ceev nrooj To speak with certainty and con-
     viction, speak convincingly, forcefully.
   hais lus plov meej To speak openly, face to face.
   hais tuag nthi To speak to the finish, finished,
     the matter settled, finalized.
   hais kiag To say definitely, decide.
   hais ob fab lus Double tongued, speak in two ways.

hais lus plhov xem Round-about talk, indirect speech,
    not coming to grips with a subject.
hais lus dov nplaig To speak difficult words hard
    to pronounce.
hais ua nqaj ua nqug Everyone talking about something
    at the same time.
hais lus plhob phij To speak worthless words.
hais lus plij ploj plij ploj Queer sounding language,
    language like the sound of bamboo bursting.
hais kom nto ntsis Tell it to the finish, carry the
    matter to a conclusion.
hais lus siab lawv To speak words despising them.
hais lus tuam mom lawv Always cursing them, can't
    see them without cursing and scolding them.
hais nraum caj qwb To speak "behind one's back."
hais lus ntog nraws To speak peculiar sounds, as
    of someone speaking a foreign language.

2. hais To dip out (cf. 'ce').
hais dej To dip water.
hais mov To dip or scoop rice out of a container,
    to serve rice for eating.
hais nkoj To row a boat.

1. haiv Of grain or corn beaten down by wind or rain and
    hence leaning over.

2. haiv To push aside with the hand.
haiv nroj To push foliage or weeds apart with the
    hand as in making one's way along an over-
    grown trail or in preparation for cutting
    it at the base (cf. 'phuab').

3. haiv Referring to those of another surname.
haiv Hmoob All Hmong of another surname.
haiv neeg Men of another surname.
sawvdaws haiv neeg All people, everybody.

1. hau To boil something in water or in liquid (contr.
    'rhaub').
hau zaub To boil vegetables, cook vegetables.

2. hau A lid, a cover (lub).

3. hau Head, the head (lub).
lub taubhau The head, head.
plaubhau Hair of the head (txoj).
nyo hau To bow the head.
ncaws hau To nod the head.
tig taubhau To turn the head around.
co taubhau To wag the head.
hau pliaj The forehead.
hau xaws The fontanelle on the head of a young child.
do do hau Baldheaded, bald.
dawb hau nrig caug White-headed, aged, hoary headed.
lub hau roob The head of the mountain, mountain top.

4. hau The leader, head person (tus).
tus hau zos The headman of a village.
tus hau rog The leader of the group that circles
    the house in mock battle at a funeral (cf. 'tuag').

5. hau
nyob ua ib hau Together in one place.

haub To lead astray (cf. 'toov,' 'ntxias').
Lawv haub kuv li menyuam nrog lawv mus. They led my
    children away with them.
Leej twg haub toov koj? Who has led you astray?

1. hauj To mix several things together. (cf. 'xyaw').
    To mix things up.

2. hauj
haujlwm Work, especially domestic work, chores.
ua haujlwm To do domestic work, to work (cf. 'ua num').
lauj haujlwm zias cia To put work aside.

3. hauj
(a) haujsam (tus) A Buddhist priest (C).
(b) hujsam (tus) A Buddhist priest (C).

4. hauj
(a) hauj yum Gunpowder (C).
(b) huj yum Gunpowder (C).

5. hauj
yam hauj ham xwm Things, business (C).

haum (cf. 'koob haum' also cf. 'hum').

haus To drink.
haus dej To drink water.
haus nrov hlawv To drink noisily.
haus hujsim To drink moderately (of intoxicants).
haus hlo To drink right away, drink immediately.

1. hauv Within, in, inside.
nyob hauv tsev In the house, at home.
nyob hauv teb In the fields, at the fields.

2. hauv
hauv qab Underneath.
(a) hauv lub qab rooj Under the table.
(b) hauv qab rooj Under the table.
hauv roob The foot of the mountain.
ntog rau hauv pem teb Fell upon the ground, stumbled
    to the earth.
hauv ntuj ntsa ntsa The dawn just before the sun
    rises (the 'underside' of the heavens alight).

3 hauv
  hauvpaus (lub) Stump, base, basis, root, origin.
  hauvpaus ntoo Tree stump.
  hauvpaus hniav Writing, written letters.
  lub hauv dej The source of a river or stream.
  tus niam hauvpaus cos The woman in charge of pounding
    rice for a funeral feast.
  hauv dej Upstream.

4. hauv
  hauvcaug Knees, the knee.
  (a) qhau hauvcaug To kneel.
  (b) txhos hauvcaug To kneel.

5. hauv
  thooj siab hum hauv One in heart, in harmony and
    in fellowship.

6. hauv
  hauv plag The rear wall of the Hmong house, the uphill
    wall of the house.
  nyob ntawm hauv plag On the rear wall.

7. hauv
  cov ua hauv qhua Those relatives who bring rice,
    paper money, etc. as gifts for the dead on
    the day before killing animals and burial.

8. hauv
  zaub ntsuab tiav hauv lawm The vegetables have formed
    clumps and are ready for picking.

9. hauv
  lub hauv roob Mountain.

haw
  (a) haw haw quav Much defecating, of a person
    having to relieve the bowels frequently.
  (b) haw quav li Much defecating, of a person
    having to relieve the bowels frequently.

1. hawb To purr.
  hawb pob Of an animal purring.

2. hawb Hoarse, hoarseness of speech, to speak indistinctly.
  hais lus hawb To speak with hoarseness.

3. hawb
  neeg tsis tshoob hawb A well-to-do person who purposely
    dresses poorly to cover up his wealth.

hawj Spirited, of animals with energy and spirit (some-
    times said 'ha').
  hawj hawj li Of a spirited animal.

hawm To show respect with both hands raised palms together
    in the fashion of the Thai greeting.

1. haws A kind of Chinese medicine used by the Hmong (in
    Chinese called 'txhob ku').

2. haws To identify as one's own (used of persons as
    'hom' is of fields).

1. hawv
  lub pas hawv A muddy hole with water running through.

2. hawv To cry out (sometimes in White Hmong but more common
    in Blue Hmong) (cf. 'qw').

3. hawv To threaten (sometimes in White Hmong but more common
    in Blue Hmong).

4. hawv Restricted p.v.int. with 'huav' (cf. Appendix 8).

1. hem To scare, to frighten, to intimidate (C).

2. hem hemcav (lub) A ship or motor propelled boat.

hee To whinny, to neigh.
  nees hee Horse whinnys, horse neighing.

1. heev Intense, severe.
  siab heev Impatient, severe, stern, harsh.
  neeg heev sawv A severe person, one prone to fight,
    quick tempered, very energetic (cf. 'neeg
    nyaum nyaum').

2. heev Used as intensive particle after verbs.
  zoo heev heev li Very very good.
  zoo tsis heev Not very good.
  loj heev Very large.

3. heev
  tus heev nyuj A large full-grown castrated bull.

hib Used for the sound of laughing.
  luag hib hib To laugh "He He."

1. hiv
  Yuav ib tug hiv thiaj mus. There must be another
    to go ahead or the others will not follow.
    (of pack animals going in a train, etc.)

2. hiv
nyob hia hiv Eaten too full, uncomfortably 'stuffed.'

hia Satiated, uncomfortably full of food.
(a) hia hia li Eaten too full, uncomfortably 'stuffed.'
(b) nyob hia hiv Eaten too full, uncomfortably 'stuffed.'

1. hiab A leech (tus).

2. hiab To weave (with rattan or bamboo, etc., not with thread).
hiab lev To weave a mat.
hiab kawm To weave a back basket.
txiav xyoob phua ncaw hiab lev To cut bamboo and split into lengths for weaving a mat.

3. hiab
hiab xab A person's face (poetical).

1. hiam To suspect, to accuse.

2. hiam
lim hiam Fierce, cruel, ferocious (C) (of men or animals).

1. hiav Scorched, toasted, almost burned (used of rice or vegetables browned but not burned black).

2. hiav The sea, the ocean.
hiav txwv The sea, the ocean.
tiv txwv hiav txwv The bottom of the sea.

1. ho Of animals losing a litter or a calf, etc. prematurely.
npua ho The sow has lost her litter.

2. ho Connective particle indicating sequence and carrying forward the action of the verb, and, and then...
Mus ho tuaj. Come again. (Common greeting to a person leaving and going to his home.)
Mus ho los. Come again. (Common greeting to a person leaving and going to a place not his home as to the fields, etc.)
Nws ho yuav sau nyiaj. And so he wants to collect money.
Nws xav noj ho ntshai. He wants to eat but is afraid.

3. ho
zeb ho Sharpening stone (lub) t.c., cf. 'hov.'

1. hob Astringent, puckery, of unripe fruit (cf. 'pluas').
noj hob hob ntsim ntsim To eat something which leaves an astringent feeling in the mouth or throat.

2. hob Of something stuck in the throat (cf. medicine that one cannot seem to swallow) (cf. 'hua').

3. hob Of the cooling sensation in the throat produced by menthol, etc.

hoj
hoj huam (tus) A kind of jungle fowl with a long flowing tail.

1. hom To mark out, to identify with a mark, mark for ownership.
hom teb To mark out an area to be made into fields for future cultivation. The usual mark is a sliver of wood cut and put into a tree or sapling horizontally.

2. hom To seal, a mark of identification (lub).
lub hom thawj A seal, a mark of identification.
ntaus hom thawj To mark for identification.

3. hom clf. for kinds or classes of things. (cf. 'yam')
ib yam ntoo One kind of Tree.
ib hom ntoo One kind of Tree.

4. hom Energetic.
hom khaj Energetic, spirited (of persons or animals) to jump for joy.

5. hom To make threatening motions.
hom rau peb mentsis Motioned toward us with a stick or with the hand as if to hit us.

hos Initial particle.
Hos zaum no kuv hais rau nej... And this time I say to you...

1. hov To sharpen on a sharpening stone.
hov riam To sharpen a knife on a whetstone.
zeb ho A sharpening stone (lub) t.c.

2. hov Used as both a question word and an emphatic to indicate "how much?" or "very much" in matters of size, length, quantity, etc.
Hov ntau li? How much?
(a) Mob ntev li cas? How long have you been ill?
(b) Mob hov ntev li? How long have you been ill?
tus tibneeg hov loj The person of very large frame, the big person.

hons Final particle.
  Yuav kuv qhia nej hons! So you need me to teach you!
  Ua li no hons. Do it like this.
  Mus txoj no hons. Go this way.
  Sawvdaws mus hons. All of us will go.

hoo nas hoo twm (tus) The red-bellied squirrel (C).

hoob hoob pob (lub) A bomb (C).
  hoob pob tawg The bomb exploded. (occasional pronunciation for 'foob pob.' cf. 'foob').

1. hu To call, to cry out, to sing.
  hu npe To call a name, to name, call by name (cf. 'daws').
  hu kom nws tuaj Call him to come.
  hu tias... Cried saying..., called saying...
  hu nkauj To sing a song.

2. hu Gluttonous, greedy (cf. 'siab hlob').
  (a) hu hu loj Of a person who eats like a glutton.
  (b) hu hu dab Of a person who eats like a glutton.
  neeg hu hu loj A glutton.

3. hu Name of a bird (named for the sound of the bird call).
  hu vaj (tus) The great hornbill.
  hu vaj xyoob (tus) Small hornbill.

1. hub Large water storage vessel (lub) (usually of stone or pottery).

2. hub A clay vessel for household use, clay pot (lub).

1. huj hujsam (tus) A Buddhist priest (C), also 'haujsam'

2. huj hujsim In moderation.
  haus hujsim To drink in moderation (of intoxicants).

3. huj hujxwv xav Intending to do whether granted permission or not, desiring to do with intensity. (cf. 'cam thawj.')

1. hum Fitting, right, suitable, appropriate (said 'haum' in Laos).
  hum nkaus Very fitting, very suitable, just right.
  hum siab Satisfied, seeing eye to eye (cf. 'dhos, raug').
  thooj siab hum hauv Oneness of heart, in heart fellowship, harmony of mind.
  tsis hum Unfitting, unsuitable.

2. hum Goods, articles (C).
  ua moj hum To do coarse work or workmanship.
  ua xim hum To do fine work or workmanship.

3. hum povhum (lub) A charm, a precious stone.

hus To gather together with the hand.
  Muab tes hus kiag los. Grab the things together with your hand.
  Muab hus los pov tseg. Gather it together with your hands and get rid of it. (as in clearing away stubble from around the rice stack before burning off the field.)

1. huv All, altogether.
  huvsi Altogether, all.
  (a) huv huv li All, altogether.
  (b) huv tibsi All, altogether.
  tag huv huv li Completely gone, all gone.
  noj huvsi Eat it all.

2. huv Clean, undefiled.
  Mov tsis huv. The rice is dirty and not fit to eat.

hua To stick in the throat (as medicine that won't go down or of things hard to swallow. cf. 'hob').

1. huab Cloud, clouds, cloudy (clf. 'tauv' or 'twv').
  ib tau huab One cloud, a cloud ('tau' t.c.)
  ib ntuj huab Clouded over sky, whole sky of clouds.
  pos huab nti Clouds all around, surrounded by cloud.
  pos pos huab Foggy (temporarily).
  (a) ib hav huab An expanse of cloud or fog.
  (b) ib plag huab An expanse of cloud or fog.
  cov huab Clouds, the clouds.
  huab ntsau tsawv Foggy, cloudy (steadily).

2. huab Varicolored (C).
  nees huab A varicolored horse, brown and white horse.

3. huab huabtais (cf. 'fuabtais') (tus) Great ruler, emperor, legendary Hmong king, king.

4. huab
  (a) huabhwm A people, a citizenry.
  (b) pejxeem huabhwm A people, a citizenry.

5. huab huabxeeb (lub) Peanut, the peanut (C).

6. huab yimhuab (cf. 'yim').

7. huab
   huablab (T) A westerner, a European (tus).

1. huaj Of an exhausted animal.
   Tus nees huaj lawm. The horse is exhausted and
      cannot go on.

2. huaj
   huajvam To flourish, to increase (cf. 'huam').

1. huam To increase, to spread, to prosper (cf. 'huajvam').
   huam loj loj mus To increase, prosper, spread.
   lo lus tuam huam Proud boastful words, 'spreading'
      words.

2. huam A craving, to crave.
   tus huam The craving.
   huam yeeb To crave opium.

3. huam Suddenly, quickly, spasm, spasmodic.
   huam tshom To jump in surprise or in being startled.
      (cf. 'ceeb nkaus').
   (a) ib sij huam Quickly, suddenly.
   (b) ib sij ib huam Quickly, suddenly.
   mob huam leej huam ceem Sudden sickness.
   huam ib tshaj ib tshaj To have spasms, a fit,
      sudden convulsions.
   huam cheej The last spasm before death.

4. huam
   chivkeeb huam yuaj In the very beginning (idiom).

5. huam
   kwvhuam Olden times, old tales.

6. huam
   hoj huam (tus) A kind of jungle fowl with long
      flowing tail.

7. huam
   kob huam Poor, poverty stricken.
   neeg kob huam A poverty stricken person.

huas To go around and ahead of.
   (a) huas ntej To go around and ahead of a person.
   (b) huas ntej ntiag To go around and ahead of
      a person.
   (c) huas tau ntej To go around and ahead of a
      person.
   (All three expressions imply forcing one's way past
      another person going in the same direction.)
   huas tau lawv ntej To go ahead of them, to go
      around them on the path.

1. huav Very dry and hard.
   huav huav li lawm Very dry and hard (of wood).

2. huav Restricted p.v.int. with 'hawv' (cf. Appendix 8).

1. hwb
   taub hwb (lub) A gourd.

2. hwb
   plhaub hwb (tus) An owl.

3. hwb
   txhem hwb txhib To separate from one another and
      forbid to marry.

1. hwj Bottle, kettle (lub) (C).
   ib lub hwj One bottle.
   lub hwj kais Teakettle (kettle with a spout).
   hwj tsib faib A type of small bottle.

2. hwj To support someone or something with the arms or hands.
   hwj taubhau To hold the head in the hands.
   hwj nws mus To support someone in walking (as in
      helping a lame or sick person).
   hwj tsis tau Cannot help him (cf. 'pab,' 'tab').
   tus hwj sawv The one who assists the shaman in his
      spirit ceremonies, the shaman's supporter.

3. hwj
   hwjtxob Black pepper.

4. hwj
   hwjtxwv Beard, the beard (C).
   tshais hwjtxwv To shave, shave the beard.

5. hwj
   hwjplhob (tsob) water lily.

6. hwj
   hwjchim (lub) Authority, air of authority, show or
      act of authority, splendor, power.
   hwjchim loj tsim txiaj Show of great power and
      authority, "miracle."

7. hwj
   hwjxwm To prepare, get ready for, care for (cf. 'tsomkwm').

8. hwj
   (a) hwj huam yees ntxwv (C) Magic, magic display.
   (b) hwj huam yees siv (C) Magic, magic display.

9. hwj
   phimhwj To honor, do deference to, respect (C)
      (cf. 'hwm').

1. hwm To reverence, to honor, respect, to defer to,
   to esteem (C).
   Yuav hwm niam txiv. Respect your parents.
   Nws tsis hwm kuv. He didn't honor my word.

2. hwm povhwm To protect, defend, guard, shelter (C).

3. hwm To pound out a thinner area of metal between two
   thicker areas. (A term used in forging metal.)

4. hwm (a) huabhwm A people, a citizenry (cf. pejxeem).
        (b) pejxeem huabhwm A people, a citizenry.

5. hwm sau meejhwm To take a census (C).
        meejhwm A census (C).

6. hwm 'tswjhwm' (cf. 'tswj').

hws Perspiration, condensed moisture.
     tawm hws To perspire.

1. hwv To graze on stubble or stalks.
   hwv nees To set horses free to graze on stubble or
   cornstalks in the fields.

2. hwv hwvtaus (rab) A hatchet (C).

3. hwv hwvcheej (lub) A guitar or dulcimer (C).

hwwv An intensive final particle (cf. 'heev').
   ntaiv qos hwwv Extremely hot.
   loj hwwv Extremely large.
   Koj kumyuj txawj xam hwwv. You certainly can
   figure things out! (somewhat satirical).

hla To cross over, go across.
     hla plaws To cross completely over.
     hla dhau mus To cross through the midst, pass over
     to the other side.

1. hlab To scald, scalding.
   hlab npua To scald a pig, pour on scalding water to
   dehair a slaughtered pig.
   dej kub hlab Scalded by hot water.
   roj hlab Scalded by hot oil.

2. hla To encircle (as a belt or sash).
   hlab siv (txoj) The red sash on a Hmong woman's apron.
   hlab ntxhoo (txoj) The ends of a Hmong woman's apron sash.
   hlab ntaub (txoj) The embroidery strip encircling a
   turban.
   txoj hlab ntawv The umbilical cord.

3. hla
   hlab pas The oesophagas.

4. hla
   khaub hlab Old clothing, rags, (cf. 'khaub ncaws'),
   ragged, worn out.

1. hlav To put forth leaves or shoots or roots.
   hlav nplooj To put forth leaves.
   hlav ntsuag To put forth shoots (as a new shoot on
   a tree stump, etc.)
   (a) hlav cag To put forth roots.
   (b) nrhau cag To put forth roots.

2. hlav A burning stick.
   hlav hluavtaws (tus) A burning stick in the fire,
   piece of burning firewood.

3. hlav
   plab hlav Sharp abdominal pain.

hlais To cut, to slice, cut with a slicing motion (contr.
   'txiav').
   hlais nqaij To slice meat.

1. hlau Iron (contr. 'kab').
   ntaus hlau To beat or forge iron.
   ntsia hlau A nail, nails.
   nchuav hlau To pour molten iron, melt iron to mould.
   niam hlau A magnet (lub).

2. hlau A hoe, the curved type of hoe used by Meo (rab).

3. hlau Clf. for strokes of the curved Hmong hoe, a hoeful
   rau hlau av Six hoefuls of earth.
   ib hlaus One hoeful (Note t.c.).

1. hlaub Pertaining to the lower part of the human leg.
   plab hlaub The lower part of the leg, particularly
       the fleshy part at the back of the lower leg.
   (a) roob hlaub The shin, the front of the lower leg.
   (b) roob qhib The shin, the front of the lower leg.

2. hlaub The warp in weaving, the long threads crossed
       by the 'txia.'

3. hlaub The upright supporting frame across which the
       more flexible strands are woven in making a basket.

hlaus t.c. cf. 'hlau' Definition No. 3.

hlauv To fall through.
   hlauv qhov lawm Fell through the hole.
   hlauv hnyuv Prolapsed bowel, hernia.

hlaw t.c., (cf. 'hlawv' Definition 2, No. 6).

1. hlaws Beads, esp. the tiny glass beads used on Hmong
       clothing (lub).

2. hlaws Bead-like.
   qhovmuag hlaws hlaws Bright shining eyes like beads
       (of persons or animals).

1. hlawv To burn something (contr. 'kub hnyiab').
   Muab hlawv pov tseg Take it and burn it up.
   hlawv ntawv To burn paper (especially paper money
       in spirit rites).

2. hlawv Used as a p.v.int. (cf. Appendix p. 469).
   As a single intensive.
   Nws haus nrov hlawv. He drinks noisily.
   In combination with other intensives:
   hlawv hlo (used with verbs 'ntxeev,' 'ua,' 'tig,'
       'tshem')

   Lawv muab qhovtxhiachaw ntxeev hlawv hlo. They
       turned everything over. (turned everything
       upside down.)
   hlawv hlias (conveying the idea of recurrence)
   looj hlawv hlias Recurring unconsciousness.
   tsis nco qab hlaw hlias To keep forgetting things
       (Note t.c. in 'hlaw' after 'qab').

3. hlawv
   hlawv thiab A form of spirit rite performed for a
       person very ill. An egg is placed at the door-
       way and made to burst by use of a charcoal ember
       in an effort to recall the departing spirit.

1. hle To take off, to remove.
   Nws muab lub hau hle hlo. He took the lid completely
       off.
   Hle kausmom. Take the hat off. Take off your hat.

2. hle Finish, to finish (in certain limited contexts).
   hle lawm Finished (also cf. the following expressions
       with the same meaning: 'tag lawm,' 'khauv lawm,'
       'dawb lawm').

hleb A coffin (lub).
   (a) lub hleb A coffin.
   (b) lub hleb ntoos A coffin.
   Nws pab ntxua lub hlob. He helped make the coffin.

hlev To extend (the tongue).
   Hlev nplaig. Put out your tongue. Extend your tongue.

1. hli The moon (lub), month (lub).
   lub hli The moon.
   lub hli no This month.
   ib hli One month (t.c.)
   ib lub hli One month.
   rau hli Six months.
   cuaj hlis Nine months (t.c.)
   kaj hli Moonlight.
   (a) qaim hli Bright moonlight.
   (b) tshav hli Bright moonlight.
   hli xiab The waxing of the moon.
   hli nqeg The waning of the moon.
   hli nra Full moon
   phua qab thoob Half moon.
   hli nraim qaib The 16th and 17th of the lunar month.
       (the time when the moon comes up after the
       chickens have gone to roost.)
   nyob nruab hlis (t.c.) Of a woman in the first month
       after childbirth.

2. hli The white of an egg.
   hli qe (lub) Egg white, the white of an egg.
   Nws noj lub hli qe tag. He ate the egg white.

hlib To take something out from the ashes of the fire.
   Muab qos hlib los noj. Take the potato out of the
       ashes to eat.

1. hlis Variant spelling of 'hli' in conformity with patterns
       of tone change outlined in Appendix 1 (cf. 'hli').

2. hlis
   paj noob hlis (tsob) The sunflower.

3. hlis
   ntoo nplooj hlis A kind of hard tree or wood used
       for making handles, etc.

hliv To pour, to pour out (cf. 'qee,' 'theej').
   (for this meaning 'laub' is more commonly used
       in Blue Meo dialect).
   Muab hliv pov tseg. Pour it out and get rid of it.
   hliv nthwv To pour out, pour.

hlias Post verbal intensive (p.v.int.) cf. Appendix 8.
   looj hlawv hlias Recurring unconsciousness.
   tsis nco qab hlawv hlias To keep forgetting things.
   tsaug zog looj hlias Very sleepy.

hliav To sharpen to a round point.
   Koj pab hliav kuv tus cwjmem. Help sharpen my pencil
       for me.

1. hlo A post verbal intensive usually indicating a
       quality of immediacy in the action of the verb.
       It usually follows right after the verb. (cf.
       Appendix 8).
   vau hlo To fall over.
   rho hlo To pull out quickly.
   nqa hlo To carry off, take, hold.
   tsa hlo To raise up.
   tig hlo To turn around.
   qhib (qheb) hlo To open up.
   zoo hlo To get well.
   ris hlo To carry on the back.
   rov hlo To return.
   keev hlo Whole, solid; 'keev hlo ci' To roast whole.
   (a) ntxeev hlo To turn over.
   (b) ntxeev hlawv hlo To turn over.
   kwv hlo To carry on the shoulder.
Also used in a similar way with many other verbs, e.g.
   mus, los, sawv, hle, ua, kaw, muab, txais, hlawv,
       noj, haus, etc. (See listings under individual
       verbs for meanings.)

The subject may appear between the verb and 'hlo'
   poob siab hlo Frightened (literally 'a fallen liver').
   tsa tes hlo To raise the hand.
As a post verbal intensive 'hlo' may either be used as
   a single word as in the illustrations above, or
   in two word combinations. The combination
   '..pes hlo' may be used with the same verbs as
       outlined above and carries the same meaning.
   ras pes hlo Startled (cf. 'dheev'), quickly awakened.
   tsa pes hlo To raise up.

The combination '..hlo li' is used as an intensive
       ending to a statement or expression.
   Kuv tsis xav mus kev no hlo li. I really don't want
       to go this way.
The p.v.int. 'hlo' is also used in combination with
   'hlawv.'
   ntxeev hlawv hlo To turn everything over, turn over.
   Lawv muab qhovtxhiachaw ntxeev hlawv hlo. They turned
       everything upside down. (cf. 'hlawv')

2. hlo To suck in the breath.
   hlo hlo To suck in the breath.

1. hlob To grow, grow up, grown up.
   Koj tus menyuam hlob zoo zoo. Your child is growing
       well.
   Tsis kheev hlob. Doesn't seem to grow well.
   Nws hlob tiav hluas. He has grown up into a young man.

2. hlob The older, the elder (in human relationships).
   tus tub hlob The eldest son.
   Nws hlob kuv. He is older than I.
   txiv hlob Father's elder brother.
   niam hlob Wife of father's elder brother.

3. hlob Forceful, great in volume, 'heavy' in volume.
   cua hlob A great wind.
   Cua tshuab hlob hlob. The wind blows with great force.
   Los nag hlob hlob li. It is raining heavily.
   dej hlob High water, great flow of water.

4. hlob Proud.
   Nws muaj muaj hlob. He is proud. (looks down on others,
       won't answer properly when spoken to, etc.)
   Nws muaj siab hlob. He is covetous, gluttonous.
       (cf. 'hu hu dab,' 'hu hu loj').
   ncauj hlob Prone to curse, always cursing (proud mouth).
   (a) sam hlob Bad language.
   (b) sam kiag Bad language.

hloo To hibernate.
   Dais hloo. The bear hibernates.

hloob Nonconversant, uninclined to speak.
   neeg hloob A person who doesn't talk much.

hloov To change, to exchange.
   Nws hloov lub npe lawm. He changed his name.
   Rov mus tsev hloov khaubncaws. Go home and change
       your clothes.

hlu To stall, stall for time (as of a person purposely
     delaying going to work until others have
     finished the job). Don't stall, go and
     help right away.
     Txhob hlu, kov tsij mus pab.

hlub To show merciful care, to love (and look after), to
      pity, to have compassion (this word implies love
      and concern particularly as expressed in looking
      after the needs of another person) contr. 'nyiam'
      concern for their parents.
      Menyuam yuav hlub niam txiv. Children should have
      Lawv tsis hlub kuv. They don't love (look after) me.
      Tsis muaj neeg hlub. No one cares for me.

hluj Post verbal intensive used in combination, '...hluj hluav.'
      xuab taw hluj hluav To "Drag the feet."
      Nws xuab taw hluj hluav tsis xav mus kiag li. He kept
      dragging his feet and didn't want to go at all.

hlua Rope, string (clf. 'txoj' for lengths) (clf. 'kauj'
      for coils)
      Muab txoj hlua khi rawv. Tie it up tightly with a
      rope.
      (a) hlua ncaws A kind of small string snare for birds.
      (b) noog ncaws A kind of small string snare for birds.

hluas Young, younger.
       hluas Young, young, younger.
       (a) hluas hluas li Quite young.
       (b) hluas ntxhias Quite young.
       hluas nraug A young man, youth (unmarried).
       hluas nkauj A young woman, maiden (unmarried).
       Nws hlob tiav hluas. He grew into young manhood.
       cov tiav hluas Young people.
       txiv hluas Husband of a woman's younger sister (or)
           husband of wife's younger sister.
       niam hluas Wife's younger sister.

1. hluav Embers, coals.
   hluav ntawv The remains of burned paper.
   hluav ncaig Wood embers, coals.

2. hluav
   hluavtaws Fire (clf. 'cub').
   Hluavtaws kub kub li. The fire is hot!
   Menyuam tsis txhob kov hluavtaws. Children should
       not handle fire.
   (a) ib plag hluavtaws A great expanse of fire.
   (b) ib ntuj hluavtaws A great expanse of fire.
   (c) ntuj tawg A great expanse of fire.
   nplaim hluavtaws Flames.
   hlav hluavtaws Lighted sticks burning in the fire.

3. hluav
   hluav hluav hluav ncuav Full of holes, pock marked.
   plhu hluav hluav ncuav Face marked with pock marks.

4. hluav Post verbal intensive used with 'hluj.' (cf. 'hluj')

1. hlw Tapering to a rounded point.
   (a) hlw zuj zus Tapering to a point, getting smaller.
   (b) me zuj zus Tapering to a point, getting smaller.

2. hlw A species of forest animal (tus).
   moj hlw A species of small rodent (tus).

hlwb Brain, marrow.
      hlwb pobtxha Bone marrow.
      Nws li hlwb tus tus. He has a good brain.
      hlwb ntag ruam Mentally dull.

hlws Crotch.
      hlws ris The crotch of the trousers.

hlwv A blister (lub), to blister.
      sawv hlwv To 'raise' a blister, blistering.
      Kuv txiav taws ib hnub, ob txhais tes sawv hlwv. I cut
          firewood the whole day and both my hands were
          blistered.

HM

hma   Wolf, jackal, wild dog-like animal.
       hma (tus) The jackal.
       hma liab (tus) Dhole dog, red fox.
       hma ntsuab (tus) The wolf.

hmab   Vine, creeper (clf. 'txoj').
       ib txog hmab ntev ntev A long length of vine.
       hmab fajkhum A jungle vine that entwines a tree,
            lives upon it and gradually strangles it.
            It creaks when first cut with an axe so it is
            used metaphorically of a person who tells lies.
            (cf. 'fajkhum').
       kua txiv hmab Grape juice (juice of the vine-fruit).

hmo   Night, a night.
       ib hmos (t.c.) One night.
       nag hmo Last night.
       hmo ntuj Night, nightime.
       ib tag hmo Midnight.
       noj hmo To eat supper (eat the night meal).
       Koj noj hmo lawm tsis tau? Have you eaten supper?
       tas hnub tas hmo All day and all night, continually.

hmob   Chicken fleas.
       hmob qaib Chicken fleas (tus).

hmov   To care for, like.
       sib hmov To care for one another, like one another.

hmoo   Tone change from 'hmoov.' (cf. 'hmoov').

hmoob The Hmong.
       Hmoob Dawb The White Hmong.
       Hmoob Ntsuab The Green Hmong (or) the Blue Hmong.
       Hmoob Quas Npab The striped Hmong (or) the armband Hmong.
       Hmoob Leeg Another name for the Green Hmong (or) the
            Blue Hmong.
       Hmoob Yob Tshuab The flowery Hmong (or Miao) as known
            from China.
       haiv Hmoob All Hmong of other surnames.

1. hmoov Powder, dust, flour.
       hmoov av Dust.
       hmoov zeb Sand.
       tshuaj hmoov Powdered medicine.
       hmoov zeb sib Chalk.

2. hmoov Fortune, luck, fate (clf. 'txoj').
       Nws tau hmoov zoo tiag tiag. He really is well off.
       muaj hmoo (t.c.) To have (good) fortune.
       txoj hmoo (t.c.) Fortune.
       pub hmoov zoo To bestow good fortune, give good luck.

3. hmoov A feast or festival (as used in Laos, not so used
            in Thailand).
       ua hmoov To have a feast or festival.

hmu   Tone change from 'hmuv,' (cf. 'hmuv').

1. hmuv A spear, a fork (rab).
       Tus tub rog nqa ib rab hmuv tuaj. The soldier came
            carrying a spear.
       diav hmuv (rab) A fork, eating fork.
       hmuv rhais plaubhau A hairpin, pin used around which
            to wind the hair.

2. hmuv Clf. for thrusts with a spear.
       nkaug ib hmu (t.c.) To pierce once with a spear,
            one thrust of the spear.

HML

We simply make note of the spelling of this consonant
cluster as used in the Laos orthography current among the
Catholics. We here spell the exact same consonant cluster
'hnl' (cf. listings under 'hnl').

HN

hnab Bag, sack, sheath (lub).
  ib lub hnab ntawv A paper bag.
  khaub hnab (lub) A small stuffed ball covered with
    cloth and used in Hmong games.
  pov khaub hnab To throw the 'khaub hnab' in games.
  hnab riam A sheath for a knife.
  hnab tsog The mantle for a pressure lamp.
  teeb hnab tsog A pressure lamp (lub).
  lub hnab nplej The head of rice, rice head.
  lub plab hnab The rice head when in the budding stage.

1. hnav To dress, to put on.
  hnav ris tsho To put on jacket and trousers, to dress.
  hnav tsoos To put on clothing, to dress.

2. hnav A certain kind of grain.

hnem hnem hnov Forgetful, absent-minded.
  (a) us hnem hnov To be forgetful, be absent-minded.
  (b) ua tem toob ua hnem hnov To be forgetful, be
    absent-minded.
  neeg hnem hnov A forgetful person.

hnee Tone change from 'hneev' (cf. 'hneev').

1. hneev The Hmong crossbow, a crossbow (rab).
  Nws xuas hneev tua rau tus liab. He killed six
    monkeys with a crossbow.
  nta hneev To set a crossbow for firing, pull a bow.
  tua hneev To shoot with a crossbow.
  qeb hnee The trigger of the crossbow (t.c.)
  taub hnee (t.c.) The body of the crossbow.
  cov thi hneev The bamboo bindings on a crossbow.

2. hneev Clf. for firings of the crossbow.
  tua ib hnee (t.c.) One shot of the crossbow.

hnia To sniff at, to smell something intentionally.
    (contr. 'hnov').
  Koj sim hnia mentsis saib puas qab. Smell this a bit
    and see if it is fragrant.

hniav Tooth, teeth, pertaining to the teeth (clf. 'tus').
  mob hniav Teeth hurt, teeth hurting.
  ib tug hniav One tooth.
  ib ncaug hniav One set of teeth (cf. 'ncauj,' also
    'lo').
  pos hniav The gums.
  hauvpaus hniav Tooth root.
  rab txhuam hniav Toothbrush.
  zom hniav To grind the teeth together, gnash the
    teeth.

rho hniav To pull teeth.
cog hniav To fit false teeth.
looj hniav To cover the teeth with gold, etc.
(a) qis hniav To clench the teeth. (also cf. 'qos').
(b) qes hniav To clench the teeth. (also cf. 'qos').
dig hniav To pick the teeth.
hniav tabmeej The incisors.
hniav kaus dev The canines and bicuspids.
hniav puas The molars, molar.
hniav txhab Wisdom tooth.
hniav taj Late teeth.
hniav cauj Early teeth.
mob hniav kuas si Gums soft and bleeding, pyorrhea.
ntxais quav hniav Clucking with the tongue, "tsk, tsk,
    tsk." "Too bad."
ob tog hniav Two sides or sets of teeth (as teeth
    set opposite each other in a hair clippers, etc.)
(a) hniav ntais ib sab lawm Tooth broken off one side.
(b) hniav khis ib sab lawm Tooth broken off one side.
tom hniav qawv Biting and gnashing of teeth.
hniav riam Knife edge.

1. hno To inject, insert a needle (cf. 'txhaj').
  hno tshuaj To inject medicine, give an innoculation.
  Thov koj pab hnov ib koob tshuaj. Please give me an
    injection of medicine.

2. hno Cooked rice (poetical).
  ua tau zaub ua tau hno Made vegetables and rice.
  noj ngaig noj hnos (t.c.) a feast (literally, time
    of eating meat and rice) This is more formal
    language as e.g. used by older people.

hnos Tone change from 'hno' (cf. 'hno' above).

1. hnov To hear (contr. 'nloog').
  Kuv tsis tau hnov dua. I have never heard it before.
  hnov lus To hear speech.
  (a) hnov sab nrov To hear a loud noise.
  (b) hnov suab sab To hear a loud noise.
  hnov dheev Heard suddenly.

2. hnov To sense, to feel pain, to feel.
  Kuv tsis hnov mob qhov twg li. I don't feel pain any-
    where.

3. hnov To sense, to be conscious of a smell or odor, to
    smell.
  Kuv tsis hnov tsw. I don't smell any odor. I'm not
    conscious of any smell.

4. hnov To be forgetful (in combination with 'hnem' or 'qauj').
  hnov qauj To keep forgetting.
  ua hnem hnov To be very forgetful.
  neeg hnem hnov A forgetful person.

hnoob hnoob nyoog Age, time (see 'hnub nyoog' which is
  more common).

hnoos To cough.
  Nws hnoos hnoos ib hnub. He's been coughing all day.
  tshuaj hnoos Cough medicine.

1. hnub Sun, the sun (lub).
  Lub hnub loj dua ntiajteb. The sun is larger than
    the earth.
  hnub tuaj Sunrise, the sun rises.
  hnub poob Sunset, the sun sets.
  sab hnub tuaj East.
  sab hnub poob West.
  tav hnub North or south (the "sides" of the sun).
  Hnub nyuav chiv tuaj. The sun has just come up.

2. hnub Day, a day, daytime.
  ib hnub One day.
  nruab hnub Daytime.
  hnub hnub Day before yesterday.
  hnub hmos Night of the day before yesterday.
  hnub caiv A day of special observance, day of taboo.
  hnub so A day of rest.
  tas hmo All day and all night.
  ob hnub tseem Two full days.
  hnub txooj Even day (woman's day).
  hnub tab Odd day (man's day).
    (The Hmong say women are born on even days and
    men on odd days.)

3. hnub Age, time.
  hnub nyoog (sometimes said 'hnub nyug' or 'hnoob nyoog')
    Age, time, years, a person's age.

4. hnub
  hnub qub Star (lub).
  cov hnub qub The stars.
  hnub qub ya Falling stars, a star "falling,"
    meteor, also the expression for "to see stars"
    as when struck by a hard blow on the head.

HNL

hnlos To dent, to be dented, to have a depressed place.
  (contr. 'su', cf. 'zuav', 'nluav')
  (a) hnlos lawm Dented, bent (as a tin, etc.).
  (b) zuav lawm Dented, bent.
  (c) nluav lawm Dented, bent.
  av hnlos A depression in the ground.

HNY

hnya To scowl, squint, frown, look sullen or gloomy.
  ntsej muag hnya hnya A scowling face.
  Thaum nws haus tshuaj iab iab nws txawm hnya hnya
    When he drank the bitter medicine he scowled.

1. hnyav Heavy, weighty.
  ob thoob dej hnyav hnyav Two heavy pails of water.
  hnyav qees Very heavy.
  (a) hnyav tog Heavy but small in bulk (as metal, etc.)
  (b) hnyav qes Heavy but small in bulk (as metal, etc.)
  (a) hnyav ya Heavy but comparatively great in bulk (as
    wood, etc.)
  (b) hnyav siab Heavy but comparatively great in bulk
    (as wood, etc.)

2. hnyav "Heavy" used metaphorically.
  siab hnyav Heavy hearted, sorrowful, distressed.

3. hnyav
  neeg cev hnyav Of a woman who easily becomes pregnant
    (cf. 'neeg tuab').

hnyev Post verbal intensive, (cf. Appendix 8).
  quaj nrov hnyev Whimpering, to whimper, cry with a
    low broken voice.

hnyiab To be burned.
  kub hnyiab Burned.
  Lub tsev kub hnyiab tag lawm. The house was completely
    burned up.
  tsw tsw kub hnyiab Smells of something burned.

1. hnyo Long-haired.
  dev hnyo A long-haired dog.

2. hnyo
  (a) ntxhov quav hnyo To make a disturbance, a tumult.
  (b) ntxhov quav niab To make a disturbance, a tumult.

hnyos To rebuke.
  Nws hnyos hnyos kuv. He scolded me, rebuked me.

1. hnyuv Intestine, intestine like, pertaining to the
    intestines (clf. 'txoj').
  hnyuv dub The large intestine.
  hnyuv dawb The small intestine.
  hnyuv ntxwm Sausage (txoj).
  hlauv hnyuv Prolapsed bowel, hernia.

2. hnyuv Male sex member, pertaining to the male sex
          member. (clf. 'tus') (cf. 'qau').
          (a) tus qau The penis.
          (b) tus hnyuv The penis.
          (c) tus hnyuv qau The penis.
          (a) hnyuv qe The testicles.
          (b) noob qes The testicles.

K

1. ka
   ka poom (lub) A can (Thai).
        (also pronounced 'kas poom').

2. ka
   txiv kalaj (lub) Olive, the olive (in Laos the
        terms used is 'txiv roj').

1. kab A written line, a line (txoj) (cf. definition No. 4)
   kuam kab Inscribe a line.
   ua kab Make a line on paper.
   sau rau kab Write on the line.

2. kab Worm caterpillar, beetle, spider, bug (tus) (many
        kinds with individual names).
   kab npauj Larva, Moth larva.
   kab txws Marbleworm, hundred legged worm.
   kab hluas nees Moulmein train worm.
   (a) kab pwj nyug Rhinocerous beetle.
   (b) kab pwj nyoog Rhinocerous beetle.
   kab laug sab Small variety of spider which makes
        a web.
   kab laug tsov Large variety of spider which lives
        in the ground and makes no web.
   kab qaus les Dragonfly.
   kab nqos vias Locust.
   kab khaub ruab Stick bug, insect resembling a stick.
   kab ntsig Hairy caterpillar which stings on contact.
   kab tuas Type of large varicolored caterpillar.
   (a) kab lauj kaub "Daddy long legs" spider.
   (b) kab raj ris laus "Daddy long legs" spider.

3. kab
   laj kab A fence (txoj).
   (a) xov laj kab To make a fence.
   (b) tuav laj kab To make a fence.

4. kab A way, a path (cf. definition No. 1).
   kab lig ntuj The Milky Way.
   kab tshis A goat path.
   kab muas lwj A deer path.
   txoj kab tsaug A porcupine trail.
        (These last three expressions and similar ones
        for other animals are used to describe trails
        over rocks or through undergrowth used by these
        animals, not the actual footprints.)

5. kab
   kabke A rite, a ceremony (txoj).
   txoj kabke ntxuav Baptism (As used in Thailand).

6. kab
   txiv kab ntxwv The orange, oranges (lub).

7. kab Steel (contr. 'hlau').
   ceem kab To temper steel.
   Muab kab ntaus ib rab riam. Take steel and make a knife.

8. kab
   tsom kab tsom kwm To care for, to look after (cf. 'tsom')

9. kab
   xwmkab The spirit paper pasted on the rear wall of a
        Hmong house (cf. 'dab', 'xwm').

10. kab clf. for "swallow" or "smoke" of opium or tobacco.
    haus ib kab yeeb To smoke one pipeful of opium.

11. kab
    kab yeeb The name of a spirit to whom incense is
        burned and whose help is sought to prevent
        illness, etc.

12. kab
    mob kab yaim Name of a certain skin disease of dogs
        and cats.

13. kab
    cov tshwj kab The ones who are appointed to serve the
        meat at a wedding or funeral feast.

14. kab
    kab ntsuj Descriptive of an animistic rite serving to
        protect the individual from the 'bite' of evil
        spirits. Water is put into a rice bowl and swung
        round the person's head.

15. kab
kab tsib Sugar cane.

kag Tone change from 'kaj' (cf. 'kaj').

1. kaj Bright, characterized by light, light.
kaj ntug Daylight.
kaj ntug txoog Dawn.
(a) kaj ntug huv Daybreak.
(b) kaj ntug plaws Daybreak.
kaj hlis Moonlight.
ntuj kaj The bright heavens.
kaj nrig Bright all around.
kaj lug Very bright.
txoj kev kaj The light, the way of light.

2. kaj
(a) kaj siab Satisfied with things, heart refreshed.
(b) lub siab kaj Satisfied with things, heart refreshed.

3. kaj Emphatic final particle.
Neb tuaj saib kaj! Come and see!

4. kaj Clf. for a "batch" of vegetables, pickles, etc.
kaj zaub no This batch of vegetables.
ib kag zaub One batch of vegetables (t.c.)

5. kaj
khaum kaj khaum kus Keeps getting caught up on something (cf. 'khaum').

1. kam Willing, agreeable.
Kuv kam thiab. I'm willing.
Kuv tsis kam mus. I won't go.
kam ntxhias Very willing, willing immediately.

2. kam Accustomed to.
Noj mov tsis kam. Unaccustomed to eating rice.
Nws sau ntawv tsis kam. He isn't accustomed to writing.

3. kam Business, affairs (tus).
Koj muaj kam dabtsi? What is your business? What do you want?

4. kam
kam paug To be pussy, to have pus, exuding pus.

kas Maggots.
nqaij ua kas Maggoty meat, the meat has maggots.

1. kav To manage, to govern, rule.
kav tebchaws To rule a nation.
Tus uas kav ntuj kav teb yog tus loj kawg nkaus.
The one who rules heaven and earth is greatest.

2. kav The stem, the body of a tree or vine as distinct from the branches; the lines in a leaf (tus).
Tus kav hmab qhuav tag lawm. The body of the vine is dried up.

3. kav The barrel of a gun.
tus kav phom The gun barrel.

4. kav The lower leg, the shin (cf. 'roob hlaub').
tus kav hlaub The shin, lower leg (cf. 'hlaub').

5. kav
kavtheej (txoj) Rattan.

6. kav
kavxwm (tus) The manager or master of ceremonies at a feast or ceremony, the one asked to be in charge of organizing the work at a wedding or funeral feast (cf. 'tshoob', 'tuag').

7. kav
kav ywm A kind of vegetable with wide leaves (tsob).

8. kav
nees faj kav (tus) A yellow horse.

9. kav
txwm kav (an expression used before verbs to indicate action persevered in regardless of advice, etc.) (cf. 'txwm').

10. kav
tsis kav No matter what (cf. 'txujkum').

kaim
kaim tom An expression used in the game of topspinning to indicate the first top is left spinning and the one thrown has gone amiss.

1. kais A pipe, a spout (tus).
lub hwj kais A teakettle (literally "pipe" kettle).

2. kais To push food into the mouth with the use of chopsticks.
kais rawg Push food into the mouth with chopsticks.

3. kais Clf. for mouthfuls by chopsticks.
Nws muab rawg noj rau kais mov. He took chopsticks and ate six mouthfuls of rice.

kau
yij kau A kind of bird something like a wild hen (clf. tus).

1. kaub Calluses, callused.
   kaub puab Calluses.

2. kaub Of hardened rice or meat, a scab.
   kaub puab mov The browned hardened rice adhering to the sides and bottom of the cooking pot.
   kaub puab nqaij Hardened browned meat sticking to the sides of the cooking pot. Also used to describe a scab.

kaug Tone change from 'kauj' or 'kaus' (cf. 'kauj' 'kaus')

1. kauj A coil, a ring (lub) (contr. 'nplhaib').
   kauj hmab Coils of vine.
   kauj xov tooj A wire coil.

2. kauj Clf. for coils or rings.
   ib kauj hlua (t.c.) a coil of rope.
   rau kauj hlua Six coils of rope.

3. kauj
   (a) tsheb kauj vab (lub) A bicycle.
   (b) tshuab kauj vab (lub) A bicycle.

1. kaum A corner (clf. 'ceg').
   ib ceg kaum One corner, a corner.
   kaum tsev Corner of the house.
   ncej kaum The corner upright posts of a house.
   mom kaum The ends of a roof.
   nyob ib leeg ib ceg kaum ntuj Widely scattered, each living in his own corner of the heavens.

2. kaum Used for the digit 'ten' in numbers 10 to 19.
   kaum tus Ten articles.
   kaum 10
   kaum ib 11
   kaum ob 12
   kaum peb 13 (etc.)

3. kaum ntaub kaum A type of sturdy black cotton cloth.

4. kaum suaj kaum To finish.
   txojlus suaj kaum The last or final word.

5. kaum tabkaum To hinder or delay.
   (a) Tabkaum koj. "I have hindered you." i.e. I have interfered with your work.
   (b) tabkaum koj li haujlwm. "I have hindered you." i.e. I have interfered with your work.

1. kaus Fang, tusk, beak (tus).
   kaus ntxhw Elephant's tusk, ivory tusk, ivory.
   kaus ncauj The beak of a bird.
   hniav kaus dev The canines and bicuspids in human teeth.
   tuaj kaus To have tusks, fangs, or canine teeth.
   Npua tuaj kaus. Pigs have tusks.

2. kaus Clf. for bites or bitefuls.
   Dev tom nws ib kaug. (t.c.) The dog bit him once.
   rau kaus mov Six bites (or) bitefuls of rice.

3. kaus A sprout or young, shoot from a plant (cf. 'yub')
   clf. 'tus.' (possibly so named because of the similarity in shape to a fang or tusk)
   kaus nplej A rice shoot.
   kaus pobkws A corn shoot.

4. kaus An umbrella, a parachute (lub).
   Nws nqa ib lub kaus mus teb. He carried an umbrella to the fields.

5. kaus To gouge out, scrape with a gouging motion.
   kaus av To gouge the earth, scrape up earth (cf. 'kuam')
   kaus qhovmuag Gouge the eye.

6. kaus
   dab tshos kaus lev. A type of ladies' embroidered collar.

7. kaus
   kausmom Hat, cap (lub).
   ntoo kausmom To wear a hat.

1. kauv To roll up (as a scroll), to wind around, entwine.
   Muab txoj hlua kauv. Wind up the rope.
   kauv pam To wrap up in a blanket.
   kauv taubhau To wrap the head in something, cover the head (cf. 'vov taubhau').

2. kauv The barking deer (tus).
   Nws tua ob tug kauv. He killed two barking deer.
   menyuam thav kauv Small half-grown barking deer.
   qev kauv txhais To "borrow the legs" of the deer; i.e. to scamper away from something quickly.

3. kauv The thin outer layer of skin; the dark outer layer of skin that is scrubbed off in dressing a slaughtered pig; dirt that adheres to the surface of unwashed skin.
   kauv taubhau Dirt on the surface of the scalp.
   kuam npua To dehair a slaughtered pig.
   kuam kauv To scrape off the black surface skin.

1. kaw To close up, to shut, to shut in.
   kaw qhov rooj Shut the door.
   kaw hlo Closed immediately.
   (a) kaw nrees Shut securely.
   (b) kaw qos nrees Shut securely.

2. kaw To saw, a saw (rab).
   Muab rab kaw kaw txiag ntoo ua tsev. Take the
      saw and saw some boards for a house.

1. kawb Curved or bent in.
   Rab hlau kawb kawb li. The hoe is curved in.

2. kawb To scold (cf. 'cem').
   (a) lam kawb To scold without reason.
   (b) lam cem To scold without reason.

3. kawb
   Tebchaws cuam cuam kawb A country of hills and
      valleys close together.

1. kawg Extremity, ended, end of, finish.
   toj kawg The bottom (end) of the hill.
   ib sim neej tsis kawg Lifelong without end.
   ib txhis tsis kawg Forever, forever without end.
   kawg kev The end of the road.
   kawg lawm Finished, ended.

2. kawg Sign of the superlative degree (also cf. 'tasnrho').
   zoo kawg nkaus Best.
   lub roob siab kawg nkaus The highest mountain.

1. kawm To study, to learn.
   kawm tsheej kiag Learned it completely.
   kawm ntawv To study books, attend school.
   kawm lus Hmoob To study the Hmong language.

2. kawm The Meo back basket for carrying, a back basket
      (lub).
   Nws ris ib lub kawm loj loj mus teb lawm. He went
      to the fields carrying a large basket.
   lub kawm qhovmuag A loosely woven basket with
      widely spaced strips of rattan or bamboo,
      used for carrying meat, storing utensils, etc.

1. kaws To gnaw, to chew upon.
   Dev kaws pobtxha. The dog gnaws the bone.
   Nees kaws kaws zaub. The horse nibbles on the grass.

2. kaws
   qav kaws A toad (tus).

1. kawv
   maum kawv The giant squirrel (tus).

2. kawv Restricted post verbal intensifier (cf. Appendix 8).
   suaj kaum kawv Finished, all gone.

ke Tone change from 'kev' (cf. 'kev').
   ua ib ke Together.
   kabke Rite, ceremony.

keb The cap of a cartridge, the small triggering charge
      inserted in the end of a shotgun cartridge (T)
      (cf. 'cos ntawv').

1. kem To separate from, to divide off, to set a boundary,
      to set apart.
   kem ib hnub To skip a day, every other day.
   kem teb To separate fields, set a boundary.
   (a) kem nkaus Separated, firmly divided off.
   (b) kem nrees Separated, firmly divided off.

2. kem A room, a division (lub).
   (a) lub kem tsev A room.
   (b) lub kem txaj A room.
   kem txhab nyiaj A treasury, room for storage of money.

3. kem
   kem plab Indigestion.

4. kem
   kem cev Syphilis, venereal disease.

5. kem tos Probably, most likely that..., because
      (this is often abbreviated to simply 'tos').
   kem tos...thiaj li... Because of this...therefore...
   Kem tos koj hais li no nws thiaj li tsis mus.
      (Probably) Because you said what you did, he
      won't go.

1. kes To scrape off, scraping off something which adheres
      to a surface.

2. kes
   kes txig To finger the cheek indicating shame toward
      someone.

1. kev Road, path, way, trail. (clf. 'txoj' for lengths;
      'tsem' for sections of road; 'ceg' for sections
      or directions of a journey)
   tho kev To make a road, cut a trail.
   luaj kev To cut down the weeds and brush along an
      existing trail in order to clear it.
   rhawv kev To level a road, put through a road for
      vehicles. Also used metaphorically for 'to
      persuade,' to force one's way through.

yuam kev To go astray, miss the trail, make a mistake.
coj kev To lead, to direct.
qaum kev Above the road on the uphill side.
qab kev Below the road, the downhill side.
lug kev To go off the trail and back to it as in passing around an obstacle.
zam kev To pass on the road (going in opposite directions.)
sawv kev mus To start on a journey.
sib txauv kev To pass one another on the road (inadvertently without seeing each other).
kev ncaim Roads that divide or separate.

2. kev Matters, business, affairs.
Koj muaj kev dabtsi? What is your business? What do you want?
Nws muaj kev ntau ntau. He has a lot of affairs.

3. kev Used to indicate "the way of..." or "the way."
Kev dab ceeblaj heev. The way of the spirits is difficult. Spirit worship is hard.
kev mob kev tuag. Sickness and death.
(a) qhia kev To teach or to explain the way, to preach.
(b) piav kev To teach or to explain the way, to preach.
zaj qhuab ke (t.c.) The song sung at death before the pipes are played and to instruct the dead how to find the right path to the ancestral home.

4. kev kevcai Custom, law, practice (txoj).
Txhob ua txhaum kevcai. Don't offend against the law.
Txoj kevcai no hais li cas? What does this law say?

5. kev kabke Rite, ceremony (txoj) t.c.
txoj kabke ntxuav The ceremony of baptism (term used by Christian Hmong in Thailand).

6. kev Used in combination to mean 'together.'
ua ib ke Together (t.c.).
Ua ib ke sib raug zoo. Be in fellowship, in harmony.

7. kev Used to kev ua "Open" to do, legitimate, permissible, lawful.
tsis to kev ua Not permissible, unlawful.

1. keeb Yeast, leaven.
xyaw keeb To add or mix in leaven in baking.
tsis xyaw keeb ncuav Cakes without leaven.
keeb ncuav Leavened bread or cakes.

2. keeb A 'watch' or a portion of time.
ntaus keeb To ring the watches of the night.
lub ntaus keeb A bell for ringing the watches.

3. keeb Basis, basic fact, the root of things (lub).
keeb puam Foundation fact (lub).
Nws hais lus tsis muaj keeb. He talks without any foundation in fact.

1. keem More than, sign of comparative degree (C), more (cf. 'haj yam').
keem chim siab More angry.
keem zoo Better.
(a) keem zoo dua Better than.
(b) haj yam keem zoo dua Better than.
Tsev pobzeb haj yam keem zoo dua. A stone house is still better (than others).

2. keem
teev keem (rab) A dibble, stick with a pointed metal end used for making holes in the ground to plant seeds or rice.

kees Clever, quick, intelligent (T). Not intelligent. Not clever.
Lub siab tsis kees.

1. keev Whole, solid.
keev hlo Whole, solid.
keev hlo ci To roast whole.
lub xauv keev A solid silver neck ring.

2. keev Used metaphorically of a solid or closed heart.
neeg keev xeeb Pig-headed, a person with a heart closed to any but his own ideas.

1. ki
tub ki Sons and daughters, children.
tseg tub tseg ki Bereft of children.

2. ki
ki qoos ki qoos Rumbling, the sound of rumbling in the stomach.

1. kib To fry in a pan or vessel with or without fat.
kib nqaij To fry meat.

2. kib
   (a) vaubkib (tus) Turtle.
   (b) vuabkib (tus) Turtle.
   vaubkib deg (tus) Water turtle.
   vaubkib nquab (tus) Land turtle.

3. kib
   laum kib tshooj Centipede (tus).

4. kib
   kib cuab To stay close at home.
   (a) neeg kib cuab One who stays much at home.
   (b) xis zeej kib cuab One who stays much at home.

kig
   zaub kig Stinging vegetation, leaves, vines, weeds,
   etc. that sting on contact.

1. kim Expensive.
   Ib phiaj xauv kim heev. A set of silver neck rings
   is very expensive.

2. kim To kneel on one knee (cf. 'txhos,' 'qhau').
   kim caug To kneel on one knee.
   kim rawv To remain keeling on one knee.

3. kim
   kimtxwv (lub) Chair, throne (C).

1. kis To spread (as a disease, etc.).
   Cov mob no txawj kis. This kind of disease can
   spread.

2. kis Rasping or tickling (as in the throat).
   kis kis qa Rasping or tickling feeling in the throat.

3. kis clf. for an open area or section.
   ib kis tsev An open area in the house.
   kis ntuj kis teb. Heavens and earth, sky and land.

4. kis
   taskis Tomorrow (cf. 'tas').

1. kiv To spin, spinning around.
   qhovmuag kiv kiv Dizzy (lit. 'eyes spinning').

2. kiv
   kiv tob (lub) Small spinning top with bamboo shaft
   used as a plaything by Hmong boys.

1. kiab A market, marketplace (lub).
   Mus nram kiab lawm. (He) went down to the market.
   nquam kiab nquam khw The marketplace (poetic).

2. kiab Quiet-mannered, good (of a child, etc.)
   menyuam kiab kiab A good child who doesn't cry, etc.

3. kiab
   yeeb yaj kiab The abode of the dead.

kiag Post verbal intensive indicating decisiveness and
   completeness. Used either singularly or as
   'kiag li' (cf. Appendix 8).
   tsis muaj kiag li Really haven't any.
   nqos kiag mus To swallow whole, swallow right down.
   ntseeg kiag lawm Believed completely.
   poob kiag lawm Fell down.
   puag kiag To fondly embrace (embrace completely with
   both arms).
   (a) sam kiag Bad language.
   (b) sam hlob Bad language.

kiaj
   kiaj kiam A boundary.
   (Note: 'ciaj ciam' is also used but the pronunciation "kaij kiam" is more common in Thailand)
   kiaj kiam teb A national boundary.

1. kiam
   kiaj kiam A boundary (cf. 'kiaj')

2. kiam To have respect for authority, to 'fear' so as to
   obey.
   Lawv tsis kiam nws. They are not afraid of him.
   (don't respect his authority).

3. kiam To accuse, to blame, to make trouble for someone
   (cf. looj koov).

4. kiam
   kwv kiam Queer, queerness, strange and somewhat
   frightening (C).

1. kiav To settle a case (without penalty), to forgive
   (cf. 'daws').
   kiav plaub To make amiable settlement of a case of
   dispute.
   kiav txim To forgive or make settlement for guilt and
   offense by talking it over but with no penalty
   or payment.

2. kiav
   kiav txhab (lub) An ulcer, an open sore.

3. kiav
   kiav xeem To change one's surname.

4. kiav
   kiav nqaij Meat cracklings.

5. kiav To seek to hinder a person from action.
   (cf. 'tshum').
   tshum kiav To seek to hinder a person from action.

1. ko A handle (tus) (of any hand implement, etc.)
   ko taus The handle of an axe, axe handle.

2. ko
   kotw Tail, the tail (tus).

3. ko
   kotaw Foot, the foot (txhais) (cf. 'taw').
   mob kotaw Foot hurts, foot ailment.

4. A final completive particle.
   Koj hais li ko... Speaking as you do...
   Referring to what you have just said.
   Txhob ua li ko. Don't do that; stop doing what you
   are doing.

1. kob clf. for showers of rain (also cf. 'phaum').
   ib kob nag One shower of rain.

2. kob
   neeg kob huam Poor, poverty stricken person.

3. kob
   Koj tes kob xwb heev. Your hands are 'skilled' in
   a worthy occupation.

4. kob
   kob sim tshuaj Tea leaves (cf. 'tshuaj swm' [C]).

koj Second person singular pronoun. "You" (singular).
   Koj mus. You go. (contr. "kos').
   Nyob tom koj. Over near you.
   Kuv hais rau koj. I tell you.
   Koj nyob qhov twg? Where are you?

1. kom To cause, bring into effect (used alone or as
   'kom xwv').
   Kuv tsis kom nws mus. I won't cause him to go.
   I won't make him go.
   Tus dev tsem tsem kom tus menyuam quaj. The dog barked
   causing the child to cry.
   Koj mus hais zoo zoo kom xwv ob tug nyob tid txhob
   cem cem. Go and speak to those two over there
   so they will stop cursing each other.

2. kom To accuse, to make official accusation at law.
   Lawv coj nws mus kom nram moos. They took him down to
   accuse him in the city. (court)
   tus yeej kom The accuser, one making the complaint.
   tus pem kom The defendant, person accused of wrong.

3. kom
   kom txwv The inner works of a watch or of a piece
   of machinery, etc.

1. kos To scribe or draw or rule a line.
   tus kos ntawv A ruler (for ruling lines).

2. kos A glancing scrape.
   Nws ntog thiab kos caj npab. He fell and scraped his
   arm.

3. kos
   sab tom kos Over there, that side over there.
   nyob ntawm kos Over there, located over there.

1. kov To handle, to touch.
   Txhob kov. Don't handle it. Let it alone.
   kov dej To play with or in the water, to fish (colloq.).

2. kov
   kov yeej To overcome, get the victory.

3. kov
   kov tsij To hasten (as used with following verbs).
   kov tsij mus Go quickly, go right away.
   kov tsij los tsev. Come home right away.
   Kov tsij khiav mus. Go quickly. "Get out!"

4. kov
   kov txwv thaum ub In the beginning, of old.
   kov txwv los From the root of things, following the
   proper way of things as originally set out.

1. koob Needle, pin, quill (rab)
   Koob mab Safety pin.
   rab koob xaws khaubncaws Needle for sewing clothes.
   lub tiv (or 'teem') qab koob A thimble.

2. koob Paternal greatgrandparent.
   yawg koob Paternal greatgrandfather.
   pog koob Paternal greatgrandmother.

3. koob To make food for another, to serve in making their
   food.
   us koob lawv To serve them by making their food.

4. koob
   koob pheej Just, equal, fair (C).

5. koob
   (a) yeeb koob (lub)   Reputation, glory, honor.
   (b) yeeb haum (lub)   Reputation, glory, honor.

6. koob
   (a) koob meej (lub)   Good name, good reputation.
   (b) meej thawb (lub)   Good name, good reputation.

7. koob
   koobxaus (lub)   Gramaphone.

8. koob
   cuam koob (rooj)   A kind of spring trap for catching
   rodents (cf. 'rooj').

9. koob
   mej koob (tus)   The middle man in wedding arrangements (cf. 'tshoob').

koog   Descriptive of an area of field, forest, or vegetation
   notably different from the surroundings.
   Lawv muab ua teb tag lawm, tshuav ib koog hav zoov
   xwb.   They made all the land into fields leaving
   only one area of forest.
   Puav leej ua hav tauj, tshuav ib koog zoo ua teb xwb.
   All is overgrown in weeds with only one area
   good for fields.
   koog pos   A patch or clump of thorns.

kooj   Locust (several varieties).
   kooj tshuab (tus)   A locust, yellowish in coloring.
   kooj txig (tus)   A black locust.

1. koom   Of action that is shared between two or more persons.
   koom ua   To do together.
   koom noj   To eat together.
   (a) nrog nws koom ua   To do with him or her.
   (b) koom nws ua   To do with him or her.
   koom ib txoj sia   To share one common life together.
   Thooj niam koom txiv, thooj pog koom yawg   Having
   the same parents and grandparents.

2. koom
   khib koom (T)   Of a deceitful person, one who
   changes his mind regarding wages, etc.
   (cf. 'com').

3. koom
   koom plig (also 'rub plig')   A special spirit rite
   or ceremony done after the New Year and before
   making new fields. A pig is sacrificed and some
   blood smeared on the backs of all the household
   members. Then a cord is tied to the pig's neck
   and drawn around all the family as a symbolic
   fence to prevent their spirits from leaving.
   Removal of the cord symbolizes removal of all
   calamity, danger, sickness, etc.

koos   koos zoo   Of a village site nicely surrounded by
   hills and mountains.

1. koov
   koov nyij   A type of fine black cloth.

2. koov
   looj koov (C)   To cause trouble, to be troublesome,
   make a fuss.

1. kub   Hot (cf. 'sov').
   kub kub li   Very hot.
   hluavtaws kub   A hot fire.

2. kub   To be burned or scalded.
   kub hnyiab lawm   Burned.
   Nws lub tsev kub hnyiab tag lawm.   His house burned
   completely.
   kub hlab lawm   Scalded.

3. kub   Used metaphorically of earnestness, "hot-hearted."
   kub siab   Earnest.
   kub siab ua   To do earnestly or energetically.

4. kub   Horns, horn of an animal   (clf. 'tus' for single horn
   and 'txwm' for a pair).
   kub twg   Water buffalo horn.
   tuaj kub   To bear horns.

5. kub   Gold.
   Nws muaj nyiaj muaj kub ntau ntau.   He has plenty of
   silver and gold.

6. kub   The opium pipe (lub).
   lub kublub   The opium pipe.
   teeb kublub (lub)   The opium lamp.

7. kub   Pertaining to distant relatives.
   kwvtij thaj kub   Distant relatives of same clan.

kug   Stripped bare of leaves and twigs.
   Kab noj ntoo kug ncos.   Insects ate the tree bare of
   leaves.

1. kuj   A particle which carries forward the action of the
   verb. Moreover, also, consequently.
   Kuv kuj tsis paub thiab.   I also do not know.
   Ua li cas kuj yog.   Whatever (you say or do) will be
   all right.
   Cov tsis zoo kuj muaj thiab.   There are bad ones as well.

2. kuj

kujyem The type of fan palm whose leaves are used commonly in roofing for Meo houses. The fruit is also edible.
ntoo kujyem The fan palm tree as above.
nplooj kujyem Roofing leaves.
txiv kujyem Palm fruit.

1. kum

twj kum (tus) The rhinocerous.

2. kum

kum khej (C) Guest, stranger (contr. 'txum tim').

3. kum

phua kum xeeb To split (a log) through the center thus obtaining wedge shaped pieces. (cf. 'phua').

4. kum

pej kum dab qus "wild" spirits (as opposed to 'dab nyeg') (cf. 'dab').

5. kum

kum yuj (cf. the ironical expression below)
Koj kum yuj txawm xam hwvv. You certainly do know how to figure things out!

kus

khaum kaj khaum kus Keeps getting caught up on something (cf. 'khaum').

kuv First person singular pronoun, "I," "me."
Kuv tsis paub. I don't know.
Nws tsis nyiam kuv. He doesn't like me.

1. kua Liquid, of a runny consistency.
kua tshuaj Liquid medicine.
kua muag Tears (contr. 'quav muag').
kua mem Ink.
kua dis Rice gruel.
kua ntxhai Rice water (poured off cooked rice).
kua yeeb Opium in liquid form.
kua mis Milk.
kua paug A thick secretion.
kua yis A thin secretion.
kua ciab, ciab mem A gummy wax used as an adhesive.

2. kua

kuatxob Red peppers, cayenne pepper.

3. kua

kua si taum Brown bean curd cakes.

4. kua

kua loos A name used to refer to the Lao people (cf. 'lostsuas').

1. kuab

xwb kuab (lub) A type of small gourd the stringy dried pith of which is used for scrubbing pots, etc.

2. kuab

txiv maum kuab (lub) The papaya (cf. 'txiv taub ntoo').

kuag Some (cf. 'txhia').
ib kuag leej Some people.
Muaj ib kuag leej mus xwb. Only some people went.

1. kuam To scrape, to scrape off.
kuam npua To dehair a slaughtered pig.
kuam kotaw To scrape off the foot.

2. kuam To scribe, to scratch.
Kuam ib kab ntawv. To scratch or draw a line.

3. kuam Clf. for a 'hand' of bananas.
ib kuam txiv tsawb A hand of bananas.

4. kuam

mov kuam Steamed corn meal.

5. kuam

kuam neeb Goat horns or simulated horns made of wood which are used in divining the mind of the spirits.
ntaus kuam To divine with the 'kuam neeb.' The horns are cast upon the ground repeatedly and the pleasure of the spirits is indicated by the way the horns lie.

1. kuas

dev kuas A type of varicolored dog.

2. kuas

mob hniav kuas si Soft and bleeding gums, a kind of mouth ailment.

kuav To wash away with a flow of water.
Dej kuav av tag lawm. The water has washed the soil away.
dej kuav kev Water washing down a path or road.

kw Tone change from 'kwv,' (cf. 'kwv').

kwj Valley, gulley (lub).
(a) kwj ha A valley, a gulley.
(b) lub hav A valley, a gulley.
kwj deg A gulley (without running water except after rain).
kwj tse The drainage ditch around a house.
kwj qaum The depression along the backbone.

1. kwm To nurture, to care for, look after (cf. 'tsom').
   tsom kab tsom kwm To nurture, to care for.
   Nws tsis mob siab kwm nws txojsiav. He doen't take
   care of his own life.

2. kwm To walk through deep water.
   Nws Kwm ntxhias mus. He went bodily through (the water).

1. kws Indian corn, maize.
   pobkws Ears of corn, corn in general (lub).
   txha kws Corncob (lub).
   paj kws Popcorn.
   plhaub kws Corn husk.
   quav kws Corn stalks.
   (a) plaub kws Corn tassels.
   (b) tw yaj pobkws Corn tassels.

2. kws A syllable used preceeding a noun to indicate an
         artisan.
   kws ntoo (tus) A carpenter.
   kws hlau (tus) A blacksmith.
   kws tshuaj (tus) A doctor or pharmacist.
   kws ntawv (tus) A 'scribe,' a scholar, secretary.

1. kwv Younger brother (tus).
   kuv tus kwv My younger brother.
   kwvtij Younger and older brothers, brethren. This
         term is also used to refer to members of one's
         own clan, relatives in one's paternal lineage.
         A man's relatives by marriage are called 'neejtsa'
         whereas after marriage a woman calls her own
         family 'neejtsa' and owns her husband's family
         as 'kwvtij.'
   kwvtij ob cag peb txhais All the people of the village,
         relatives and otherwise.
   kwvtij thaj kub Distant relatives of the same clan.

2. kwv Friend, companion.
   kwvluag A good friend, companion.

3. kwv To carry on the shoulder.
   Peb mus kwv ntoo ua tsev. We are going to carry logs
         to erect a house.

4. kwv Clf. for shoulder loads (cf. Definition No. 8).
   ib kw dej One shoulder load of water (t.c.)
   rau kwv Six shoulder loads.

5. kwv To turn aside from.
   kwv ntswg To turn the nose away in disgust.
   kwv nuj nqe To refuse to repay a debt owed.

6. kwv Queer, peculiar (C).
   kwv kiam Queer, peculiar (C).
   muaj kwv kiam To be queer; it is queer.

7. kwv
   kwvhuam Old tales, traditions, olden times.
   hais ib zag kwvhuam To tell an old tale.

8. kwv A portion, a part (cf. 'tsoom'), also (cf. definition
         No. 4).
   rau kwv Six parts.
   ib kw One part (t.c.).
   Used in expressing fractions, etc.
   Tag ib kw tshuav ib kw. Half gone. (t.c.).
   Zoo ib kw, tsis zoo xya kwv. Only one eighth is good.

9. kwv
   kwvlam Probably, almost, approximately (cf. 'tamfaj')
         also (cf. 'kwvyees' below).
   Kwvlam yog nws ua tiag. Most probably it was he that
         did it.

10. kwv
    kwvyees To guess, probably, unpracticed (cf. 'nyaj').
    (a) kwvyees hais To guess, to give a guess.
    (b) kwvyees nyaj To guess, to give a guess.
    kwvyees ua To do without practice, guess at doing.

11. kwv
    kwv txhiaj (zaj) A serenade or ballad; especially as
         sung by boys and girls to each other.
    hais kwv txhiaj To sing ballads, to serenade.
    Note: This expression is sometimes spelled 'khwv txhiaj'
    For reference: We also include here the other types
         of Hmong songs.
    khawv chab Another type of boy-girl song but without
         the long drawn-out notes typical of 'kwv txhiaj'
    zaj tshoob Wedding songs.
    lus taum Old folks songs.
    txiv xaiv Funeral songs, songs of death.

KH

khab
  khab seeb Empty, barren, uncluttered, roomy.
  lub tsev khab seeb An empty uncluttered house,
    a roomy house.
  neeg khab seeb A childless person.

1. khaj Of forcible vigorous speech.
  (a) neeg khaj lus One who speaks forcibly.
  (b) neeg khaj thawj One who speaks forcibly.
  tso khaj thawj rau.. To speak forcibly with
    weighty words to someone as e.g. to drive
    him away and frustrate his intended purpose.

2. khaj Energetic, spirited (of persons or animals)
  hom khaj to jump for joy.

1. khav Proud, boasting, boastful.
  Tsis txhob khav. Don't boast.
  lub siab khav theeb A proud 'heart.'
  (a) khav txiv To boast.
  (b) khav qhuas To boast.
  Nws khav qhuas nws li zoo xwb. He only boasts of
    his own goodness.

2. khav A raised porch (cf. 'qab tsag').
  qab khav A raised porch (cf. 'qab tsag').

3. khav
  Txhob khav thwj lawv tej pub mov nej noj. Don't rely
    upon others to provide your food.

4. khav
  khavloom (tus) The governor (T).

5. khav To covet; to seek after.
  Nws khav pw tsaug zog xwb. He only wants to sleep.

1. khais A plow (rab).

2. khais A slight feeling in a tooth indicating developing
    pain.
  Kuv tus hniav khais khais li. My tooth is beginning
    to give me trouble.

khau Shoe, shoes (clf. 'nkawm' for pairs).
  ib nkawg khau One pair of shoes.
  rau khau To wear shoes.
  khau caj ntswm Chinese cloth shoes with upturned
    toes, traditionally used in burial.

1. khaub Of articles crossing each other, crossed.
  (a) khaublig ntoo (tus) A wooden cross, the cross.
  (b) ntoo khaublig (tus) A wooden cross, the cross.

2. khaub To wind around, encircle, wind up.
  khaub zig To wind around.
  txoj hmab khaub khaub zig ntoo The vine encircles the
    tree.
  Muab txoj hlua khaub zig. Wind up the string.

3. khaub A dry branch or stick (tus).
  khaub nplawm (or 'tshum') qhovmuag Hit in the eye by
    a branch or stick.

4. khaub
  khaub ruab (rab) A broom.
  Muab khaub ruab cheb tsev. Take the broom and sweep
    out the house.
  kab khaub ruab (tus) An insect resembling a stick.

5. khaub
  khaubncaws Clothing.
  hnav khaubncaws To wear clothing, to dress.
  Note: This word is also used to refer to menstruation.
  (a) yawg khaubncaws To menstruate.
  (b) coj khaubncaws To menstruate.
  (c) yawg cev To menstruate.

6. khaub
  khaub hlab Rag, ragged, old clothing, worn out
    (of clothing, baskets, etc.)
  Muab ib txog khaub hlab rau kuv. Hand me a rag.
  khaub khaub hlab Ragged, worn out.

7. khaub
  khaub hnab (lub) A small stuffed ball covered with
    cloth and used in Hmong games. At the New Year
    it is thrown between teams of boys and girls in
    a game of forfeits.

8. khaub
  khaub thuas The common cold, to have a cold (often
    used in combination with 'sab foob' which is
    the equivalent expression in Chinese.)
  sab foob khaub thuas To have a cold.

1. khauj A shell of an animal, turtle, mollusk, etc. (lub).
  khauj khaum A shell (as above).
  khauj khaum taubhau The skull.

2. khauj
  khauj tsiav To hit with the knuckle.

1. khaum Caught upon, caught fast.
   khaum nrees Caught fast.
   Ntoo khaum nrees saud. The tree is caught fast up
     there. (and can't fall though it has been
     chopped through).
   khaum kaj khaum kus Keeps getting stuck (as when
     carrying an article of unwieldy length.)

2. khaum To fix upon, to settle.
   foom khaum To settle the fate, 'fix' a fortune.

3. khaum Shell of an animal, etc. (cf. 'khauj' above).

4. khaum Greedy, selfish, jealous (cf. 'qia dub').
   cuajkhaum

5. khaum.
   txhab khaum (lub) The gunstock.

6. khaum
   (a) teev phaj The box in which the small balance
       scales is kept.
   (b) teev khaum (lub) The box in which the small
       balance scales is kept.

khaus Itchy.
   khaus khaus li Very itchy.
   khaus cau "itchy hands" Used to refer to a person
     who must always be up to some mischief or
     evil deeds as stealing, etc.

1. khauv Finished.
   khauv lawm Finished (same as 'dawb lawm,' 'tag
     lawm,' 'hle lawm').

2. khauv
   khauv zeeg cua Whirlwind.

khaw Tone change from 'khawv,' (cf. 'khawv').

1. khawb To scratch out, to dig, to hoe.
   khawb av. To hoe the ground.
   khawb qhov To dig a hole.
   khawb qua tsev To level a house site (cf. 'ncaws av').
   khawb qees To keep on digging.

2. khawb A hook, a buckle, to hook on or hook together
     (lub).
   khawb xauv The clasp on a neck ring, chain fixed to
     the ends of the ring.

1. khawm A button, to button (lub).

2. khawm
   hais lus khawm lus To swear to a fact, take an oath.

3. khawm To embrace.
   sib khawm To embrace one another (used by young
     people but not a very elegant expression).

1. khaws To pick up, gather.
   Muab khaws cia. Pick it up and store it away.
   khaws nraim To pick up things (as a regular custom).
   khaws nkaus To pick up.
   khaws txiv To pick up fallen fruit.
   taug kev khaws taw qhuav Picks up things as he goes
     along (i.e. for nothing, without labor).

2. khaws
   khaws xyeem (cf. 'ntxab ntxawm').
   khaws xyeem ua To do something taking advantage of
     what someone has already done or prepared.

1. khawv Clf. for mouthfuls (also cf. 'kaug') (C).
   rau khawv Six mouthfuls.
   ib khaw One mouthful (t.c.).

2. khawv
   thov khawv To beg, ask for alms or food.

3. khawv
   pov khawv Satisfied, enough (with the sense, "I'm
     sick of it.")

4. khawv
   pom khawv To tell of the evils of other people,
     to inform on someone's offences.

5. khawv
   khawvkoob Magic.
   ua khawvkoob tij lim To do wonderful magic.

6. khawv
   khawv chab A type of boy-girl song (cf. 'kwv txhiaj').

7. khawv
   fwv khawv (lub) A natural pass or gateway through the
     jungle or landscape where wild game will usually
     be forced to travel.

8. khawv
   ua timkhawv To witness, bear testimony (cf. 'tim').

1. khej The crocodile (tus) (T).

2. khej
   kum khej (C) (cf. 'kum').

khem   muj khem Notches made in wood and used by the Hmong
        in certain patterns as a limited form of
        communication.
        hlais muj khem To make such notches, to cut notches.

khee   t.c. from 'kheev' used as a clf. (cf. 'kheev').

1. kheej   Round, circular (contr. 'pluav').
        Lub khaub hnab kheej kheej li. The ball is round.
        taubhau kheej lam A round head.

2. kheej   Entire, whole (in special expressions).
        kuv lub cev kheej My whole body, entire person.

kheem   To recline, lie down (cf. 'pw').

khees   To finish off the little bit remaining, to deal with
        completely.
        Khees kiag ua. Finish it all. (of field work, etc.)
        Khees huvsi. (eaten) All gone.
        Khees tsis huv. Not (eaten) clean. Residue on the
        plate.

1. kheev   To be willing, to be inclined to.
        Kuv kheev mus. I'm willing to go.
        Tsis kheev ua. Unwilling to do. (or) Unwilling for
        another person to do.
        Kheev hlob zoo. (He) is growing well.
        Kheev nws tuaj... If only he would come....
        (cf. Cia nws tuaj... Let him come.)

2. kheev   Clf. for bunches of onions, garlic, etc.
        (varies with 'khee' according to rules of tone change).

khi   To bind, to tie up.
        khi rawv Bound tightly.
        Muab nws khi! Tie him up!

1. khib   Irritated, offended, to offend, to annoy, resentful.
        khib lub siab Irritate, annoyed, aroused.
        siab khib khib Offended, irritated, annoyed.
        khib siab "Tight hearted" in the sense of not
        willing to lend money, etc.

2. khib   A carrying frame for carrying wood, etc. on the
        back. (rab)
        Nws ris rab khib mus txiav taws. He went with a
        carrying frame to cut firewood.

3. khib   To end or put a stop to.
        hnoos tsis paub khib Coughed without stopping.
        cem tsis khib Cursed or scolded constantly.
        tsis paub khib Intensely or without stopping.
        tshem tau khib To leave provisions of food, etc. for
        guests and strangers.

4. khib   tshuaj khib (lub) A mortar (for grinding peppers, etc.)

5. khib   Khib liab (T) Dirty, disgusting (cf. 'qias neeg').

6. khib   Khib koom (T) Of a person who changes his mind
        especially regarding wages, etc.

khis   To break a piece off (cf. 'ntais').
        khis lawm Nicked (as a knife hitting a nail).
        Hniav khis ib sab lawm. (My) tooth is chipped or a
        piece has broken off one side.

khiab   To tie up with a band in a special way. To tie a
        sash about the waist and then between the legs
        before it is tucked in, in the manner of the Thai
        in former days.
        khiab tw Tail band on a horse harness.
        khiab txia Chest band on a horse harness.
        daim sev khiab menyuam A band of cloth used to shield
        an infant carried on the back from the sun
        (cf. 'nias').

khiam   Natives of India (T) (tus).

khiav   To run, to go quickly, to depart (cf. 'plau').
        khiav lawm Ran away (cf. 'plau lawm').
        Nws khiav ya ntxiag mus. He fled away. "Flew off."
        khiav quj qees Ran slowly, fled slowly.
        khiav hlo Got completely away.
        khaiv ntsuj mus Went away.

1. kho   To heal.
        kho mob To heal sickness.
        kho zoo lawm Healed up, gotten well.

2. kho   To fix, to arrange, repair.
        Muab lub teeb kho kom zoo. Fix the lamp.

3. kho   To reforge or repair metal knives, etc. that have
        been chipped or blunted. (cf. 'phiaj').

4. kho   Lonely, melancholy, filled with longing and nostalgia,
        homesick.
        kho kho siab Lonely, homesick (cf. 'seev').

5. kho   khov kho (cf. 'khov'). Very steady, very firm.

1. khob   To rap, to knock with the knuckle.
        Khob qhovrooj. Knock on the door.

2. khob A small cup for drinking wine or whisky (cf. 'pib txwv') (C).
   ib khob cawv One cup of whisky.

khom To rest upon, rely upon.
   khom To rest upon (as a beam resting on two uprights, etc.).
   vamkhom To rely upon, to trust in (C).

1. khov Steady, firm.
   (a) khov khov Very steady, very firm.
   (b) khov kho Very steady, very firm.

2. khov Thick (of liquids), having viscosity.

3. khov To congeal, congealed (cf. 'nkoog').

4. khov To instruct in a special sense, as to help or teach a crime witness how to bear testimony, to 'fix' a witness.

khoo Old and thin (of old persons, animals, etc.)
   Khuvleej tus pojniam khoo khoo. Have pity on the old emaciated woman.

1. khoob Empty, hollow.
   lub xauv khoob A hollow neck ring.
   neeg khoob xeeb (C) "Hollow-hearted" person, i.e. one who is teachable, ready to listen.

2. khoob To call together.
   khoob menyuam To call children to come.

khooj Knees bent tight together, doubled up.
   zaum khooj ywb To sit squatting on the heels.
   khooj To be doubled up (in pain) or on the knees with the head to the ground as when injured in the abdomen.

1. khoom Leisure, ease, idle time (cf. 'xyeej').
   Kuv tsis khoom ua. I have no time to do it.
   dim plhuav khoom haujlwm Leisure time free from work.

2. khoom Freely.
   khoom pub To freely give (without charge).

3. khoom Goods, baggage (T).
   tu khoom To pack goods in preparation for travel.
   thauj khoom To carry goods by horse or conveyance.

khoos To fail to enter the flesh (as of a knife stroke or a bullet that glances off.)

1. khoov To stoop, to bend over.
   khoov nkoos To bend over, stoop.
   (a) tibneeg khoov khoov A hunchback, person with a permanent stoop.
   (b) tibneeg caws caws A hunchback, person with a permanent stoop.
   (a) ntoo khoov A tree bent or leaning.
   (b) ntoo rawv A tree bent or leaning.

2. khoov
   txhiaj khoov... It would be better if... (cf. 'yim').
   Txhiaj khoov txhob yug los. Better if he hadn't been born.

1. khub Encrusted.
   khub khub dub dub Dirty and encrusted (with mud, etc.)
   khub laujkaub lawm The pot has a thick encrustation on the bottom surface or the inside.

2. khub To admit, to acknowledge.
   Kuv khub npau li no xwb. (You accuse me of such and such but...) I'll only admit to so much.

khuj Fortune (lub).
   muaj ib lub khuj To have a fortune.
   khuj zoo; khuj phem Good or evil fortune as told by a fortune teller.

khum (cf. 'fajkhum').

1. khuv
   khuvleej (C) To pity, to have compassion.

2. khuv
   khuvxim (C) What a pity, too bad.

3. khuv
   khuv cev Having scanty menstruation.

4. khuv
   Kuv tsis khuv hais. I don't want to say anything lest it aggravate the situation.

khuab Alternate pronunciation for 'khuam.' (cf. 'khuam').

khuaj
   Khuaj mub The Khamu people, a tribe found mostly in Laos.
   Khuaj phaib The Tin people, a tribe found in Laos and in certain parts of N. and E. Thailand.

1. khuam Caught upon something, hung up (sometimes said 'khuab').
   Ntoo khuam lawm. The tree is caught and can't fall.
   khuam kausmom To hang up a hat.
   khuam cheem To retain someone, to engage in conversation, etc. so as to keep a person from leaving. (cf. 'lawj').
   khuam ntab khuam ntuv khuam xeeb khuam tshaj Betwixt and between, caught between two uncertainties.

2. khuam
   khuam siab Lonely, missing others.

khw nquam kiab nquam khw Market, marketplace (poetic and archaic, not in common speech).

1. khwb To cover up, cover over (as with a hand, with a vessel, etc.)

2. khwb Upside down, with the face or mouth downwards.
   pw khwb rwg To lie on the stomach with face down.
   puag khwb rwg To hold (an infant) on its tummy.

3. khwb
   khwb teeb (lub) A plaited bamboo stool, typical low bamboo stool used in Hmong homes and made something in the shape of an inverted vessel.

khwm thomkhwm Socks (clf. 'nkawm' for pairs).
   rau thomkhwm To wear socks.

khws To imitate, to follow an example (cf. 'xyaum').
   Nws ua khws khws Huabtais tus yamntxwv. He followed the example of the king.

1. khwv Bitter toil, bitter experience, hardship (C).
   sawm khwv To endure bitterness and hardship.
   khwv khwv tawm tawm Very toilsome.
   Khwv koj. I have troubled you. "Excuse me." (cf. 'tabkaum koj').

2. khwv khwv txhiaj (cf. 'kwv txhiaj').

la Tone change from 'lav,' (cf. 'lav').

lab huablab (T) A westerner, a European (tus).

1. lag To be deaf, deafness.
   lag ntseg Deaf, deaf ears.

2. lag
   lag zeb A smooth surface of exposed rock.

3. lag
   uab lag (tus) A kind of wild black bird.

4. lag
   ua lag ua luam To do trade, to do business.

1. laj One hundred thousand as a numerical unit.
   ib laj One hundred thousand.

2. laj Mountain ridge.
   taug laj mus To walk along the ridge.

3. laj Cool, to cool off.
   Nws lub cev sov pheej tsis laj. He has a fever that won't go down.
   laj laj siab To "cool off," abate anger.

4. laj
   ceeblaj Difficulty, trouble, troublesome.

5. laj lajkab (txoj) A fence.
   xov lajkab To erect a fence.

6. laj laj muag Cross-eyed.

7. laj laj zoov The beginning of the jungle, jungle edge.

8. laj lo laj lo luav All plastered up with mud and dirt.

9. laj roob laj The pole laid lengthwise on the roof peak of a house in the crotches of poles which hold down the leaf thatch.

10. laj ntoo toov laj (tus) A type of long-fronded palm.

11. laj
    (a) kuv laj nloog   I'm tired of hearing it.
    (b) kuv nkees nloog   I'm tired of hearing it.

12. laj
    txhiam laj txhiam xwm   Vegetables (cf. 'txhiam').

13. laj
    (a) Nws sab tsis taj laj.   He hasn't yet discussed the
        matter or has not concluded the discussion on it.
        (cf. 'sablaj').
    (b) Nws tsis tau sablaj.   He hasn't yet discussed the
        matter or has not concluded the discussion on it.
        (cf. 'sablaj').

14. laj
    tus phijlaj (cf. 'phij').

1. lam   Foolish, haphazard, untrue, with no regard for facts.
    lam hais   To speak foolishly, speak with no regard
        for the facts (cf. 'txeev lam hais').
    lam ua   To do haphazardly, do **poorly**.
    lam tau lam ua   To do any old way, do haphazardly.

2. lam   Upset, in turmoil.
    (a) tebchaws lam   A nation in turmoil.
    (b) tebchaws lwj   A nation in turmoil.
    lub siab lam   Heart upset, heart in turmoil.
    loj lam   Calamity, travail, trouble.
    luj lam tam   Poverty stricken, calamity stricken.

3. lam   Bright, glistening, glittering.
    lam lam li   Bright, glittering.

4. lam   lwvlam   Probably (cf. 'tamfaj').
    Kwvlam nws yuav los.   Probably he will return.

1. las   An ounce.
    ib lag (t.c.)   One ounce.
    kaum las   Ten ounces.
    ib txiaj   One tenth of an ounce (cf. 'txiaj').
    ib fiab   One one hundredth of an ounce.
    ib poom   One pound.

2. las   To put down in salt, to salt.
    las ntsev   To put down (meat, etc.) in salt.

3. las   Exclamatory final particle.
    Koj ua tau diam tiag las.   You can really accomplish
        things.

4. las   Castrated.
    tus las npua   Large castrated pig.

5. las   The second period of weeding the fields (contr. 'dob').
    las yeeb   To weed the opium the second time.
    las nplej   To weed rice the second time.

6. las
    pw las tshav   To sleep under the open sky.

7. las
    rab chaws las   A metal rod used in making holes in
        wood after heating in the fire.

8. las
    hais tsuag las   (cf. 'tsuag').

9. las
    tauv las tshuj tshuav (cf. 'tauv').

1. lav   Raw.
    noj lav   To eat raw meat, eat raw.
    ua lav npua   To make minced raw pork and spices.

2. lav   To guarantee.
    lav tau   To guarantee.
    lav ntxhias (cf. 'pob ntxhias')   To guarantee.

3. lav   To bear responsibility for, to take unto one's self.
    lav txim   To bear sin, to bear the responsibility for
        sin, to take the full weight of sin.
    Yexu lav peb lub txim mus.   Jesus bore our sin.
        (cf. 'nres').
    Koj yuav lav vaj lub tebchaws los ua hmoov.   You shall
        have a part in the kingdom.

4. lav   A place prepared for a group to sleep or sit.
    Pua ib lub lav rau lawv pw.   Prepare a place for them
        to sleep.
    Pw ib la. (t.c.)   Sleep in a line.

laig   To offer food to the spirits to eat.
    laig dab   To set aside food and invite the spirits
        to eat.
    laig rau noj   To offer to spirits to eat.
    Note: This word 'laig' is also used in place of the
        word 'noj' (to eat) in rough speech or cursing.
        (cf. 'loob').

laij   To plow.
    laij liag   To plow paddy fields. (cf. 'liaj' which is
        usually read 'liag' in this expression).
    laij av   To plow the ground.

1. laim   Lightning (cf. 'xob').
    xob laim   Lightning.

2. laim   To twitch, flutter.
    qhovmuag laim laim   Eyes twitching, eyes affected with
        spasm of fluttering.

3. laim To cast away, cast aside, throw away.
   (a) laim ntias To cast away, throw away.
   (b) laim rhees To cast away, throw away.
   (c) laim pov tseg To cast away, throw away.

1. lais
   Phis lis phais lais An expression used as a post verbal intensifier indicating something done haphazardly, aimlessly, foolishly.

2. lais
   lais txhiam xwm To plant vegetables.

lau The male of birds and poultry (contr. 'poj').
   ib tug lau qaib A cock, a rooster.

1. laub
   sib laub To push and pull on opposite ends of a stick.

2. laub
   laub zeb daus To flatten and smooth thread with a stone roller, a process in preparing hemp thread for weaving.

3. laub To pour, to pour out.
   Note: This word is sometimes used by White Hmong but it is more common among the Blue Hmong. (cf. 'nchuav' and 'hliv' which are more commonly used by White Hmong.

1. laug To sustain a long drawn out note in song, etc.
   laug suab ntev To sustain a note.
   quaj laug laws To cry loud and long.

2. laug
   chaub laug To crawl on one's belly (cf. 'chaub').

3. laug Cross stitch type of embroidery.
   laug nplooj suab Cross stitch embroidery.

4. laug
   (a) tij laug (t.c. from 'laus') (cf. 'laus').
   (b) dab laug (t.c. from 'laus') (cf. 'laus').

5. laug
   ciblaug (lub) An open basket for carrying earth, refuse, etc.

6. laug
   (a) kab laug sab (cf. 'kab').
   (b) kab laug tsov (cf. 'kab').

1. lauj Pertaining to the left side, left (contr. 'xis').
   txhais tes lauj The left hand.
   sab lauj (t.c.) The left side.

2. lauj To withdraw or retract.
   lauj tes To retract the hand.
   Nws lauj kiav tes ntaus. He drew back his hand to hit.

3. lauj To put aside.
   (a) lauj haujlwm zias cia Put the housework aside (to attend to something else).
   (b) muab lauj tseg Put the housework aside (to attend to something else).
   lauj num mus Lay the work aside and go.

4. lauj A completive particle.
   Tsis yog lauj! No!
   Lawv lawm lauj. They have gone.
   Los lauj. Has come.
   Yog li kuv hais ntag laux. Just as I said! (t.c.)

5. lauj
   lauj kaub (lub) Cooking pot.

6. lauj
   lauj vaub Lengths of knotted hair.

7. lauj
   nqe lauj (tus) A wooden hook to hang articles on in the home.

8. lauj
   mus lauj taw To walk on the heels.

9. lauj
   laujpwm (cf. 'loojpwm').

1. laum To bore (cf. 'tho').
   laum qhov To bore a hole.

2. laum Cockroach (tus).

3. laum
   laum kib tshooj (tus) Centipede (pronounced 'laum kev tshooj' in Laos).

4. laum To strangle, to press close upon (cf. 'zawm').
   pos laum nplej The thorns strangle the rice.
   nroj laum nplej The weeds strangle the rice.

5. laum To plug, to put an object into a hole to stop it up.
   Lawv muab ntiv tes laum hauv qhovntseg. They put their fingers in their ears.

6. laum
   raus laum tshauv To rub bamboo arrows in the hot
      ashes to soften them for straightening.

7. laum
   sub laum (cf. 'sub').

8. laum To tickle.

1. laus Old, aged (of persons or animals), elder (contr. 'qub').
   neeg laus laus An aged person.
   (a) laus neeg The village "elders," older persons
       whose counsel is respected.
   (b) cov txwj laus The village "elders," older
       persons whose counsel is respected.
   (c) cov txwj cov laus The village "elders," older
       persons whose counsel is respected.
   laus nkoos Very old.
   tij laug (t.c.) Older brother.
   dab laug (t.c.) Mother's elder brother.
   niam laus Wife's elder sister.
   txiv laus Husband of wife's elder sister.

2. laus Lower in sound or tone.
   suab laus laus A low voice.
   tsov quaj laus nkoos The tiger gave a low growl.

3. laus
   plab laus The stomach region (cf. 'plab mog')
      (also 'plab laug' t.c.).

4. laus
   raj ris laus (tus) A kind of long-legged spider.

law
   sib law In a row next to each other (as a row of
      shops, etc.)

lawb
   lawb menyuam To have a miscarriage.
   Note: This is offensive language.

lawd (cf. 'lawm,' also cf. Introduction pp. xxii-xxiii).

1. lawg Hail, hailstones (lub) (cf. 'daus xib daus npu').

2. lawg To collide. (cf. 'npug').
   sib lawg Head on collision.
   Ob lub tsheb ya mus lawg. Two cars collided.

1. lawj To forcibly detain, forcibly restrain.

2. lawj A bamboo guest platform in the home (lub).

3. lawj
   nees txov lawj A brown horse.

4. lawj
   lawj faj Sulphur.

1. lawm Completed, sign of completed action or past tense.
   tuag lawm Died, dead.
   tag lawm Finished, completed.
   mus teb lawm Went to the fields.
   Peb mus lawm. We are going. (i.e. the start of our
      departure has been accomplished.)

2. lawm To go, to depart, leave.
   Lawm lawm los tsis tau? Have they gone yet?
   Lawm tim lawv lawm. (they) have gone over there to
      them.
   Lawv lawm lauj. They have gone.

3. lawm
   neeg lus lawm plias A person quick of speech.

4. lawm P.v.int. (Cf. 'luj').

1. laws To strip off (cf. 'tev').
   laws maj To strip hemp bark off the reed.
   muab laws tawv To skin, to strip the skin off.

2. laws
   puv nco laws Filled rounded over (cf. 'puv').

3. laws
   quaj laug laws To cry loud and long.

1. lawv Third person plural pronoun, they, them.
   Lawv tsis paub. They don't know.

2. lawv To follow.
   lawv qab To follow after, follow behind.
   Lawv peb qab. Follow us.

3. lawv To drive something ahead.
   lawv nyuj To drive cattle (cows).

4. lawv To flush with water, to wash down.
   muab dej lawv Wash it down with water (cf. swallowing
      medicine, etc.)

5. lawv Diarrhea.
   lawv plab Diarrhea (cf. 'raws plab,' 'thoj plab').

6. lawv To pound or forge metal to lengthen it.

le (cf. 'lev').

1. leg To imitate, follow the way or example of another
   (cf. 'xyaum').
   leg koj txoj kev Go your way.
   tsis leg Yexu kev Does not follow Jesus' teaching.
   tsis leg haujlwm Doesn't do work.

2. leg
   pab leg To help (cf. 'pab').

3. leg
   vwm loj vwm leg To reel around in a drunken manner.

lej Nose (cf. 'ntswg' which is the more common word).
   ntswg lej Mucus from the nose.

1. lem To warp, to turn backward.
   lem tes To turn the arm backward, twist the arm.
   lem taw To turn the ankle or twist the foot.
   lem caj dab To twist the neck.
   (a) lem nqe To argue price.
   (b) nyom nqe To argue price.

2. lem ceeb The lengthwise rafter of a house
   (cf. 'tsev').

1. les
   xooj les Surprised, startled, in wonder and amazement
   (cf. 'ruaj zog' 'yoob zog').

2. les
   kab qaus les (tus) The dragon fly.

3. les
   lev les (rab) Small reed flute made by children as
   a plaything.

1. lev Plaited bamboo mat (daim).
   This mat is used for sleeping, to spread things
   on to dry and to beat the rice on in harvesting.
   hiab lev To weave or plait such a mat.
   phua ncau hiab lev To split the bamboo for weaving
   a mat.
   daim lev pua pw A mat to sleep on.

2. lev Used as a clf. for things spread out on a mat.
   ib le nplej One matful of rice (t.c.)

3. lev
   rab lev les (cf. 'les').

4. lev
   dab tshos kaus lev A type of ladies' embroidered
   collar.

lee
   lee lee ntswg Of a person the bridge of whose nose
   extends far up toward the forehead.

1. leeb
   neeg loj leeb A wanderer, a person prone not to stay
   at home (cf. 'neeg luj luas').

2. leeb
   leeb nkaub (tus) A parakeet.

1. leeg Vein or artery (txoj).

2. leeg A seam in clothing or sewing (tus) (cf. 'leej').

3. leeg
   tsaug tsaug leeg Weak, lacking physical strength.

4. leeg
   Hmoob leeg Another term for the Green (or Blue) Meo
   (cf. 'Hmoob ntsuab').

1. leej Clf. for persons (this clf. is only used for persons
   and is perhaps more polite than 'tus' which may
   also be used for various animate objects. cf. 'tus').
   kaum leej Ten persons.
   ib leej One person (t.c.)
   Leej twg Who?
   leej txiv Father.

2. leej Effective (as of medicine, etc.)
   Cov tshuaj no tsis leej. This medicine isn't effective.
   Hais li cas kuj tsis leej. No matter what he said it
   had no effect.

3. leej A line, a line of objects, a seam in clothing or
   sewing.
   ua ib leej Put them in a line, make a line.
   leej leej A seam in clothing or in sewing (tus).

4. leej To admit, to be willing to.
   tsis leej hais I'm not willing to say.
   Deb deb li, kuv tsis leej tuag. It's too far so I'm
   not willing to come.

5. leej
   leej leej li Clearly, truly (cf. 'tiag tiag li').

6. puav leej All, altogether.
   Cov dub tsis muaj, puav leej liab xwb. There are no
   black ones, all are red.

1. leem To pave, to put a solid coating on something
   (cf. 'plia' 'pleev').
   leem kev To pave a road.
   leem qua tsev To put in a concrete floor.

2. leem
   tuam thawj leem (C) Chief soldier, general.

3. leem
   leem nees To take a horse out to play.

1. lees To acknowledge, to accept, to receive (cf. 'lav').
   lees lub txim To acknowledge guilt, to confess sin.
   Yexu lees pab lub txim Jesus has borne our sin.
   (i.e. Jesus has acknowledged our sin and guilt
   as resting upon Him.)

2. lees Post verbal intensifier of restricted use.
   ntswj lees Very twisted.

1. li Particle used after nouns or noun expressions to
   indicate "pertaining to," "belonging to,"
   "having connection with." Used in this way it
   is the common way for indicating possession.
   kuv li Mine.
   lawv li Theirs.
   ntiajteb li. Belonging to the world, the world's.

2. li Particle used after verbs or verbal expressions to
   indicate "like," "as," "after the manner of."
   zoo li no Like this.
   Ua zoo li no. Do it like this.
   ua li no So, In that case, That's the way it is.
   Ua li no mas kuv yuav tsis mus. Well in that case
   I won't go.
   kub kub kub li Very hot.
   Nws tuaj sai sai li. He came quickly.

3. li Particle used in combination with post verbal
   intensives, usually also bearing its meaning
   "like" or "as." Compare the following expressions in Appendix 8 p. 468.
   kiag li; li ub; li no; hlo li; li ntag.

1. lib
   lib lib av Of children playing in the mud.

2. lib
   lib nyug (tus) The brown fish-owl.

1. lig Late, tardy.
   Lig lawm, mus tsis txog. It's late, we won't be able
   to get there.

2. lig
   mob lig Scabies, the "itch."

3. lib To wind on a spool.
   lig xov Thread wound on a spool, sewing thread.

4. lig
   kab lig ntuj The milky way.

1. lij To bore a hole, to enlarge a hole (cf. 'tho').
   lij koob txam A drill (clf. 'tus' for the bit; 'rab'
   for the whole tool).

2. lij
   cov Lijxub The Lisu tribespeople.

1. lim Tired, weary (C).
   Kuv lim lim li, ua tsis tau. I'm tired and can't do it.

2. lim To filter, to strain.
   lub lim A strainer, a filter.

3. lim
   lim hiam Fierce, cruel (C).

4. lim
   tij lim Effective, having strength. (cf. khawv koob)

1. lis To settle cases of dispute.
   Muab lis (or 'hais,' or 'txiav' or 'kiav') tag lawm.
   (The case) has been settled.

2. lis Post verbal intensive of restricted use.
   daj lis Very yellow (cf. Appendix 8).

3. lis Used in the post verbal intensive expression 'phis
   lis phais lais' (cf. Appendix 8 p. 468).

4. lis
   lis xaiv Gossip.
   neeg lis xaiv (tus) A gossip, one who tells tales on
   others.

1. liv Of flat objects spinning on edge, to spin a coin, etc.

2. liv
   xisliv (daim) A straw mat, straw sleeping mat (C).

3. liv
   pum liv (raj) A flute, a horn with finger holes.

1. liab Red.
   liab liab Very red.
   liab dhoog Dark red, crimson, color of congealed blood.
   liab ploog Very red.
   hnub liab ploog Sunset.
   liab tseb Light red, not very red.
   liab txiv tsuav Pink, bright pink.
   liab vog Speckled or figured red.
   liab qab Naked, nude.
   qos liab The sweet potato (lub) (cf. 'qos').
   menyuam mos liab (or iam liab) A new baby, young babe.

2. liab The short-tailed monkey, Rhesus monkey (tus).
   txiv thais liab A large male monkey.

3. liab
   hma liab (tus) Dhole dog, red fox (cf. 'hma').

4. liab
   liab npog muag (tus) The sloth.

5. liab (T) Dirty (cf. 'qias neeg'), disgusting.
   khib liab (T) Dirty (cf. 'qias neeg'), disgusting.

liag The rice sickle, small curved implement for cutting grain (rab).

1. liaj Paddy field, field for wet-crop cultivation (clf. 'zeg').
   laij liaj To plow paddy fields (t.c.)
   liaj qhua Dry paddy field.
   ua liaj To make paddy fields, cultivate paddy fields.
   lub nras liaj qhua Dry fields, a dry wilderness with dry fields and rolling hills.

2 liaj Lands, territory.
   liaj ia Lands, territory.
   liaj ia tebchaws Fields and land, territory.

3. liaj To close with a bar or bolt.
   liaj qhovrooj To bar or bolt the door.

1. liam To blame, to wrongly accuse.
   liam rau nej Wrongly accused you.
   liam ub liam no rau luag tej Blaming others for all kinds of things.

2. liam Ruined, destroyed, in turmoil.
   liam sim Ruined, destroyed (cf. 'puas tsuaj').
   ua lwj ua liam To do recklessly, without purpose.
   tebchaws lwj liam Land in turmoil.
   ua chib chawj puaj liam (C) To do recklessly, do poorly, create turmoil.
   (cf. 'ua xya chawj yim liam' which is the Hmong expression equivalent to the above which is from the Chinese although both expressions are used.)

3. liam Bare spots bereft of hair especially in animals.
   liam txwv Bare hairless spots.
   dev liam txwv A disease of dogs resulting in such spots.
   ua liam txwv qas ntsuav To do poorly, sloppily.

4. liam
   tsis liam fab Doesn't suit me, don't like.
   tsis liam fab ua Don't want to do.

1. lias A thin piece of silver ornamentation worn as decoration (cf. 'daim').

2. lias P.v.intensive (cf. Appendix 8).
   dawb lias Not very white, off white.
   pheej lias Level measure, level full.
   tiaj lias Level.

3. lias A pre-verbal connecting word (cf. 'nyaj').
   Nej lias puav leej nyob zoo pauj? Are you all well?
   Nyaj nws lias yuav pab. I think probably he will help.

1. lo To stick to, stick on, stuck to.
   lo nkaus Stuck to, stuck together.
   lo nrees Firmly stuck.
   lo lo av Stuck up with mud.
   lo lo mov Stuck up with food, food on the face.
   lo laj lo luav All plastered up with dirt and mud.

2. lo Clf. for words or for mouthfuls.
   lo lus no This word.
   kaum lo lus Ten words.
   ib los lus One word (t.c.).
   ib los hniav One mouth full of teeth, one set of teeth.

lob To grab and pull with the hand (cf. 'rub').
   (a) lob los To grab and pull.
   (b) rub los To grab and pull.

1. log A wheel (lub).

2. log To spin, to set something spinning, to spin around.
   thob log To spin, set something spinning.

3. log
   log cam (lub) A wooden chopping block.

4. log To bury something in the ground (cf. 'los').
   Muab log hauv av. Bury it in the ground.

1. loj Large, great (of quantity, area, or status).
   tsev loj loj A large house.
   tus tibneeg hov loj The person of large frame.
   hwjchim loj Great authority.

2. loj Completive particle (cf. 'los').
   (a) mus lawm Has gone.
   (b) mus lawm loj Has gone.
   (c) lawm loj Has gone.

3. loj
   (a) loj faj (lub) A prison.
   (b) tsev loj faj (lub) A prison.

4. loj loj cuj (lub) A shackle, to shackle, an ankle ring.

5. loj loj lam Calamity, travail.

6. loj loj xov cem huvsi To scold the group for one man's fault.

7. loj loj leeb Wander about.
   neeg loj leeb A wanderer, one who is prone not to stay at home.

1. lom Poisonous, pertaining to poison.
   tshuaj lom Poison, poisonous medicine.
   lom neeg To poison someone.

2. lom To tan leather, to soak in strong solution.
   muab tshuaj lom daim tawv To tan leather.

3. lom txuj lom Spices, condiments, food flavorings (cf. 'txuj').

4. lom lom zem (C) Noisy and crowded, lots going on, revelry.

5. lom lom vab vàb The sound of revelry, noise and talking so loud one cannot hear anything else.

1. los To return, to come (back to a place where you reside, contr. 'tuaj').
   Koj mus qhov twg los? Where have you been? Where have you been and come from?
   Mus ho los. Come again. (common polite phrase said to one leaving and going to a place which is not his home, from which he will return).
   los qujqees To return slowly and steadily.
   Los qhov no. Come here.
   los hlo Returned (cf. 'los lawm,' 'los hlo lawm').
   (a) los los To return to, returned.
   (b) los lov To return to, returned.
   (a) los lawm Has returned (for a time).
   (b) los lawm loj Has returned (for a time).
   los loj Is just returning.
   los lauj Has come.

2. los Used as a secondary verb. The King of heaven
   Vajtswv ntuj tsim peb los. created us.

3. los Interrogative particle, particle indicating "or," "or not."
   Koj mus thiab los? Are you going too?
   Lawv lawm los tsis tau? Have they gone or not?
   Koj muaj nplej los koj muaj txhuv? Have you hulled or unhulled rice?
   Koj puas yuav mus los tsis mus? Are you going or not?

4. los To bury (persons) contr. 'log'
   Muaj plaub tug kwv tus tuag mus los. Four carried the corpse and buried it.

5. los To flow (in certain contexts only, cf. 'ntws').
   los ntshav To bleed, bleeding.

6. los Used in referring to the order of children's birth after the Chinese fashion (C).
   los tuam The firstborn.
   los lwm The second child.
   los xab The third child.
   los xwm The fourth child.
   (and so on, using the Chinese numeration).

7. los lossis Very, intensively (C).
   lossis zoo Very good.
   lossis loj Very large, huge.

8. los Sometimes the interrogative 'los' is used with 'sis.'
   Koj mus los sis tsis mus? Are you going or not?
   Koj hnov los sis tsis hnov? Have you heard or not.

9. los lostsuas The Lao people (cf. 'phwv nyeeb' and 'kua loos').

10. los los pav (tus) (C) Manager, employer, master.

11. los los yuaj (tus) The large back teeth of a horse that appear after 3 years.

1. lov To break in two, to break off.
   lov ntho Broken in two (as a stick or bone).

2. lov los lov (cf. 'los').

lox (cf. 'los'. The 'x' intonation gives an added sense of surprise or wonder. cf. Introduction p. xxii-xiii)
   Koj tuaj lox? You've come? (to my surprise).
   Koj pom lox? You mean you can see it?

loo   Crops
    ua qoob ua loo   To do crops, to raise corn and
        rice, etc.
    qoob loos   Crops (t.c.)   (also said 'qoob loo').

1. loob   Small wild animal   (cf. 'npua,' 'zaj npuas').

2. loob   Deaf   (used only in ridicule, comparing a deaf
    person to a 'loob,' a pig-like animal which
    appears deaf and stupid).

3. loob   Coarse language for 'hnav'   To wear.   Used only
    in scolding.   (cf. 'laig').

1. loog   Numb, insensitive.

2. loog   Courtyard, large fenced enclosure (lub).
    rooj loog   Gate of the courtyard.

1. looj   To fix, to arrange.
    looj hniav   To fix a tooth, cover a tooth.

2. looj   Unconscious.
    looj hlawv hlias   Recurring unconsciousness.
    tsaug zog looj hlias   Very sleepy.

3. looj   pwm (lub)   (C)   Tuber, root vegetable (cf. 'lauj
    pwm').

4. looj   koov   To make a fuss, make trouble   (cf. 'kiam')
    (C).

5. looj   tes   Gloves   (also called 'rau' sometimes).

loom   Khavloom (tus)   (T)   The governor.

1. loos   miaj loos (lub)   A woven basket of the type used by
    Meo for storing clothing, etc.

2. loos   lees (lub)   (T)   A school.

3. loos   phwv nyais npas (lub)   (T)   Hospital.

4. loos   qoob loos   (cf. qoob).

5. loos   loos dua ib tom   Do it over again, fix it again.

1. lub   Clf. for articles characterized by bulk or roundness.
    lub ntuj   The sun.
    lub pobzeb   A stone.

2. lub   To chafe, a rubbing which becomes uncomfortable.

3. lub   tuj lub (lub)   A wooden spinning top, toy top.
    ntaus tuj lub   To play the game of spinning tops, each
        trying to knock down the others (commonly played
        at New Year's time).

1. lug   To detour.
    (a) lug kev   To detour, go off the path and return to
        it as when passing an obstacle.
    (b) lug kev mus   To detour, go off the path and return
        to it as when passing an obstacle.
    lug mus   To detour on another trail or road.
    Lawv lug pem lawm.   They took another trail up the hill.
    lug nees   A side trail for horses.

2. lug   Post-verbal intensive   (restricted).
    pawg lug   Many grouped together.
    kub lug   Hot.
    kub siab lug   Zealous, earnest.
    du lug   Very smooth.
    qheb lug   Opened.
    kaj lug   Very bright.
    tshab lug   Clear through.

1. luj   Heel, elbow.
    lub taws (t.c.)   Heel of the foot.
    luj khau   Heel of a shoe.
    luj tshib   Elbow   (cf. 'yas npab').

2. luj   To weigh.
    luj teev   To weigh in a balance scale.

3. luj   The mongoose (tus).

4. luj   lujtxwv (tus)   (C)   A mule, the mule.

5. luj   txiv puv luj   (lub)   The pineapple.

6. luj   mab luj   (lub)   The Thai style brass gong.

7. luj   luj lam tam   Poverty-stricken.

8. luj
   (a) ua luj luas To be a wanderer, a person who seldom stays home.
   (b) ua neeg loj leeb To be a wanderer, a person who seldom stays home.

9. luj P.v.int. (cf. Appendix 8).
   hais luj laws To speak without expression.

1. lum
   lum nplej To stack rice sheaves on a rack for drying.

2. lum One dozen (T).

1. lus Words, speech (clf. for single words 'lo' for sayings 'txoj,' for speeches 'zaj.')
   ib los lus One word (t.c.) Say it all at once.
   ua ib zag lus hais (t.c.) Say it all at once.
   lus dev Cursing, filthy language.
   paj lug (t.c.) Proverb, "flowery speech."
   Piv lus Illustration, figurative language.
   nriav lus Plain speech, straight language as opposed to flowery or figurative speech.
   hais lus To speak, to talk, to say words.
   lus cov Words difficult to say or pronounce.
   txuas lus To converse.
   lus pivtxwv An illustration, a figure of speech, parable.
   txiv lus To interpret.
   ua txiv lus To speak on behalf of another.
   pej yam lus Foreign languages, unfamiliar speech.
   lus plhov xem Round about speech, speaking indirectly to soften the approach.
   nkaw lus To speak forcibly, to command.
   hais lus khawm lus To swear to a fact, take oath.
   niag lus Flattery.
   ua niag lus hais To flatter.
   txhais lus To translate, to explain (cf. 'txiv lus').
   ('cev lus' sometimes used in this sense also.)
   muj vam lus Old fashioned language, ancient speech.
   (a) lus xaus Term for words of completion, final particles.
   (b) lus tag Term for words of completion, final particles.
   lus plhob phij Worthless words, foolish speech.
   hais lus tub qaug neeg To speak disparagingly.
   (a) ta timkhawv To witness concerning.
   (b) hais tim lus To witness concerning.
   lus tuaj dab ros A joke, words causing laughter.
   (a) lus cuav qaub Lies, lying.
   (b) lus dag Lies, lying.
   hais lus nraim nkoos Speak secretly.
   hais lus taum To tell stories in song style.
   (a) tso lus To agree to, give permission.
   (b) pluam lus To agree to, give permission.

   lus mos lus tuaj pos Hypocritical language, soft sounding but with a "thorny" meaning.
   neeg lus lawm plias A person quick of speech, fast talker.
   (a) hais lus taj tsawv Slow of speech.
   (b) hais lus nrho nrhuj nrhawv Slow of speech.

2. lus P.v.int. after 'xiav,' (cf. 'xiav').

1. luv Short.
   Txiav luv mentsis. Cut it off a bit shorter.
   lub siab luv luv Short-tempered, impatient (cf. 'tws').

2. luv
   phom luvxoom (rab) Shotgun.

1. luab To borrow on interest (cf. 'txais').

2. luab To slip, slide aside.
   taw luab Foot slipped (taking some ground or mud with it from a loose or muddy surface.) (contr. 'luam').

3. luab
   (a) nyuj luab tsheb Oxcart, ox pulling a cart.
   (b) nyuj luag tsheb Oxcart, ox pulling a cart.

1. luag To laugh (cf. 'tuaj dab ros').
   luag tawg ntho To break out laughing
   luag nyuj nyav To smile.

2. luag To drag along the ground.
   Luag mus pov tseg. Drag it away and get rid of it.
   (a) nyuj luab tsheb Oxcart, ox pulling a cart.
   (b) nyuj luag tsheb Oxcart, ox pulling a cart.

3. luag Companion.
   kwvluag Very good friend, constant companion (tus).
   (a) Tsis muaj neeg ua luag. No companion.
   (b) Tsis tau luag. No companion.

4. luag Others, sometimes used for 'lawv,' third person plural pronoun. (cf. 'lawv').
   (a) luag tej Others, other people.
   (b) lawv tej Others, other people.
   (a) luag zej zos Other villages.
   (b) luag zej luag zos. Other villages.

5. luag Like, the same as (cf. 'luaj').
   yuav luag ib yam Almost exactly the same.
   sib luag Similar, the same, equal to each other.

1. luaj To cut vegetation with a brush knife, to clear off weeds.
   luaj teb To cut down weeds and brush in the fields, to begin preparing new fields for planting.
   luaj kev To cut down the vegetation along a path.
   luaj nroj To cut down the weeds.

2. luaj Like, The same as, similar to (cf. 'luag').
   luaj li no Like this.
   Luaj li cas? Like what? What's it like?
   Ua li cas koj hlub peb luaj no? How is it you love us like this?

3. luaj Emphatic particle.
   Mob ua luaj! It hurts terribly!
   loj ua luaj Huge.

4. luaj luaj zus Clear through, (to do, go, speak, etc.) right through. Go all the way through.
   Ua luaj zus mus huvsi.

5. luaj luaj tuam Careless (cf. 'liam sim'). (t.c.)
   neeg luaj thuam A person careless with belongings, etc.

6. luaj
   (a) pob av luaj (lub) Anthill.
   (b) pob av muas yis tib (lub) Anthill.

1. luam Business, trade.
   ua lag ua luam To do trade, do business.
   tub luam A merchant, a trader.

2. luam To swim.
   ua luam dej To swim.

3. luam To slip, to slide (due to slippery surface) (contr. 'luab').
   taw luam Foot slipped.
   luam khaubncaws To iron clothing.

4. luam To mill grain in a motorized rotary mill.
   luam txhuv To mill rice.

5. luam luam yeeb Tobacco, cigarette (tus).
   haus luam yeeb To smoke tobacco.

6. luam luam ntawv To print with a rotary press, mimeograph.

1. luas luas nqaij To separate fat meat from the lean.

2. luas
   (a) ua luj luas (cf. 'luj').
   (b) ua neeg loj leeb (cf. 'luj').

3. luas tsev xuas luas (cf. 'tsev').

1. luav A donkey (tus).
   (a) tus luav The donkey.
   (b) tus luav nees The donkey.

2. luav A rabbit (tus).
   (a) tus luav The rabbit.
   (b) tus luav nas The rabbit.

3. luav lo laj lo luav Plastered up with mud and dirt.

lw An open way in the jungle or high grass indicating where someone has gone before although not a regular trail.
   txoj lw Such a way.

1. lwg Dew.

2. lwg To strip off.
   lwg nplooj To strip leaves off a branch, bamboo, etc. a few at a time.

3. lwg cua moj lwg xib kaw A great wind (cf. 'cua').

1. lwj Rotten, decayed.
   lwj ntsuav Putrid, gangrenous.
   lwj nthwb Rotten and mushy.

2. lwj Windbox, blacksmith bellows (lub). (Also called 'foob xab' after the Chinese).
   lub tsev lwj hlau Blacksmith shed or shop.

3. lwj To render rotten, to destroy.
   lwj tebchaws To cause uprising or revolution.
   tus lwj tebchaws A revolutionary.
   (a) tebchaws lwj Nation in turmoil, nation at war.
   (b) tebchaws lwj liam Nation in turmoil, nation at war.
   ua lwj ua liam To destroy, to do recklessly and to no purpose, to make a mess of things.
   neeg lwj An evil person, a "rotten" individual.

4. lwj muaslwj (tus) The Sambar deer.

5. lwj Phwj lwj A tribe in Laos (variously said 'Phwj lwj' or Phwv lwj') (T).

1. lwm Second, another, next in order (C).
   lwm zaus The next time, a second time.
   los lwm The second born child.
   lwm hnub Another day.

2. lwm Clf. for times, occasions.
   nyeem ib lwm Read once, read one time.

3. lwm A term used in spirit ceremonies.
   lwm qaib To wave a live chicken over the head of
   a wife on bringing her into her husband's home;
   to call the woman's spirit to come and abide in
   her husband's home and clan.

4. lwm haujlwm Domestic work (cf. 'hauj').

1. lws To pillage and rob.
   lws nyiaj To steal silver, steal money.

2. lws The eggplant (lub).
   lws liab The red eggplant.
   lws dawb The white eggplant.
   lws qeb Type of small eggplant.

lwv sib lwv To contest in song singing to see who can
   better the other.

M

1. mab People who dwell on the plains (other than Hmong and
   familiar Chinese and tribes).
   mab daum Plains people.
   mab suav Plains people and Chinese.
   koob mab (tus) A safety pin (pin used by plains folk).
   mab luj Thai style brass gong.
   mab qus Wild people, aborigines, the Yellow Leaf tribe.

2. mab A species of animal, civet.
   mab txho The Palm civet. (There are also other members
   of the species called 'mab nkawb' and 'mab dais').
   mab nyooj The civet cat growls.

mag To be ensnared or trapped, to trap or snare, to catch.
   mag hlua To snare with a rope.
   mag lawv nplawm To receive a beating from them,
   caught and beaten.

1. maj Hemp.
   laws maj To strip the bark off the hemp stalks.
   txhiab maj To dry the hemp by the fire to ready it
   for stripping.
   plhaub maj Hemp stalk.

2. maj In a hurry (C), busy.
   siab maj To be in a rush, in a hurry, heart in a
   state of anxiety to rush off.
   maj heev Very much hurried, very busy.

3. maj Exclamatory final particle.
   Nej mus saib maj! You go and see!

4. maj Large silver coin, a silver "dollar," large coins
   as used in Laos (lub).
   ib lub txiaj maj One silver dollar.

5. maj majmam Slow, slowly, gradually, after a while (C).
   Majmam mus. Go slowly.
   Majmam kuv yuav mus thiab. After a while I'll go too.
   Nws majmam tuaj ze mentsis. He gradually came closer.

1. mam majmam (cf. 'maj' above).

2. mam Particle indicating lapse of time, something to take
   place first. "and then"
   Cia nws xub tuaj kuv mam mus. Let him come first and
   then I'll go.
   Ob peb hnub mam mus. (We will) go in two or three days.

(a) ib mentsis   A very short time
(b) ib ntsis   A very short time.
(c) ib mechim   A very short time.
(d) ib chim   A very short time.
me yaus   This humble person   (A polite term sometimes
   used in referring to oneself.)

2. me

menyuam (tus)   Child, children   (cf. 'me' Definition
   No. 1).
menyuad   Alternate spelling of 'menyuam' in certain
   contexts.   (cf. Introduction p. xxii-xxiii).
menyuam ntxaib   Twins.
xeeb menyuam   To be pregnant, have a child in the womb.
lub tsho menyuam   The afterbirth, placenta.
nchuav menyuam   To abort, miscarriage.
menyuam ntsuag   An orphan, an adopted child.
menyuam tsaub   An illegitimate child.
qhuab menyuam   To discipline a child.
khoob menyuam   To call children to come.

1. mej

tus mej koob   The middleman in wedding arrangements.
   (cf. 'tshoob')   (also 'mej zeeg').

2. mej

mejrum (lub)   A low, round, plaited bamboo or rattan
   table made by tribes in Laos and sometimes
   used by the Hmong.

1. mem   Ink (C).
   kua mem   Liquid ink.
   cwjmem (tus)   A pen.
   cwjmem ntoo   A pencil (tus).

2. mem
   ciab mem   (cf. 'kua ciab')   Wax, a sticky wax used by
      the Meo as an adhesive   (cf. 'ciab').

3. mem
   mem tes   The pulse (sometimes said 'meem tes').
   mem tes ntoj   The pulse pulsates.
   seev mem tes   To feel the pulse   (cf. 'tshuaj').
   mem tes nkaum lawm   Can't feel the pulse.
   (a) mem tes tsis dhia   No pulse, no pulsations.
   (b) mem tes tsis ntoj   No pulse, no pulsations.

4. mem
   mem toj   A crack or vein in the rock of a hillside.

5. mem   To guess, to think out.
   (a) Mem tsis tau.   Couldn't think of it.   (cf. 'xav,'
      'nyaj').
   (b) Mem tsis tshwm.   Couldn't think of it.   (cf. 'xav,'
      'nyaj').
   Mem tau.   Guessed it.   Thought of it.

---

3. mam
   (a) mam auv (lub)   (T)   The pumelo.
   (b) txiv mam auv.   The pumelo.

mas   Particle indicating a slight pause in speech similar
      to the English comma.   Often used as an initial
      particle at the beginning of a sentence similar to
      carry forward the action similar to "And..."
      or "Well..."   (cf. 'ces').
   Mas ob peb hnub nws yuav tuaj.   And in a few days he
      will come.
   Hais li cas mas kuv xav tias kuv tsis yuav.   No matter
      what you say, I'm afraid I don't want it.

maij   Clf. for bolts of cloth (T).

1. maim   To flinch, draw back from danger or to avoid being
          struck.
   maim phom   To flinch when firing a gun.

2. maim
   phiv kauv maim (T)   (cf. 'phiv').

maiv   A girl's name.

maub   To grope, to feel one's way in the dark.
   maub mus   To go along by feeling one's way.

1. maum   The female of animals   (cf. 'txiv')   (contr. 'poj').
          (not of humans or of birds).
   tus maum npua   The sow.

2. maum
   txiv maum kuab (lub)   Papaya   (also 'txiv taub ntoo').

3. maum
   taub maum (lub)   Pear-shaped, fist-sized vegetable
      growing on a vine above ground. It is green
      with a somewhat rough exterior and a white
      marrow-like center.

4. maum   A term sometimes used to call young female children
          instead of using the given name.

5. maum
   maum kawv (tus)   The giant squirrel.

1. me   Little, diminutive, small, small amount (size or
        quantity).
   Pub me me rau kuv.   Give me a little bit.
   mentsis   A little bit.
   Pub mentsis rau kuv.   Give me a little bit.
   mentxhais (tus)   A girl child.
   metub (tus)   A boy child.

6. mem
   us mem muj qus Knocked out, not clearly conscious.

7. mem
   nees ntaus ntxwm mem The horse rears and kicks with both hind legs.

1. mes A small species of bee which makes honey (cf. 'muv,' 'ntab').

2. mes
   mes es The sound of bleating goats or sheep. Used by children as a name to refer to sheep or goats. (This is perhaps more commonly said 'mias ias').

meeg
   tabmeeg In front of, face to face, openly (C).
   tabmeeg hais lus To speak face to face, speak openly.

1. meej Clear (of ideas, speech, sight, etc.) (C).
   pom tsis meej Can't see clearly.
   feeb tsis meej Can't distinguish clearly.
   hais meej meej To speak clearly.

2. meej
   meejpem To understand, be clearly conscious (C).

3. meej
   txhiaj meej The spirit articles above the door (C) (cf. 'txhawb txheej').

4. meej Name (C).
   (a) koob meej (lub) Good name, reputation (C).
   (b) meej thawb (lub) Good name, reputation (C).
   sau meej hwm To take a census (C) (In Laos this is pronounced 'sau mej hwm').

5. meej
   Cawv meej lawm. The whiskey is used up. (polite language used at a feast).

6. meej Soft, easily formed or bendable (contr. 'nkig').

1. meem A layer, clf. for layers of cloth.
   meem hauv Lining, inner layer of cloth.
   meem saum Outside layer of cloth.

2. meem To pave, to fill out the low places and bring all to one level.

3. meem Dazed, not fully conscious.
   meem lawm Dazed, half conscious.

4. meem Ten thousand (T) (cf. 'vam').
   ib meem Ten thousand.

5. meem
   meem txom Provoking, irritating, provoked in heart.

6. meem
   xwbfab puajmeem (C) Every direction, to the four winds (cf. 'plaub ceg ntuj').

7. meem
   txhiaj teeb meem To speak in riddles, a riddle.

8. meem
   yejmeem (cf. 'yej').

9. meem
   meem tes (cf. 'mem tes').

1. mim A woman's name.

2. mim
   txhij txiv mim The Pleiades.

mis The female breast (lub).
   ob lub mis The two breasts.
   kua mis Milk, secretion of the breast.
   nyuj mis Cow's milk.
   lub txiv mis The nipple.

miv Cat, the domestic cat (tus).

miaj
   miaj loos (lub) (cf. 'loos').

mias (cf. 'mes es') The sound of the goat's cry and therefore used by children as a name for goat or sheep. (cf. 'tshis').

1. mob Pain, sickness (clf. 'tus' for a case of illness, type of sickness) (clf. 'phaum' for epidemics; clf. 'lub' for a tumor).
   mob teb hlob Epidemic, pestilence.
   mob kis An infectious disease.
   kis mob To spread disease.
   mob npaws Malaria, chills and fever.
   ua mob teb Birth pangs, travail in birth.
   mob aws A common infectious disease in chickens.
   mob rwj Carbuncle (also 'mob npuag faj').
   mob faj A boil.
   mob npuag Blood poisoning, infection.
   mob txeeb zig Bladder stones, hard to urinate.
   mob sis teeb Small pimples secreting water.
   mob fab A fit or coma after eating something which doesn't agree.

mob yuas Coma coming on as an illness becomes severe.
mob kab yaim A skin disease of dogs and cats.
mob tuaj leeg Of a skin infection spreading.
mob huam leej huam ceem A sudden sickness.
mob tsam chim Of exhaustion and pain as after hard exercise.
mob muas faj A sickness with pain all over, no fever.
kem cev Syphilis, venereal disease.
(a) mob yeeg A kind of venereal disease with pussy discharge.
(b) mob cas A kind of venereal disease with pussy discharge.

2. mob To be "hurt" in the affections.
mob siab Hurt in heart (literally in the liver), grieved, sorry, distressed.
Mob kuv siab heev. It really hurt me.
siab mob ib zag One time of sorrow or grief.
mob siab ua To do earnestly.
('mob siab' can be used for expressing earnestness in almost any action. cf. 'siab').
hais lus rho plaub mob nqaig To speak words that hurt people like pulling hair or cutting flesh.

1. mog Wheat.

2. mog
plab mog The lower abdominal region (contr. 'plab laug').

3. mog A completive particle used for gentle commands or admonitions and emphasis.
Nyob twjyws mog. Please be still.
Mus ob peb hnub tuaj mog. Do come back soon.

4. mog
taum mog Pea, peas (lub).

1. moj Final particle in exclamations and questions.
Leej twg yuav pab moj? Who will help?

2. moj
ua moj hum To do coarse or heavy work (contr. 'xim hum').

3. moj
plhom moj To fool around, to speak or do rashly. (cf. 'plhom').

4. moj
ntxias moj tuam To braid braids.

5. moj
cua moj lwg xib kaw A great wind (cf. 'cua').

6. moj
rooj moj sab A wilderness, a wild area of mountains and trees.

1. mom Of water rising and filling the stream bed.
Mom kiag sab saum. The water is coming over the top.

2. mom
mom kaum The ends of a roof.

3. mom
kausmom (lub) Hat, cap.

4. mom
hais lus tuam mom Threatening, arrogant language.

1. mos Fine, small (of writing, embroidery, etc.) (contr. 'ntxhib').

2. mos Young and tender.
(a) menyuam mos mos A young child.
(b) menyuam mos liab A young child.
mos mos ntsuab ntsuab Of young green vegetation.

3. mos To squash or squeeze into a pulp as in preparing certain vegetables.

4. mos To massage.
mos plab To massage the abdomen.

5. mos
mos nplej To rub rice off the stalk with hands or feet.

6. mos
mos qhovmuag To rub the eyes.

7. mos
yoov mos dab (tus) The horse fly.

8. mos Of soft polite speech.
lus mos Soft polite speech (contr. 'lus tshawv').

1. mov Cooked or steamed rice, rice ready for eating.
noj mov To eat, to eat rice.
cub mov To steam rice.
txhws mov To spread out the cooked rice.

2. mov
mov kuam Steamed corn meal cooked corn meal.

3. mov
txiv mov poj (lub) The coconut (T).

moo   News, report, information, reputation.
       nto moo To receive news, get a report.
       hnov moo tuaj To hear news.
       Kuv nug koj moo. I asked news of you.
       xyav moo To spread a report.
       tso moo To tell news, give a report.
       txwv kav tso moo To tell it to everyone, spread
            abroad.
       npe nto moo Name spread abroad, of great reputation.
       moo cua (lub) A radio.
       moo zoo Good news, good reputation.
       tu moo To make an end of it, cease reports of it
            to do once for all.

1. mooj   Childless, barren.

2. mooj   To deceive, to keep from understanding.
       Dab mooj lawv lub siab. The spirits deceived them.
       mooj lawv lawm Deceived them, blinded their minds.

moos   The plain, the area down off the mountains (lub).
       Sometimes also used in the sense of a particular
       city or market on the plain. (T).
       Kuv mus nram moos. I am going to the plain. (or)
       lub moos The city, the market in the town.
       lub moos The city, the market, the plain.

moov   To chew with the gums, to eat without teeth.

mub   Fleas (contr. 'tuv').
       dev mub (tus) The flea.

1. muj   xeeb mujmum Great grandchild (tus).

2. muj   hlais muj khem To cut notches in wood in certain
            patterns as a limited means of communication.

3. muj   mujvam lus Old fashioned language, obscure language.

4. muj   ua mem muj qus Not clearly conscious, knocked out.

5. muj   xov muj tim To prepare a large trap for game. An
            area is fenced off and a trap set at the entrance.
            A strong young tree is cut and set to spring or
            fall on the victim.

1. mum   To push something along by one end (cf. 'tsij').

2. mum   mujmum (cf. 'muj').

mus   To go, to depart.
       (a) mus lawm Gone, has gone.
       (b) lawm loj Gone, has gone.
       (c) mus lawm loj Gone, has gone.
       (a) Mus qhov twg lawm? Where has he gone?
       (b) Dua twg lawm? Where has he gone?
       mus quj qees To go slowly and deliberately.
       nyimno mus lawm Is going now.
       mus nraim To go straight, to follow straight.

muv   Bee, honey bee (tus).
       zib muv Honey.
       muv doom Large edible species of honey bee (tus).
       Listed below are the other various kinds of bees and
       wasps. (also cf. each individual listing).
       ntseeb A very small species of wasp.
       nkawj Wasp, small wasp.
       mes A small honey bee.
       ntab Another species of honey bee.
       daiv Large species of bumble bee.

1. muab   To take in the hand, take hold of, to give with
            the hand, to give, to hand over.
       Muab rau kuv. Give it to me.
       Muab ob tug nees khi. Tie the two horses. (lit.
            Take the horses and tie them.)
       Muab tsis cuag. Beyond reach, cannot grasp it.

2. muab   To harvest.
       muab nplej To harvest rice.

3. muab   To arrest, to catch or take someone.
       Lawv muab tus tubsab los tsis tau? Have they taken
            the thief?

muad   (cf. 'muam,' see Introduction pp. xxii-xxiii).

1. muag   Face, pertaining to the face.
       ntsej muag (lub) The face.
       qhov muag (lub) The eye, eyes (cf. Definition No. 2).
       txaj muag To be ashamed.
       ceb muag Dirty face.
       txiav muag To have nothing to do with, to refuse to
            look at another because of hatred, etc.
       ntxeev muag A forceful expression used to describe
            one who has completely turned aside from or
            against even his own kinsfolk.
       ua neeb muag dawb A form of spirit worship calling on
            a greater spirit to chase out a lesser.

(a) pom ntsej pom muag To see the face.
(b) pom ntsej muag To see the face.
dub muag txig mus To go straight on oblivious of others.

nkauj muag pag (tus) A prostitute (lit. Flowery faced woman).

2. muag Pertaining to the eyes (using 'muag' as a shortened form of 'qhov muag,' cf. definition No. 1).
qe muag To shut the eyes.
rua muag To open the eyes wide.
plaub muag Eyelashes, eyebrows.
qheb muag Open eyes.
ib ntsais muag One twitching of the eyelid, blink.
ntsiab muag (lub) The pupil of the eye.
daim tawv muag Eyelid.
kua muag Tears.
quav muag Excretion which fills the corners of the eyes.
nraug zeeg muag Dizzy.
qhov muag ntseg ntsos Eyes in vacant fixed stare.
ploj muag ntais Disappeared from sight.
qhov muag tawv tawv Heavy eyed, sleepy eyed.
ib lub twm qhov muag One eyed, one eye missing.
npog muag To cover the eyes.
qhov muag txaij Cannot see clearly.

3. muag To sell (contr. 'muas').
Muab muag rau lawv. Take it and sell it to them.
muag lawm Sold.

4. muag Soft, pliable, weak (cf. 'phom').
(a) lub cev muag zog Body has no strength, weak in body.
(b) lub cev ntshaus zog Body has no strength, weak in body.
neeg yeem muag One who responds to patient teaching. (contr. 'tawv').
siab muag muag Teachable, humble.

muaj To have, to possess.
Kuv tsis muaj. I have none. I don't have.
nws muaj nws Idiom meaning 'he has his own' or 'there are some such.'
Tibneeg zoo nws muaj nws, tibneeg tsis zoo nws muaj nws thiab There are some good people and there are some bad people, too.
Nws muaj hlob. He has a proud heart.

muam Sister (as called by her brothers) (contr. 'vivncaws').
muam npaws The name used by a man to refer to his female cousins of a different surname, i.e. female children of his mother's brothers and sisters and of his father's sisters. (cf. kinship chart Appendix p. 495).

1. muas To buy (contr. 'muag').
Koj muas qhov twg los? Where did you buy it?
muas los To buy, to buy in.

2. muas
muaslwj (tus) The Sambar deer.

3. muas
muastxwv (lub) A bullet, cartridge.

4. muas
mob muas faj (cf. 'mob').

5. muas
(a) pob av luaj Anthill (lub).
(b) pob av muas yis tib Anthill (lub).

6. muas
cuam muas Doesn't meet together properly, e.g. one side slanted and the other straight.

ML

The consonant cluster spelled 'ml' in the orthography used by the Roman Catholics among the Hmong in Laos is spelled 'nl' herein. (cf. 'nl' for listings).

N

1. na   Final interrogative particle.
         Nej puas paub na? Don't you know?

2. na   nalika (lub) Watch, wristwatch (T).

1. nab Snake, worm, snake like.
         nab (tus) Snake.
         cua nab (tus) Earthworm.
         nab muaj taug Poisonous snake (any species).
         ntses nab (tus) the eel, an eel.
         nab hab sej (tus) The python.

2. nab
         nab qa (tus) A lizard.
         nab qa nqhuab Dry land lizard, iguana.
         nab qa dev Type of large lizard.
         (b) nab qa tuaj txoob A type of small lizard.
         (c) nab qa tsiav A type of small lizard.

1. nag Rain (clf. 'kob' for showers, 'phau' for a period
         of rain).
         (a) los nag To rain.
         (b) ntuj los nag To rain.
         ntub ntub nag To be wet with rain.
         nag tshauv Drizzling rain.
         los nag hlob hlob Downpour, heavy rain.
         nag xob nag cua Storm, tempest, rain wind and
              lightning.
         los nag tuam tuam Heavy rain.
         nag tshia Rain blows in.
         los nag xuj xuav A light rain.
         (a) nag tshauv zawg ziag Drizzling.
         (b) nag tshauv ntsuag ntseb Drizzling rain.

2. nag Yesterday.
         nag hmo Last evening.

3. nag nagkis (or sometimes 'naskis') The day after tomorrow.

1. naj Exclamatory particle.
         Tom cov nyuag teb naj! Over the fields!

2. naj A stick with gummy sap put on it to snare birds.

1. nam To stalk, to walk or steal along furtively and
         stealthily.
         nam mus To go along stealthily.

2. nam To encroach upon.
         nam teb To encroach on someone else's fields.

---

nas Rodent, rat (tus).
         nas tsuag (tus) Mouse, house rat.
         nas ncuav (tus) A type of squirrel.
         nas ciav (tus) The zebra squirrel.
         (a) nas ncuav txaij (tus) Chipmunk.
         (b) nas ncuav ciav (tus) Chipmunk.
         nas ntxhw (tus) The large guinea pig.
         nas hoo twm (tus) The red-bellied squirrel.

nav The runt, the last born of a litter, smallest of a
         litter.
         tus thawj thiab tus nav. The first and the last.

nau Term used for a foolish person in scolding.
         dab ntaus nau May the spirits beat him.

nawj Completive particle of emphasis.
         Nej tsis txhob muab lub cev pub rau dab nawj! Don't
              give your body to the spirits!

ne   Final interrogative and exclamatory particle.
         Koj tsis paub ne? Don't you know?
         Kuv twb hais rau nej no ne! I did tell you!
         Note: This particle is sometimes said 'nej' or 'nev.'
              (cf. 'nej' 'nev')

1. neb Second person dual pronoun ("you two persons") (cf.
         'nej')
         Neb mus qhov twg? Where are you (two persons) going?

2. neb P.v.int.   (cf. 'nuj').

1. nej Second person plural pronoun (for three or more
         persons).
         Nej mus qhov twg? Where are you (three or more)
              going? (cf. 'neb').

2. nej Final interrogative and exclamatory particle
         (cf. 'ne').
         The tone on this particle may vary with the emphasis.
         The word is usually 'ne' but may become 'nej'
              if emphasized.
         Koj tsis paub nej? Really! Don't you know? You
              mean you don't know?

nem ua nem nuv quv Describing a person who is silent
         after a scolding because he doesn't know what
         to say.

nev Final interrogative particle.   (cf. 'ne')
         Zab yog tus twg nev? Who is Zab?

nee Tone change from 'neev,'   (cf. 'neev').

1. neeb Friendly or familiar spirits (cf. 'dab').
   The shaman seeks the aid of the 'neeb' and is possessed
   by them in his sorties into the spirit world to
   seek out and do battle with the 'dab' who may
   have caused sickness, etc.
   (a) tus neeb The shaman.
   (b) tus txiv neeb The shaman.
   ua neeb To do spirit worship, do spirit rites.
   ua ib thaj neeb To do one session of spirit rites.
   ua neeb ua yaig Fuller term for spirit rites.
   txoov neeb The greatest of the 'neeb.'
   Siv Yis The head or leader of the 'neeb.'
   nruas neeb The spirit gong (lub).
   txiab neeb The metal ring with metal pieces which
      is jingled by the shaman in calling the spirits.
   kuam neeb (cf. 'kuam' Definition No. 5).
   thaj neeb The spirit shelf, shelf against the rear
      wall of a Hmong home where articles of spirit
      worship are kept.
   rub sab neeb The spirit articles attached to the
      under side of the roof.
   ua neeb muag dawb A form of spirit worship calling
      on a greater spirit to chase out a lesser.
   neeb koos plig (cf. 'koos' Definition No. 1).

2. neeb A species of large tree used to make boards for
   the spirit shelf (tus).

3. neeb To hurt slightly.
   pheej neeb neeb Keeps on hurting a little bit.

neeg Person (tus) (cf. 'neej').
   neeg zoo A good person.
   tibneeg (tus) Person.
   haiv neeg People of another surname, outsiders.
   ib zeej tsoom neeg All persons, all people.
   neeg xam txeem A person who does a bit of work and
      then puts the rest off onto others.
   neeg keev xeeb Pigheaded, one with a mind closed to
      all but his own ideas.
   dab neeg Folklore, tradition, story, legend.
   menyuam neeg ntiajteb no The children of men, the
      people of earth.
   neeg khoob xeeb (C) Teachable, ready to listen to
      others.
   neeg txog lig One who regrets too late.

1. neej Fortune, estate, a person and all he possesses (lub).
   ua zoo neej In good fortune, well off, has enough
      food money and animals, etc.
   ua neej To prosper, be well.
   tsis zoo neej Not well off, poorly, unfortunate.
   tsa koj ua neej To set you up in house and goods, etc.
   tsawv neej To tell the fortune (e.g. by trying to
      stand a coin on an egg, etc.)

   (a) ib sim neej A lifetime, for a lifetime.
   (b) ib sim li A lifetime, for a lifetime.
   rooj neej (lub) The side door of a house (cf. 'rooj').

2. neej
   neejtsa A man's relatives by marriage or a woman's
      blood relatives after she becomes married.
   kwvtij neejtsa All relatives, blood relatives and
      relatives by marriage.

3. neej
   txivneej (tus) A man, a male individual.

neem The spirits of the woods or the spirits of hunting
   which some serve in order to gain skill and
   success in hunting.
   (a) coj neem To serve or worship the hunting spirits.
   (b) coj dab neem To serve or worship the hunting
      spirits.
   neem ntxhib (and) neem mos Two different kinds of
      hunting spirits each with its observances.
   Note: Those who worship or serve these spirits (coj
      dab neem) use some special evasive language to
      deceive the spirits and avoid calamity or ill
      fortune. For example:

Evasive Term	Plain Speech	Meaning
hle lawm lauj	ua tag lawm lauj	Finished
tshav ntuj lawm	nquag lawm	Recovered
hov txuas	noj su	Eat lunch
nqia hnyuv	tshaib plab	Hungry
hov taus	ntov ntoo	Down a tree
los so	los noj mov	Come and eat
peb xuas kab	peb mus tsev	We go home.

1. nees Horse (tus).
   nees nra Horse pack saddle (or 'nra nees')
   tawb nees (lub) Horse pack baskets.
   nees hee Horse whinnys, horse neighs.
   ncaim nees A young female horse having had no young.
   maum nees A mare that has had a colt.
   sam nees Castrated horse, to castrate a horse.
   rov nees Horse kicks out with both hind legs.
   Terms for Hmong horse harness:
   cuam txwv nees The pack frame which fits over the
      pack saddle (see above).
   xauv nees The bit.
   phab xyoob Chest band ('txees nees' is archaic term
      but sometimes used).
   phij chob The leather rope for tying baskets and
      loads.
   khiab tw The tail strap.

Types of Horses:
  nees txov lawj Brown horse.
  nees faj kav Yellow horse.
  nees huab Brown and white horse.
  nees vwb Black horse.
  nees kub hnyiab Dark horse, part black and brown.
  nees txheeb A dappled horse.

2. nees Used in combination for numbers 20 to 29.
  nees nkaum 20.
  nees nkaum ib 21 (etc.)

3. nees A stretcher.
  ua nees To make a stretcher (carry the dead).

4. nees (cf. 'dais').
  dais nees (cf. 'dais').

5. nees (cf. 'tsho').
  dab tshos hneev nees (cf. 'tsho').

6. nees daj dua (tus) A kind of small animal with a
  Yellow back, something like a large squirrel.

neev Footprint, hoofprint, pawprint.
  neev taw Footprint
  ib nee taw One footprint (t.c.)
  neev nees Horse hoofprint.
  neev npua teb Hoofprints of the wild pig.
  Note: This word is sometimes said 'hneev'

1. nim Particle used before the verb to indicate immediacy
  of action. "Just then," "immediately," "just as"
  Nws nim los los kua muag. Just then he began to cry.

2. nim
  nimno Now.
  tab nimno mus From now on.
  Nimno kuv yuav mus. Now I am going.
  Nimno koj nyob qhov twg? Where do you live now?
  Note: This word varies in different speakers between
  'nimno,' 'nyiamno,' 'nyimno,' and 'niamno.'

3. nim
  nimno i...; no i...; nimno uas; no uas These expressions
  are often used to fill in pauses in running conversation as "..er..." in English.

niab ua ntxhov quav niab To raise tumult, do violence.

niad (cf. 'niam,' See Introduction pp. xxii-xxiii).

1. niag Large, great, major.
  lub niag nroog Capital city, major city.
  tus niag dej The large river.
  lub niag tsev The large house, palace, temple.
  ua niag tuam tshawj chim To be great enemies.
  ib niag daim One large flat surface.
  (a) niag tshais About 9 to 10 AM.
  (b) tav niag tshais About 9 to 10 AM.
  (a) niag su Noon.
  (b) tav su Noon.
  qhov niag tod The big place yonder.

2. niag Used in terms of familiarity.
  niag yawg Familiar term of address for males.
  Nyob zoo pauj niag yawg? How are you friend?
  niag pog Familiar term of address for females
  (for older women).
  niag pog laus Familiar term used by older men for
  their wives, "my old woman."

3. niag
  ua niag lus hais To speak flattery, to flatter.

4. niag
  txhiab niag tim puas xyoo (cf. 'txhiab').

niaj Each, every.
  Niaj hnub niaj hnub tuaj. (He) comes every day.
  niaj hmo Each night, every night.
  niaj zaus Each time, each occasion.

1. niam Mother (tus).
  Kuv tus niam. My mother.
  niam txiv Parents.
  pojniam Woman (tus), wife.
  Kuv tus pojniam My wife (lit. "my woman").
  niam tub txiv nyuag Idiomatic way of saying "parents
  and children."
  niam fam txam (cf. 'tuag').
  niam hauvpaus cos (cf. 'tuag').

2. niam Used for "the wife of..." in describing relationships.
  niam tais (tus) Maternal grandmother (or) wife of
  maternal grandfather's brothers.
  niam tij Wife of an older brother.
  niam hluas Wife's younger sister.
  Note: There are many other such kinship terms. (cf.
  Appendix p. 484 and Charts in Appendix pp. 493-497.)

3. niam
  niam hlau A magnet.

1. nias To press down, to press upon.
   nias ntiag To press down completely.
   nias nkaus To press, press down.

2. nias
   daim nias menyuam A band of cloth to tie a child for carrying on the back (cf. 'khiab').

1. no A noun of location; This (place, time, person, thing) (cf. 'ntawm')
   hnub no This day, today.
   qhov no This place, here.
   lub tsev no This house.
   li no This way, like this.

2. no Cold (of the weather) (cf. 'txias').
   no no li It's cold.

3. no i (cf. 'nim' Definition No. 3).

1. nog To pack goods, tie things up for transport.
   nog nees nra To pack goods on a pack saddle.

2. nog To forage, to graze.
   nog zaub To graze, forage, feed in pasture.

1. noj
   noj mov To eat rice, to eat.
   noj tshais To eat breakfast.
   noj su To eat lunch.
   noj hmo To eat supper.
   (a) noj peb caug To eat the New Year feast.
   (b) noj tsiab To eat the New Year feast.
   noj nplej tshiab To eat a meal in celebration of the first new rice of the season.
   noj qees Keeps on eating slowly.
   rawm noj In a hurry to eat.
   noj tsuag tsuag Eat quickly.
   noj qab nyob zoo Well off, prosperous and eating well.
   noj tshoob To eat the wedding feast (cf. 'tshoob').
   cov noj xwm Leaders, elders, wise men (C).

2. noj To consume, to "eat" figuratively.
   noj tshaj thawj To make profit.
   lawv noj mentsis They take a bit of profit or tax.
   lub tshuab noj roj The machine uses oil or gasoline.

nom Official, officer (tus).
   cov nom tswv Officials, the officers.

nos ntsuag nos Orphaned and penniless.

1. noo Damp or moist of itself (as of earth, sugar, etc.) (cf. 'ntxooj').
   av noo noo Damp moist earth.

2. noo
   (a) ua noo Feeling of weakness of impending illness.
   (b) ua noo ntxiag Feeling of weakness of impending illness.

1. noob Seed (lub).
   tseb noob To scatter seed broadcast.
   noob zaub Vegetable seeds.

2. noob
   noob qes (lub) The testicles (cf. 'qau').
   noob qes thoob tshaj Inguinal hernia.

noog Bird (tus).
   (a) noog ncaws A snare for birds.
   (b) hlua ncaws A snare for birds.
   noog w Quail (tus).

nooj A curse word, unsavory language; the Chinese equivalent of the Hmong 'phev.'

noos Measure of width; the distance between the end of the thumb and the end of the extended first finger.

noov Blue Hmong term for the penis. (cf. 'qau') Sometimes used also by the White Hmong.

nug To ask, to question.
   nug tias... Asked saying...
   Nws nug tias, "Koj puas mus thiab?" He asked, "Are you going also?"
   (a) nug kiag To ask straightforwardly.
   (b) nug zoj tias To ask straightforwardly.
   ua nug rau nws To rely on him (cf. 'vamkhom'), i.e. to depend on one person to answer all sorts of questions.

1. nuj
   nplua nuj (tus) A rich person.
   ua nplua nuj To be rich or to become rich.

2. nuj nqe A debt.
   kwv nuj nqe Unwilling to repay a debt.
   luab nuj nqe To borrow on interest.
   ris nuj nqe To hold a debt for a long time, to keep on refusing to pay a debt.

3. nuj
   hav zoov nuj xiab Wild jungle.

4. nuj P.v.int. (cf. Appendix 8).
   hais nuj neb To speak in a whining voice.

num Work, labor, chores (cf. 'haujlwm').
   ua num To do work or labor.
   lauj num mus To lay aside the work and go.
   Note: This word is used more among the Blue (Green)
         Hmong, the more common White Hmong term is
         'haujlwm.'

nus Brother (tus) (as called by his sisters).
   nus kwv Younger brother (as called by his sister).
   nus tij Older brother (as called by his sister).

1. nuv A hook, catch; to hook, to catch with a hook.
      (clf. 'rab' for a large hook held in the hand)
      (clf. 'tus' for a small fish hook).
   (a) ib tug nuv A small hook.
   (b) koob nuv A small hook.
   nuv ntses To catch fish with a hook.

2. nuv
   ua nem nuv quv (cf. 'nem').

3. nuv
   hab nuv tseg (cf. 'hab').

nuam nuam yaj To bend backward and look, "stretch the
   neck" and look around.

1. nwj To kiss, a kiss.
   Muab nws nwj kiag ib zaug. Kissed him once.

2. nwj A slave.
   ua nwj ua qhev To be slaves, be a slave (cf. 'qhev').

nwm Tus nwm tshis A young female goat without young.

nws Third person singular pronoun. He, she, it.
   Nws tsis mus. He, she or it won't go.

ncab To straighten (cf. 'yeb') (cf. 'ncaj').
   ncab duav To stretch oneself, straighten the back.
   ncab dua ntsag Obstinate, unbending.

ncag
   pos ncag A little tree cut and used at New Year time
      in spirit ceremonies. A live chicken is tied
      to it and the family encircles the tree, the
      aim being to keep them from misfortune the
      coming year.

1. ncaj Straight.
   (a) Ncaj qha mus. Go straight on.
   (b) Ncaj nraim mus. Go straight on.
   ncaj nraim, ncaj nrwb nraim, ncaj ncees, ncaj qha All
      these terms are used for "perfectly straight."

2. ncaj Morally honest and upright, morally "straight."
   (a) siab ncaj Morally honest and upright, righteous.
   (b) siab ncaj ncees Morally honest and upright, righteous.
   (c) siab ncaj siab ncees Morally honest and upright,
       righteous.
   ua ncaj ua ncees To be honest, be righteous.

1. ncas A small musical instrument which when placed close
      to the mouth gives tones from a metal tongue
      struck with the fingers, a jew's harp (rab).
   ncas tooj Such an instrument of brass.
   tshuab ncas To play such an instrument.
   Note: The 'ncas' is usually only used in courting.

2. ncas
   ua raj ncas (cf. 'pobkws').

ncav To stretch the hand or stand on tiptoe.
   ncav tes To stretch one's hand to get something.
   ncav taw To stand on one's toes.
   ncav tsis cuag Can't reach even on tiptoe.

ncai dab tshos ncai (cf. 'tsho').

ncaib A species of tree the bark of which may be used to
   make a potion to poison fish. (tus).

ncaig Coals, embers.
   (a) ncaig Wood embers.
   (b) hluav ncaig Wood embers.
   tsis ciaj ncaig Won't burn, won't hold fire.
   "plaub qaib tsis ciaj ncaig." "Chicken feathers will
      not hold any fire or make coals." An idiomatic
      expression meaning "It won't amount to anything."

1. ncaim To separate from, to divorce, to divide.
   sib ncaim To divorce, two persons or things separate.
   kev ncaim Roads that separate.
   (a) ncaim npoj To separate the group.
   (b) ncaim luag To separate the group.

2. ncaim
   tus ncaim nees (cf. 'nees').

ncais Forceps, tweezers (tus).
   ncais rho hwjtxwv Tweezers for pulling whiskers.

1. ncau To put forth as branches, to bear as branches,
      to branch from.
   ncau ceg To put forth branches.
   tsis ncau ntawm tus ntoo mus Does not branch from
      the tree.

2. ncau A length of bamboo or rattan split for use in tying
      (clf. 'pluaj').
   phua ncau To split lengths of bamboo or rattan.
   zaws ncau To strip the cut lengths of bamboo or
      rattan to make them thin.

ncaug (t.c. from 'ncauj') (cf. 'ncauj').

1. ncauj Mouth, mouthlike opening (lub); pertaining to
      the mouth.
   qhovncauj (lub) The mouth.
   di ncauj The lips.
   (a) gheb qhovncauj To open the mouth.
   (b) rua qhovncauj To open the mouth.
   (a) qhaws qhovncauj To close the mouth.
   (b) qos qhovncauj To close the mouth.
   tiag ncauj To curse, to scold.
   ncauj hlob Prone to curse.
   qaub ncauj Spittle (t.c.)
   nto qaub ncaug To spit (t.c.)
   (a) ntxub ncaug To hate bitterly (t.c.)
   (b) ntxub ntxaug To hate bitterly (t.c.)
   tsa ncauj Began by saying, opened his mouth saying.
   tso ncauj Permit, allow.
   qhovncauj tawm Canker sores.
   npuas ncauj Froth at the mouth.
   kaus ncauj qaib Chicken beak.
   tim ncauj ntsees tham To speak face to face.
   (a) neeg ncauj liab ncauj sai A person who talks a
      lot and says all he thinks.
   (b) neeg ncauj txua A person who talks a lot and
      says all he thinks.
   ncauj ke The entrance to a road, mouth of a road.
   lub ncauj hub The mouth of the pot.

2. ncauj Clf. for sets or mouthfuls of teeth.
   ib ncauj hniav One set of teeth.

ncaus
   vivncaus (tus) Sister (as called by her sisters).
   niam ncaus (tus) Wife of a man's younger brother.

ncawb Intentional foolish talk.
   (a) lus dab tuag Foolish talk.
   (b) lus ncawb Foolish talk.

ncawg To enter.
   qaib ncawg cooj Chickens enter the roost.
   tsiaj ncawg nkuaj Animals enter the stable.

1. ncaws To kick.
   Menyuam Hmoob sib ncaws. Hmong children play at kicking
      one another. (a kind of friendly foot boxing)

2. ncaws To hoe the ground, clear the ground of weeds and
      roots with a hoe.
   ncaws teb To clear a field.
   ncaws av To hoe the earth, clear a site.
   ncaws nroj To clear out the weeds.
   ncaws tsev Clear a site for a house (cf. 'khawb qua
      tsev').
   Qab teb peb xub ncaws, nkauj nyab peb xub aws. We were
      the first to clear fields and the first to
      claim the prospective daughter in law. (idiom
      for "We have first rights.")

3. ncaws To nod, dip the head.
   ncaws hau To nod the head, to nudge with the head
      as an animal.
   ncaws nruj nris Nodding the head.
   ncaws ncaws dab ntub To doze, nod the head in sleep.

4. ncaws To peck as a fowl, to peck off or peck at with the
      beak (cf. 'thos').
   qaib ncaws The chicken pecks.
   zaub qaib ncaws A kind of leafy vegetable with saw-
      tooth edge leaves.

5. ncaws
   khaubncaws Clothing (cf. 'khaub').

6. ncaws
   (a) hlua ncaws A snare for birds.
   (b) noog ncaws A snare for birds.

nce To ascend, to go up.
   nce toj To go up the hill, to climb.
   nce zog mus To gain or increase in strength.
   sib nce Term used for the sex act in animals.
   Note: With the above connotation this word is used
      in foul language.

nceb Mushrooms, tree fungus.

1. ncej Frame, upright post, pillar, post in a house frame (tus).
   ncej kaum Corner posts of a house.
   (a) ncej tsev Center posts of a house holding up the ridge pole.
   (b) ncej ru Center posts of a house holding up the ridge pole.
   ncej cos The upright posts of a rice foot-mill.
   ncej ntos The frame of the simple Meo loom.
   ntiv ncej Forked stick for a slingshot.
   ncej dab The main pillar or post of the house; one of the main pillars which upholds the ridge pole and where the spirits of the household are supposed to reside. The 'ncej dab' must set on the ground and not on a board floor. Guests must not sleep at the foot of the 'ncej dab.' The placenta of male children are buried at the base of the 'ncej dab.'

2. ncej
   ncej puab (tus) Thigh, upper leg of a person.

ncem toj (tus) A kind of small fruit bearing tree. The berries are reddish in color.

nceeg Clf. for a kingdom or a dynasty.
   ciaj ib nceeg vaj To establish a kingdom or dynasty.

ncees Post verbal intensifier (cf. Appendix 8).
   ncaj ncees Straight, upright, just.
   siab ncaj ncees Morally upright.
   ua ncaj ncees To do fairly, do justly.

nceev A species of large hardwood tree with bark somewhat red. (tus)

ncig To encircle, to go completely around, a turn, one turn around.
   ua ib ncig To do one turn around.
   hmab ncig ntoo The vine encircles the tree.
   ncig lawv lub qhov nyob All around where they were.
   ncig ncig ua num Working around the house.

ncia To sob, to catch the breath as in sobbing.

1. nciab Post verbal intensifier (cf. Appendix 3).
   (a) dub nciab Very black, perfectly black.
   (b) dub txig Very black, perfectly black.

2. nciab Outsiders (poetic).
   Zaub tsis yog ntxuag, nciab tsis yog luag. Vegetables are not suitable for a feast and outsiders are not suitable for companionship.

1. nco To remember.
   nco qab To remember, to recall what is past.
   tsis nco qab lawm Forgot, forgotten, unconscious.
   nco qas ntsoov To fix in memory, remember well.
   (a) nco dheev To suddenly call to mind, suddenly remember.
   (b) nco dhuj dheev To suddenly call to mind, suddenly remember.
   nco zoj To remember.
   nco txog To think of, remember.
   nco tias To remember that...
   (a) tsis nco qab hlaw hlias To keep forgetting things, absent-minded.
   (b) hnov qauj To keep forgetting things, absent-minded.
   Nco koj tshav ntuj. "Thanks very much." I remember you with appreciation.

2. nco To miss, to long after one absent.
   Kuv nco nco koj. I miss you.

3. nco Combined with 'laws' as a restricted p.v.int. (cf. Appendix 8).
   puv nco laws Filled rounded over (cf. 'puv').

ncoj To shake, to shiver (cf. 'tshee' which is more common).
   ncoj tho To shake, shiver.

ncos
   noj ntoo kug ncos (cf. 'kug').

ncov Peak, mountain top (lub).
   lub ncov roob Mountain peak.
   nto ncov roob To cross the mountain top.

ncoo Pillow, the place where the head is placed in reclining or lying down.
   lub hauv ncoo A pillow.
   hauv ncoo The region where the head is placed in lying down.
   muab rau ncoo To place as a pillow.

ncooj Descriptive of a group sleeping close together to keep warm.

ncu To place beside the fire to steam and soften.
   ncu mov To place rice beside the fire to steam.

ncuj P.v. Intensifier (cf. Appendix 8).
   ncaws hau ncuj nco Nodding the head in sleep.

ncus Descriptive of throbbing pain.
   ncus ncus li Throbbing pain.

ncuv Post verbal intensifier (cf. Appendix 8).
hnub dai npoo ncuv Sunset, sun hanging on horizon.
lub siab nka ncuv In despair.

ncua Clf. for the suitable distance for a gun or bow shot.
ib ncua phom Distance for a gun shot.
ib ncua hneev Distance for a crossbow shot.

1. ncuav A steamed cake (lub); especially cakes of beaten
cooked rice or of ground corn flour, etc.
ncuav tsuam A steamed cake pressed into shape.
qe ncuav Egg-shaped steamed rice cake.
keeb ncuav Steamed cakes made with leaven.

2. ncuav Pock mark.
hluav hluav ncuav Full of small depressions.
plhu hluav hluav ncuav Pock marked face.

3. ncuav (cf. 'nas').
nas ncuav (cf. 'nas').

4. ncuav A slap, strike with the palm of the hand.
(a) ib tawg ncuav One slap.
(b) ib ncuav pias One slap.

ncw Bearing fruit abundantly, prolific fruit bearing.
txi txiv ncw ncw li Bears fruit abundantly.

ncwb noog ncwb (tus) A species of small yellow bird.

ncwm To hold incense in the hand and circle it around the
chicken or animal being sacrificed in spirit
worship.

NCH

1. ncha To spread abroad, announce, spread forth (of sound,
news).
ncha ntws To sound forth (used also as a p.v.int.)
lub suab nrov ncha ntws Sounded forth with a great
noise, the sound resounded.
hais ncha mus txog luag zej zos Announced it to the
neighboring villages.

2. ncha Used as a post verbal intensifier, (cf. Appendix 8)
nrov ncha ntws Resounding (see Definition No. 1 above)
ncha nthi (A two-word post verbal intensifier used
to amplify verbs where loudness is a feature
and where a group is involved as in a tumult
or commotion.) (cf. 'zom zaws').
ua ncha nthi To do with noise and commotion.
qw ncha nthi Of a crowd shouting.
nrov ncha nthi Noise of a crowd, etc.

nchav Vigorous.
ua nchav To do with vigor.
lus nchav Vigorous forceful speech (cf. 'lus loj').

nchaiv A given name for men.

nchauv Smoky (cf. 'ncho').
tsw nchauv To smell smoky.

nchi Flatulence.
ceev ceev nchi nchi Flatulence, feeling of being full
though not having eaten.
nchi plab Flatulence, gas in the stomach.

nchias
nchias taw On tiptoe.
Nws mus nchias taw. He walked on tiptoe.

ncho To produce smoke, to smoke.
ncho pa To produce smoke, make smoke.
Hluavtaws ncho ncho pa. The fire is smoking.

nchos To shake something, to shake in the hand, to jiggle.
nchos menyuam To shake or jiggle a child as in play
or in putting it to sleep, etc.
nchos nchos plab A method of relieving stomach pain
by jiggling the abdominal region.

1. nchuav To pour out.
Muab dej nchuav pov tseg. Pour the water away.
dej nchuav nthwv The water spilled.
nchuav hlau To melt iron to mold, pour iron into
the mold.

2. nchuav To abort, miscarry.
   (a) nchuav cev To abort, miscarry (of humans).
   (b) nchuav menyuam To abort, miscarry (of humans).

NK

1. nka Skinny, lean (of animals) (contr. 'yuag').

2. nka
   lub siab nka ncuv Heart in despair.

1. nkag To crawl, to go beneath.
   nkag hauv qab To go underneath.
   nkag rooj To go beneath the table.
   nkag pem teb To crawl on the ground.
   nkag qhawv qho lawv qab To go unwillingly, e.g. one
      dragged off to an unhappy marriage. (to "go
      along crawling").

2. nkag
   nkag siab To understand (lit. "to enter the heart").
   Koj puas nkag siab? Do you understand?
   (a) Kuv tsis nkag siab. I don't understand.
   (b) Tsis nkag kuv siab. I don't understand.

nkaj The indigo plant, indigo dye as used by the Hmong.

nkaib
   (a) hais nkaib To lie, to deceive.
   (b) hais dag To lie, to deceive.

nkais
   nas nkais (tus) Small yellowish-red rodent. Somewhat
      smaller than a squirrel but with a similar bushy
      tail. (cf. 'nas').

1. nkaub Yolk.
   nkaub qe (lub) Egg yolk (cf. 'qe').

2. nkaub
   hais nkaub To lie, to deceive.

3. nkaub
   leeb nkaub (tus) The parakeet.

1. nkaug To pierce, to stab.
   Nws muab hmuv hlau nkaug lub plab. He stabbed him in
      the stomach with an iron spear.

2. nkaug Restricted post verbal intensifier with 'ntsim'
   niaj no nkaug ntsim Of persons cold and shivering.

1. nkauj Young unmarried female, mature female having had
      no young.
   hluas nkauj Young woman, unmarried girl (tus).
   nkauj fa Adulteress (tus), one who runs away from
      her husband.
   (a) nkauj muag paj Prostitute (tus).
   (b) pojniam ntiav Prostitute.
   nkauj npuas Young female pig (tus).
   (a) tiav nkauj To come to young womanhood, girl
      past puberty.
   (b) ua nkauj To come to young womanhood, girl past
      puberty.

   nkauj qaib A pullet, young hen (tus).
   nkauj ntsuab nraug nas Legendary first woman and man.
   nkauj nyab A corncob doll, a doll (tus).

2. nkauj Handsome, beautiful.
   zoo nkauj Beautiful.

3. nkauj A song, melody (zaj).
   (a) hu nkauj To sing, sing a song.
   (b) hais nkauj To sing, sing a song.

1. nkaum To withdraw something back, to recede into.
   Nab nkaum hauv qab zeb lawm. The snake receded under
      the rock.
   mem tes nkaum lawm The pulse has disappeared, can't
      feel the pulse.

2. nkaum Used in combination with 'nees' for numbers 20
      to 29.
   nees nkaum 20.
   nees nkaum ib 21, etc. (cf. 'nees').

1. nkaus A restricted post verbal intensifier (cf. Appendix p. 471) Used singly or in combination 'pes nkaus.'
   kawg nkaus Superlative degree, ended, completely.
   zoo kawg nkaus The best, intensely good.
   hum nkaus Fitting.
   yam nkaus Like, similar to.
   ceeb nkaus Startled.
   lo nkaus Stuck to.
   ti nkaus Very close together.
   Note: These illustrations are some common examples of the use of p.v.int. 'kaus.' It is also used with the verbs listed below. See the individual verbs for the meaning.

cuag	ntsiab	tim	txaws
kem	puv	twb	txij
khaws	puv ntug	thooj	txiv
nias	puab	tsawv	txheem
npuaj	puag	tsuam	zoo
nres	puas	txais	
nthos	tib	txaus	

2. nkaus Single, only.
   Ib tug nkaus xwb los? Only one?

nkaw (This is a legal term) To put aside a cause of complaint, etc. for further consideration at a later date.

nkawd (cf. 'nkawm,') (cf. Introduction pp. xxii-xxiii).

1. nkawg Concerning gossip.
   nkawg lus Gossip, to gossip.
   tus nkawg lus A gossip, a spy, one who listens to others' conversation secretly and reports to outsiders, etc. (cf. 'taug xaiv').

2. nkawg
   ib nkawg t.c. (cf. 'nkawm').

nkawj A wasp (cf. 'muv').
   lub taub nkawj A wasp's nest.

nkawm A pair (clf. for pairs).
   Nkawm hais li cas? What did the two of them say?
   ib nkawg A pair (t.c.)
   nkawm khau Pair of shoes.
   txij nkawm An engaged person or couple.

nkawv Sometimes used to refer to bites by animals, etc.
   tib nkawv One bite, bitten once.

nkeeg t.c. from 'nkees' (cf. 'nkees').

nkees Lethargic, lazy, disinclined to act.
   nkees nkees nqa li Weak and lethargic.
   (a) nkees nloog Disinclined to listen, "tired of hearing it."
   (b) laj nloog Disinclined to listen, "tired of hearing it."
   nkees ua Disinclined to do.
   tub nkeeg (t.c.) Lazy.
   kev mob kev nkeeg (t.c.) Sickness and lethargy.
   ua dab tub nkeeg (t.c.) To have Malaria, (so called because of the lethargy with it.)
   "Tub nkeeg muaj tub nkeeg ntuj." The lazy man has his own time. (proverb)

nki ib nyuag nki xwb (I just touched you) a little bit (and then you cry!)
   Note: This is language used by children.

1. nkig Brittle, crisp (contr. 'zooj').
   nplej nkig The rice is hard and firm in the hull.

2. nkig
   ua nkog ua nkig Vascillating, unsteady, to do carelessly or poorly.

3. nkig
   liab nkog nkig Dull red.

nkim To waste, to use without purpose.
   nkim zog To waste strength, useless effort.
   nkim nyiaj To waste money.
   nkim hnub nyoog To waste time.

nkis Restricted p.v.int. (cf. Appendix 12).

nkiag siab nkiag Sharp memory, good memory.

nkog ua nkog ua nkig (cf. 'nkig' Definition No. 2).

1. nkoj A boat (lub), (usually a hand-propelled boat) (contr. 'hemcav').
   nkoj tog The boat sinks.
   nkoj deg (t.c.) A boat (lub).
   nkoj cua An airplane, aircraft (lub) (cf. 'dav hlau').
   txheeb nkoj To pole a boat.
   (a) hais nkoj To row a boat.
   (b) hais dej To row a boat.
   (c) nquam nkoj To row a boat.

2. nkoj To uproot
   nkoj cag (tree) uprooted.

nkos Muddy.
      nkos nkos li Muddy.
      av nkos Mud.

nkoog To congeal, congealed (cf. 'khov').

nkoos Restricted post-verbal intensifier (cf. Appendix 8 p. 471)
      nraim nkoos Hidden.
      hais lus nraim nkoos To speak secretly.
      laus nkoos Very old; of sounds low in tone.
      khoov nkoos Stooped, bend over.
      xauj nkoos Bent over to peek.

nkoov Twisted (as a rope, etc.) (cf. 'ntswj').
      Ntswj kom nkoov. Twist it like a rope.
      nkoov hlua To twist a rope.
      nkoov kav (cf. 'nplej').

nkuj Restricted p.v.int. (cf. Appendix 8).

nkua Clf. for strikes with the fist.
      (a) Ntaus nws ib nkua. (He) struck him once.
      (b) Ntaus nws ib teg. (He) struck him once.

nkuag (cf. 'nkuaj') (t.c.)

nkuaj A stable, a pen or enclosure (lub).
      nkuaj nees A horse stable.
      rooj nkuag Stable door (lub) (t.c.)
      tsiaj ncawg nkuaj Animals enter the pen.

nkuav tua tshwb nkuav To kill (game) close at hand.

nkham To go on all fours, crawl on all fours.

nkhas (cf. 'nrov').

1. nkhaus Crooked, having a crook or bend.
      Kev nkhaus nkhaus li. The road is crooked.

2. nkhaus Not straightforward, dishonest.
      Nws lub siab tsis ncaj siab nkhaus nkhaus. He has a crooked heart.

nkhawb Soot, carbon, carbon residue that gathers on the boards or roof over a Hmong open fireplace.

nkhawv Restricted post verbal intensifier. (cf. Appendix 8).
      nqhis dej nkhawv To be very thirsty.

nkhib A crotch, angle formed by the parting of two legs or branches.
      nkhib teg Crotch of the fingers (t.c.)
      ntoo muaj nkhib Trees have crotches.

nkhis Restricted post verbal intensifier. (cf. Appendix 8, p. 475).
      nrov nkhis nkhoos The sound of things hollow (cf. 'nrov').

nkhoob The sound of a dog barking.
      nkhoob nkhoob Sound of a dog barking ("Woof Woof!")

nkhoos Restricted post verbal intensifier with 'nrov.' (cf. 'nrov,' 'nkhis' Also Appendix 8, p. 475).

npaj To provide for, to prepare, to prepare for (cf. 'pam').
npaj nqaij npaj mov To provide food, prepare food.
Npaj tau yug lub cev xwb. To provide for one's body only.
npaj siab To prepare the heart (as for instruction, etc.)

npam Used for the "Baht," unit of Thai currency, tical (T) (lub).

1. npau To bubble up, to boil.
Dej npau npau. The water is boiling.

2. npau To be angry, to "boil" with anger.
(a) npau siab To be angry.
(b) npau lub siab To be angry.
(a) npau taws To be angry.
(b) lub siab npau taws To be angry.
npau vog Sudden burst of anger.

3. npau
npau suav A dream
ua npau suav To dream.

npaub A given name for women.

1. npaug t.c. from 'npaum,' (cf. 'npaum').

2. npaug
ua npuav npaug tshaws (cf. 'pobkws').

npauj Moth (tus).
tus npauj The moth.
tus kab npauj The moth larva.

1. npaum Equal, equal to, as much or as many as.
(a) npaum li As much as this.
(b) npaum li no As much as this.
Muaj npaum no xwb. Only this much, that's all I have.
zoo sib npaug Equally good (t.c.)
faib sib npaug Divide equally (t.c.)
ua num sib npaug zos To do an equal amount of work.

2. npaum Used after numbers to express mathematical increase or multiplication in geometric ratio such as doubling, tripling, etc.
ua ob npaug Twice as many, doubled (t.c.)
peb npaug Tripled (t.c.)
rau caug npaum 60 times as many.

1. npawg Term used for male cousins of a different surname, i.e. male children of mother's brothers and sisters and of father's sisters. (tus) (cf. kinship charts, Appendix 11).

NL

nlog The sound made by a tiger when startled.

nlom An idol, an image (tus).
pe nlom To worship idols.

nloog To listen, to hearken to, give attention to (contr. 'hnov').
nloog tias... What (I) heard was...
(a) nloog zoj To listen well.
(b) nloog zoo zoo To listen well.
nloog tsis tshab Didn't hear clearly, can't hear clearly.
nloog lus To listen to what is said, to obey.
nloog mob To be conscious of pain (give attention to) to listen with a stethoscope.

nluas Sickly, weak.
lub cev nluas nluas Weak sickly body.

nluav Dented (cf. 'hnlos.' 'zuav').
(a) nluav lawm Dented.
(b) hnlos lawm Dented.
(c) zuav lawm Dented.

NP

npab Arm.
caj npab The human arm, the upper arm.
yas npab Elbow (cf. 'luj tshib').
tooj npab Bracelet (lub).

npag Stout and strong physically, muscular (contr. 'rog').
Note: This is a better term to use of persons than 'rog.'

3. npo Restricted post verbal intensifier (cf. Appendix 8).
   puv npo Completely full.
   Note: 'puv npo' is used figuratively also whereas
         the similar term 'puv nkaus' is used most of
         things literally filled.
   Kuv lub siab puv npo. My heart is full.
   tsau npo Filled, satisfied.

1. npog To cover something over, to cover so as to hide.
   Roob nphau los npog lawv. The mountain slid down and
         covered them.
   liab npog muag (tus) The sloth, a sloth.

2. npog A bad omen, pertaining to taboo (cf. 'chov,' 'xu').
   (a) ua chov Is an evil omen, is taboo.
   (b) ua npog Is an evil omen, is taboo.
   (c) ua xu Is an evil omen, is taboo.
   Note: There are many things considered in this category
         by the Hmong such as any snake or bird or wild
         animal entering a house, a dog on the roof, a
         litter of one piglet, etc. Where such things
         are encountered they must be met by suitable
         appeasement to the spirits.
   vij dab vij npog - troubled by evil omens and spirits

3. npog
   siab nphau npog Very angry (lit. "heart turned over").

npoj Flock, brood (cf. 'pab'), a group gathered together.
   ib npog qaib One flock of chickens (t.c.)
   qaib npoj A flock of chickens.
   ncaim npoj To separate the flock, to separate the
         group.
   sawvdaws poog npoj All come together in one group or
         one flock.

npos Teb nyob npos npos. The fields lie in a hollow.

npoo The edge of a precipice, cliff edge.
   dai npoo ncuv Hung on the edge, of anything hung or
         balanced on the edge of a cliff or about to fall
         over a precipice.
   Hnub dai npoo ncuv Sunset, the sun "hung" on the
         horizon.

npoog To build up the ground around plants or trees.

1. npoos A kind of tree pitch used for lighting.
   taws npoos To carry a pitch torch, to use pitch for
         lighting (cf. 'tsau roj').

2. npoos Clf. for sides of folded cloth.
   ib npoos ntaub One side of folded cloth.

2. npawg Of another clan, friendly term used in greeting
         others of the same age whom you do not really
         know, "friend." (tus)

npawj Restricted post verbal intensifier after 'nrov'
   (cf. 'nrov').

npawm To shape, to carve, to shave off a board (cf. 'tws').

1. npaws To pinch with the knuckles, pinch off with the
         knuckles.
   npaws zaub hau To pinch or break off short lengths
         of leafy green vegetables into a pot for
         boiling.

2. npaws Chills and fever (clf. 'tus' for one chill
         and temperature).
   ua npaws To have chills and fever.
   mob npaws Malaria, illness characterized by chills
         and fever, to be sick with such illness.

npawv Rounded off and not really straight as e.g. of a
         dull wedge or of teeth worn off.

npe Given name, name (lub).
   ib lub npe A name, one name.
   Nws lub npe hu li cas? What is his given name?
   (a) daws npe To give a name.
   (b) hu npe To give a name.
   (c) tis npe To give a name.
   hu tuav npe To call by name.
   poob npe To lose one's name or reputation.
   npe nto moo Name or reputation spread abroad.
   Tuav npe txog ntawm kwj tse. No sooner had we said
         his name than he appeared.
   npe ntawv Letters, alphabet.

npeeg To miss the mark (as in firing a gun, etc.)

npees To slip over (a term used in sewing).

1. npis A given name for men.

2. npis Naturally stout and strong (cf. 'npag').

npiaj Restricted post verbal intensifier after 'nrov'
   (cf. 'nrov').

1. npo To pick out of, to lift out of (as from water, etc.)
   npo tawm los To lift or dip out of (the water).

2. npo To restrain, to restrain the bowels or urine.
   npo zis To restrain urination.

npu   daus xib daus npu Snow.

npub Dull, not sharp.
Rab taus no npub npub li. This axe is dull.

npug
ntiv npug (cf. 'qeej').

1. npuj To hammer, to pound, to batter, bump hard against.
Muab npuj kom ncaj. Pound it until it is straight.
Tsheb sib npug. The cars collided. (t.c.) (cf.
'sib lawg').

2. npuj A trap for animals consisting of a sharp
spear of bamboo, etc. set horizontally to
spring when released so as to kill the game.

3. npuj
npuj npaim (tus) Butterfly.

npuv Fine powder, very finely powdered.

1. npua Pig, pertaining to pigs (tus).
taw npua Boar, old male pig used for breeding.
maum npua Sow.
nkauj npuas (t.c.) Young female pig having had no
young.
las npua Large castrated pig.
quab npuas (t.c.) Young castrated pig.
pub npua To feed the pigs.
npua ho Pig has lost a litter.
npua tshom Pig rooting, pig digging to find food.
tus cuamtxwv npua Half grown castrated pig.
npua teb Wild pig, wild boar.

2. npua To wrap around the body, to wear wrapped around.
sev npua The back apron on a woman's outfit.
(cf. 'sev').

3. npua
zaj npuas (t.c.) (tus) A small wild animal having a
body similar to a pig but nose and feet similar
to a dog. Nests in the ground. (cf. 'loob').

npuab To massage, to lay the hands on (contr. 'npuaj').
npuab plab To massage the stomach.

1. npuag Serious infection.
mob npuag Infection, blood poisoning.
mob npuag faj A carbuncle (also 'mob faj').

2. npuag A kind of expensive cloth.
ntaub tsuj ntaub npuag Fine cloth.
hnav tsuj hnav npuag To dress in finery, dress in
expensive clothing.

1. npuaj To pound with the hands.
npuaj plab To pound the stomach region with the hands
to relieve pain. (contr. 'npuab').
npuaj teg (t.c.) To clap hands.

2. npuaj
npuaj nkaus Touching, stuck together (cf. 'lo nkaus').

1. npuas Bubbles, foam, bubble (lub).
ib lub npuas dej A water bubble.
npuas ncauj Foam from the mouth.

2. npuas
sib npuas (t.c. from 'npua') (cf. 'npua' Definition
No. 2).

1. npuav To hold in the mouth.
npuav rawv To hold tightly in the mouth.
muab npuav Place it in the mouth.
muab nyiaj npuav To place a silver coin in the mouth
of a dead person. This is part of the preparation for burial providing money for passage
into the land beyond death.

2. npuav
ua npuav npaug tshaws (cf. 'pobkws').

NPH

1. nphav To knock or touch against accidentally.
2. nphav Used as a restricted post verbal intensifier with 'nrov' (cf. 'nrov').

1. nphau To tip over.
   roob nphau los The mountain slid down (lit. "tipped over").
2. nphau Turbulent (of running water).
   dej nphau nphwv Turbulent water.
3. nphau nrig nphau Of persons or animals turning over on the back.
   nees nrig nphau Horse rolling on its back.
4. nphau siab nphau npog Very angry (lit. "heart turned over").

nphaws Restricted post verbal intensifier. (cf. Appendix 8).
   ntaug nphaws lawm Decreased in intensity (of illness storm, fire, etc.)

nphiv Restricted post verbal intensifier with 'nrov' (cf. 'nrov').

npho Restricted post verbal intensifier. (cf. Appendix 8)
   cais npho To separate, each go his own way.

nphob Dirty, soiled, musty.
   ntaub nphob nphob Cloth soiled, not new cloth.
   kev nphob nphob Road in poor condition.

1. nphoo To throw or scatter with the hand.
   nphoov av To throw dust, scatter dust.
   nphoov ntsev rau nqaij Scatter salt on the meat.
2. nphoo Post verbal intensifier (cf. Appendix 8).
   neeg coob nphoo ntxoj nphoo ntxuas A great crowd.

nphoob Restricted post verbal intensifier (cf. Appendix 8).
   pham nphoob - very fat (of animals)

nphoov Restricted post verbal intensifier after 'nrov' (cf. 'nrov').
   ntog nrov nphoov Fell down with a resounding crash.

nphuab pos nphuab A kind of thorn.

nphwv Restricted post verbal intensifier (cf. Appendix 8).
   dej nphau nphwv Turbulent water.

NPL

nplas Restricted post verbal intensifier (cf. Appendix 8).
   plag nplas Disorderly.
   ci nplas An expanse of brightness (cf. 'vus').
   qaij nplas To avoid, steer away from, lean from.

1. nplav Gradual slope.
   nplav toj A hill with a gradual even slope.
2. nplav Used with 'nplem' as a restricted post verbal intensifier.
   nce nplem nplav Gradual ascent (cf. 'nplem').

1. nplai Fish or reptile scales (cf. 'nplais').
   nplai ntses Fish scales.
   nplai nab Snake or reptile scales.
2. nplai Sections of a citrus fruit.
   ib nplais txiv lwj zoov One section of pomelo (t.c.)

nplaig The tongue (tus).
   hlev nplaig Put out the tongue.
   nplaig txhav Can't speak clearly, tongue-tied.
   lus dov nplaig Words hard to enunciate.

1. nplaim Surface, expanse.
   nplaim hiav txwv Surface of the sea.
   nplaim dej Surface of the water.
2. nplaim Flame.
   (a) nplaim taws Flames of fire.
   (b) nplaim hluavtaws Flames of fire.
   nplaim teeb Lamp flame.
3. nplaim Petal
   nplaim paj ntoo Flower petals.
4. nplaim The reed of a wind instrument.
   nplaim tooj Brass reed as used in the 'qeej' or other wind instrument.
   raj nplaim A flute.

nplais nplais taws Wood chips (cf. 'nplai').

nplaum Glutinous, gluey, sticky.
   nplaum nplaum li Gluey, sticky.
   nplej nplaum Uncooked glutinous rice (cf. 'nplej').

nplawg Combined with 'ntias' to form a two word restricted
    post verbal intensifier. (cf. Appendix 8)
    The use of this p.v.int. adds to the verb the
    sense that the action is done by many persons
    together.
  zaum nplawg ntias Sat down together.
  cem nplawg ntias All began to scold.
  los nplawg ntias All returned together.
  Also used with the following verbs: (See individual
    entries for the meanings.)

  ua   nplej   tuaj   qw
  hais   quaj   txeeb   nyiav
  ntaus   thuam   khiav   lawm

1. nplawm To whip, to beat, to inflict stripes.
  rab nplawm A stick for beating, a whip.

2. nplawm Clf. for blows, lashes.
  ib nplawg One lash with the whip (t.c.)
  kaum nplawm Ten blows.

nplaws Restricted post verbal intensifier with 'npliag'
    (cf. 'npliag').

nplej Unhulled rice (whether standing in the field or cut)
    (contr. 'txhuv,' 'mov'). (clf. 'lub' for a
    kernel, 'tes' for a sheaf).
  teb nplej Rice field (t.c.) (dry field rice).
  ib teg nplej A sheaf of rice (t.c.)
  ntaus nplej To thresh rice.
  (a) hlais nplej To harvest rice.
  (b) muab nplej To harvest rice.
  yaj nplej To winnow rice.
  npluag nplej Rice chaff.
  (a) quav nyab nplej Rice straw
  (b) quav nplej Rice straw.
  tshav quav nplej To cut the rice stubble for burning.
  xua nplej Rice bran.
  lum nplej (cf. 'lum').
  kaus nplej Rice sprout when it first appears (tus)
  yub nplej Young rice sprouts, rice seedlings.
  hnab nplej The head of rice (lub).
  nplej txhawv txhij The rice has come to a head.
  (a) dob nplej To weed the rice fields.
  (b) dob teb nplej To weed the rice fields.
  noj nplej tshiab (cf. 'noj') To eat a meal in
    celebration of the first newly harvested rice.
    Relatives are invited in, a chicken killed and
    thanks given to the spirits as all in the home
    take part in the feast.

Note: Below are the terms descriptive of the various
    stages in the growth of rice.
  nplej ua koob nto av Rice sprout just appearing.
  nplej ua duav phuaj One leaf has formed.

  nplej dauv tw qaib The leaves are bending over.
  nplej txij hauvcaug Up to the knees.
  nplej txij duav As high as the waist.
  (a) nplej nqus yas The stem has formed.
  (b) nkoov kav The stem has formed.
  nplej ua plab hnab Seed pod has formed.
  nplej paim tshaws lawm The growing heart has appeared.
  nplej ziab pag tshaws The kernels begin to form.
  nplej rau txhuv Soft kernels have formed.
  nplej too The rice is filling out.
  nplej daj qab hnab The rice kernels are ripening
    at the top of the head.
  nplej siav nto nqob The rice is ripe to the base of
    the head.

nplem Used with 'nplav' as a two-word restricted post verbal
    intensifier. (cf. Appendix 8).
  nce nplem nplav Gradual ascent.

npleem To slip sidewise off a surface (as when pressure is
    added from above, e.g. a hand slipping off the
    edge of a table).

1. nplij To comfort, to console (cf. 'deev').
  nplij lub siab To comfort the heart.
  Nplij nws mentsis kom nws txhob quaj. Comfort him a
    little so he will not cry.

2. nplij A restricted post verbal intensifier with 'nrov'
    (cf. 'nrov').

npliv Small silver coins used for ornamentation (lub).
  txiaj npliv (and) txiav cub Two types of small Indo-
    Chinese coins worn by the Hmong for decoration.

1. npliag Exact, accurate, precise
  xyaum npliag npliag li To follow exactly, do exactly
    as told.
  hais lus tsis npliag To speak inaccurately.

2. npliag Restricted post verbal intensifier in combination
    with 'nplaws'. (cf. Appendix 8).
  ntub nag npliag nplaws Soaking wet.

npliaj Given name.

1. nplias Given name for a girl.

2. nplias
  txiv nplias (lub) A kind of fruit.

nplo slightly used (of clothing, etc.)
  lub tsho nplo A jacket slightly worn.
  ris tsho qub nplo zog Clothing slightly used, worn
    but not old.

nplog A word used in derogatory speech, probably referring to the anus. (cf. 'nplos').
This word is sometimes used in referring to the people of Laos (plains dwelling Lao) by the Hmong in Laos but the Hmong in Thailand speak of the Lao as 'Lostsuas' and consider 'nplog' derogatory.

nploj Restricted post verbal intensifier after 'nrov' (cf. 'nrov').

nplos Socket (lub), a hole for the handle of an implement. (cf. 'nplog').

nploog T.c. from 'nplooj' (cf. 'nplog').

1. **nplooj** Leaf (daim), leaf-like, pertaining to the leaf, frond.
   nplooj kuj yem Fan palm fronds used for roofing.
   cuam nplooj To fix palm leaves or fronds between lengths of split bamboo to make sections for roofing.

   ntoo hlav nplooj The tree puts forth leaves.
   zeeg nplooj Sheds its leaves.
   ntoo nplooj hlis A type of hardwood tree useful for making strong handles, etc.

2. **nplooj** Clf. used for certain vital organs.
   (a) nplooj siab The liver.
   (b) lub siab The liver.
   nplooj ntsws The lungs.
   ib nploog siab (t.c.) One liver, one "heart". (cf. 'siab').

3. **nplooj**
   (a) nplooj pus The shoulder blades.
   (b) duav pus The shoulder blades.

4. **nplooj**
   tsov nplooj suab (tus) The Bengal tiger.

5. **nplooj**
   laug nplooj suab Cross stitch embroidery.

nploos The short-quilled porcupine (tus) (contr. 'tsaug').

1. **nplua** To impose a fine or penalty, to judge or condemn.
   nplua nyiaj To impose a fine, to fine.
   nplua lub txim To judge sin, to fix penalty for transgression.

2. **nplua** slippery.
   Kev nplua nplua. The road is slippery.
   nplua roj Oily, slippery with oil or wax.

3. **nplua**
   ua nplua nuj To be rich.
   tus nplua nuj The rich man.

npluag Chaff (contr. 'xua').
npluag nplej Rice chaff.

npluas The water leech (tus) (cf. 'hiab').

npluav The side of a knife.
npluav riam The broad surface side of a knife.

NPLH

nplhaib A ring, finger-ring (ntiv).
ib nti nplhaib One finger-ring (t.c.)
ntiv nplhaib no This ring.

nplhib Restricted post verbal intensifier with 'nplhob' (cf. Appendix 8).
ntses nti nplhib nplhob The fish wriggled and twisted (on the hook).

nplho Restricted post verbal intensifier (cf. Appendix 8).
Nws chaws nplho mus hauv tsev. He quickly went into the house. He "ducked" into the house.

nplhob Restricted post verbal intensifier (cf. 'nplhib').

nplhos To stab, to stick with a knife, to kill by piercing.
nplhos npua To stick a pig, kill a pig by piercing.

NQ

1. nga To lift with the hand, to carry in the hand or hands, to hold in the hand, take in the hand.
   nga hlo To take in the hand.
   nga dej To carry water in a vessel held in the hand.
   nga rawv To take or carry firmly in the hand.

2. nga
   nkees nkees nga li Weak and lethargic.

1. ngag Of things or persons gathered together in a group, of group action.
   ib ngag lus Unanimous, all telling the same story, of words grouped together into a verse or saying, etc.
   ua ib ngag cem Of many persons scolding another at the same time.

2. ngag Used as a restricted post verbal intensifier.
   raj puab raj xyu nrov ngag ntxhias Horns and trumpets sounding loudly together.

1. ngaj Horizontal beam, rail (tus) (cf. 'tsev') (contr. 'yees').
   ngaj tsev Horizontal beam for a house.
   ngaj ru The ridgepole.
   ngaj tsuag The long horizontal side beams of a house.
   tsheb ngaj Railroad (cf. 'tsheb').

2. ngaj
   ngaj qaum The backbone.

3. ngaj
   hais ua ngaj ua ngug Everyone talking about something.

ngaig T.c. from 'ngaij' (cf. 'ngaij').

1. ngaij Meat, flesh (of animals, birds, humans, nuts and fruit).
   ngaij rog Fatty meat.
   ngaij ntshiv Lean meat.
   tseev ngaij To cut up meat in suitable portions after slaughtering.
   txhoov ngaij To cut up meat in small pieces.
   tsuav ngaij To mince meat very fine.
   ngaij pluas Meat not good, meat going rotten.
   thooj siav thooj ngaij Of one flesh and blood.
   hais lus rho plaub mob ngaig (t.c.) To speak words that hurt (like pulling hair and cutting flesh).

2. ngaij Used in referring to wild game.
   ngaij nruab nrag Wild game, wild meat.
   ngaij pos Animals of prey, animals that prey upon others.

ngaim Narrow.
   kev ngaim ngaim li A narrow road.

ngawm To heal, of flesh or bone healing.

1. nqe Price, wage, debt.
   Note: This word is sometimes pronounced 'nqi'
   Yuav li cas nqe? What price are they wanting?
   them nqe To pay a price, repay a debt.
   tshuav lawv li nqe To owe them a debt.
   (a) nyom nqe To argue price
   nqe tes Wages for hand labor.
   (b) lem nqe To argue price.
   luab nqe To borrow on interest.
   kwv nuj nqe Unwilling to pay a debt.
   rob nqe To seek payment of a debt.
   ris nqe To hold a debt for a long time, keep on refusing to pay a debt.
   nqe taw tuaj Traveling expenses in coming.

2. nqe To hook a finger or toe on something.
   nqe kotaw To hook the foot on something and stumble.

3. nqe
   nqe lauj (tus) Wooden hook to hang things on in the home.

nqeg To wane or abate.
   Note: This word is sometimes pronounced 'nqig'
   hli nqeg The waning of the moon.
   dej nqeg The water abates, flood abates.

1. nqes To descend, to come or to go down.
   Note: This word is sometimes pronounced 'nqis'
   nqes hav To go down the hill.

2. nqes One half of a Hmong poetic couplet.
   Ob nqes ua ib txwg. Two halves make a couplet.
   (cf. 'tshooj,' 'zaj,' 'txwm').

nqee (cf. 'qhoob').

nqeeb The long tough grass used to make thatch for roofing.
   vov nqeeb To cover a house with 'nqeeb' thatch.
   cuam nqeeb To fix grass thatch into lengths for roofing.
   hav nqeeb A valley or expanse of 'nqeeb'

nqia Thin in the middle and thicker at the ends.
   nqia hnyuv (cf. 'neem').
   duav nqia nqia Person with a small back.
   neeg nqia nqia A small thin person, thin-waisted person.

Page 171:

nqob   The part of the rice stalk just under the head.
       nqob npleg (t.c.) The upper part of the rice stalk.
       siav nto nqob (cf. 'nplej').

1. nqos   To swallow.
          nqos kiag mus   To swallow whole, swallow completely.

2. nqos   The weaving shuttle (rab).

3. nqos   Clf. for passes of the shuttle in weaving.
          ib nqog (t.c.)   One pass of the shuttle.

4. nqos
          nqos cos   The crossbeam of the rice footmill (cf. 'cos').

5. nqos
          kab nqos vias (tus)   The locust.

nqov   The bellowing of a cow.
       nyuj nqov   The cow bellows.

nqug   hais ua nqaj ua nqug   Everyone talking.

nqus   To suck, inhale, absorb, draw in, attract to (as a
       magnet).
       lub nqus dej   A pump for water (cf. 'txhuav').
       Paj txawj nqus dej.   Cotton can soak up water.
       nqus yas (cf. 'nplej').
       tus nqus dej   A drinking tube or straw.

nquab   Dove, pigeon (tus).
        Note: There are many kinds, some of these are listed.
               Fuller descriptions will have to be obtained
               from the people.
        nquab dais   "Bear" dove, a large variety.
        nquab dawb   The white dove.
        nquab ntsuab   A greenish variety of dove.
        nquab liab   A red variety.
        nquab kho siab   Dove with a plaintive lonely cry.
        nquab poj mab   A striped variety.
        nquab plhuaj taub tawg   Dove with a cry that sounds
               like these syllables.
        nquab lib rwg   Another type of dove.

1. nquag   To recover from illness, to get well.
           Nws nquag lawm tsis tau?   Has he recovered or not?

2. nquag   Energetically, with vigor, actively (contr.
           'nkees').
           nquag nquag ua num   To work energetically, ready to
               work.

Page 172:

1. nquam   To transport.
           nquam nra   To transport goods; especially to transport
               goods by vehicle or boat.

2. nquam
           cov nquam qauv   The pallbearers.

3. nquam   To row a boat.
           nquam nkoj   To row a boat   (cf. 'nkoj,' 'txheeb').

4. nquam
           nquam kiab nquam khw   Market, marketplace (poetic).

nquas   Restricted post verbal intensifier (cf. Appendix 8).

nqws   Missing a limb of the body.
       nqws tes   Missing one arm.
       nqws taw   Missing one foot.

NQH

nqha   Of a dry area having only few trees and little or no
       green undergrowth.
       hav zoov nqha   Such an area of the forest.

nqhis   To thirst, to have an intense desire for (cf. 'tshaib')
        Kuv nqhis dej.   I am thirsty for water.
        nqhis dej nkhawv   Extremely thirsty.
        nqhis nqaij   To have a desire for meat, hunger for meat.
        Note: This word is sometimes said 'nqhes.'

nqho   Post verbal intensifier (see 'nqhug').

nqhug   Restricted post verbal intensifier with 'nqhos.'
        (cf. Appendix 8).
        nthe sib nqhug nthe sib nqhos   To cry out very loudly.

1. nqhuab   To dry up (as a stream, pond, etc.).
            nqhuab tag lawm   Dried up.

2. nqhuab   Pertaining to dry land as opposed to water.
            vuab kib nqhuab (tus)   Dry land turtle.
            nab qa nqhuab (tus)   Dry land lizard, iguana.
            nruab nqhuab   On land.

NR

1. nra Goods, baggage, a bundle of goods (lub), a pack load.
   nra nees A horse pack or a pack saddle (lub).
   thauj nra To transport goods by animal.
   nquam nra To transport goods by vehicle or boat.

2. nra Clf. for packs, loads.
   ib nras One load (t.c.)

3. nra
   hli nra Full moon.

nrab Half, one half, mid (horizontal) (contr. 'ntav').
   ib nrab One half.
   nruab nrab Middle, center, midst.
   nyob nruab nrab In the middle, in the midst.

nrad (cf. 'nram' and Introduction pp. xxii-xxiii).

1. nrag
   nqaij nruab nrag Wild meat, wild game.

2. nrag
   mus nram plawv tiaj nrag Went down into the midst
      of the level country.

nraj The white pheasant (tus).

nram Downhill, down below, noun of location (for t.c.
      cf. Introduction p.
   Kuv mus nram lawv los. I have been and come from
      down below.
   nram qab dej Downstream.
   nram qab kev The downhill side of the trail.
   mus nyob nrad Went to stay below (t.c.)
   nyob nram moos Staying down on the plain.
   nram ntej The period of time up until now.
   nram ntej nram ntxov Previously.

1. nras A large broad level area (lub).
   lub nras liaj qhua An area of dry flat fields or
      a dry uncultivated area with rolling hills, etc.

2. nras t.c. from 'nra' (cf. 'nra' Definition No. 2).

nraig nraig mov To "clean up" the table, clear the table of
      rice, food, etc.

1. nraim To hide, hidden.
   tsiv nraim To hide oneself.
   nraim nkoos Hidden.
   hais lus nraim nkoos To talk secretly.
   hli nraim qaib (cf. 'hli').

2. nraim Used with other words in two word restricted post
      verbal intensifiers. (cf. Appendix 8).
   ua tib nraim To do exactly according to direction.
   mus tib nraim To go exactly straight.
   ncaj nrwb nraim Exactly straight.
   ua nrwb nraim To do exactly according to direction.

3. nraim A single word restricted post verbal intensifier.
      (may be used with or without 'qos' preceeding,
      i.e. 'nraim' or 'qos nraim') (cf. Appendix 8 p. 472).
   Note: This intensive adds the idea of fixedness, sted-
      fastness and straightness to the character of
      the verb.

   ncaj nraim Straight through, perfectly straight.
   raws nraim Follow strictly, follow stedfastly.
   sawv nraim Standing in one place fixedly.
   nrog nraim Always accompanying.
   xyuas nraim To study faithfully, follow plan.
   mus nraim To follow straight on, go straight on.
   lawv nraim To follow straight on.
   khaws nraim To gather up things faithfully, as a
      habit.

nrau To bump or push with the head or horns, to butt.
   nrau av To dig or push up earth as an animal does
      with its horns.
   nyuj sib nraus (t.c.) bulls fighting each other.
   tsheb nrau av A bulldozer (lub).

nraub nraub qaum The back, especially the region of the
      back between the shoulders and above the waist
      (cf. 'duav') (lub).
   mob nraub qaum My back hurts.
   nraud (cf. 'nraum') (cf. Introduction pp. xxii-xxiii).

1. nraug Pertaining to unmarried men.
   hluas nraug A young unmarried man (tus).
   zoo nraug Handsome.
   nraug vauv (tus) Bridegroom (cf. 'qhua vauv').
   nraug xwb Bachelor, unmarried man.
   nkauj ntsuab nraug nas (cf. 'nkauj').

2. nraug
   nraug zeeg muag Dizzy (cf. 'muag').

nrauj To divorce, to separate off from.
   Nws muab pojniam nrauj lawm. He divorced his wife.
      He put his wife away.
   tsis nrauj hnub tsis nrauj hmo Unceasing day and
      night.

nreej The large flat flanging root structures at the base
       of certain types of trees. (clf. 'daim').
   ib daig nreej ntoos (t.c.) A section of
      flanging tree root.

nrees Restricted post verbal intensifier used either as
       a single word or in the combination '-qos nrees')
       (cf. Appendix 8, p. 472) This word often adds
       to the verb the idea that the action involved
       has continued in a fixed state for some time.
       See the following illustrations.
   (a) ruaj nrees Firm steady, enduring.
   (b) ruaj qos nrees Firm, steady, enduring.
   (a) txhav nrees Stiff, hard.
   (b) txhav qos nrees Stiff, hard.
   lub siab txhav nrees Hard hearted.
   (a) kaw nrees Closed tightly.
   (b) kaw qos nrees Closed tightly.
   Note: In each case 'qos' may be used as above.
      kem nrees Divided off
      chob nrees Pierced.
      ntsia nrees Nailed.
      khaum nrees Caught fast.
      nias nrees Pressed down.
      lo nrees Stuck on.
      ntog nrees Fallen down, stumbled.

nrib Slightly opened up (e.g. as a cut or a crack).
   nrib pleb Just a little cracked.

1. nrig To support oneself with the aid of a cane or stick.
   nrig pas mus To walk with the aid of a stick.

2. nrig A stick or cane for use in walking.
   ib tug pas nrig A cane, a walking stick.
   tus cwj nrig A rod, a staff.

3. nrig
   dawb hau nrig caug Old and hoary-headed, aged.

4. nrig The fist (clf. 'lub') Clf. for blows with the fist.
   ntaus nrig To hit with the fist.

5. nrig
   nrig nphau To roll over upside down, somersault
      (of persons or animals).
   nees nrig nphau Horse rolls over on its back.
   nrig nphau ntsos Rolled over quickly.

6. nrig Restricted post verbal intensifier. (cf. Appendix 8).
   (a) kaj nrig Very bright.
   (b) kaj lug Very bright.
   tshav ntuj nrig Bright all around, bright sunshine.

---

nraum Noun of location, outside (for t.c. cf. Introduction
       pp. xxii-xxiii).
   nraum zoov Outside, out of doors.
   nraum nraub qaum Behind one's back.
   sab nraud (t.c.). The outside, the side without,
      the back of a book, etc.
   Nws mus nraud lawm. He went outside.

1. nraus Weak and feeble.
   nraus zus nraus zus To become weaker and more feeble.
   (cf. 'pheej si si' Both expressions used of
      people who grow old and feeble.)

2. nraus
   ntuj nraus Used to refer to places extremely distant.
      On the other side of the earth, the "regions
      beyond."

nrawg Used with 'nroos' as a two word restricted post
       verbal intensifier. (cf. 'nroos' Cf.
       Appendix 8).
   paub sib nrawg nroos To know equally well.

nrawm Quickly, swiftly (cf. 'sai,' 'tsuag,' Contr. 'qeeb').
   Txhob hais lus nrawm nrawm li. Don't talk so fast.

nraws
   hais lus ntog nraws To speak peculiar sounds as of
      one speaking a foreign language.

nrawv Used witn 'nroos' as a two word restricted post verbal
       intensifier. (cf. 'nroos' cf. Appendix 8).
   tuaj nrawv nroos Coming one after another.

nre To pleat.
   nre tiab To pleat a skirt.

1. nres To stand erect, stand upright, to cause to stand
        erect.
   Nres ntawm koj Stand where you are.
   (a) nres nkaus To support upright.
   (b) txheem nkaus To support upright.

2. nres To bear the full weight of, bear full responsibility
        for.
   Yexu nres peb lub txim. Jesus has borne the full
      weight of our sin.

1. nreeg Aerial tree roots.
   ib nreeg ntoo An aerial tree root.

2. nreeg
   nreeg taum Bean or pea poles, stakes for beans. (tus).

nris Restricted post verbal intensifier with 'nruj' (cf. 'nruj').

nriaj To pull apart with force.
nriaj hlua kom tu Pulled the rope in two.

1. nriav Plain speech.
nriav lus Plain speech (as opposed to figurative)

2. nriav Restricted post verbal intensifier.
xyab nriav Stretched out flat.

nro Murky, containing foreign matter.
dej nro nro Murky water, water containing foreign matter.

nrob The breast or chest (especially when referring to game or animals) (cf. 'siab').
Tua hauv nrob. Shoot it in the breast.

1. nrog With, to accompany.
Kuv nrog koj mus. I'll go with you.
nrog nraim To always accompany, to stay close beside.

2. nrog From (in the sense "to obtain from").
Kuv nrog koj yuav ob daig nyiaj. I want two bars of silver from you.
Kuv nrog ob tug thov tau ib daig ntaub. I borrowed a length of cloth from the two.

3. nrog To drip.
dej nrog The water is dripping.
nrog ib tee ib tee Drips one drop at a time.

4. nrog The flat inside area of a winnowing tray, (clf. for a trayful.)
lub nrog vab The inside of the winnowing tray.
ib nrog vab nqaij One tray full of meat.

5. nrog
lub nrog cev The inner area of the body.

nroj Vegetation, weeds.
nroj tsuag Vegetation.
luaj nroj To cut down weeds.
dob nroj To pull weeds.
hav nroj Uncultivated fields, fields of weeds.

nros nros taus Rebellious, perverse, refusing to obey simply because told to do so.

nrov Loud, loudly, noisily.
nrov quaj qees A great resounding noise.
suab nrov A loud voice.
(a) hnov suab sab Heard a loud noise.
(b) hnov sab nrov Heard a loud noise.
Note: The word 'nrov' may be followed by any one of a category of post verbal intensifiers which serve to emphasize the character of the sound or noise indicated or to imitate the sound. Below is an illustrative list. There are undoubtedly many more examples.

nrov hlawv Noisy drinking.
nrov hnyev Whimpering.
nrov lis loos Loud droning.
nrov nkuaj (A sound we have not identified).
nrov nkuav Break something brittle.
nrov nkhas The sound of hitting a wall.
(a) nrov nkhis nkhoos Hitting a wall or a hollow tree.
(b) nrov nkhoos Hitting a wall or a hollow tree.
nrov npawj Noise of hitting something flying.
nrov nphiv nphav Sound of tree chopping.
nrov nphoov A resounding fall, tree falling.
nrov nplaj Clapping hands.
nrov nplij Sound of a baby pulling off the nipple.
nrov nploj Falling into water.
nrov nqag ntxhias Loud noise (cf. trumpets, etc.)
nrov nrawj Hitting something hard.
nrov nreev Metal hitting on metal.
nrov nrhawj Sound of a rope tearing.
nrov nrhij nrhawj Sound of several strands tearing.
nrov nta vos Sound of a gunshot.
nrov ntwg Sound of hitting hollow ground.
nrov ntws Great noise (as of a great crowd).
nrov ntoo ntws Loud droning noise.
nrov ntsiaj Sound of metal on metal.
nrov ntxhe hav ntws Sounding a long distance.
nrov ntxhias A great noise.
nrov pag Sound of falling into mud.
nrov poog Sound of stepping on solid ground.
nrov ploom Sound of object dropping into water.
nrov qis qawv Sound as of knuckles cracking.
nrov **rhij rhuaj Sound of dry leaves crackling.**
nrov tawg ntho Sound of something bursting.
nrov **theb** Noise of hitting something flying.
nrov tsej (A noise we have not identified).
nrov txij txej Sound of sucking.
nrov tawj (A noise we have not identified).
nrov nthuj nthav Sound of weaving on a loom.

1. nroo To sigh.

179

2. nroo A restricted post verbal intensifier used in combination with 'ntws.' (cf. Appendix 8) This combination is used especially in describing sounds characterized by humming, droning, etc. (e.g. thunder, distant vehicles, a crowd, etc.)
ua nqaij ua cawv nroo ntws To have a big feast.
xob quaj nroo ntws Rolling thunder.

nroog Thickly inhabited area, large city (lub).
lub niag nroog The capital city, the great city.

nrooj Restricted post verbal intensifier (cf. Appendix 8).
hais ceev nrooj To speak forcibly, convincingly.

nroos Used in two word combinations as a restricted post verbal intensifier. (cf Appendix 8).
tuaj nrawv nroos Many coming one after another.
paub sib nrawg nroos To know equally well.

nru The uvula (tus).
nru qaij (The uvula to one side) Cannot speak clearly.

nrug Separated from, having separated.
nrug lawm Separated (as of boards shrinking, etc.)
qhov tsev nrug Crack in the wall of a house.
nrug zog Disconnect, separate (contr. 'twb') (as of a switch, etc.).
nyob nrug deb Living apart, living at some distance.
kev nrug deb Far away from, separated far away.

1. nruj Taut, drawn tight (contr. 'taug').
hlua nruj A tight rope.
mob nruj nruj li Swollen and hard area.
kua mis nruj tuaj Of a woman's breast milk coming in, breasts hard with milk.

2. nruj Of an intense and impetuous nature.
siab nruj siab heev Impatient, impetuous, intense.

3. nruj A two word restricted post verbal intensifier with 'nris'. (cf. Appendix 8).
ncaws nruj nris Nodding the head.
nyo nruj nris Bending over.
tsaug zog nruj nris Nodding in sleep.

4. nruj
ua nruj nriaj Near to death.

nrua A small bamboo stick split at one end, used as an instrument to make noise to chase chickens, etc. (rab).

180

1. nruab Midst, middle, center (cf. 'nrab').
nruab nrab Middle, center, midst.
nyob nruab nrab In the midst, in the middle
nruab hnub Daytime, in the day, during the day.
nyob nruab thiab In the womb, unborn babe.
ib txhis nruab thiab From birth, from the womb on.
nqaij nruab nrag Game, wild meat.
nruab nqhuab On land.
nruab deg On the sea (t.c.)
cov nruab zog Those in the villages (t.c.)
nyob nruab hli Of a woman during the first month after childbirth.

2. nruab Flattened out bamboo.
tsoo nruab To crush bamboo flat.
tsuav nruab To split and flatten bamboo for weaving into walls and floors, etc.

3. nruab
nruab xaub A type of trap for game. A pit is prepared on a game trail and set with sharpened bamboo spears. It is then covered with a split bamboo covering and earth so that an animal will fall into the pit unawares.

nruag T.c. from 'nruas' (cf. 'nruas').

1. nruam To reap with a small curved instrument called a 'vuv' held in the palm of the hand.
nruam nplej To reap rice in this way.
nruam noob yeeb To reap opium seed in this way.

2. nruam To omit, to skip over, to leave out.
Txhob nruam ib hnub. Don't skip a day.
Txhob nruam ib yam li. Don't omit any.

nruas A drum or a gong. (lub)
ntaus nruas To beat a drum or gong.
nruas tuag A death drum, drum beaten at death.
nruas neeb A gong used in spirit rites.
qws nruas Drumstick, stick to beat a gong (tus).
tsa qeej nruag (t.c.) To begin playing the pipes and beating the drum at a funeral.

nruav Txhob nruav. Don't mention it. (or it might happen!)

1. nrwb To seek after, to hunt.
mus nrwb nqaij To go hunting.
mus nrwb tub sab To hunt for thieves.
mus nrwb hluas nkauj To seek after young ladies.

2. nrwb Used with 'nraim' as a two word post verbal intensifier (cf. Appendix 8, p. 469).
   ua nrwb nraim To do perfectly according to pattern.
   ncaj nrwb nraim Perfectly straight.

nrwg Slack (of rope, etc.) (cf. 'taug').

nrws To bore, to make a hole in a tube, etc.
   nrws pobntseg To pick the ear, to clean the ear.

NRH

nrha maj mam nrha To go about slowly (as in endeavoring to care for oneself when ill and with no other help).

nrhab Bur (lub), prickly seed pods that cling to clothing.
   lo lo nrhab Burs clinging to clothing.
   plhws nrhab To brush off the burs.

nrhav A species of thorny tree (tus).

1. nrhau The ribs in an umbrella (tus).
   tus nrhau kaus Umbrella rib.

2. nrhau The upright ribs around which the lengths of bamboo or rattan are woven in basket making.
   nrhau kawm (tus) The ribs of a basket.

3. nrhau To put forth roots (not as common as 'hlav').
   (a) hlav cag To put forth roots.
   (b) nrhau cag To put forth roots.

nrhawj Restricted post verbal intensifier (cf. Appendix 8).
   tu nrov nrhawj Sound of a strand of rope breaking.
   tu nrov nrhij nrhawj Sound of several strands of rope tearing (cf. 'nrov').

nrhawv Restricted post verbal intensifier used with 'nrhuj' (cf. 'nrhuj' Also cf. Appendix 8).

nrheev Restricted post verbal intensifier (cf. Appendix 8).
   sawv nrheev To stand straight up (cf. 'ntsug').
   sawv nrhuj nrheev To stand up with difficulty, to stand slowly (as of an infant just learning to walk).

nrhij Restricted post verbal intensifier with 'nrhawj.' (cf. 'nrhawj').

nrhiav To seek, to search for.
   Koj mus nrhiav ib lub pobzeb loj loj. Go and look for a large stone.

nrho Restricted post verbal intensifier (cf. Appendix 8).
   Note: This word adds the idea of completed or finished action.
   tagnrho Ended, final, completely.
   zoo tagnrho Completely good, best quality.
   tu nrho Parted in two, broken.
   tu siav nrho To die.
   tu siab nrho Highly offended.
   txhua nrho All, completely.
   txij nrho Reaching to.
   de nrho Peeled off.
   hais lus nrho nrhuj nrhawv Slow of speech (cf. 'taj').

nrhoob Leggings, puttee, leg wrappings (clf. 'txhais').
   rau nrhoob To put on leg wrappings.

nrhuj A restricted post verbal intensifier used in connection with other intensifiers. (cf. Appendix 8).
   sawv nrhuj nrheev (cf. 'nrheev').
   (a) hais lus nrhuj nrhawv Slow of speech (cf. 'taj').
   (b) hais lus nrho nrhuj nrhawv Slow of speech (cf. 'taj').

1. nta To pull a bow, to set a spring or a trigger.
   nta hneev To pull back a crossbow for firing, the crosspiece of a crossbow.
   nta npuj (cf. 'npuj').
   nta faiv fuaj kom cig. Light the Flashlight.

2. nta Middle toe or finger (cf. 'ntav').
   ntiv taw nta Middle toe.
   ntiv tes nta Middle finger.

3. nta T.c. from 'ntav' (cf. 'ntav').

4. pab nta To help.

5. nta Post verbal intensifier after 'nrov' (cf. 'nrov')
   phom nrov nta vos The sound of a gun firing.

1. ntab To float.
   ntab saum nplaim dej To float on the water.

2. ntab A species of bee (tus) (cf. 'muv').

3. ntab The loose fold of skin hanging below the neck of Brahman cattle (daim).
   nyuj ntab Fold of skin on cattle as above.

4. ntab To glance off, to ricochet.
   cua ntab saud lawm The wind sweeps over above.

5. ntab
   khuam ntab khuam ntuv Betwixt and between (cf. 'khuam').

1. ntag Used either as a single word or more commonly in the combination '...li ntag' as an unrestricted post verbal intensifier. (cf. Appendix 8).
   Tsis muaj li ntag. (I) haven't any at all.
   Yog ntag! Yes, indeed!
   Tsis txawj dim li ntag. No escape!

2. ntag
   hlwb ntag ruam Mentally dull.

1. ntaj A sword (rab).
   hniav ntaj The edge of the sword.
   ntsis ntaj The point of the sword.
   kev ntsis ntaj ntsis phom Death by violence.
   rab ntaj dab Short wooden swords strung over the door as protection against spirits.

2. ntaj Clf. for strokes with a sword.
   ib ntag One stroke with the sword (t.c.)

1. ntas Ripples, small waves, to make ripples (contr. 'twv').
   dej ntas The water is making small waves.

2. ntas A carrying pole, shoulder pole (tus).
   kwv ntas To carry with a shoulder pole.
   ib tug ntas kwv dej (t.c.) Pole for carrying water.

3. ntas
   suav kwv ntas The constellation Orion.

ntav One half of a vertical measurement (contr. 'nrab').
   (a) ib nta (t.c.) One half (vertical).
   (b) ib nyuag (t.c.) ntav One half (vertical).
   ib nta ntuj One half of the heavens, one strata of heaven, in the midst of the heavens.

1. ntais To break a piece off, broken off (cf. 'khis').
   ntais hniav Tooth broken off.
   ntais rhe Broken.
   ntais pobkws To pick corn, break off corn ears.
   Rab riam ntais lawm. The knife edge is broken.
   lub siab ntais rhe Broken "heart."

2. ntais A cigarette lighter (lub).
   yaj hauv tooj A cigarette lighter.
   zeb ntais Lighter flint.

3. ntais Restricted post verbal intensifier (cf. Appendix 8).
   (a) ploj ntais Disappeared.
   (b) ploj muag ntais Disappeared.
   fos ntais Covered up.
   tsaus ntuj ntais Nightfall, darkness.
   dua ntais Much better.
   Note: The word 'dua' (passing, surpassing) is used after a verb to express the comparative degree. (cf. 'dua') The addition of 'ntais' intensifies the comparison ("much better") and the two words are often used together in the manner of a two word post verbal intensifier. Thus:
   zoo dua ntais Much better than.
   loj dua ntais Much larger than.

1. ntaiv Extremely hot (cf. 'kub').
   (a) kub ntaiv ntaiv li Extremely hot.
   (b) ntaiv qos hwv Extremely hot.

2. ntaiv A ladder (tus).
   taw ntaiv Steps of a ladder.

ntau Many, much.
   Nws muaj nyiaj muaj kub ntau ntau. He has lots of silver and gold.

ntaub   Cloth (clf. 'daim' for lengths).
ntsuas ntaub To measure cloth.
ntaub tsuj ntaub npuag Expensive cloth, fine cloth.
ntaub kaum A type of durable black cotton cloth.
paj ntaub Embroidery.
ib chaws ntaub One weaving of cloth, one full length
    in the loom.

ntaub koov nyij A type of fine black cloth.
hlab ntaub The strip of embroidered cloth worn on
    the turban (txoj).

1. ntaug To pound or stamp with fist or foot.
ntaug taw To stamp the feet.

2. ntaug To decrease in intensity.
ntaug nphaws lawm To decrease in intensity (of
    illness, storm, fire, etc.)

1. ntaus To strike, to beat, to hit, to thresh, to fight.
    (cf. 'phob,' 'xa,' 'peg').
sib ntaus To fight together, to fight.
ntaus ntxhias Suddenly hit.
ntaus yeej To win a fight.
ntaus nruas To beat a drum or a gong.
ntaus nplej To thresh rice.
ntaus nrig To hit with the fist.

2. ntaus To imprint, to mark.
ntaus cim To make a mark of identification or to aid
    memory (cf. 'thuam yeem').
(a) ntaus taub teg To make a fingerprint.
(b) thuam yeem tes To make a fingerprint.
ntaus yeem To stamp or mark with a seal.
ntaus hom thawj To make a mark of identification,
    in spirit rites to make some mark as a bit
    of extra cloth sewn on the back of a jacket
    to show who is included in the rite.

3. ntaus To convey.
(a) ntaus xov To convey a message.
(b) ntaus ib kab xov To convey a message.
hais lus ntaus xov To convey a verbal message.
ntaus xov mus To send a message.

4. ntaus To play an instrument by striking or plucking.
ntaus hwvcheej To play a guitar or dulcimer.

5. ntaus To draw from a well.
ntaus dej To draw water from a well.

6. ntaus
cov ntaus thawj The elders, the leaders, respected
    persons.

7. ntaus
ntaus yeeb To roll the opium in preparation for smoking.

8. ntaus
siab ntaus yau Pessimistic, looking for the worst.
siab ntaus yau ntshai Timid and afraid.

ntauv
(a) dej ntem ntauv Lukewarm water.
(b) dej sov so Lukewarm water.
sov ntem ntauv Lukewarm.

ntawd (t.c. from 'ntawm')   (cf. 'ntawm' also Introduction
    pp. xxii-xxiii).

1. ntawg To divine concerning the dead.
ntawg rau tus tuag To divine whether the spirit of
    the deceased is ready to take his leave or not.
ntaus txhib ntawg To make small sharpened bamboo
    horns which are used to divine concerning the
    deceased.

2. ntawg
nroo ntawg Of a deadfall trap falling.

ntawm A noun of location indicating nearby, location nearby,
    or location at a particular time, place, person,
    or thing nearby; there, that way, that time,
    that person, etc. (cf. 'no') (For t.c. cf.
    Introduction pp. xxii-xxiii).
Used by itself it indicates location near the speaker.
Nws nyob ntawd. (t.c.) He is there nearby.
Nyob ntawd. (t.c.) There.
Followed by a noun it signifies location at the place
    indicated.
ntawm lub tsev At the house.
ntawm lub tsev no At this house.
ntawm phab ntsa At the wall, on the wall.
ntawm no Here, at this location.
Used with verbs it identifies the movement as to or
    from the person, place, or object indicated.
Tuaj ntawm kuv. Come to me.
Mus ntawm tsev. Go to the house.
ntawm tsev mus Go from the house...
ntawm qhov no mus tsev Go from here to the house.
Used following a noun or a word indicating time it
    serves to particularize the time, person,
    place or thing upon which attention is focused.
ob tug ntawd (t.c.) Those two persons.
ob hnub ntawd (t.c.) Those two days; those days.
hnub ntawd (t.c.) That day.
thaum ntawd (t.c.) At that time, then.

ntem (cf. 'ntauv').

ntes To catch, to catch hold of something pursued.
    ntes qaib ntes npua To catch chickens and pigs.

ntev Long, lengthy (of time, objects, life, patience, etc.)
    txoj hlua ntev ntev A long rope.
    Qhov ntev Length.
    Qhov ntev yog li cas? What is the length?
    lub siab ntev Patience.
    tos ntev ntev li Waited a long time.

ntees Funeral rites, death ceremonies (lub) (cf. 'tuag')
    ntees ploj ntees tuag To hold funeral rites.
    lub ntees tuag Funeral rites, pertaining to the
        time when all are gathered at a funeral.

1. nti To writhe, to wriggle, toss to and fro as in sleep
    or delirium (cf. 'phov', 'da').
    ntses nti nplhib nplhob The fish wriggled.

2. nti To chip, splinter off in layers, pry off a thin layer.
    Txhob muab kiav txhab nti. Don't peel off the scab.

3. nti To get rid of from the mouth, to spit something
    out (but not forcibly) (cf. 'nto').
    Nti pov tseg. Spit it out.

4. nti Restricted post verbal intensifier. (cf. Appendix 8).
    ntuj tsaus nti Darkened sky.
    pos huab nti Surrounded by clouds.

ntig (t.c.) (cf. 'ntim').

1. ntim Small Chinese style rice bowl (lub).
    ib lub ntim One rice bowl.
    ib ntig mov (t.c.) One bowl of rice.

2. ntim To pour or place inside of something else.
    Muab ntim hauv lub phav. Put it into the can.

ntis To ward off, to protect from (cf. 'tiv').
    nits nag ntis cua To protect from wind and rain.

1. ntiv Digit, a finger or toe (tus).
    ntiv tes Finger.
    ntiv taw Toe.

2. ntiv To snap or flick with the finger.
    ntiv ya To flick something away with the finger.

3. ntiv Finger-like.
    ntiv roj hmab A slingshot.
    ntiv ncej The forked stick for a slingshot.
    ntiv qeej The bamboo pipes in a set of Hmong pipes.
        (cf. 'qeej').

Txij thaum ntawd los txog hnub no... From that time
    until today.
    tus ntawd (t.c.) That person.
    qhov ntawd (t.c.) That place.
    tamsim ntawd (t.c.) Immediately at that time.
    The expression '...li ntawd' is used to indicate "in
    that way" following verbs.
    ua li ntawd In that way.
    hais li ntawd Saying it that way.
    Yog li ntawd. That's the way it is.

ntaws
    (a) pij ntaws (lub) Umbilicus, the navel (cf.
      'ntawv').
    (b) lub ntaws Umbilicus, the navel (cf. 'ntawv').

1. ntawv Paper (clf. 'daim' for sheets), book (clf.
    'phau'), letter (clf. 'tsab').
    sau ntawv To write.
    txiaj ntawv Paper money.
    txaug ntawv To pierce paper with a rounded chisel
      for use as spirit money in spirit rites.
    hlawv ntawv To burn paper money in spirit rites.
    sau ib tsab ntawv To write a letter.
    ntawv fajlem (cf. 'faj').
    thav ntawv Frame for making paper.
    nruab ntaw (t.c.) In books, on paper.
    txawj ntawv Literate, able to read and write.
    nws ntawv tes His writings.
    nyeem ntawv To read.

2. ntawv
    txoj hlab ntawv The umbilical cord (cf. 'ntaws').

nte To get warm by a fire.
    nte taws To get warm by a fire, be near a fire.

1. nteg To lay eggs.
    Qaib nteg qe. The chicken has laid an egg. Chickens
    lay eggs.

2. nteg
    hnub rooj nteg thaum ub Previously, before, long ago.

ntej Before in time or location, previous, ahead.
    us ntej mus To precede, to go ahead.
    Koj ua ntej. You go first. You go ahead.
    noj ua ntej To eat ahead, eat first.
    nram ntej Previously, the period up till now.
    nram ntej nram ntxov Previously, earlier.
    huas ntej To go around and ahead of another.

ntiab To drive away, to drive out.
Ntiab tus dev kom khiav. Drive the dog away.

1. ntiag The front surface, the presence of, bosom (lub).
   xubntiag (lub) The bosom, the presence of.
   pw hauv xubntiag Reclined on his or her bosom.
   ntiag tsho Front panel of a jacket.
   ib ntiag ntuj The whole heaven and earth.
   sab ntiag The front surface (as of a book) (contr. 'nraum').

2. ntiag Restricted post verbal intensifier (cf. Appendix 8).
   nias ntiag To press down completely.
   huas ntej ntiag To pass around in front of.

ntiaj
   ntiajteb (lub) The earth.
   ntiajteb qaum ntuj The heavens and the earth.
   (cf. 'ntiag,' 'ib ntiag ntuj').

1. ntias Used as a single word restricted post verbal
   intensifier (cf. Appendix 8).
   pub ntias Filled.
   (a) ua ntias Cast away, cast aside.
   (b) laim ntais Cast away, cast aside.

2. ntias Used as a two word restricted post verbal intensifier
   with 'nplawg,' (cf. 'nplawg').

1. ntiav To hire.
   ntiav ua zog To hire for manual labor.
   (a) pojniam ntiav (tus) A prostitute.
   (b) nkauj muag paj (tus) A prostitute.

2. ntiav Shallow.
   dej ntiav Shallow water.

1. nto To spit out forcibly (contr. 'nti') To spit at.
   nto qaub ncaug To spit, to spit out spittle.

2. nto To reach to, arrive at a point, to extend to.
   nto roob To reach the mountain top.
   nto ncov roob To reach the mountain peak.
   nto laj Reach the mountain crest, cross the ridge.
   ua tsis nto Hasn't reached full development (as
     of an illness that has not yet shown the full
     symptoms).
   nto ntsis To the tip, to the end, to completion.
   Ua kom nto ntsis. Complete the job.
   Hais kom nto ntsis. Finish the disucssion.
   nto luag To complete.
   Ua teb kom nto luag. Finish the field work.

3. nto To send or receive news, report or fame and reputation.
   npe nto moo Of great reputation, name spread abroad.
   moo nto tuaj News has been received.
   nto moo tias... Have heard news that...
   nto moo phem Has a bad name or reputation, have
     received bad news.

ntob To hit the mark (cf. 'raug').

1. ntog To stumble and fall, to fall down.
   ntog nrov nphoov Fell down with a resounding fall.
   ntog nreem Stumbled and fell.

2. ntog To roll over and over, roll along (cf. 'dov').
   Kuv thawb ntog. I pushed it and set it rolling.
   Nws ntog nws. It rolls along by itself.

3. ntog Used after 'pw' similar to a post verbal intensifier.
   pw ntog To lie prostrate.

4. ntog
   hais lus ntog nraws (cf. 'nraws').

ntoj To pulsate (as of blood in the veins, etc.)

1. ntom To fit close together, tight fitting.
   ntom ntom li Fitting close together (as boards in a
     wall, etc.)
   kho ntom ntom To fix so it fits well.

2. ntom
   ntom kab (cf. 'pobkws').

1. ntos The loom, weaving machine (lub). (cf. 'ntuag,'
     'seb,' 'ntxaiv,' 'xov')
   ua ntos To weave on the loom.
   ua ntos nthuj nthav The noise of working the loom.
   ncej ntos The upright frame of the loom.
   ntos ib tog tuaj To weave one roll of cloth.

2. ntos To think of, call to mind (cf. 'xav,' 'nco').
   (a) ntos tsis txog Can't think of it, cannot recall.
   (b) xav tsis txog Can't think of it, cannot recall.
   ntos tsis txhua Didn't think through completely.

1. ntov To chop down, to fell.
   ntov ntoo To cut down a tree or trees.
   (a) ntov pheej tsab To cut a tree from both
     sides until it falls.
   (b) ntov txo ntswg To fell a leaning tree
     by cutting one side till it splits off.
   ntov ib cim ntoo (cf. 'cim').
   ntov qees To keep on felling trees.

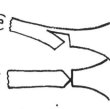
(a)   (b)

2. ntov To throw (water or liquid).
   ntov dej To throw water.
   Muab dej ntov hluavtaws. Throw water on the fire.
      Quench the fire.
   dab ntov ntshav The spirits sealing someone's fate
      by sprinkling blood upon him. This is said
      in superstition if blood is discovered on a
      person's clothing without explanation.

1. ntoo Tree (tus), wood.
   ces ntoo Branches.
   cag ntoo Roots.
   cev ntoo (lub) Trunk of a standing tree.
   cav A fallen log.
   tawv ntoo Bark.
   pob ntoos (t.c.) (lub) Tree stump, stump of a
      fallen tree.
   paj ntoos (t.c.) Flowers.
   nplooj ntoos (t.c.) Leaves.
   hauvpaus ntoo The base of a standing tree, or the
      stump of a fallen tree.
   qab ntoos (t.c.) At the foot of the tree.
   lub hleb ntoos (t.c.) A coffin.
   tus kws ntoo A carpenter.
   phua ntoo To split logs.
   txiag ntoo (daim) Boards.
   tws ntoo To smooth wood with an axe or knife.
   tshav ntoo To plane wood.
   ntsis ntoo The crown of a tree, ends of branches.
   duas ntoo Notch made in felling a tree (lub).
   nplaim ntoo Wood chips.
   Note: There are many names for the great variety of
      trees. We list a few.
   ntoo peeb lab The Areca palm.
   qheb A species of hard durable wood similar to
      oak. There are several sub-species.
   ntoo qhuav plawv A durable tree with red heart wood.
   ntoo daj tawv A large tree with yellow wood below
      the bark.
   ntoo kuj yem The fan palm whose leaves are used for
      roofing.
   ntoo nplooj hlis A species of hard wood used for
      handles, etc.
   ntoo tawv ntxhw A tree with a tough rough bark.
   ntoo toov laj A type of palm with long fronds.
   ntoo txiv roj Olive tree (tree with fruit producing
      oil, an adopted term).
   ntooj (cf. 'ntooj') Kind of tree.

2. ntoo To wear on the head, to carry on the head, to carry
   overhead as an umbrella.
   ntoo kaumom To wear a hat.

ntoog
   ntoog ntoog mob Long illness with no relief, to let
      the illness run its course.

ntooj A species of large tree, the bark is coarse and the
   wood is very suitable for use in making water
   buckets (tus).

ntoos T.c. from 'ntoo' (cf. 'ntoo').

1. ntu A period of time, a period of a few months (cf.
      'yav').
   ntu no This period of time.
   ib ntus One period of time (t.c.)

2. ntu Clf. for lengths or sections of road, lengths of
      train, stripes or bands of cloth or of color, etc.
   ib ntus tsheb One long section of train (t.c.)
   ib ntus kev One section of road (cf. 'tawm').

1. ntub Wet, to be wet, soaked.
   ntub nag Wet with rain.
   ntub nag npliag nplaws Soaking wet with rain.
   ntub ntub dej Wet with water.

2. ntub To sleep, to doze (cf. 'pw,' 'tsaug zog').
   ua dab ntub To sleep.
   qaug dab ntub To doze.
   ncaws ncaws dab ntub To doze, nod the head in sleep.
   ntub ntsiag zog To be really asleep.
   Nws pw ib hmos tsis tuaj ib tug dab ntub. He lay down
      all night but didn't sleep a wink.

1. ntug The light of day, bright day, morning (in the sense
      when daylight appears) (cf. 'ntuj').
   kaj ntug The light of day, morning, tomorrow morning.
   kaj ntug no This morning.
   kaj ntug txoog Early dawn.
   (a) kaj ntug plaws Daybreak.
   (b) kaj ntug huv Daybreak.

2. ntug The edge, the shore, the bank of a river or stream
      (lub).
   ntug dej The shore.
   ntug hav The level banks of a stream or river.

3. ntug T.c. from 'ntuj' (cf. 'ntuj')

4. ntug To grow, to enlarge (of tubers and roots only).

5. ntug
   kev plaub kev ntug Litigation and cases of dispute.

1. ntuj The sky, the heavens (lub).
   hmo ntuj Night (contr. 'nruab hnub').
   tsaus ntuj Darkness (contr. 'kaj ntug').
   qab ntug liab ploog Sunset.
   ib lub qab ntuj Everything under the heavens.
   plaub ceg ntuj Every direction, the four directions.
   hauv ntuj West.
   qab ntuj East.
   tav ntuj North and south.
   lub caij ntuj A season (cf. 'caij').
   ntuj ntawg This region.
   ntuj nraus The distant region, 'regions beyond'
        (cf. 'nraus').
   ntuj los nag To rain, raining.
   ib ntiag ntuj The whole heaven and earth.
   lub qaum ntuj The high heavens.
   ib nta ntuj (cf. 'ntav') (t.c.)
   ntiajteb qaum ntuj Heaven and earth.
   ntuj qeg Earthquake.
   (a) ib roog ntuj A far country, a far distant place.
   (b) ib ntxees ntuj A far country, a far distant
        place.
   (a) hauv ntuj ntsa The first light of dawn.
   (b) hauv ntuj ntsa iab The first light of dawn.

2. ntuj Clf. for something of vast expanse as the heavens.
   ib ntuj hluavtaws A great expanse of fire.
   ntuj tawg An expanse of fire, "hell."

ntus T.c. from 'ntu' (cf. 'ntu').

1. ntuv
   nyob plim pliaj ntuv (cf. 'plim').

2. ntuv
   khuam ntuv (cf. 'khuam').

ntua Restricted post verbal intensifier (cf. Appendix 8).
   Note: This intensive adds the idea of immediacy to the
        action of the verb.
   zaum ntua To sit down.
   los txog ntua Just came, just arrived, just returned.
   daj ntua tuaj Came straight to.
   Nws txhos ntua ntawm nws xubntiag. He stuck it in the
        ground right at his feet.

1. ntuag To tear, to be torn (as of cloth, etc.)
   (a) ntuag lawm Torn apart.
   (b) ntuag rhe lawm Torn apart.

2. ntuag Hemp thread (cf. 'maj').
   saws ntuag To twist hemp thread.
   tshuab ntuag A spinning wheel, to spin hemp thread.
   tis ntuag Stick fixed with a handle in the middle
        so that thread can be wound around both ends
        in a figure eight.

1. ntuas To exhort, to rebuke (especially as of one person
        to another face to face).

2. ntuas To speak or chant at great length in doing spirit
        worship.

ntuav To vomit, to throw up.
   tshuaj ntuav An emetic.

1. ntwg Clf. for things carried on a string, etc.
   ib ntwg nqaij A portion of meat carried on a string
        or on the end of a piece of split bamboo or
        rattan.

2. ntwg A restricted post verbal intensifier after 'nrov'
        (cf. 'nrov').

ntwj
   qhov ntwj (lub) A hole in the ground where the earth
        is sunken in of itself (cf. 'saus').

1. ntws To flow.
   Dej ntws nram hav The water flows down the valley.
   ntshav ntws nto Blood flowing out.

2. ntws Restricted post verbal intensifier after 'nrov'
        (cf. 'nrov').
   'nrov ntws,' 'nrov nroo ntws,' 'nrov ntxhe hav ntws'
        cf. 'nrov'

3. ntws Restricted post verbal intensifier as a single word.
   ncha ntws To spread abroad.
   poog ntws To gather together in a group.

NTH

ntha A person's waist, the soft flesh in a person's side below the ribs.

nthab The large storage platform overhead in a Meo home (lub).
Muab rau saum nthab. Put it on the storage platform.
lub qab nthab The smaller storage shelf immediately over the fire (cf. 'tsuav ntxaij').

1. **nthav** Restricted post verbal intensifier (cf. Appendix 8)
   (a) poob nthav To fall down.
   (b) poob kiag To fall down.
   siab poob nthav To be fearful, startled, suddenly afraid, distressed or discouraged (cf. 'ntshai zog').

2. **nthav** Restricted post verbal intensifier after 'nrov' (cf. nrov').

nthaw To sprout from the ground.
Ntsuag xyoob nthaw kaus. The bamboo sprout has appeared.

nthaws Restricted post verbal intensifier (cf. Appendix 8).
rog nthaws Very fat (of animals).

nthe To cry out loudly, to shout at someone or something.
nthe nthe nrov nrov To shout loudly.
nthe 'tawg ntho Suddenly yelled.
nthe 'sib nqhug nthe sib nqhos To cry out very loudly.

nthee To toss or mix together and fry in fat, to scramble.
nthee qe Scrambled eggs.
ncuav nthee roj Cakes made by scrambling with fat.

1. **nthi** A single word restricted post verbal intensifier (cf. Appendix 8).
   tuaj nthi Completely, to the greatest degree.
   tuag nthi Finalized, really dead.
   tsuj nthi To step on, to tread under foot.
   pw nthi To lie down.
   ploj nthi To disappear (cf. 'ploj ntais').
   tsuj nthi ntawm taw tseg To put under foot, to put a matter completely aside.
   nyiam tuaj nthi To greatly love.
   siab tuag nthi Well satisfied with.
   hais tuag nthi Finished discussing, settled.

2. **nthi** Used as a two word restricted post verbal intensifier with 'ncha' (cf. 'ncha nthi').

1. **ntho** Single word restricted post verbal intensifier (cf. Appendix 8).
   lov ntho To break in two, broken.
   ti ntho Very close together.
   tawg ntho Burst, burst open.

2. **ntho** Used with 'tawg' as a two word restricted post verbal intensifier.
   nthe tawg ntho (cf. 'nthe').
   luag tawg ntho Broke into laughter.
   quaj tawg ntho Broke out into weeping.
   nyiav tawg ntho Broke into wailing.
   cem tawg ntho Suddenly began scolding.
   Note: Also so used with the following verbs: 'hawv,' 'nrov,' 'qw.'

nthos To grasp with two hands (cf. 'muab,' 'ntsiab,' 'tsawv').
   nthos nkaus Grasp with the two hands.
   Nthos tus ntses. Grab the fish.

nthuj Restricted post verbal intensifier with 'nrov' (cf. 'nrov.').

nthua To hoe out, to dig out.
   nthua nroj To hoe out weeds.
   nthua yeeb To hoe opium fields.

nthuav To unfold, to open out as a book, to unroll.
   muab lub siab nthuav ntxeev To "open" one's heart.

nthw T.c. from 'nthwv' (cf. 'nthwv').

nthwb Restricted post verbal intensifier (cf. Appendix 8).
   lwj nthwb Rotten and mushy.

1. **nthwv** Clf. for gusts of wind.
   ib nthw cua (t.c.) One gust of wind.

2. **nthwv** Restricted post verbal intensifier (cf. Appendix 8).
   Muab hliv nthwv Pour it out.
   Dej nchuav nthwv. The water has spilled.

NTS

1. ntsa Wall.
   (a) phab ntsa Wall, side wall, house wall.
   (b) ntsa Wall, side wall, house wall.
   Muab dai ntawm phab ntsa. Hang it on the wall.
   sab ntsa vaj nraud Outside the garden wall.

2. ntsa Shining, to shine.
   (a) hauv ntuj ntsa ntsa The first light of dawn on the horizon.
   (b) hauv ntuj ntsa iab The first light of dawn on the horizon.

3. ntsa Used as restricted post verbal intensifier with 'iab'
   hauv ntuj ntsa iab The first light of dawn on the horizon.
   ci ntsa iab Bright and glittering.

ntsab To kill to eat.

1. ntsag The buttocks (cf. 'caj tw').

2. ntsag Obstinate.
   ncab dua ntsag Obstinate.

1. ntsaj To groan, to moan.
   mob ntsaj ntsaj li. Groaning in pain.
   qw qw ntsaj ntsaj To cry and groan.

2. ntsaj A type of small portable fish trap.
   ntsaj ntseg Small portable fish trap (t.c.).

ntsaig To gather things up in order to put them away. (as in clearing up after a meal or clear a table of books, etc.)
   Muab ntsaig cia. Put things away.

1. ntsais Side, sidewise, profile.
   pw ua ntsais To lie on one's side.
   ib lub ua ntsais A triangle.
   thais ua ntsais To take a profile photo, take a side view.
   ua ntsais ntaub To sew in a triangular pattern.

2. ntsais To blink the eyes.
   ntsais muag To blink.
   ib ntsais muag In the twinkling of an eye, one blink.

1. ntsau To be foggy or cloudly.
   huab ntsau tsawv Steady fog or cloudiness (contr. 'pos pos huab' which may be just passing cloudiness).

2. ntsau T.c. from 'ntsauv'

3. ntsau Of a cock's comb which is spread out somewhat (cf. 'ib').
   qaib ib ntsau Cock's comb spread out.

1. ntsaub To put the sticks of a fire close together at the burning end so as to build up the fire.
   ntsaub taws To put the sticks of a fire close together at the burning end so as to build up the fire.
   (a) sib ntsaub As sticks of wood together in a fire, i.e. dwelling together in casual relationship.
   (b) sis ntsaub As sticks of wood together in a fire, i.e. dwelling together in casual relationship.

2. ntsaub
   taubhau ntsaub hau ntsees Head lower than the body.

ntsaum Ants, the ant (tus).

1. ntsauv Of bees buzzing or swaming, to cluster or swarm around.
   Huab ntsauv lub roob. The clouds surround the mountain.

2. ntsauv Clf. for stems of flowers.
   ntsauv paj no This stem of flowers.
   ib ntsau paj One stem of flowers (t.c.)

ntsawj Spray, to spray.
   dej ntsawj Water rising in spray.
   pa ntsawj Steam rising.
   Cua ntsawj dej ntas. The wind blew the water into waves and spray.

ntsawm To strike out forcibly with the hand or arm (as in anger or when under spirit influence, etc.)
   ib ntsawg One thrust with the arm (t.c.)

ntsaws To stop up, to plug up, plugged, stuck.
   ntsaws qhov ntsej To stop up the ears.
   Nalika ntsaws lawm. The watch has stopped and won't go.

ntsawv To multiply by division of the roots, of trees and plants that increase in this way.

1. ntse Sharp (contr. 'npub').
   riam ntse hau A sharp pointed knife (contr. 'tw').
   Muab rab riam hov kom ntse. Sharpen the knife.

2. ntse Clever.
   neeg ntse A clever person.
   neeg ntse ntxeev A person who is overly clever, clever and deceitful.

ntseb Used with 'ntsuag' as a two word restricted post verbal intensifier. (cf. Appendix 8, cf. 'ntsuag').

1. ntseg Erect, vertical, steep (of a roof).
sawv ntseg Stand erect, stand upright.
hnub ntseg Noon, the sun directly overhead.

2. ntseg T.c. from 'ntsej' and 'ntses' (cf. 'ntsej' and 'ntses').

3. ntseg Fixed, steady.
qhov muag ntseg ntsos Fixed stare, eyes vacant.
caj dab ntseg ntsos Stiff neck, neck fixed and steady.

1. ntsej The ear, pertaining to the ear.
pobntseg The outer ear (lub) (t.c.)
qhov ntsej The ear canal (lub).
taug taug ntsej Hurts the ears (as a loud noise).
taub ntseg The ear lobe (lub) (t.c.).
qhws ntseg Type of long elaborate ear ring (lub).
mob ntsej rag Earache, ear hurts without apparent reason.
tsis quav ntsej Doesn't listen, pays no attention.
tsis to ntsej Can't understand (doesn't enter my ear).

2. ntsej Pertaining to the face (cf. 'muag')
ntsej muag The face (lub).
pom ntsej pom muag To see the face, to see someone face to face.

ntses Fish (tus).
muab ntses To catch fish.
nuv ntses To catch fish with a hook, fish hook.
vas ntses A fishnet (lub).
lub puav ntses Fishnet (as said in Laos).
yawm ntses To scoop up fish with a basket.
tawb cuab ntses A woven fish trap similar to a basket (lub).
ntsaj ntses A type of small portable fish trap (lub).
ntses nab An eel (tus).
roj ntses Fish oil, also the name used for a candle from the mistaken idea that it is made of fish oil (tus).

ntsev Salt.
las ntsev To put something down in salt, to salt.
daw daw ntsev Very salty (contr. 'tsuag').
qab qab ntsev Tasty with salt, salty.

ntseeb A small species of wasp. (tus) (cf. 'muv').

ntseeg To believe.
ntseeg kiag lawm Believed truly, really believed.
ntseeg tias... Believe that...
Kuv tsis ntseeg tias nws yuav los. I don't believe that he is coming.

ntseej The chestnut.
ntoo ntseej Chestnut tree (tus).
txiv ntseej Chestnuts (lub).

1. ntsees
tim ncauj ntsees tham To speak face to face.

2. ntsees Restricted post verbal intensifier (cf. Appendix 8).
taubhau ntsaub hau ntsees Head lower than the body.

3. ntsees Variant rendering of 'ntsoov' which is used as a restricted post verbal intensifier with 'ntsuj' (cf. 'ntsuj' and 'ntsoov').
(a) tos ntsuj ntsoov To wait.
(b) tos ntsuj ntsees To wait.
Also sometimes used as a variant spelling of the post verbal intensifier 'nrees' (cf. 'nrees').

ntsib To meet, to encounter.
sib ntsib Of two persons meeting each other.
ntsib kev ceeblaj To meet up with trouble.

ntsig T.c. from 'ntsim' (cf. 'ntsim').

1. ntsim Peppery, pungent, stinging.
Zaub ntsim ntsim li kuv tsis noj. I do not eat food heavily flavored with peppers.
zaub ntsig A kind of pickled peppery vegetable prepared from the tops of mustard greens (t.c.).
qab ntsig Any kind of caterpillar having hairs which sting on contact.
noj hob hob ntsim ntsim (cf. 'hob').

2. ntsim
(a) txiaj ntsim (lub) A gracious gift, a kind or gracious act, favor.
(b) txiaj ntsig (lub) A gracious gift, a kind or gracious act, favor.
pauj txiaj ntsim rau To make return for a favor.
txiaj ntsha txiaj ntsim A favor, gracious act.

3. ntsim Used as a restricted post verbal intensifier with 'nkaug'
niaj no nkaug ntsim Of persons cold and shivering.

ntsias Dwarfed, of persons very small in body frame.

ntsiav
  ntsiav pobkws Kernel of corn (maize) (lub).
  ib ntsia pobkws One kernel of corn (t.c.) (cf. 'ntsiab').

ntso Restricted post verbal intensifier (cf. Appendix 8).
  rau siab ntso To apply the heart steadily to.

ntsog T.c. from 'ntsoj' (cf. 'ntsoj').

ntsoj Pertaining to orphanhood (cf. 'ntsuag').
  kev ntsoj kev ntsuag Orphanhood, penury, destitution.
  tub ntsog tub ntsuag Orphans (tus) (t.c.)

1. ntsos Hiccough.
  ua ntsos To hiccough, hiccup.

2. ntsos Restricted post verbal intensifier (cf. Appendix 8)
  ntseg ntsos Fixed, steady.
  nrig nphau ntsos Rolled over onto the back.
  paj paws ntsos Jump, jump up.
  caws qia ntsos Jump, leap.
  dhia ntsos Jump, leap.
  sib zog ntsos Energetically, with vigor.
  ntshav txuas qos ntsos Blood spurting, hemorrhage.

ntsov The hump on the back of a Brahman bull (lub).

ntsoog Restricted post verbal intensifier with 'ntxaws.'
  tsoo tawg ntsoog ntxaws Crushed, smashed, rendered completely useless.

ntsooj
  nas ntsooj A kind of jungle rodent (tus).

ntsoos Weak, sickly.
  ntsoos ntsoos li Weak and sickly in body.
  qaib ntsoos A sickly chicken.

1. ntsoov Restricted post verbal intensifier (cf. Appendix 8)
  Note: This p.v.int. is frequently used with verbs of perception. It adds the idea of fixedness or steadiness. It may be used as a single word p.v.int. or preceded by 'qos' or 'qas' or in the combination 'ntsuj ntsoov'
  (a) nco qas ntsoov To remember well.
  (b) nco ntsoov To remember well.
  ntsia ntsoov To stare at.
  pom ntsoov To see well.
  paub ntsoov To know well.
  vam ntsoov To hope steadily.
  saib ntsoov To look at intently.

1. ntsis A moment, a little bit, a small amount.
  mentsis A little, a little bit.
  (a) ib ntsis In a moment, a moment, a very short time.
  (b) ib mentsis In a moment, a moment, a very short time.

2. ntsis To comb.
  ntsis plaubhau To comb the hair.

3. ntsis Tip, tendril, the growing tip of branches or vines (lub).
  ntsis ntaj Point of the sword.
  ntsis phom End of the gun barrel.
  kev ntsis ntaj ntsis phom Death by violence.
  ntsis kub End of a horn.
  ntsis plaubhau End of a strand of hair.
  ntsis hmuv End of a spear.
  ua nto ntsis To do to completion (for other uses of 'nto ntsis' cf. 'nto').

1. ntsia To nail, a nail (tus) (cf. 'teem').
  ntsia hlau A nail (lit. "iron nail") (tus).
  ntsia nrees To nail firmly.
  muab ntsia dai vias To hang up with a nail.
  muab ntsia saum ntoo To crucify.

2. ntsia To gaze at, to stare.
  Txhob ntsia ntsia kuv. Stop staring at me.
  ntsia ntsoov To stare at, to look steadily at.

3. ntsia T.c. from 'ntsiav' (cf. 'ntsiav').

1. ntsiab To grasp with the hand.
  ntsiab tes To grasp the hand of another.
  ntsiab nkaus To grasp, to grasp the arm. (cf. 'tsawv nkaus,' 'nthos nkaus').

2. ntsiab A kernel, the pupil of the eye, the heart or essence of a matter (lub).
  ntsiab muag The pupil of the eye (lub).
  lub ntsiab npleg A kernel of rice.
  phum lub ntsiab To give the essence of a matter, to get at the root of things.
  lus tseeb ntsiab True words, words that get to the heart of things.
  phum ntsiab Clearly stated (cf. 'meej').

ntsiag Still, quiet.
  ntsiag to Still, silent, perfectly quiet.
  Note: This idea is also extended to mean "ineffective" in the case of medicine, etc.
  ntub ntsiag zog Really asleep, asleep and quiet.

xyuas ntsoov To study intently.
(a) tos ntsoov To wait.
(b) tos ntsuj ntsoov To wait.
suav ntsoov hnub To count the days.

2. ntsoov To be fixed, remain steady.
taubhau ntsoov mus To go straight on, eyes fixed ahead.

1. ntsu To accumulate, to gradually pile up.
maj mam ntsu To pile up slowly (as snow or ashes).

2. ntsu
ntsu quav zaj Slippery mossy rock (lit. "dragon dung").

ntsub To strain in defecating.
ntsub ntsub li Hard to defecate, strain in relieving the bowel.

1. ntsug Vertical, also length as opposed to 'tav' of breadth when referring to the measurements of large flat things such as blankets, etc.
thoob ntsug A water bucket (lub), tall wooden bucket.

2. ntsug Restricted post verbal intensifier (cf. Appendix 8).
sawv ntsug To stand upright, stand erect (cf. 'nrheev').

1. ntsuj The human spirit or soul, spirit or soul (cf. 'plig' and contr. 'dab') (tus).
(a) tus ntsuj tus plig The soul, the spirit.
(b) tus ntsuj plig The soul, the spirit.
kab ntsuj (cf. 'kab').
Note: Both 'ntsuj' and 'plig' are used to refer to the soul or spirit and there is no apparent distinction. Some say there are as many as seven or twelve human "souls" but most Hmong regard man as having three:

(a) ntsuj duab The "shadow soul" that stands guard at the grave after death.
(b) plig duab The "shadow soul" that stands guard at the grave after death.
(c) ntsuj xyoob ntsuj ntoos The "shadow soul" that stands guard at the grave after death.
(a) ntsuj qaib The "chicken soul" that is reincarnated. This soul also takes flight most easily as when a person is frightened or falls and a chicken must be sacrificed to call it back.
(b) plig qaib The "chicken soul" that is reincarnated. This soul also takes flight most easily as when a person is frightened or falls and a chicken must be sacrificed to call it back.

(c) ntsuj noog The "chicken soul" that is reincarnated. This soul also takes flight most easily as when a person is frightened or falls, and a chicken must be sacrificed to call it back.
(a) ntsuj nyuj The "cow soul" that goes to 'yeeb yaj kiab', the abode of the dead.
(b) plig nyuj The "cow soul" that goes to 'yeeb yaj kiab' the abode of the dead.
(c) nyuj rag The "cow soul" that goes to 'yeeb yaj kiab' the abode of the dead.

2. ntsuj Clf. for portions of a field, tracts of land.
ib ntsuj teb One portion of field.

3. ntsuj Restricted post verbal intensifier (cf. Appendix 8).
khiav ntsuj Ran off, departed.
rov ntsuj Returned.

4. ntsuj Restricted post verbal intensifier used with 'ntsoov' or 'ntsees' (cf. 'ntsoov' and 'ntsees').

ntsum A given name for women.

ntsuv Restricted post verbal intensifier (cf. Appendix 8).
mob siab ntsuv Earnest, zealous, with dedication.
mob siab ntsuv ua To do with earnestness (cf. 'siab').
mob siab ntsuv qhia To teach with zeal and interest.

1. ntsua A measurement of distance.
ib ntsua muag kev One sight of road, the length of road one can see in one view.
ib ntsua muag ntuj The distance between one's eyes and the horizon.

2. ntsua Restricted post verbal intensifier (cf. Appendix 8).
mob siab ntsua In earnest, zealous (cf. 'siab').

ntsuab The color green, greenish blue, the color of vegetation.
(a) Hmoob ntsuab The Green Hmong or the Blue Hmong.
thaib ntsuab A soldier (tus) (as used by Hmong in Thailand).
ntsuab xiab Very blue.
Note: For colors see Appendix p. 484.
nws ntsuab ib sab qhov muag He had a black eye.

1. ntsuag A short sprout of bamboo or of a tree. (cf. 'kaus').
ntsuag xyoob Bamboo sprouts.

(a) phum ntsuav Wasted.
(b) phum lam ntsuav Wasted.
dag ntsuav Cheated, lied.
yaj ntsuav Melted away.
ua liam txwv qas ntsuav To do poorly, carelessly.

1. ntsw To taunt, to provoke.
Nws muab hluavtaws ntsw ntsw lawv. He poked a fire-
brand at them to taunt them.

2. ntsw To dip something into a liquid.
Muab ncuav ntsw ntsw suav thaj. Dip the rice cake
into some brown sugar syrup.

1. ntswg Nose, pertaining to the nose.
qhov ntswg (lub) The nose, nostril.
(a) caj ntswm The bridge of the nose.
(b) caj ntswg The bridge of the nose.
so ntswg To wipe the nose.
txhaws ntswg Stuffed up nose.
(a) taub ntswg The tip of the nose.
(b) txiv ntswg The tip of the nose.
kwv ntswg To turn the nose away in disgust.

2. ntswg T.c. from 'ntswj' (cf. 'ntswj').

3. ntswg
ntov txo ntswg (cf. 'ntov').

1. ntswj To twist, twisted, to wring (cf. 'xuab').
ntswj lees Very twisted.
sib ntswg To wrestle (t.c.) (cf. 'qhau').

2. ntswj Clf. for twists, clf. for strands in a twisted
rope.
Xuab hlua ua ob ntswg. (t.c.) Twist the rope into
two strands.

1. ntswm
neeb ntswm A kind of edible tree fungus.

2. ntswm
caj ntswm (cf. 'ntswg').

1. ntsws The lungs (clf. 'nplooj').
tas siab tas ntsws Patient.
Siab tsis qhuav dej, ntsws tsis qhuav ntshav. A
proverbial expression used of one who makes much
of a small matter and who refuses to let it go
at that.

2. ntsws To wither.
ntsws zog To wither.

2. ntsuag Without parents, without wife or husband, destitute,
orphaned or widowed (cf. 'ntsoj').
ua ntsuag lawm Left destitute, orphaned, abandoned.
menyuam ntsuag An orphan (tus).
tub ntsog tub ntsuag Orphans.
yawg ntsuag Widower (tus).
(a) poj ntsuag Widow (tus).
(b) poj ntsuam Widow (tus).
cov ntsuag nos Orphans.

3. ntsuag Restricted post verbal intensifier with 'ntseb'
los nag tshauv ntsuag ntseb A drizzling rain.

4. ntsuag
tsab ntsuag Hypocritical.
neeg tsab ntsuag Hypocrites (tus).
tsab ntsuag ua To pretend, put on a big show to
impress people.

5. ntsuag
ntsuag qaub A rhubard-like vegetable sour in taste.

ntsuam
(a) poj ntsuam A widow (tus) (cf. 'ntsuag').
(b) poj ntsuag A widow (tus) (cf. 'ntsuag').

1. ntsuas To measure, to measure cloth, measure a person's
worth, etc.
ntsuas ntaub ua tsho Measure cloth for a jacket.
ua ntsuas tu siab hwv Became very offended.

2. ntsuas The praying mantis (tus).

3. ntsuas To chew a little and then spit out.

4. ntsuas A kind of sweet edible stalk similar
quav ntsuas to sugar cane.

5. ntsuas
lub ntsuab phoo A lock.

1. ntsuav To meet, to converge.
sib ntsuav To converge, meet together as of two
mountains or ridges converging.

2. ntsuav Restricted post verbal intensifier (cf.
Appendix 8, p.473.
Note: This word may so be used alone or preceded
by 'qas' or 'qos'.
lwj ntsuav Putrid, decayed.
txab ntsuav Dirty, soiled.
qias ntsuav Dirty, disgusting.

NTSH

1. ntsha A spear or knife set up at a sharp angle in a
   trap so as to catch game.
   cuab ntsha To set such a trap.

2. ntsha
   txiaj ntsha txiaj ntsim (cf. 'ntsim').

ntshav Blood (cov).
   los ntshav To bleed.
   ntshav ntws nto Blood flowing freely, copious
     bleeding.
   ntshav tuag Congealed blood.
   ntshav txuas qos ntsos Spurting blood, hemorrhage.
   doog ntshav A blood clot under the skin.

ntshai To fear.
   kev ntshai Fear.
   cuab ntshai To begin to fear.
   ntshai zog To fear.
   ntshai tias... Fear that...
   siab ntaus yau ntshai Timid and afraid.

ntshaub A species of tree whose wood does not easily
   split or rot. It is valued for use in making
   water buckets. (tus)

1. ntshaus Weak, sickly (cf. 'ntshov').
   lub cev ntshaus ntshaus Body sickly and weak.
   ntshaus zog Weak.
   ntshaus raws Weakness in the knees resulting in
     stumbling and falling.
   ntsej muag ntshaus zog Face "fallen" as after a
     scolding or bad disappointment.

2. ntshaus Restricted post verbal intensifier with 'ntshiv'
   (cf. Appendix 8).
   to qhov ntshaus ntshiv Full of tiny holes.

ntshauv Head lice (tus) (cf. 'tuv').
   riab ntshauv Small head lice, lice just hatched.

ntshaw To covet, to long for what belongs to another
   person.

ntshawb
   caj pa ntshawb ntshawb li Choking, cannot get one's
     breath (especially when due to gas or odor,
     etc.).

ntshawv Restricted post verbal intensifier with 'ntsheeb.'
   (cf. Appendix 8).
   khiav ntshawv ntsheeb Running and jumping.

ntsheeb Restricted post verbal intensifier (cf. 'ntshawv').
   khiav ntshawv ntsheeb Running and jumping.

ntshis
   ib pliag ntshis An instant, in an instant.

1. ntshiv Lean, fleshy (contr. 'roj,' 'rog').
   nqaij ntshiv Lean fleshy meat (contr. 'nqaij rog').

2. ntshiv A splinter.
   ntshiv ntoo A wood splinter (tus).
   ntshiv xyoob A bamboo splinter (tus).

3. ntshiv
   paus ntshiv Of things pourous.
   nceb paus ntshiv A kind of large mushroom.

4. ntshiv Restricted post verbal intensifier with 'ntshaus'
   to qhov ntshaus ntshiv Full of tiny holes.

ntshiab Clear, fresh.
   dej ntshiab ntshiab Clear fresh water (contr. 'nro').
   siab ntshiab A clean clear heart, a transparent person.

ntshov Restricted post verbal intensifier (cf. Appendix 8).
   lub cev ntshaus ntshov Body weak and without strength.

1. ntshua Clf. for hanks of thread or for flowers that
     hang in strands.
   ntshua no This hank of thread.
   ib ntshuas xov One hank of thread (t.c.)

2. ntshua Restricted post verbal intensifier (cf. Appendix 8).
   to siab ntshua To understand.
   tsoo to ntshua To break open a big hole.

ntshuab The otter (tus).

209

ntxa A grave, pertaining to the brave (lub).
  (a) lub ntxa The grave.
  (b) lub qhov ntxa The grave.
  toj ntxas Graveyard, cemetery, hillside where the dead are buried. (lub) (t.c.)
  rooj ntxas The door of a grave (lub) (t.c.)

ntxab
  ntxab ntxawm An expression used immediately preceding the verb to indicate taking advantage of something which has already been done or provided for. The expression 'khaws xyeem' is similarly used. Both are common but 'ntxab ntxawm' is of Chinese derivation. (cf. 'khaws xyeem').
  ntxab ntxawm ua To do what another has already done for you.
  Peb ntxab ntxawm hais Vajtswv Ntuj li lus xwb. We are saying what God has already spoken.

1. ntxas Crooked teeth.
  ntxas ntxas kaus Crooked teeth (of animals or persons but impolite to use of another in his or her presence).

2. ntxas T.c. from 'ntxa' (cf. 'ntxa').

ntxaib Twin, double.
  phom ntxaib (rab) A double-barreled gun.
  menyuam ntxaib Twin children.
  cov thi ntxaib Double bamboo binding.

ntxaig T.c. from 'ntxais'

1. ntxaij (lub) Platform over the fire to dry things on (cf. 'nthab').
  tsuav ntxaij

2. ntxaij The tail of an arrow, tail fin of an arrow.
  ntxaij xub The tail of an arrow.

3. ntxaij A mesh of bamboo or other material.
  ib daig ntxaij hlau Screening, wire mesh (clf. 'daim').

1. ntxais To suck, to nurse (cf. 'nqus').
  ntxais mis To drink at the breast.
  ntxais quav hniav To suck through the teeth or against the back of the teeth as in the Western way of expressing "too bad." In Hmong it is more an expression of anger.

210

2. ntxais To sting, to smart (as of medicine in an open cut, cut, etc.)

3. ntxais To withdraw something from.
  (a) ntxais los To withdraw something from (as from the eye, etc.)
  (b) nqus los To withdraw something from (as from the eye, etc.)
  (c) rho los To withdraw something from (as from the eye, etc.)

4. ntxais Close together.
  Ob tus dav hlau ib ntxaig mus. The two airplanes flew close together (t.c.)

1. ntxaiv A spinning spindle, bobbin (tus).

2. ntxaiv
  tshuab ntxaiv A reel made of two crossed poles on a spindle and upon which the thread is wound.
  qaiv ntxaiv To hang the thread on the 'tshuab ntxaiv.'

ntxau White specks on the face (lub).

1. ntxaug Skinny, thin (this is used more commonly in Green Hmong [Blue Hmong]).

2. ntxaug Restricted post verbal intensifier (cf. Appendix 8).
  (a) ntxub ntxaug To hate bitterly.
  (b) ntxub ncaug To hate bitterly.

3. ntxaug
  dab ntxaug A certain spirit greatly feared by the Hmong. He has certain places of abode in the jungle and the Hmong are afraid of calamity if he is disturbed. Often when epidemic or widespread calamity arises it is attributed to having met with and disturbed 'dab ntxaug.'

ntxawg Youngest son, a pet name often used for little boys (cf. 'ntxawm' which is used for girls).

1. ntxawm Youngest daughter, pet name for little girl.
  muam ntxawm Youngest sister (as called by her brothers).

2. ntxawm
  txiv ntxawm Father's younger brother.

3. ntxawm
  niam ntxawm Wife of father's younger brother. (cf. kinship charts Appendix 10 p. 494).

4. ntxawm
   ntxab ntxawm (cf. 'ntxab').

1. ntxaws Restricted post verbal intensifier (cf. Appendix 8)
   (a) txhua ntxaws Completely, thoroughly.
   (b) ntxaws ntxaws Completely, thoroughly.
   nrhiav txhua ntxaws To seek thoroughly.
   hais txhua ntxaws To tell completely.

2. ntxaws Restricted post verbal intensifier with 'ntsoog'
   (cf. 'ntsoog').

ntxee To cross over.
   ntxee roob To cross over the ridge (cf. 'nto').

ntxeem To pass through a crisis.
   ntxeem kom dhau Pass through the crisis.
   Nyias ntxeem nyias li. Each must pass the crisis
   himself. Each must pass the test. Each must
   fend for himself.

ntxees
   (a) ib ntxees ntuj A far country, a distant place.
   (b) ib roog ntuj A far country, a distant place.

ntxeev To roll over, to turn over, to change over.
   ntxeev hlo Turn over.
   ntxeev hlawv hlo To overturn several things at
      once.
   ntxeev siab To turn against, to change the mind,
      have a change of heart.
   ntxeev dua siab tshiab To repent, have a new heart.
   nthuav ntxeev To open (the heart) and change to a
      new way.
   ntxeev tiaj To lie on one's back, fall over on
      one's back.
   ntxeev muag (cf. 'muag').
   ntxeev tis qaib To tie a chicken's wings together
      to tie a person's hands behind his back.

ntxi A word used in cursing, vile language.

ntxig To insert into a hole or opening (e.g. putting the
   finger into a ring or a hole, etc.)
   Nws muab ntxig rau hauv lawm. He inserted it inside.

1. ntxim To be effective, to meet the point of need (as
   medicine, etc.).
   Tshuaj tsis ntxim. The medicine is not effective.
   (cf. 'leej').
   Ib tug mob ntxim ib yam tshuaj. Each ailment has its
   own medicine.

2. ntxim
   ntxim siab ua To do earnestly, wholeheartedly
   (cf. 'rau siab ua').
   (a) ua ntxim siab To do what is desired, do what
      is pleasing.
   (b) ua hum siab To do what is desired, do what
      is pleasing.
   Ua ntxim nws lub siab. Do it in the way that pleases
      him.

1. ntxiv To repair, to fix up, to mend (especially when it
   involves making up something that is lacking),
   to patch up.
   ntxiv tsev To patch up the roof of a house.

2. ntxiv To make up what is lacking.
   ntxiv nplej To fill in the bare places in a planted
      rice field with new seed.
   ntxiv nqe To make up a debt, make up payment.
   rov ntxiv To make amends for.

3. ntxiv To add to.
   Lwm zaus muaj ntxiv. There will be more next time.
      ("to be continued").
   tsis xav noj ntxiv Don't want to eat any more.
   Txhob ua txhaum ntxiv. Don't sin again.

ntxiab A type of trap for game. (clf. 'rooj') (cf. 'rooj'). A lithe
   cuab ntxiab To construct such a trap. A lithe
      sapling is cut and pinned down in the middle.
      The thicker end is then pinned up on a trigger
      set to release easily when an animal passes
      beneath. The other end of the sapling is
      raised and braced up to provide tension.

ntxiag Restricted post verbal intensifier (cf. Appendix 8).
   ua noo ntxiag A feeling of impending sickness.
   ya ntxiag To fly away.
   tseev zam ntxiag To dress in fancy clothing.

1. ntxias To deceive, to entice. Don't entice others
   Txhob ntxias neeg ua txhaum. Don't entice others
      to do wrong.

2. ntxias To persuade, to coax.
   ntxias menyuam To persuade children by giving them
      goodies to eat, etc.

3. ntxias To braid.
   ntxias moj tuam To braid hair braids.
   ntxias hlua To braid rope.

ntxos Fibrous, as of food very hard and fibrous, also of the sides of a wooden wedge roughened and pulpy after use in splitting hard logs.

ntxob A word used in bad language and cursing.

ntxov Early.
  sawv ntxov Early morning.
  nram ntej nram ntxov Earlier, previously.
  Yuav mus ntxov ntxov li. We'll go quite early.
  Ntxov lig nws yuav los. Sooner or later he will come.

ntxoo (cf. 'ntxoov').

ntxoog (cf. 'dab' p. 28).

ntxooj Damp, moist, to become dampened or moist of itself as of ground or vegetation in damp weather or bedding during rainy days, etc. (cf. 'noo').

ntxoov Shaded, cloudy, overcast.
  ntxoov ntxoo Cloudy, overcast sky.
  Hav pos ntxoov lawm. It was overshadowed by the weeds and thorns.

ntxub To hate.
  (a) ntxub ntxaug To hate bitterly.
  (b) ntxub ncaug To hate bitterly.
  kev ntxub Hatred.

ntxuag Pertaining to that which is eaten along with cooked rice which is the basis of each meal.
  ntxuag mov To eat along with the rice.
  ua me ntxuag To eat bits and pieces, eat only a little of this and that.
  Noj mov ntxuag kua muag. To weep while you eat (to have tears with your rice, expressive of real sorrow).

ntxuaj To wave, to fan, to flap (cf. 'ntxuam').
  ntxuaj taws To fan a fire.
  ntxuaj nplej To fan paddy rice in winnowing.
  (a) ntxuaj teg To wave or motion with the hand.
  (b) co tes (t.c.) To wave or motion with the hand.
  qaib ntxuaj tis The chicken flaps its wings.
  vab ntxuaj (lub) A winnowing fan.

1. ntxuam A fan, a hand fan (rab) (cf. 'ntxuaj').

2. ntxuam A species of small bird with a large fan-like tail (tus).

ntxuav To wash, to wash out a vessel, to wash something off in water or other liquid (contr. 'ntxhua').
  ntxuav tes To wash the hands.
  ntxuav cev To take a bath, wash the body.
  txoj kabke ntxuav Baptism, rite of washing.
  ntxuav yias To wash out the pan.

1. ntxwg
  dab ntxwg nyoog (cf. 'dab' p. 28).

2. ntxwg T.c. (cf. 'ntxwj').

ntxwj Clf. for boulders.
  Ib ntxwj (or Ib ntxwg) niag zeb. A large boulder, a large jutting out rock.

1. ntxwm
  hnyuv ntxwm Sausage (txoj).

2. ntxwm
  nees ntaus ntxwm mem Horse rears and kicks with its hind legs.

ntxws
  muaj muaj ntxws Of a person with large buttocks.

ntxwv A syllable added to many Hmong nouns which come from the Chinese. It is an adopted Chinese nominal ending (cf. 'txwv').
  txiv kab ntxwv An orange (lub), oranges.
  yam ntxwv An example, an illustration.
  daim thav ntxwv A loincloth.
  yaj ntxwv A sheep (tus).
  xeeb ntxwv Grandchildren.
  vaj ntxwv King (tus).
  tav ntxwv Courage, boldness.

NTXH

ntxhab Steep, sharply inclined. This is a steep trail.
Txoj kev no ntxhab ntxhab.

1. **ntxhai** Bleached, having lost its natural pigment.
tuag ntxhai Of flesh that has lost color, of flesh that is shrivelled and whitened from immersion in water.
neeg tuag ntxhai An albino, one whose flesh is an unnatural color.

2. **ntxhai** The water that is poured off cooked rice.
kua ntxhai It is often served as part of the morning meal.

ntxhais Young girl, a girl (tus), daughter (tus).
mentxhais Little girl (tus).
Nws muaj ib tug tub ob tug ntxhais. He has one son and two daughters.

1. **ntxhe** A loud noise, to sound loudly, to resound.
lub suab ntxhe tuaj A voice sounded.

2. **ntxhe** Restricted post verbal intensifier after 'nrov' (cf. 'nrov').

1. **ntxheb** A given name for girls.

2. **ntxheb** The decorative rim or fringe just below the mouthpiece of the Hmong musical pipes. (cf. 'qeej') It is usually made of tortoise shell.

1. **ntxhee** Swift and turbulent.
dej ntxhee dej tsaws tsag Swift and turbulent water.

2. **ntxhee** Used as a post verbal intensifier (cf. Appendix 8)
dej tsaws ntxhee Swift and turbulent water.
kiav plaub kom nce ntxhee To make peaceful settlement of dispute or litigation.

ntxheev Not sticky, easily separated, not adhesive or sticking.
plaubhau ntxheev ntxheev Hair easily combed.

ntxhi To whisper.
sib ntxhi To whisper together.
ntxhi tias Said in a whisper.
sib ntxhi pes tus thuam kuv Kept whispering things against me.
lub siab ntxhi chiv (cf. 'chiv').

ntxhib Coarse, rough (of language, writing, weaving, sewing, also of poor grain, etc.) Contr. 'mos'
sau ntawv ntxhib To write poorly.
ntxhib txhuv Hulled rice not thoroughly cleared of hulls.
lus ntxhib Coarse language.
(a) neem ntxhib (cf. 'neem').
(b) neem mos (cf. 'neem').

ntxhia A sharp knife-like pain.
mob ntxhia To have a very sharp pain.

ntxhiab Odor, pungent smell.
Tsw tsw ntxhiab. It has a distinctive and pungent odor.

ntxhias Restricted post verbal intensifier.
nrov ntxhias Very loud.
kam ntxhias Willing immediately.
plhaw ntxhias Jumped suddenly.
kwm ntxhias To go through deep water.
plos ntxhias To go through shallow water.
(a) pob ntxhias To guarantee.
(b) lav ntxhias To guarantee.
ntaus ntxhias To hit, to strike.
hluas ntxhias Young.

ntxhiav A given name for women.

1. **ntxhov** Weedy and overgrown (cf. 'fab').

2. **ntxhov** Luxuriant, thick in growth.
plaub ntxhov ntxhov Thick fur, thick hair.

3. **ntxhov** Unsettled, disturbed and restless.
siab ntxhov Unsettled and restless heart.
ua ntxhov quav niab To raise tumult, do violence.

1. **ntxhoo** A given name for women.

2. **ntxhoo**
hlab ntxhoo (txoj) The ends of a woman's apron sash.

3. **ntxhoo** A branch or a bamboo stick set in the ground at certain spirit rites. (tus)

ntxhua To scrub, to wash by scrubbing or pressing (contr. 'ntxuav').
ntxhua khaubncaws To wash clothes, specifically to wash by scrubbing or by the common Hmong method of pressing the clothes against a rock with the hands or with the feet.

ntxhuab Moss (cf. 'ntxhuav').
   ntxhuab ntoo Tree moss.
   ntxhuab av Moss on the ground.

1. ntxhuav Clumps of moss or short grass (cf. 'ntxhuab').
   pobzeb tuaj ntxhuav Short grass on the rocks.

2. ntxhuav Hairy, mossy.
   tsov ntxhuav A lion (tus).
   ntxhuav pobkws Corn silk.

ntxhw The elephant (tus).
   ntoo tawv ntxhw A type of tree with rough bark
      (cf. 'ntoo').
   tawv ntxhw Elephant hide.
   kaus ntxhw Ivory, elephant's tusk.

NY

1. nyab Daughter-in-law (tus) (cf. Appendix pp. 484-485,
   496) (also Cf. 'tshoob') (see Definition
   No. 4 below).

2. nyab Flood, to flood.
   dej dag nyab A flood of water.

3. nyab
   (a) quav nyab npleg Rice straw (cf. 'nplej').
   (b) quav nplej Rice straw (cf. 'nplej').

4. nyab
   tis nyab Wife of a woman's older brother (tus)
      (cf. Definition No. 1 above).

nyag (cf. 'nyaj').

1. nyaj Long-tailed monkey, the Leaf Monkey (tus).
   Nyaj caws qia. The monkey leaps.

2. nyaj To suspect, to guess, to be doubtful of, probably.
   (cf. 'xav,' 'mem,' 'kwv yees') (sometimes
   said 'nyiaj').
   Nyaj tsis tau. I cannot see through it, cannot guess.
   Nyaj yog nws xwb. I suspect it is he.
   Nyaj ho **tsis** ua. I doubt if (he) will do it.
   Nyaj yuav pab saj. Probably (he) will help.
   Saib los nyaj kuv tus kwv lias yuav pab. The way I
      look at it my brother probably will help.

3. nyaj
   (a) plhu ua plhu nyaj Crestfallen, completely dis-
      couraged, face dark and fallen (cf. 'siab
      puas tsus').

nyas To stalk, to approach stealthily.
   tubsab nyas tuaj. The thief sneaked up on them.

nyav To smile (cf. 'luag').
   luag nyuj nyav To smile.

nyais phuv nyais Headman, official (tus) (T).

nyaum Severe, stern, prone to fight (as a bad dog, etc.),
   harsh.
   Tus nom nyaum nyaum li kav lawv. The official ruled
      them very harshly.

nyawj The Shan people (sometimes heard said 'nyuj').

nyaws To twist or turn something (not as common as 'qoj').

nyeg Domesticated, tame (contr. 'qus').
   nyuj nyeg, npua nyeg Domestic cows and pigs.
   nyuj qus Wild cow or ox.
   (a) dab nyeg Domesticated spirits (cf. 'dab').
   (b) dab qus Wild spirits (cf. 'dab').

1. nyem To grasp firmly, to close the hand, clench the fist.
   nyem tes To close the hand, clench the fist.
   nyem ceev ceev To clasp firmly, hold tightly.

2. nyem
   nyem ib lo lus To give a firm or strict word or
      order.

3. nyem
   txomnyem Destitute, impoverished, suffering calamity.

nyeeb   cov phwv nyeeb   The northern Thai (contr. 'lostsuas').

1. nyeem   To read.
    nyeem ntawv   To read books, to read.
    tsis txawj nyeem ntawv   Cannot read.

2. nyeem   Thick (of liquids), having relatively great
    density or consistency (contr. 'sab').

nyij   koov nyij   A type of fine black cloth.

1. nyim
    nyimno   (a variant rendering of 'nimno') (cf. 'nimno').

2. nyim   A preverbal intensifying particle often indicating
    continuous action in the verb.
    Kuv nyim hnov. I keep hearing...
    Nws nyim quaj.   He kept crying.
    Nws nyim hais li ntawd.   That's what he keeps saying.
    Kuv nyim hle hlo xauv.   So I took off my neck ring.

nyiag   To steal secretly (contr. 'txhav'), to do secretly.
    Nws nyiag kuv lub xauv.   He stole my neck ring.
    nyiag ua   To do secretly.
    nyiag kev khiav   To secretly escape, abscond.

1. nyiaj   Silver, silver money, money (clf. 'daim' for
    bars and ingots).
    Kuv tsis muaj nyiaj.   I have no money. (lit. "no
    silver").
    nyiaj txiag   Money, silver money.
    poob nyiaj   To lose money (t.c.)
    muaj muaj nyiaj   Wealthy.
    nyiaj daim   Bars of silver.
    nyiaj dai (cf. 'dai').

2. nyiaj   A silver neck ring (lub) (cf. 'xauv').
    (a) ib lub nyiaj   A silver neck ring.
    (b) ib lub xauv   A silver neck ring.
    (a) ib phiaj nyiaj   A set of silver neck rings.
    (b) ib phiaj xauv   A set of silver neck rings.

1. nyiam   To like, to favor, to care for (contr. 'hlub').
    Kuv tsis nyiam.   I don't like (it).
    Nws puas nyiam koj?   Does he like you?

2. nyiam   A variant rendering of 'nimno'   (cf. 'nimno').
    nyiamno

1. nyias   Thin, not thick, measuring relatively little
    between opposite surfaces (contr. 'tuab').

2. nyias   Cloth for carrying a baby on one's back. (daim).

3. nyias   Each, each one.
    Nyias muaj nyias npe.   Each has his own name.
    Nyias muaj nyias.   Each is its own, each is different.

nyiav   To wail, to lament (contr. 'quaj').
    Particularly used of wailing at a funeral.

nyo   To bow, to bend over.
    nyo hau   To bow the head.
    nyo nruj nris   To bend over.

1. nyob   To reside at, to be located at, to be alive (located
    on the earth).
    nyob hauv tsev   To be at home, in the house.
    tsis nyob lawm   Not here, (or) deceased.
    (a) nyob dag   To be idle, to hang about doing nothing.
    (b) nyob dag nyob u   To be idle, to hang about doing
    nothing.
    nyob ib leeg xwb   Alone, living by oneself.
    nyob dawb nyob do   To live without doing any work.

2. nyob   Repeated twice this word indicates the passage of
    a period of time.   After a while he will come.
    Nyob nyob nws yuav los.   After a while he will come.
    Nyob nyob tsis pom lawm.   After a time it just dis-
    appeared.

3. nyob   Used with 'tsam' in the expression 'nyob tsam' to
    mean shortly, before long, soon.
    Txhob noj, nyob tsam rov qab mob tuaj.   Don't eat
    anything or you will soon have pain again.

nyog   Fitting, suitable, appropriate, likely.
    tsim nyog   Of value, worthwhile.
    tsim nyog ua   Worth doing.
    tsim nyog yuav   Worth obtaining or buying.
    yuav nyog   Suitable to purchase or obtain.
    siv nyog   Usable, suitable for use.
    haus nyog   Drinkable, suitable for drinking.
    Hnub no tsim nyog los txog.   It is likely that (he)
    will come today.
    Tsis nyog tuaj.   Hasn't yet come.   (when by this time
    we thought he would be here.)
    (a) yuav tsis nyog   Cannot obtain it, can't buy it.
    (b) yuav tsis tau   Cannot obtain it, can't buy it.
    (c) yuav tsis yeej.   Cannot obtain it, can't buy it.
    Tsuav tamfaj koj qheb nyog txoj kev rau kuv.   Well
    then maybe you can provide a suitable solution.

nyoj To boil down, to cook away the liquid and leave only
      the solid or residue.
      nyoj yeeb To boil down the raw opium.
      nyoj suav thaj To boil down the sugar cane syrup.

1. nyom Grass (cf. 'tauj').
      lub hav nyom A grassy valley.

2. nyom To pry, to lever (as to pry something open or to
      lever a log into position).
      To act with leverage (as of a load unevenly balanced
      that exerts force or leverage to one side).

3. nyom To debate, argue, seek to move another from his
      position.
      nyom nge To argue price.
      sib nyom To argue together, to debate.

1. nyos Restricted post verbal intensifier (cf. Appendix 8).
      ua qaj qaug nyos To be sound asleep and snoring.

2. nyos
      ua nyos pliv Children's language for playing at
      hiding by covering one's eyes.

nyoo To be willing, to agree (T) (cf. 'kam').

1. nyoog hnub nyoog Age, time, a person's age (lub).
      (sometimes said 'hnub nyug' or 'hnoob nyoog').

2. nyoog dab ntxwg nyoog (cf. 'dab' p. 28).

nyooj To hum, of nasalized sounds, of feline annimals
      growling.
      nyooj qhov ntswg A nasal sound, to hum.
      mab nyooj The civet cat growls.
      tsov nyooj laws The tiger growls.

1. nyoos Fresh, green (of timber, vegetables, water,
      etc.).
      ntoo nyoos Freshly cut wood.
      dej nyoos Fresh water (unboiled).

2. nyoos Fresh, uncooked (of meat, etc.)
      nqaij nyoos Uncooked meat.

1. nyug (cf. 'nyoog').

2. nyug T.c. from 'nyuj' (cf. 'nyuj').

1. nyuj Cow, bull, pertaining to the cow (tus).
      nqaij nyug (t.c.) Beef.
      nyuj ngov The cow bellows.
      tus xob nyuj The bull kept for breeding.
      nyuj qus Wild ox, the Gaur.
      tus xyuas nyuj Young cow having had no young, heifer.
      twm nyuj A wild bull which goes about on its own.
      sab nyuj Wild bulls which go about in pairs.

2. nyuj
      (a) nyuj vab tuam teem Name of a certain spirit
          (cf. 'dab').
      ua nyuj dab An animistic ceremony for a deceased
          parent. A cow is killed in sacrifice to the
          deceased the idea being to repay the parent
          for the milk and food she or he has expended.
          This ceremony is performed by certain groups
          of Hmong and not by others. When it is performed
          it is often quite some time after the death
          and it constitutes the last of the funeral
          rites.

nyuad menyuad (cf. 'menyuam' and Introduction pp. xxii-xxiii).

nyuag T.c. from 'nyuam' (cf. 'nyuam').

nyuaj Difficult (T), (cf. 'ceeblaj').
      Note: This is also sometimes said 'nyuab.'

nyuam Small, little, negligible (contr. 'niag').
      menyuam Child (tus), children.
      ib nyuag qhov A little bit, a little place (t.c.)
      lo puav nyuam xwb Only a few words.
      ob peb nyuag hnub A few days (t.c.)
      (a) ob nyuag hnub ntawd These past few days (t.c.)
      (b) ob peb hnub ntawd These past few days (t.c.)
      ib nyuag vuag dua In a very short time (t.c.)
      niam tub txiv nyuag Parents and children (t.c.)
      ib nyuam qhuav A moment, a short time.
      nyuam qhuav mus Just went, went just a moment ago.
      nyuam qhuav tuaj Just came, arrived this moment or
          just a moment ago.

nywj A type of spirit which seeks to bring about repetition
      of former calamity or evil. (tus) These spirits
      are feared hovering in the vicinity where one
      has died or been in an accident, etc.

P

1. pa   Air, breath, gas.
   ua pa   To breathe.
   pem pa To hold the breath.
   tsis dim pa To choke, can't get one's breath.
   caj pas Throat (t.c.)
   hlab pas Oesophagus (t.c.)

2. pa   Clf. for breaths.
   ua ib pas To take one breath (t.c.)
   tshuab ib pas To blow one breath (t.c.)

1. pab   To help, to assist.
   Thov koj pab kuv. I beg you to help me.
   pabcuam To help, to assist (C).
   (a) pab leg To help, to assist.
   (b) lab nta To help, to assist.

2. pab   Clf. for a group or a flock.
   ua ib pab ib pab To be in groups.
   Pab yaj A flock of sheep.

1. pag   (cf. 'dib' for 'dib pag').

2. pag   lub pag lub xaus A term used to refer to all death ceremonies. To play the pipes, beat the drum and make sacrifices for the dead.

1. paj   Flower, flowery, cotton.
   paj ntoos Flower (clf. 'ntsauv' for one stalk) (t.c.) (clf. 'tsob' for a cluster).
   tawg paj To put forth flowers, to flower.
   paj noob hlis Sunflower.
   paj ntaub Embroidery.
   paj kws Popcorn.
   paj lug Proverb, flowery speech.
   tawg paj hais To speak proverbs.

2. paj   paj yeeb Pink or light lavender color.

3. paj   paj plhu Face, cheek (cf. 'plhu').

4. paj   paj paws To jump, to jump up and down (cf. 'dhia').
   ua paj paws ntsos To jump up.

5. paj   tsis muaj paj tshab mus No money or food with which to make a journey.

1. pam   A blanket (daim).
   muab pam vov To cover with a blanket.
   kauv pam To wrap in a blanket while sitting or standing.
   pam tab A thin blanket.
   pam rwb A quilt.

2. pam   To prepare, to provide for (cf. 'npaj').
   pam mov To provide rice, provide a meal (also 'pam zoj').
   pam ib tsum mov To set out a feast.

3. pam   Funeral rites, especially those rites conducted in the house.

4. pam   pamthawj (tus) A wooden mallet for splitting logs.

5. pam   Clf. for passes of urine or feces.

1. pas   A staff, a rod (tus)
   pas nrig Staff, walking stick.

2. pas   A lake (lub).
   (a) lub pas dej The lake of water, the lake.
   (b) lub pas zaj The lake of water, the lake.
   lub pas av A mudhole, a "lake" of mud.
   lub pas hawv A muddy hole with water running through.

3. pas   T.c. from 'pa' (cf. 'pa' ['hlab pas' and 'caj pas']).

1. pav   To bind, to tie into a package, to tie around, wrap up.
   (a) pav tsev To bind on the side boards of a house with rattan strips.
   (b) pav ncej To bind on the side boards of a house with rattan strips.

2. pav   (a) pav txhwj A hoe, mattock (rab).
         (b) choj txhwj A hoe, mattock (rab).

3. pav   los pav (tus) Manager, boss (C).

4. pav   pav ywj The loose fat adhering to a pig's stomach and intestines.

paig Wattle, loose fleshy skin hanging from the throat of a fowl.
   qaib paig txig A species of chicken having a large wattle.

1. paim To excrete, of liquids or semi-liquids breaking
   forth.
   paim paug To excrete pus.
   paim dej Water excreting from a wound.
   dej paim Of water breaking through a dam.

2. paim Of things other than liquids breaking forth.
   paim tshaws lawm (cf. 'nplej').
   yuav paim quav (lit. "it will excrete feces") A
      colloquial expression meaning "the truth will
      out," "The thing is sure to come to light in
      due time."

paiv A given name.

pau A loosely woven frame of bamboo strips to place things
   on for steaming (lub).
   lub pau ncuav Such a frame to steam rice cakes
      over a cauldron.
   lub pau tsu Such a frame set into the bottom of
      a rice steamer.

paub To know
   Kuv paub ntsoov. I know well.
   Kuv paub tias... I know that...
   paub dheev To know suddenly.
   paub sib nrawg nroos To know equally well.

1. paug Pus.
   (a) kam paug To exude pus.
   (b) los paug To exude pus.
   kua paug Pus.
   paug paim lawm The pus has drained.

2. paug Dust, dusty, dirty with dust.
   paug paug li Dusty.
   paug paug plaus plav Dusty, dust settling over every-
      thing.
   dej paug paug li Dirty water.

3. paug Restricted post verbal intensifier after 'dawb'
   dawb paug Perfectly white (cf. Appendix 8).

1. pauj To make return for an obligation or indebtedness.
   pauj zog To return an obligation of physical labor
      (contr. 'pauv zog' To help another in labor).
   pauj txiaj ntsim rau To make return for a favor
      or gift.
   pauj yeem To make return on a promise of sacrifice
      made to the spirits (cf. 'fiv').

2. pauj To avenge.
   pauj tau To avenge, take revenge (cf. 'rob caub').

3. pauj Exclamatory and interrogative final particle.
   Nej nyob zoo pauj? Are you well?
   Yaid, ntshai kuv txiv sawv pauj! Gracious, I'm
      afraid my father has risen!

paum The vulva, the external parts of the female genital
   organs whether human or animal.   (clf. 'lub').
   (contr. 'qau') (cf. 'lub pim').
   (a) tsoob pim The sex act (whether human or animal).
   (b) tsoob paum The sex act (whether human or animal).
   (c) sib tsoob The sex act (whether human or animal).

1. paus
   hauvpaus (lub) Stump, basis, root, origin (cf. 'hauv').

2. paus Abdominal gas.
   tso paus To pass gas through the anus.

3. paus
   paus ntshiv Porous, of things porous.
   neeb paus ntshiv A large species of mushroom.

pauv To exchange (cf. 'txauv').
   pauv zog To help another in manual labor with the
      understanding of help in return (cf. 'pauj').
   Lub no tsis zoo, muab pauv yuav ib lub zoo. This
      one is no good, exchange it for a good one.

1. pawg A stack, a pile (cf. 'pawv').
   pawg nplej no This rice stack.
   ib pawg taws One pile of firewood.

2. pawg Used with 'lug' as a two word restricted post
   verbal intensifier indicating that the action
   of the verb concerns many persons or things
   grouped together. (cf. Appendix 8).
   zaum pawg lug Many sitting together.
   muaj pawg lug To have a great quantity of.
   nyob pawg lug Residing together.
   ua pawg lug Many persons doing together.
   (also with the verbs 'cia,' 'qw,' 'pov,' 'txiav,' etc.)

pawj A curse word, vile language.

paws
   paj paws To jump (cf. 'paj') (cf. 'dhia').

1. pawv To stack, to pile up (cf. 'pawg').
   pawv nplej To stack rice sheaves.

2. pawv Colloquial among the Hmong of N. Thailand for "No!"
   (cf. 'tsis') This is especially common among
   children and young people.

pe To bend in worship or reverence, to bow to the ground on the knees with the hands raised in worship, to worship.
    pe ntuj pe teb To worship the heavens and the earth.

1. peb First person plural pronoun indicating three or more (cf. 'wb').
    Peb tsis mus. We (three or more persons) are not going.

2. peb The number three. (used with 'caug' to indicate the thirties).
    Peb tug tibneeg. Three people.
    Peb caug Thirty.
    noj peb caug To eat the "thirtieth," eat the New Year Feast.

3. peb
    peb txheej peb tis Great numbers, a great crowd.

ped (cf. 'pem' also cf. Introduction pp. xxii-xxiii).

1. peg To hit, to beat.
    Txhob peg nws. Don't beat him.

2. peg
    dab peg A spirit producing symptoms like epilepsy.
    (a) qaug dab peg To have epilepsy, to have an epileptic fit.
    (b) mob dab peg To have epilepsy, to have an epileptic fit.

3. peg
    teb peg Dry fields for farming on the flat plains.

1. pej Strange, other than ordinary (cf. 'pem').
    pej yam lus Other languages, foreign languages strange speech.
    pej kum Other, strange.
    pej kum tebchaws Other lands, other countries.
    pej kum dab qus Wild spirits, strange spirits as distinguished from 'dab nyeg.'

2. pej
    pejthuam A tower, a pagoda (tus).

3. pej
    pejchum Aluminum.

4. pej
    (a) pejxeem A people, the populace, those governed as distinct from the officials (C).
    (b) pejxeem huabhum A people, the populace, those governed as distinct from the officials (C).

1. pem Uphill from, above, on the uphill side (contr. 'nram').
    pem ub Way up there.
    (a) puag pem Way up there.
    (b) puag pem ub Way up there.
    Nws nyob pem zos. He is up in the village.
    nyob pem teb Up in the fields (cf. 'poob pem teb').
    nyob pem te Over in the village nearby.
    nyob pem tej hav zoov Over in the jungle.
    pem qaum kev The uphill side of the trail.

2. pem In some idioms this word is used to indicate location nearby without the connotation of above or uphill.
    poob pem teb Fell upon the ground, fell to the earth.
    Note: Used as a noun of location this word may vary with the pronunciation 'ped' subject to conditions outlined in Introduction pp. xxii-xxiii.

3. pem Other, different from, out of the ordinary (cf. 'pej').
    pem lus Vague speech, figurative speech.
    pem lub tebchaws Another country, a different country.

4. pem
    meejpem (cf. 'meej') (C).

5. pem To restrain, withhold.
    pem pa To hold the breath.

6. pem
    tus pem kom The defendant, person accused or wrong.

1. pes
    pes tsawg How many, how much (cf. 'tsawg').
    Muaj pes tsawg? How much is there?
    Koj yuav pes tsawg tus? How many do you want?

2. pes A post verbal intensifier used only in connection with other intensifiers as a combination.
    (cf. Appendix 8, p. 470).
    ras pes dheev Startled.
    lub siab xob pes vog In fear of punishment, afraid.
    pes hlo (cf. 'hlo').
    pes nkaus (cf. 'nkaus').

1. peeb
    ntoo peeb lab The Areca palm whose fruit is chewed with the beetle leaf (tus).

2. peeb
    phaj peeb The mediator in a dispute, one who tries to assist in settlement before going to court. (tus).

3. peeb Soldiers (tus) (C). (cf. Hmong 'tub rog' and 'tuamham' from the Thai).

1. peem To force oneself to do something one feels physically unable to do.

2. peem xijpeem (cf. 'xij').

1. peev Money capital, money which is yours to use or invest.
   (a) peev Capital funds (C).
   (b) peev txheej Capital funds (C).
   poob peev To sell at a loss.
   rho lawv peev Using their capital.

2. peev peevxwm Ability, cleverness, skill (C) (cf. 'txujci').
   Kuv tsis muaj peevxwm ua. I haven't the skill to do it.
   peevxwm tsim txiaj Worthwhile demonstrations of ability, "miracles."

3. peev peev choj Rice flour noodles.

1. pib pibtxwv (lub) A very small handleless cup, a Chinese wine cup (cf. 'khob') (C).
   ib pib tshuaj A small cup of tea or medicine.

2. pib To begin (cf. 'chiv').
   Nws pib hais tias... He began by saying... (cf. 'chiv kiag hais tias!..').

pij pij ntaws (lub) The umbilicus, the navel.

pim The vulva, the external parts of the female genital organs whether human or animal. (cf. 'paum') (clf. 'lub').
   (a) lub pim The female sex member (cf. 'ple') (contr. 'qau').
   (b) lub paum The female sex member (cf. 'ple') (contr. 'qau').
   (a) tsoob pim The sex act.
   (b) tsoob paum The sex act.
   (c) sib tsoob The sex act.

1. piv To compare.
   piv lus hais To give a comparison, to illustrate.
   pivtxwv An illustration, a comparison, a picture (C).
   lus pivtxwv Figurative speech.
   ua pivtxwv To make a comparision, to draw a picture.

2. piv ua puab ua piv (cf. 'puab').

piab An adze or hewing hatchet (rab).

piag
   (a) piag deg A clam.
   (b) pliag deg (lub) A clam.

1. piam Spoiled, useless, broken (cf. 'puas').
   Lub teeb piam lawm. The lamp is broken.

2. piam piam thaj White sugar (C).

3. piam
   (a) piam iav A kind of grass or short vegetation.
   (b) piam liaj A kind of grass or short vegetation.

4. piam piamsij Destroyed (cf. 'puas tsuaj').

1. pias Millet.
   ncuav pias Steamed cakes made of millet.

2. pias ib ncuav pias One slap with the palm of the hand.

3. pias qhua pias Measles.
   mob qhua pias To have measles.

1. piav To explain, to demonstrate (cf. 'qhia').
   piav kev To explain the way, to preach.
   piav zoj To explain.
   piav tias.. Explained saying...
   piav taw tes To dance.

1. po The spleen (tus).

2. po ntoo po A rotten tree (tus).

1. pob Lump, round or ball-like.
   ib pob A small package (C).
   ib lub pob A lump.
   zaub pob Head cabbage.
   ua pob To form a knot or a lump.
   hoob pob (lub) A bomb.
   (a) pob av luaj An anthill.
   (b) pob an muas yis tib An anthill.

2. pob The first syllable in many nouns especially those characterized by roundness or bulk. (clf. 'lub' for all).
pobzeb A stone, stone.
pobtxwv Bulk, frame.
pobcaus A knot (a firm knot, not a slipknot) (cf. 'rhaus').
(a) pobtsuas (t.c.) Cliff, rock mass.
(b) tsua Cliff, rock mass.
pobntseg Ear.
pobtxha Bone.
pobkws Ear of maize or Indian corn (cf. Definition No. 9).
pob ntoos Stump of a fallen tree.

3. pob A joint.
pob xyoob The joint in bamboo.
pob qej txha A bone joint.
pob teg Wristbone.
pob taws Anklebone.

4. pob To crumble.
lub tshuaj pob tag The pill of medicine crumbled.
(a) toj pob A landslide.
(b) pob rhe A landslide.

5. pob
pob pob li Smoky.

6. pob Troublesome, mischievous.
txhoj pob

7. pob Of an animal purring.
hawb pob

8. pob
(a) pob ntxhias To guarantee.
(b) lav ntxhias To guarantee.

9. pob
Note: For convenience we list the common terms relating to the growth and use of 'pobkws' (maize or corn) (cf. entries under 'kws').
ntais pobkws To pick corn.
ntsia pobkws Corn kernels.
ntxhuav pobkws Corn silk.
tw yaj pobkws Corn tassels.
plhaub kws Corn husk.
quav kws Corn stalk.
pobkws taj Late corn.
pobkws cauj Early corn.
pobkws nplaum liab A type of red glutinous corn.

Note: Below are the stages in the growth of corn.
ua raj ncas The stem appears from the ground.
dauv tw qaib The leaves have begun to bend over (like a cock's tail).
txij hauvcaug As high as the knee.
txij dua As high as the waist.
ua nplooj qoov tshaws The leaves fully formed.
ua npuav npaug tshaws The heart of the stalk has begun to appear.
ua tw yaj tshaws The tassels appear on the top.
ua nplais taws The corn pods appear.
ua ntxhuav liab The corn silk is becoming red.
tsam pom The corn pods are filling out.
(a) tuag ntxhuav The silk is drying off.
(b) yeeb ntxhua (t.c.) The silk is drying off.
ua pos nyuj The corn kernels are forming.
ntom kab The kernels are fully outlined.
(a) siav Ripe (shiny husks).
(b) ci plhaub vog Ripe (shiny husks).
daj daj plhaub Drying corn pods on the stalk.

pog Paternal grandmother, or paternal grandfather's brother's wife (tus) (cf. kinship chart, Appendix p. 494).
phauj pog Paternal grandfather's sister.
niag pog Familiar term of address for an old woman.
(a) niag pog laus "grandma" or "old woman", a familiar term used by an older man for his wife.
(b) pog laus "grandma" or "old woman," a familiar term used by an older man for his wife.

1. poj Female (of birds or of humans) (contr. 'maum' and 'txiv').
pojniam Woman (tus).
poj qaib Hen (tus).
poj ntsuag Widow (tus).
pojniam tub se Wife and children.
muab rau poj ntoo ris Figurative expression concerning a mother who neglects her child.
poj ntxoog (cf. 'ntxoog').

2. poj
txiv mov poj The coconut (lub) (T).

3. poj
poj co (lub) The common earring worn by Hmong women.

4. poj
tebchaws (or 'hav') quav poj An expanse of land once inhabited but now only weeds and scrub vegetation.

1. pom To see.
   (a) pom kev To see, to see the way.
   (b) pom kev To see, to see the way.
   pom ntsoov To see well, to be looking at.
   pom dheev To suddenly see.

2. pom
   pom khawv To tattle, to report on the evil of others.

3. pom
   pomtxwv The panther (tus).

1. pos Thorns
   pos hmab Thorns on a vine.
   pos ntoo Tree thorns.
   hav pos An expanse of thorny vegetation.
   pos tshauv txi A type of small thorn.
   tuaj pos To have thorns.
   lus mos lus tuaj pos Nice sounding words but with
      a "thorny" or harsh meaning and intent.

2. pos The gums.
   pos hniav The gums.

3. pos To hold the finger over an opening.
   pos ntswg To hold the nose closed.
   pos To "play" an instrument where the fingers are
      held over openings to control the escape of air.
   pos qeej To finger the Hmong musical pipes.

4. pos
   pos ncag (cf. 'ncag').

5. pos
   pos pos huab Foggy (temporarily).
   pos huab nti Surrounded by clouds.

6. pos
   nqaij pos Animals of prey, animals that prey on
      other animals and humans.

7. pos
   tsw pos Of meat that smells slightly old but not
      really spoiled.

1. pov To throw.
   pov tseg To throw away, to dispose of by any means.
   tua pov tseg To kill.
   Muab hlawv pov tseg. Burn it up.
   pov rhees To throw.
   pov khaub hnab (cf. 'khaub').

2. pov To guarantee, to act as a guarantor.
   tus povthawj An intermediary, a guarantor (also
      'pov zeej'). This terms has also been used for
      a Jewish "priest."

3. pov
   pov khawv Satisfied, sufficient (often with the
      connotation "fed up").

4. pov
   povhwm To protect, defend, guard, shelter (C).

5. pov
   povhum (lub) A charm, a precious stone.

6. pov
   pov ib lo lus hais To send word, give an order.

1. poo To rob, to pillage (Lao or Thai language but used
      by Hmong) (cf. Hmong 'txhav,' 'nyiag').

2. poo Variant rendering of 'poog' (cf. 'poog').

1. poob To fall down, to fall from a height (cf. 'txeej').
   poob plhuav To fall down.
   (a) xeeb poob Fell into.
   (b) tij yim poob Fell into.
   (a) poob nthav To fall down completely (cf. 'nthav').
   (b) poob kiag To fall down completely (cf. 'nthav').

2. poob To fall in a moral or figurative sense.
   poob npe To lose one's reputation.
   poob zog To be discouraged, to be without strength
      from fear or discouragement.
   poob siab hlo Frightened.
   poob zoo To be lost in the jungle.

1. poog All gather together in a group (some say 'poo').
   Cov yaj poog nkuaj. The sheep entered the fold.
   Sawvdaws poog npoj. All came together in a group.
   Xuas zeb poog ntws rau nws. Threw a handful of stones
      at him.

2. poog A restricted post verbal intensifier with 'nrov'
      (cf. 'nrov').

poom A pound, ten 'lag' (cf. 'lag') (T).

poov The "mother" of yeast or vinegar.
   poov xab Leaven, yeast (lub).

1. pub To give (free of charge), to hand to.
   Muab pub kuv. Give it to me.
   Pub rau nws yuav. Give it to him as a gift.

2. pub To allow, to permit.
Kuv txiv tsis pub kuv mus. My father won't let me go.
Tsis pub ua. It is not permitted to do that.

1. puj
puj sis Does not (C).
Nws puj sis hlub yus thiab. Doesn't he also love
you?

2. puj
puj daub (tus) A species of bird.

3. puj
cuab xeeb puj teem Confused and uncertain (cf. 'cuab').

1. pum
pum liv Small bamboo flute (rab).

2. pum
neeg tshum pum One who seeks to hinder another from
taking action (cf. 'tshum').

1. pus
(a) duav pus Shoulder blades.
(b) nplooj pus Shoulder blades.

2. pus To escape with all or part of the trap or rope or
arrow, etc. still attached (a term used in
catching game).

3. pus A five gallon tin, a large tin can (lub).

1. puv Full, filled.
puv puv li Filled.
puv nkaus Completely filled (of vessels).
puv npo Completely filled (of the heart, etc.).
puv nco laws Filled and running over, filled and
rounded over as a basket of grain.
puv pheej lias Level full.
puv ntug nkaus Full to the edge.
puv ntias Filled all through (as of a room filled
with sound, with furniture, etc.)

2. puv
txiv puv luj The pineapple (lub).

1. pua Hundred.
rau pua Six hundred.
ib Puas One hundred (t.c.)
(a) ib puas tsav yam A great variety, all kinds of.
(b) ib puas tsav A great variety, all kinds of.

2. pua To prepare a level place on the ground, to prepare
a flat surface, to spread on a flat surface.
pua pobzeb To pave with stone.
pua chaw pw To prepare a sleeping place, to put down
bedding to sleep, make a place to lie down.
daim lev pua pw A sleeping mat.

1. puab Close to, in close relationship with, to remain in
close relationship with something. (cf. 'tshob').
(cf. Definition No. 11).
plig puab cev The spirit remains in the body.
puab nkaus Very close to (also 'puab rawv').
siab tsis puab Not very earnest about something,
doesn't have close at heart.
Nws lub siab puab Yexu tiag tiag. He is really
close (in fellowship) with Jesus.

2. puab
ncej puab Thigh, upper leg.

3. puab
puab tais The groin.

4. puab
puab tsiag The chin, jaw.

5. puab
kaub puab Calouses, scab.
kaub puab mov Hardened rice on the sides of the pot.

6. puab
thoob puab A cloth bag carried over the shoulder.

7. puab To mould or form with the hands (in Laos said
'npuab').
Nws muab av puab coj los ua ib tug nlom. He made
an idol out of earth.
Puab ua ncuav. (He) made rice cakes.

8. puab
txob puab Of a child whimpering and difficult to
control or comfort, fussy, troublesome.

9. puab A bamboo horn, trumpet (rab).

10. puab
ua puab ua piv All over, covering the whole.

11. puab
tus puab rooj puab ntsa One who hangs around the
house and table of another (cf. Definition No. 1).

1. puag To embrace, to hold in the two arms.
   (a) puag lias To embrace.
   (b) puag kiag To embrace.
   puag nkaus To embrace.
   puag rawv To keep on embracing, hold in embrace.

2. puag Intensive pre-nominal particle for terms of time or distance.
   (a) puag pem Far up the hill.
   (b) puag pem ub Far up the hill.
   puag tim Way over there.
   puag thaum ub A very long time ago.

3. puag To set on eggs.
   Qaib puag qe. The hen is setting.

4. puag A measure of rice, as much as can be held in two hands.

5. puag Just now, just a moment ago (sometimes 'puas ta').
   puag ta no Just now, this moment.
   puag ta mus Just left.

1. puaj
   xwm fab puaj meem In every direction (C) (cf. 'plaub ceg ntuj').

2. puaj
   chib chawj puaj liam (cf. 'chib').

3. puaj
   xyoob puaj tsw tsev Green bamboo for the walls of a house.

4. puaj
   puas txwv puaj tiam From the beginning of mankind (C) (cf. 'cuaj txheej cuaj tis').

5. puaj
   taum puaj yem A variety of long string beans (C).

1. puam The small lengthwise rafters of a house. (cf. 'tsev') (tus).
   tw puam The small lengthwise pole fastened under the eaves of a house to hold the roofing.

2. puam
   tshav puam An expanse of open ground.
   tshav puam suab zeb An expanse of stony ground.

3. puam
   suab puam A gravel bank, sand and gravel or small stones deposited by a stream.

4. puam
   keeb puam (lub) A foundation fact, basis.

1. puas Interrogative particle.
   Koj puas paub? Do you know or not?
   Koj puas mus? Are you going or not?
   Note: This may be used along with other question forms.
   e.g. 'koj puas paub lawm tsis paub?' Do you know or not?
   Puas yog? Isn't that so? Yes or no?

2. puas Destroyed, useless, spoiled (cf. 'piam').
   Puas lawm. Spoiled, useless.
   ua puas tsuaj To destroy, render useless, to perish (sometimes said 'puam tsuaj') (cf. 'piamsij').

3. puas T.c. from 'pua' (cf. 'pua').
   ib puas tsav yam (cf. 'pua') (t.c.)
   txhiab niag tim puas xyoo Hundreds and thousands of years, a very long time, (t.c. from 'pua').

4. puas
   hniav puas Molar teeth (cf. 'hniav').

5. puas Close to, nearby.
   puas nkaus Next door, very near by.
   sib puas ciam To have a common boundary.

6. puas
   puas txwv puaj tiam (cf. 'puaj').

7. puas
   (a) siab puas tsus Completely discouraged, everything gone wrong.
   (b) siab poob tag Completely discouraged, everything gone wrong.

8. puas
   ua plhu puas nyag (cf. 'plhu').

9. puas
   puas ta (cf. 'puag ta').

1. puav Occasional, some.
   zaum puav Sometimes, occasionally.
   tus puav Some persons (or some of any noun taking the Clf. 'tus').
   lub puav Some things (any noun taking Clf. 'lub').
   pub puav sijhawm Sometimes.

2. puav
   puav leej All, altogether (cf. 'leej').

3. puav The bat (tus).

4. puav To gather, to bring together.
Puav npua los. Gather the pigs together.
lub puav ntses A fishnet (so called by Hmong in Laos).
puav ntses To catch fish (so called by Hmong in Laos).

5. puav
puavpheej An article of evidence.
Muab puavpheej tseg lawm. (He) gave an article to
seal a venture. (e.g. a ring to seal an engage-
ment, etc.)
Note: The placenta which is buried after birth is
regarded as a 'puavpheej' which is taken at
death to the final abode as evidence of parentage).

pw To recline, to lie down (cf. 'kheem').
pw nthi To lie down.
pw ntog To lie prostrate.
pw tsaug zog To lie down in sleep, to sleep.
pw ntxeev tiaj To lie on the back.
pw ua ntsais To lie on the side.
pw khwb rwg To lie on the stomach (cf. 'kheem').

pwg xub pwg Shoulder.

pwj kab pwj nyug (tus) The rhinocerous beetle.

1. pwm Mildew.
tuaj pwm To be mildewed, become mildewed.

2. pwm
cwjpwm (cf. 'cwj').

3. pwm
looj pwm (cf. 'looj').

1. pwv To train an animal to harness, to train an animal
to work.

2. pwv To add to (cf. 'tsav,' 'txhab').
pwv rau To add to.

1. phab A wall, a flat vertical surface, a side.
ib phab A wall, a surface or side (cf. 'phab ntsa').
phab tav A person's side.
phab ntsa A wall, the wall of a house.
phab tsuas A rock surface, cliff face.

2. phab
phab xyoob Chest band on a horse harness (the
archaic term for this item is 'txees nees')
(cf. 'nees').

3. phab An area or region of the heavens, one of the
directions.
phab hnub tuaj The east.

1. phaj An age group, generation.
phaj txiv The older generation, "fathers."
phaj hluas The younger generation, young people.

2. phaj A flat plate (lub).
phaj teev The plate to hold articles being weighed
on a balance scale.
yeeb phaj A plate used to place opium upon.

3. phaj To set forth, declare.
phaj txoj kevcai To set forth rules or laws.

4. phaj
phaj peeb (tus) An intermediary in a dispute, one
who tries to assist in settlement before going
to law about it.

5. phaj
phaj qhovtxhiachaw The process of moving house, etc.

6. phaj
xamphaj (cf. 'xam').

7. phaj
phaj txhawm To save, set aside (cf. 'txhawm').
Nws ho phaj txhawm tau thaum twg mas nws thiaj li
them koj thaum twg. He will pay you when he
has saved enough money.

pham Fat, chubby (commonly used in referring to babies or
children, impolite when used of adults).
(cf. 'rog' and 'npag').
pham nphoob - very fat (of animals, etc.)

phav A box or tin can (lub), a small box or can.

1. phaib
khuaj phaib The Tin tribe.

2. phaib Used by itself this word is used as a curse word.

1. phais To cut open, to incise.
   phais qaib To butcher a chicken, cut open a chicken.
   phais plab To cut open the stomach, to perform a
      surgical operation.

2. phais Used by itself this word is also used as a
      curse word.

3. phais
   phis lis phais lais Aimless, foolish, careless.
   hais phis phais lais To talk nonsense.

phau Clf. for books, volumes.
   Phau ntawv no loj loj. This is a very large book.

phauj Father's sisters (cf. kinship charts p. 494).
   phauj pog Paternal grandfather's sister.

phaum Clf. for a time of rain, an epidemic or time of
      sickness, a time or occasion.
   ib phaum nag A time of rain (contr. 'kob' the clf.
      for a single shower).
   ib phaum mob One time of sickness, an epidemic.

phaw Referring to certain large male animals.
   phaw muas iwj Large male deer.
   phaw twm Large male water buffalo.
   phaw nyuj qus Large male gaur or wild ox.

phawv Large plaited bamboo storage bin (lub), (for rice,
      etc.)
   phawv nplej A rice storage bin (as above).

pheb Of wood or metal that has been spread, split or softened
      by pounding. (cf. the top of a chisel or wedge).
   Pheb lawm, tsis zoo siv. It has been beaten to a
      pulp and is useless.

phem Evil, wicked (contr. 'zoo').
   ua phem To do evil.
   hais phem To speak evil.
   Phem zoo yus yog Hmoob. Whether for better or for
      worse we still are Hmong.

phev A curse word, vile language.

1. pheeb To lean against, to lean over.
   pheeb phab ntsa To lean against the wall.
   tsev pheeb suab A "leanto", a temporary shelter
      (lub), shelter made of leaning branches.

2. pheeb To "lean" figuratively, i.e. to find excuse
      (cf. 'ib').

1. pheej Repeatedly, regularly, continually (cf. 'sij' and
      'nyim').
   pheej mob Keeps getting sick.
   pheej tsis los Still hasn't returned, still has not
      come (although called for).
   Nws pheej noj tshuaj pheej tsis zoo. He keeps taking
      medicine but gets no better.
   pheej mus pheej hais lus Walking and talking.
   Note: This is common idiom for two simultaneous
      activities.
   pheej sis Continually weak and sickly, not really
      well.

2. pheej
   pheej lias Level measure (e.g. a level basketful) (C).

3. pheej
   koob pheej Fair, equal, right, just, "on the level."

4. pheej
   pheejyig Cheap (C), inexpensive.

5. pheej
   puavpheej (cf. 'puav').

6. pheej
   ntov pheej tsab To fell a tree by cutting in from
      both sides until it falls over. (cf. 'ntov').

pheev menyuam pheev riam Of children playing with knives.

1. phij
   phijxab (lub) A large box, especially the common
      large tin box used by Hmong for storage purposes (C).

2. phij
   phijchob (txoj) The leather thong for tying baskets
      to a pack saddle.

3. phij
   phua cem phij To split (boards) off the side of a
      log rather than through the middle.

4. phij
   hais lus plhob phij To speak worthless words.

5. phij
   neeg zoo phij sam siab com viab "Hypocrites" (persons
      with a good skin but a crooked heart).

6. phij
   phijlaj (tus) The friend or helper of the bridegroom,
      the "best man" (cf. 'tshoob').

7. phij
   phij vias (cf. 'vias').

1. phim   To match, fitting, suitable (cf. 'hum').
   tsis sib phim   Does not match, unsuitable.

2. phim
   phim thabntxwv   To lean or depend on others; of a lazy person who relies on help from the industrious.

3. phim
   phimhwj (C)   To honor, to respect, to do deference to, also to wonder at, to stand in awe of.

phis
   phis lis phais lais   (cf. 'phais' Definition No. 3).

1. phiv   To scratch out, to eliminate (cf. 'thuam').
   Muab phiv tseg.   Scratch it out.

2. phiv   To offend, to do wrong (T).
   phiv kauv maim   To break the law (T).

phiab   A bowl or basin (lub).
   lub tais phiab   A bowl or basin with a protruding edge such as an enamel washbasin.

1. phiaj   Clf. for sets.
   ib phiaj nyiaj   A set of silver neck rings.
   ib phiaj tswb nyiaj   A set of silver bells.

2. phiaj   A small slab or sheet of solid material.
   phiaj zeb   A slab of stone, a slate for writing.

3. phiaj   The slab of bone marked with combinations of fortune and worn on a string around the neck for use in divining lucky days, etc. (clf. 'daim').

4. phiaj   To reforge or repair metal knives and axes, etc. that have been blunted or chipped in use. (cf. 'kho').

5. phiaj   The square of plaited bamboo set up outside a home to warn strangers not to break taboo by entering. Usually this is because of sickness in the home, because the shaman has set a time of taboo, or because a mother is still in her first month after giving birth.

6. phiaj
   neeg tsis tshoob phiaj txwv   Spoken of a person who is wealthy but who purposely dresses poorly to conceal his wealth.

1. phob   To use up, to waste (cf. 'phum lam').
   muab phob tas   Used it up, wasted it completely.

2. phob   To hit.

3. phob   Clf. for sheets of skin or leather (cf. 'daim').

4. phob
   phob tis   A wing (cf. 'tis').

5. phob
   ib phob tsig cuab noog   A noose or snare to catch birds.

6. phob
   phob fab   The work of moving and preparing new fields, etc. (cf. 'fab').

1. phoj   To creep off after being injured, etc. (of animals or human beings).

2. phoj
   phojxom   Itchy all over (infrequently used).

1. phom   A gun (clf. 'rab').
   xuas phom tua   To kill with a gun.
   tsom phom   To aim a gun.
   qeb phom   Gun trigger.
   ntsis phom   End of the gun barrel.
   tus kav phom   The gun barrel.
   lub txhab khaum phom   The gunstock.
   maim phom   To flinch when firing a gun.
   tua phom   To fire a gun.
   phom thaib   A rifle.
   phom luvxoom   A shot gun.
   yaj phom   A revolver, an automatic, a pistol.
   kev ntsis ntaj ntsis phom   Death by violence (by gun or sword).
   tus tsav phom   (cf. 'tuag').

2. phom   Clf. for shots of a gun.
   tua ib phom   To fire a gun once, fire a shot.

3. phom   Soft, pliable, in contrast to hard or brittle (cf. 'muag').

phos
   phosxoos   A meeting, a special gathering (Thai).

phov   To writhe, to roll or toss to and fro as in delirium or in fitful sleep. (cf. 'da', 'nti').
   phov phov   To writhe to and fro (as above).
   phov nkuaj   Of an animal causing trouble in his pen striving to get out.
   phov ub phov no   To make a fuss, getting into various kinds of mischief.

1. phoo A lock.
   ntsuas phoo (lub) A lock.

2. phoo T.c. from 'phoov' (cf. 'phoov').

1. phooj A tent.
   tsamphooj A tent (sometimes also used for a mosquito net) (clf. 'lub').
   vijtsam Mosquito net (C) (clf. 'lub').

2. phooj tsev timphooj A field house, temporary house or shelter.

3. phooj phoojywg A friend (C), (clf. 'tus').

phoom To bump against.
   ti ti phoom phoom Crowded together so that bumping is unavoidable, descriptive of a crowd of people close together.
   sib phoom Bumped together.

phoov Clf. for a handful.
   ib phoo tes A handful (t.c.)
   muab ob phoo tes qee mentsis nplej Take out two handfuls of rice (t.c.)
   yuav rau phoov Six handfuls are needed.

1. phum Clf. to give (cf. 'pub').
   phum pub To give.
   Yuav phum pub it tug pab. (He) will give someone to help.
   (This word is used in this sense in Laos but is seldom so used among Thailand Hmong. 'pub' by itself is used.)

2. phum phum ntsiab Clearly (cf. 'meej').
   phum lub ntsiab To speak clearly, to give the "essence" of things, to give the whole truth, to go right to the heart of matters.

3. phum phum lam Wasteful (cf. 'phom').
   phum lam ntsuav Very wasteful.
   neeg phum lam Of a person who wastes things and never saves.
   siv nyiaj phum lam ntsuav To waste money extravagantly.

phuv phuv nyais Headman, official (tus), (Thai).

1. phua To split open, to split "to pass through the midst."
   phua ntoo To split a log.
   phua txiag ntoo To split boards.
   phua plaws To split through.
   phua plaws nruab nrab lawv To push through a crowd.
   phua qab thoob Half moon.
   phua cem phij To split (boards) off the side of a log rather than through the middle.
   phua kum xeeb To split (boards) by splitting through the center of the log in wedges.

2. phua hais phua plhawv To speak openly (cf. 'tabmeeg').

3. phua phua kev To render judgment.

phuab phuab nroj To push foliage or vegetation apart with the hands as in making one's way along an overgrown trail or in reaping grain. (cf. 'haiv').

phuaj A raft (lub).
   lub phuajtxwv A raft.
   duav phuaj An oar.

phuam A cloth, a rag or cloth for a particular use, (clf. 'daim'), the black cloth head dress worn by Hmong women as a kind of turban.
   ntoo phuam To put on the headband or turban, to wear a headband.
   phuam ntxuav muag (daim) A wash cloth, face cloth.

1. phuas Curds.
   phuas taum The curds in the making of bean-curd.

2. phuas The portion remaining or spit out when something is chewed (e.g. sugarcane).

phwj To ferment, to boil over.

phwv A people (Thai) (sometimes also pronounced 'phuj' and 'phwj').
   phwj lwj A Laotian tribe, the 'lwj' people.
   phwv nyeeb The Northern Thai.
   phuj nyeeb The Northern Thai.

PL

pla Of a flock of animals scattering, to scatter or flee.

1. plab The stomach, the stomach region, abdomen (lub).
   lub plab The stomach.
   (a) lawv plab Diarrhea.
   (b) raws plab Diarrhea.
   (c) thoj plab Diarrhea.
   kem plab Indigestion.
   tswm plab To stop up the bowels.
   tshuaj tswm plab Medicine to stop diarrhea.
   nchi plab Flatulence, feeling of fulness though
      not having eaten much.
   mob plab Pain in the stomach region.
   thais plab To take a laxative, to purge the bowels.
   vom vom hauv lub plab A churning in the stomach
      producing gradual weakness.
   zais zais plab Enlarged abdomen as in a child that
      has had intestinal parasites.
   (a) plab laus The stomach region.
   (b) plab laug (t.c.) The stomach region.
   plab mog The lower abdominal region.
   npua plab To massage the stomach region.
   npuaj plab To gently pound the stomach region to
      relieve pain (pound with the hand).
   (a) zaws plab Term for massaging the stomach region.
      (cf. 'npua plab').
   (b) mos plab Term for massaging the stomach region.
      (cf. 'npua plab').
   (c) zuaj plab Term for massaging the stomach region
      (cf. 'npua plab').
   nchos plab Relieving stomach pain by mechanical
      means, shaking or pinching the skin, etc.
      (cf. 'nchos').
   mob plab zaw Cholera or dysentery.
   plab hlav Sharp abdominal pain.

2. plab Abdominal region regarded as a seat of the
   intelligence.
   (a) plab loj Wise or intelligent (literally having a
      large abdomen and heart).
   (b) plab plaw loj (from 'plawv') Wise or intelligent
      (literally having a large abdomen and heart).

3. plab
   plab hlaub The lower part of the human leg, particu-
      larly the fleshy part at the back of the leg.

4. plab
   ua plab ua plus Of one who doesn't stay at home.

5. plab
   plab hnab The seed pod in the forming of a head of
      rice (cf. 'nplej').

1. plag Pertaining to the uphill or rear side of a house.
   nyob hauv plag At the rear of the house (on the
      uphill side), at the rear wall.

2. plag
   plag nplas Disorderly.

3. plag T.c. from 'plas' (cf. 'plas').

plam To come untied, to come loose, to come apart or slip
   off.
   Plam taw lawm. My foot slipped out from under me.
   plam plhuav Came off, came completely undone.

1. plas The owl (tus).

2. plas Clf. for a wide expanse.
   plas teb A large field.
   ib plag teb One large field (t.c.)
   ib plag hluavtaws A large expanse of fire.

1. plav An empty cartridge shell (T).
   lub plav muastxwv Empty cartridge shell (T).

2. plav
   paug paug plaus plav Dusty (cf. 'paug').

plau To depart, to run away.
   plau lawm Ran Away (cf. 'khiav lawm').

1. plaub The numeral four.
   plaub fab Square, the four 'corners' of the earth.

2. plaub Litigation, cases of dispute, cases at law (clf.
   'tshaj', 'txub' and 'rooj').
   kev plaub kev ntug Trials and accusations, litigation.
   txob plaub To meet with litigation, to be charged
      in a law case.
   xeeb plaub To give rise to litigation.
   hais plaub To discuss a case of dispute or a case at
      law.
   txiav plaub To fix settlement in a law case (done
      by a headman, judge, or official).
   (a) tu plaub To make amiable settlement of a case
      of dispute or litigation, especially where
      settlement is made by a middleman "out of
      court."
   (b) kiav plaub To make amiable settlement of a case
      of dispute or litigation, especially where
      settlement is made by a middleman "out of
      court."

3. plaub Hair, fur, feathers (clf. 'tsos' for hairs).
   plaubhau Hair of the head.
   plaub muag Eyelashes, eyebrows.
   ib tug plaub A feather.
   qaws plaubhau To twist the hair into a topknot in the style of Hmong women.
   rho plaub To pluck out the hair.
   hais lus rho plaub mob nqaig (cf. 'nqaij').
   plaubhau sawv tsees The "hair on end" (also 'plaubhau xob vog').
   Plaub qaib tsis ciaj ncaig (cf. 'ciaj').

1. plaus (cf. 'pluas').

2. plaus
   paug paug plaus plaw Dusty (cf. 'paug').

plaw T.c. from 'plawv' (cf. 'plawv').

plaws Restricted post verbal intensifier contributing the idea of suddenness to the action of the preceding verb. (cf. Appendix 8).
   kaj ntug plaws Daybreak.
   tawm plaws To come out.
   dim plaws Escaped.
   Used similarly with the following verbs: (cf. the individual listings for the meanings.)
   tshab, thoob, cig, ya, phua, dhau, hla, sam

1. plawv The heart (lub).
   lub plawv The heart (physical organ).
   plab plaw loj (t.c.) Having much wisdom or intelligence (lit. a large stomach and heart).

2. plawv In the midst of, in the heart of.
   nyob plawv zoov In the heart of the jungle.
   nyob hauv plawv hiav txwv In the heart of the sea, in the middle of the ocean.
   plawv ntoo The "heart" of a tree.

3. plawv
   qhuav plawv (tus) A kind of durable tree or wood. The wood is reddish in color.

ple A word used in cursing, vile language. (cf. 'pim,' 'plev,' and 'tus ple').

pleb To crack, a crack.
   tawg pleb To crack open, to split open in a crack.
   Tawg pleb lawm. It has cracked.
   nrib pleb Just a little bit cracked.

ples T.c. from 'plev'.

plev To sting, an insect sting.
   ib ples One sting (t.c.)
   tus ple The stinger, an insect proboscis.
   Dabtsi plev koj? What has stung you?

plees Brazen, impudent, shameless.
   hluav nkauj plees plees li A shameless young woman.
   kwv txhiaj plees Bawdy or lewd songs.

pleev To swab, to apply with a swab or brush, to apply a liquid or oil coating to a surface (contr. 'leem' or 'plia').
   Muab tshuaj pleev kuv ntiv tes. Paint some medicine on my finger.

plig The human spirit or soul, spirit or soul (cf. 'ntsuj' and contr. 'dab') (clf. 'tus').
   Note: Both 'ntsuj' and 'plig' are used to refer to the soul or spirit and there is no apparent distinction.
   (a) tus ntsuj tus plig The soul, the spirit.
   (b) tus ntsuj plig The soul, the spirit.
   For the three kinds of "souls" (plig duab, plig qaib, and plig nyuj) cf. the distinctions listed under 'ntsuj.'
   tso plig To "release" the spirit. This is the name given to a ceremony performed for persons who have died. It may be performed soon after death or delayed for years afterward, but it is regarded as a duty which must be performed by the living for the dead if spirit rites are to be completed. Sacrifices are made during the ceremony. The animals, etc. which necessarily were offered to the deceased at the funeral for him or her to take into the spirit world are regarded as delaying progress and reincarnation. Hence, the need for further ceremony to release the spirit from the burden being carried.
   koom plig (or 'rub plig') A special spirit rite performed after the New Year and before making new fields. (For description cf. 'koom').

plig An onomatopoetic syllable used with 'ploj' in describing certain sounds.
   plij ploj plij ploj The sound of bamboo bursting as when a bamboo grove is burning.
   hais lus plij ploj plij ploj Descriptive of strange sounding language. (speech like bamboo bursting).

plim To throw the head back (cf. 'pliaj').
   plim pliaj To throw the head back.
   zaum plim pliaj To sit with the head thrown back.
   (a) nyob plim pliaj ntuv With the head thrown back facing up.
   (b) plim pliaj u With the head thrown back facing up.

plis Leopard cat, wildcat (tus).
  Nag hmo plis tom ob tug qaib. Last night a leopard
    cat killed two chickens.

plia To paint, to apply a liquid or non-solid coating.
  plia To apply a liquid or non-solid coating.
  pleev To swab.
  leem To apply a solid coating or surface (cf. 'meem').
  Muab av plia rau. Put a layer of earth on it.

pliab Shallow, flattened out (as of a shallow or flat
    dish, etc.)
  pliab pliab ntswg Having a flat nose.

1. pliag A moment, an instant.
  ib pliag An instant, a moment, suddenly.
  ib pliag ntshis An instant, in an instant.

2. pliag A clam (lub).
  (a) piag deg A small clam, also the piece of shell
    on which opium is rolled in preparation for
    smoking.
  (b) piag deg A small clam, also the piece of shell
    on which opium is rolled in preparation for
    smoking.

3. pliag Restricted post verbal intensifier. (cf.
    Appendix 8).
  ploj pliag To disappear, to go out of sight.

pliaj The forehead.
  hau pliaj The forehead.
  plim pliaj To throw the head back (with the fore-
    head turned upward).
  nyob plim pliaj ntuv With the head thrown back and
    facing upward.

plias Restricted post verbal intensifier with 'lawm.'
    (cf. Appendix 8).
  neeg lus lawm plias A person quick of speech, a
    fast talker.

pliav A scar.
  caws pliav A scar.

1. plob To hunt for game.
  Nws mus plob hav zoov lawm. He went hunting.

2. plob
  Dais tsiam plob. The bear jumps down (from the tree).

1. ploj To disappear, to become lost, lost to sight.
  poob ploj lawm Fell and disappeared, lost.
  ploj nthi Disappeared completely.
  ploj lawm Disappeared.
  ploj muag ntais Disappeared from sight.
  (a) ploj pliag Disappeared.
  (b) ploj ntais Disappeared.

2. ploj An onomatopoetic syllable used with 'plij.'
    (cf. 'plij').

plos To go through shallow water or through grass or under-
    growth where there is no path, to wade.
  plos ntxhias hauv lub pas dej mus. Waded through
    the pond.

1. plov An empty cartridge shell (lub).

2. plov
  hais lus plov meej To speak plainly, to speak openly.

3. plov
  qhov muag plov nkaus Eyes sealed shut.

ploog Restricted post verbal intensifier (cf. Appendix 8).
  hnub liab ploog Sunset.
  liab ploog Very red, bright red.

1. plooj Blurred, indistinct, not clearly visible.
  plooj plooj li Blurred, not distinct.
  plooj qhov muag Blurring to the eyes.

2. plooj To join pieces together edge to edge.
  plooj sev To put the edging on an apron.
  plooj phab ntsa To join into a wall.

plus ua plab ua plus Of one who doesn't stay at home.

plua (a) plua tshauv Dust.
  (b) plua av Dust.
  nyob saum plua tshauv av On the dusty ground,
    e.g. a dusty road.
  tawm plua tshauv tog There where the dust is rising.
  plua plav - dust which settles on things
  plau plav (alternate spelling for 'plua plav')
  paug paug plaus plav - dusty

pluaj Clf. for split lengths of rattan or bamboo for weaving
    or tying.
  pluaj ncau Rattan lengths.

1. pluag Poor, to be poor.
  neeg pluag pluag A poor person.

2. pluag T.c. from 'pluaj' or 'pluas' (cf. 'pluaj' and 'pluas').

1. pluas Puckery to the mouth, astringent, of unripe fruit (cf. 'hob').
txiv pluas Unripe fruit, puckery fruit.
ngaij pluas Meat not good, meat going spoiled.

2. pluas Clf. for a meal or a dose.
ib pluag mov One meal of rice (t.c.)
Muab tshuaj ua rau pluas noj. Take the medicine in six doses.

pluam To relinquish, release.
pluam lus To agree to, to give permission.
lub tsho pluam tsis tau A retained placenta.

1. pluav Having corners, i.e. not round (contr. 'kheej'). Thus a hexagonal or octagonal shaped piece of wood, etc. would be called 'pluav.'

2. pluav Descriptive of wood changing shape when drying.

3. pluav Sometimes used as a clf. for beans (cf. 'taum').

PLH

1. plhaub A shell, a case or a small box (clf. 'lub').
plhaub qe An egg shell.
plhaub muastxwv A cartridge shell.
plhaub kws Corn husks.
plhaub maj Hemp stalks.
plhaub taub dej A water bottle, a canteen.

2. plhaub The owl
plhaub hwb The owl (tus).

plhaw A jump.
dhia ib plhaw Made a jump, leaped up, to jump.
nqe plhaw Jumped down.
dhia tib plhaw Made one jump, made a single leap.
plhaw ntxhias Jumped suddenly.
tib plhaw mus Went with a jump.

plhawv Restricted post verbal intensifier. (cf. Appendix 8).
tawg plhawv To burst forth.
Tawg plhawv ib lub npuas dej tuaj. A bubble of water came up.
hais phua plhawv To speak openly (cf. 'tabmeeg').
Nws tsiv plhawv lawm. He suddenly moved away.

1. plhe
raj plhe le A trumpet.

2. plhe
plhe ncauj Lips portruding, a protruding mouth.

3. plhe A syllable used in cursing, vile language.

plhis To change form, of an insect which emerges from the chrysalis stage in a new form by stripping off the old covering, to strip off the old body and emerge in a new one.

1. plhob
hwj plhob The water lily.

2. plhob
hais lus plhob phij To speak worthless words.

plhom plhom moj Foolish, reckless, rash, unrestrained.
plhom plhom moj Of a horse galloping about loose.
plhom moj hais To speak foolishly or rashly;
plhom moj lam dag tibneeg To tell foolish lies.

plhov hais lus plhov xem To speak circuitously, to speak of something indirectly so as to soften the effect.

plhu Cheek, the cheeks (clf. 'lub' or 'sab').
ib sab plhu One cheek.
paj plhu Cheeks, face.
fee plhu To turn the cheek, turn the face away.
plhu hluav hluav ncuav A face marked with pockmarks.
(a) ua plhu puas nyag A dark and crestfallen face.
(b) plhu ua plhu nyaj A dark and crestfallen face.
muaj plhus To have respect or honor, to have "face"
(also meaning 'to be bold or brazen') (t.c.)
tsis muaj plhus Has lost respect, has no pride or honor (t.c.)

plhus   T.c. from 'plhu' (cf. 'plhu').

plhuaj   plhuaj taub (lub) A gourd, especially a gourd used for carrying water.

plhuav   Restricted post verbal intensifier. (Cf. Appendix 8).
tso plhuav To relinquish, to put down, to release.
plam plhuav Came undone, came off.
poob plhuav Fell, fallen down.
txhais plhuav Of a trap springing, sprung.
tso siab plhuav To relax, to put one's heart at rest.
dim plhuav Escaped.
dim plhuav khoom haujlwm Free from work, at leisure.

plhws   To stroke, to caress, to rub lightly, to brush off.
plhws tsho To brush a jacket.
plhws nrhab To rub off the burs clinging to one's clothing.

Q

1. qa   The back of the throat, the inner throat.
txhaws qa A stuffed up throat.
(a) pob yeeb qa The Adam's apple,
(b) pob qa The Adam's apple.
kis kis qa A raspy or itchy throat.

2. qa   Pertaining to lizards.
nab qa One of many kinds of lizards (tus).
nab qa tsiav A type of small lizard (tus).
nab qa nqhuab Dry land lizard, the iguana (tus).

1. qab   Sweet in taste, pleasant to the taste.
qab qab zib Sweet as honey.
qab xob (cf. 'xob').
noj tsis qab - Unpleasant to eat, tasteless

2. qab   Pleasant to the feelings.
qab siab Happy, at ease, satisfied in heart.
tsis qab siab Ill at ease, unhappy about something.

3. qab   Under, underneath, at the base of, the lower side of.
hauv qab Underneath, under.
hauv lub qab roog Under the table.
hauv tsob qab ntoos At the base of the tree, under the shade of the tree.
hauv lub qab roob At the foot of the mountain.
hauv lub qab pobzeb Under the rock.
qab kev The downhill side of the trail or road, the lower side of the trail (contr. 'qaum kev').
nram qab kev Down below the trail.
qab deg Downstream.
qab tsuas Base of the cliff.
ib lub qab ntuj All under the heavens.
qab ntug liab ploog Sunset (red at the base of the heavens).
qab tsib taug The area just below the house, outside and on the downhill side of the house.

4. qab   Behind, that which is behind.
lawv qab To come behind, to follow.
Nws lawv kuv qab tuaj. He followed me here.
tom qab After, afterward, behind.
Nws thim tom qab He turned back.
taug qab To follow after another person, to follow another's footsteps.
liab qab Naked.

5. qab   To return, go back, go backward.
rov qab To return.
tshwm rov qub qab mus Returned the way he came.
thaub qab To go backward.

6. qab   To remember.
nco qab To remember.

7. qab   Usefulness, worthwhileness.
qabhau Usefulness, worthwhileness.
tsis muaj qabhau Worthless, of no use.
Tsis pom qab mus. I don't know how to go.
Tsis pom qab ua li cas. I don't know what to do.

8. qab   qab qwj A spiral style of Hmong embroidery.

9. qab   qab khav A porch (lub) (raised porch above ground level.)

10. qab   qab tsag A porch (lub) (lower down than 'qab khav').

11. qab   qab thoob Half-moon, half-moon in shape (like the boards forming the bottom of a wooden bucket).

12. qab
    ntiv tes rwg qab The little finger (tus).
    ntiv taw rwg qab The little toe (tus).

qag Axle, swivel.
    qag tswb nees The clapper in a horse bell.

qaj Snoring.
    ua qaj To snore, snoring.
    ua qaj qaug nyos Sound asleep and snoring hard.

qas Used with 'ntsoov' or 'ntsuav' as a restricted post
       verbal intensifier. (cf. 'ntsoov' and 'ntsuav'
       Also cf. Appendix 8, pp. 257.
    nco qas ntsoov To remember well.
    yaj qas ntsuav To disappear suddenly.
    ua liam txwv qas ntsuav To do poorly.

1. qav Frog, the frog (tus).
    qav kaws Toad, the toad (tus).

2. qav Food (rice and vegetables and meat).
    ib diav qav A spoonful of food.
    ua ib.roog qav loj To put on a big feast.

qaib Chicken, pertaining to chickens.
    tus qaib The chicken.
    tus poj qaib The hen.
    tus lau qaib The rooster.
    qe qaib Chicken eggs.
    qaib nteg qe Chickens lay eggs.
    qaib tsauj The chicken cackles.
    qaib cuab The hen clucks.
    qaib qua The rooster crows.
    qaib quaj The chicken cries out in fright.
    nkauj qaib A pullet, a young hen.
    qaib rheeb kab Chicken scratching for worms.
    qaib tseev Type of chicken with curled feathers
       that protrude from the body.
    twm qaib A lone chicken, the only one hatched.
    (a) ib pab qaib A flock of chickens.
    (b) ib npog qaib A flock of chickens.
    qaib ncawg cooj Chickens go to roost, chickens
       enter the roost.
    ntxeev tis qaib To tie a chicken's wings together
       behind its back, used also of tying a person's
       hands behind his back.
    (a) saib qaib To divine by observing the position
       of the feet and bones of a slain chicken.
    (b) saib tshiav thawj To divine by observing the
       position of the feet and bones of a slain
       chicken.
    lwm qaib (cf. 'lwm').

kooj kub lub lug The sound of a cock crowing.
khaum khaum The sound of a hen clucking.
pom qaib pom qaib The sound made by a hen when she
   has laid an egg.

qaij To lean, to be inclined to one side, slanted.
    qaij hlo Leaning, leaning to one side.
    hnub qaij Afternoon (sun declining).
    sau qaij To write on the slant.
    qaij nplas mus To steer away from, to avoid, to lean
       away from.

1. qaim To hold under the armpit, to carry under the arm.
    qaim hauv qhov tsos To hold under the armpit,
       clasp under the arm.

2. qaim
    (a) qaim hli Bright moonlight.
    (b) tshav hli Bright moonlight.

1. qais The collar bone (tus).

2. qais Clf. for skeins of thread or rope, a skein.

2. qais
    ua qais To belch, to eject wind or stomach gas.

qaiv To hang thread on the cross-frame or 'tshuab ntxaiv'
    qaiv ntxaiv To hang thread on the cross-frame or
       'tshuab ntxaiv'. (cf. 'ntxaiv').

qau The penis, the male organ of copulation (tus).
    (referring to the organ in humans or animals).
    (cf. 'pim,' 'noob qes,' 'tsoob').
    'tus qau' is the term used by adults referring to the
       male sex member. It is also used as vile
       language in cursing. The term 'tus hnyuv'
       or 'tus hnyuv qau' is also used but more by
       children or of children. The following terms
       are listed here for comparison:
    (a) sib tsoob Term for human coition or copulation,
       the sex act.
    (b) tsoob pim Term for human coition or copulation,
       the sex act.
    (c) tsoob paum Term for human coition or copulation,
       the sex act.
    (a) tshov Copulation in animals.
    (b) sib nce Copulation in animals.
    (a) mob qau Vile language used by children.
    (b) mob pim Vile language used by children.

1. qaub Sour.
    zaub qaub Pickled cabbage.

2. qaub
   qaub ncaug Spittle.

3. qaub To gradually bend something over (as a tree, etc.),
   to gradually coax or entice another into action.
   Lawv qaub nws ntseeg. They coaxed him to believe.

4. qaub
   cuav qaub No good, useless, of no account.

1. qaug To fall over with the roots still in the ground
   (as of grain beaten down by wind or rain).

2. qaug Weak and tottering.
   qaug qaug zog Weak, tottering, unsteady on the feet.
   qaug lawm Tottered and fell, fainted.
   qaug doj qaug de Tottering, unsteady, reeling from
   side to side.
   qaug cawv Drunk, intoxicated, reeling from drink.
   qaug tshuaj Reeling and unsteady on the feet from
   effects of taking medicine.
   qaug dab ntub Nodding with sleepiness, sluggish and
   unsteady due to sleepiness, drowsy.

3. qaug
   (a) mob dab peg Epilepsy, to have an epileptic fit.
   (b) qaug dab peg Epilepsy, to have an epileptic fit.

4. qaug
   ua qaj qaug nyos (cf. 'qaj').

5. qaug To despise, to disparage.
   tub qaug To despise.
   hais lus tub qaug neeg To speak disparagingly of
   others, to speak despising words.

1. qauj Fail to hatch out (contr. 'daug').
   ge qauj An egg that has failed to hatch.

2. qauj To keep forgetting things. (also 'tsis
   hnov qauj To keep forgetting things. (also 'tsis
   nco qab hlaw hlias').

1. qaum The back.
   nraub qaum The back, the region of the back between
   the shoulders and above the waist (lub) (cf.
   'duav').
   qaum tes The back of the hand.
   qaum taw The top of the foot.
   qaum tsev At the back of the house.
   nkaj qaum The backbone.
   kwj qaum The "valley" or depression of the backbone
   region.

2. qaum
   qaum kev The uphill side of the road or trail
   (contr. 'qab kev').
   pem qaum kev Up above the trail.

3. qaum
   qaum ntuj The high heavens.
   ntiajteb qaum ntuj The heavens and the earth.

4. qaum To swindle.

1. qaus To have a white spot in the eye.
   qhov muag qaus lawm The eye has a white spot in it.

2. qaus
   kab qaus les The dragonfly (tus).

1. qauv Pattern (as a pattern used in doing embroidery)
   (tus).
   saib qauv To study the pattern, to follow a pattern
   in doing embroidery.

2. qauv
   cov nquam qauv The pallbearers (cf. 'tuag').

1. qawg Startled, started in fright.
   tib qawg Startled, started in fright.

2. qawg
   sib qawg T.c. from 'qawm' (cf. 'qawm').

qawj To wear a depression in something.
   (a) qawj To wear a depression in something (as when
   an ulcer eats into the skin or of a road worn
   down by use).
   (b) qawj qees To wear a depression in something (as
   when an ulcer eats into the skin or of a road
   worn down by use).

qawm To be on very intimate terms, to have and show
   affection for.
   sib qawg (t.c.) Of two persons holding hands on
   parting and showing signs of affection.

1. qaws To roll up (to roll up a sleeve or trouser leg, etc.)
   qaws ceg ris To roll up the trouser leg.
   qaws plaubhau To roll the hair into a topknot in the
   fashion of Hmong women.

2. qaws Of a group gathering together, to gather into a
   group.
   Neeg coob coob qaws tuaj. A great many people gathered.

1. qawv Restricted post verbal intensifier either used by
   itself or after 'qos' (cf. Appendix 8).
   tom hniav qawv Biting and gnashing of teeth.
   tom hniav qos qawv To clench the teeth, gnash the
   teeth.

2. qawv Restricted post verbal intensifier after 'nrov'
   nrov qis qawv The sound as of knuckles cracking.

1. qe Egg, like an egg, pertaining to an egg, a cocoon.
   ib lub qe An egg (clf. 'lub').
   nteg qe To lay eggs.
   puag qe To set on eggs.
   Qaib puag qe. The hen is setting on her eggs.
   qe daug The eggs hatch.
   hli qe The white of the egg.
   nkaub qe Egg yolk.
   plhaub qe Egg shell.
   ib zeg qe One nest of eggs, one setting of eggs.
   (a) noob qes (lub) The testicles (cf. 'qau').
   (b) hnyuv qe (lub) The testicles (cf. 'qau').

2. qe To shut (of eyes, etc.) (cf. 'kaw').
   qe muag To shut the eyes.

1. qeb (Note that this pronunciation is sometimes heard
   as 'qib') A step (vertically) (cf. 'theem').
   ib qeb ib qeb mus To go up one step at a time.

2. qeb Trigger.
   qeb hnee (t.c.) The trigger of a crossbow.

3. qeb A certain type of grain.

1. qeg (Note that this is sometimes heard as 'qig') To
   consume, to use up.
   qeg (or 'qig') hnub nyoog To use time, to waste time.
   qig hnub nyoog li Time consuming.
   taws roj av qeg Burns the kerosene quickly, uses a
   lot of kerosene.

2. qeg To quake, earthquake.
   ntuj qeg Earthquake (also 'ntiajteb qeg').

3. qej Short in stature.
   qej taub Short in stature.
   neeg qej taug A short person.

1. qej (also 'qij') Garlic.

2. qej
   pob qej txha A bone joint.

1. qes (also 'qis') Low.
   Txhob ua tsuaj ntxaij qes qes. Don't make the shelf
   over the fire too low.

2. qes Sprained.
   pobtxha qes lawm A sprained joint.

3. qes
   noob qes T.c. from 'qe' (cf. 'qe').

1. qev (also 'qiv').
   qev To borrow, to lend to.
   Kuv qev koj rab taus. I'm borrowing your axe.
   Thov muab koj rab taus qev rau kuv. Please lend me
   your axe.
   qev kauv txhais To "borrow the legs of a deer" i.e.
   to flee from something.

2. qev
   choj qev A swinging bridge (as of rattan, etc.)

1. qee Some, a portion of.
   qee leej Some people.
   qee zaus Sometimes.

2. qee To take some portion away from a larger quantity, to
   put a portion aside.
   qee dej To pour off a bit of water (cf. 'theej'
   and 'hliv').
   Muab qee ua ib pawg ib pawg. Take and divide it
   into piles.
   Muab ob phoo tes qee mentsis nplej. Take out two
   handfuls of rice.
   tus uas qee qhovtxhiachaw One who pilfers little bits.

qeeb Slowly, slow, clumsily (contr. 'nrawm').
   mus qeeb qeeb li Goes awfully slowly.

qeeg To quake, earthquake (pronunciation as used in Laos)
   (cf. 'qeg').
   ntiajteb qeeg Earthquake (as said in Laos).

qeej The Hmong musical pipes (rab) (cf. 'tshov').
   tshov qeej To blow the pipes.
   ntiv qeej The bamboo pipes
   set into the stock of
   the Meo pipes.

1. qees Restricted post verbal intensifier used either by
   itself or in the combination 'qos qees.' It
   contributes the idea of constancy or continuity
   to the action of the verb. (cf. Appendix 8, p. 474).
   hais qees To continue talking.
   ua qees To continue doing.
   qawj qees To wear a depression.
   cem qees Kept scolding.
   quaj qos qees Kept crying.
   thov qos qees Kept asking for.

Also with the following verbs: (see the individual entries for the meanings).
noj, khawb, ntov, nkag, pab, hnyav, tos, chim,
tuaj, mus, rov, los, ntaus, khiav

2. qees Restricted post verbal intensifier in the combination 'quj qees' which adds the idea of being slow and steady to the character of the verb. (cf. Appendix 8, p. 469).
rov quj qees Slowly returned.
chim quj qees Gradually his anger rose.
hais quj qees Spoke slow and deliberately.
tos quj qees Waited patiently.
khiav quj qees Slowly departed.
Used similarly with the following verbs (cf. the individual listings for meanings).
mus, los, tuaj, ntaus, ua

3. qees Restricted post verbal intensifier used in the combination 'qog qees' (cf. Appendix 8 and cf. 'qos qees' above).
quaj qog qees To cry loudly.
ua qog qees Of many persons doing things together (cf. 'ua zom zaws').

qeev Phlegm.
Kuv nti tau hnoos qeev ntshav los. I spit up bloody phlegm.

qi (cf. 'qe').

qig (cf. 'qeg').

qij (cf. 'qej').

qiv (cf. 'qev').

1. qis (cf. 'qes').

2. qis hniav To clench the teeth.

3. qis Post verbal intensifier used in combination with 'qawv' after 'nrov.' (cf. Appendix 8).
nrov qis qawv Sound as of knuckles cracking.

1. qia
caws qia A jump, to jump, to leap.
nyaj caws qia The monkey leaps.
caws qia ntsos Leaped, made a leap.
dhia ib caws qia sawv ntsug Stood up with a jump.

2. qia
qia dub Selfish (cf. 'cuajkhaum').
neeg qia dub A selfish person, stingy person.

qiab
sib qiab Hooked together.

qiag The separation between boards in a wall, crack in a wall.

qiaj A species of tree (tus).

1. qias Disgusting, dirty, repelling.
qias qias neeg Disgusting to a person.
qias qias txab txab Disgusting and dirty.

2. qias
qias hli Bright moonlight.

qiav To make a shoulder on a knife blade to fit the handle.

1. qog To mimic, to imitate in ridicule.

2. qog A carbuncle, a large inflamed lump producing no pus (lub), a glandular swelling. He has an inflamed Nws mob ib lub qog hauv qhov tsos. swelling in his armpit.

2. qog Used in combination with 'qees' as a restricted post verbal intensifier (cf. 'qees').

qoj To twist or to turn something.
Muab lub nalika qoj ceev ceev. Wind the watch tight.

1. qos To close (cf. 'kaw').
qos (or 'qhaws') qhov ncauj Close the mouth.
qos nkaus kaus Close the umbrella.

2. qos Any of a large variety of tubers.
qos liab (lub) The sweet potato.
qos yaj ywv (lub) The white potato.
Note: Here we list the names of other kinds of tubers whose specific description in English we are not able to give.
qos tau teeb   qos ntshov
qos ntoo ntus   qos faiv
qos do

3. qos A restricted post verbal intensifier used in combination with 'qees' and 'qawv.' (cf. 'qees' and 'qawv').

4. qos It is also used as a p.v.int. with certain other
verbs although this is more common in Blue
(Green) Hmong speech.
ntaiv qos hwv Extremely hot.
Nws muab siab qhia qos zog tiag. He really has a
heart to teach.
See also listings under the verbs:
ntsoov, nrees, ntsuav, nraim, nrog

qov Yuav muab koj qov. I'll kill you.

qoob Field crops (grain, etc.)
ua qoob To do field work, to raise crops.
qoob loo Grain, crops.
ua qoob ua loo To raise crops, to farm, do field
work.

1. qoos Able, effective, productive, having results.
Nplej tsis qoos. The rice has not filled out in the
kernel.

2. qoos
ki qoos ki qoos Rumbling, the sound of rumbling in
the stomach (Thus a post verbal intensifier
after 'nrov.' Cf. 'nrov')

1. qoov A kind of reed like vegetation the heart of which
is edible.

2. qoov
ua nplooj qoov tshaws (cf. 'pobkws' p. 231).

qub Old (of inanimate objects) (contr. 'laus').
lub qub zos The old village.
qub txeeg qub teg Old things, old articles, e.g.
things left to children by the parents.
qub mov Old cooked rice.
qub teb qub chaws Old or original place.
txoj qub ke The old way.
tshwm rov qub qab mus Went back the way he came.
Note: Unlike most modifying words this word precedes
rather than follows the word modified.

1. quj Restrictive post verbal intensifier used in combination with 'qees.' (cf. 'qees').

2. quj Yuav muab koj quj I'll kill you. (cf. 'qov').

1. qus Wild, untamed (contr. 'nyeg').
tsiaj qus Wild animals.
nyuj qus Wild ox (tus).
dab qus Wild spirits of the jungle as contrasted
'dab nyeg' the spirits of the home. (cf. 'dab').
mab qus Wild people, uncivilized people of the
jungle who have no houses or villages such
as the "Yellow Leaf" tribe in Thailand.

2. qus
ua mem muj qus Not clearly conscious, knocked out.

quv
ua nem nuv quv (cf. 'nem').

1. qua To crow.
qaib qua The cock crows.
qaib qua ib tsig The cock crowed once.

2. qua To level a site, level a plot of ground, a house site.
khawb qua tsev To level a house site.
qua tsev Site for a house.

quab
quab npuas Young castrated pig (tus) (t.c.).

1. quaj To cry aloud, to weep aloud (contr. 'los kua muag').
Txhob quaj. Stop crying.
quaj quaj taug li Always crying (of children).
quaj tawg ntho Broke out in loud crying.
nyim quaj quaj tias... He cried and said...
quaj ngus ntswg dhawv dhev Wept loudly and bitterly.
quaj laug laws To cry loudly.
quaj nrov hnyev To whimper, whimpering.

2. quaj To growl, to squeal.
Tsov quaj laus nkoos. The tiger growled.

3. quaj To make a loud noise, a loud noise.
xob quaj Thunder.
tsheb quaj tse The truck rumbled on, sound of a
motor vehicle.

quam
tus quam yej caws A type of triggering device for
a deadfall trap using a heavy stone.

1. quas To come in between.
quas lus To add words to an expression so that it
sounds smooth and complete.
quas lawm Came in between.

2. quas
   quas hli Bright moonlight (cf. 'qaim hli' and
   'tshav hli').

3. quas
   Hmoob quas npab The striped Hmong.

1. quav Feces, excrement (clf. 'pam' for passages of
   'quav').
   ua ib pam quav Had one elimination.
   tso quav To defecate.
   cem quav Constipated.

2. quav Used figuratively of evil, that which is bad and
   distasteful.
   txuas quav Makes up evil, tells a lot of lies.
   yuav paim quav The evil will come out in due time.

3. quav Excretion.
   quav muag Excretion from the eyes (contr. 'kua
   muag').

4. quav Straw, grain stubble, stalks.
   (a) quav nplej Rice straw.
   (b) quav nyab npleg Rice straw.
   quav kws Corn stalks.
   quav yeeb Dry stalks of the opium plants (cf. 'quav'
   Definition No. 5).
   quav ntsuas A kind of sweet edible stalk.
   tebchaws quav poj An expanse of land once inhabited
   but now just grown over with scrub vegetation.

5. quav To crave.
   quav yeeb To crave opium (cf. 'quav' Definition
   No. 4).
   quav cawv To crave intoxicating drink.

6. quav To fold or break into two equal lengths.
   Muab txoj hlua quav. Fold the rope into two equal
   lengths.
   (a) quav ceg To fold one's legs under one.
   (b) caws ceg To fold one's legs under one.

7. quav
   ua ntxhov quav niab To raise tumult, do violence.

8. quav
   tsis quav ntsej Doesn't listen, pays no attention,
   disregards, having no interest in or concern for.

9. quav
   ntxais quav hniav (cf. 'ntxais').

qw To cry out loudly, to rant, shout, rave.
   qw tawg ntho Shouted out suddenly.

qwb The back of the neck.
   qhov qwb The depression at the back of the neck.
   caj qwb The backbone ridge at the back of the neck.
   hais nraum caj qwb To speak behind one's back.
   ua tuv txias tom caj qwb Speaking evil behind my
   back (like body lice biting my neck!)

1. qwj The snail (clf. 'lub').
   qwj yeeg A snail.

2. qwj Spirals of embroidery.
   qab qwj A spiral pattern type of embroidery.

1. qws A club, a stick (rab).
   qws nruas A drumstick, stick to beat the spirit gong.
   qws txob A pestle (rab), pestle for crushing pepper,
   etc. in the small stone mortar.

2. qws A type of trap wherein a tree is set to fall and
   scare the game into a pit set with bamboo
   spears (ntsha) (clf. 'rooj').

qwv
   qwv nplooj To make a loud noise by blowing on a
   leaf or a blade of grass.

QH

1. qha To dry over or near the fire for a long time, to
   smoke something to preserve it. (contr. 'sub').
   qha nqaij To smoke meat.

2. qha A restricted post verbal intensifier. (cf. Appendix 8).
   ncaj qha Perfectly straight.

qhab The rafters, the narrow slanting poles in the roof of a Hmong house to which the leaves or covering is secured.
  qhab tsev The rafters, the narrow slanting poles in the roof of a Hmong house to which the leaves or covering is secured (cf. 'tsev').
  sam qhab To put the rafters on.

qhav Khavloom (tus) (T) The governor.

1. qhaib Crossed one over the other, entwined.
  sib qhaib Of fingers crossed one over the other.

2. qhaib Ntuj yeej qhaib tus ntxhais ntawd cia rau koj lawm. Heaven has already promised the girl to you.

1. qhau To fall flat, to fall over, fall to the ground (of an article that has been standing).

2. qhau hauvcaug To kneel (cf. 'txhos' and 'kim').

3. qhau qhau cai "The case falls" Term used to describe the failure of a case at law.

4. qhau sib qhau To wrestle (trying to see who can make the other fall over) (cf. 'ntswj').

qhaub cuab qhaub A type of snare for large wild game made with a bent tree as a spring and a rope as a snare. (clf. 'rooj') (cf. 'rooj').

1. qhauv Ground corn, etc. for pig food.
  npua noj qhauv Pigs eating pig food.
  npua qhauv Pig food.

2. qhauv thiab qhauv (cf. 'thiab').

1. qhaws To close (of the mouth, etc.)
  qhaws qhovncauj Close the mouth (also 'qos qhovncauj').

2. qhaws raws Weak and hardly able to walk.

qhawv Post verbal intensifier, restricted, (cf. Appendix 8).
  nkag qhawv qho lawv qab (cf. 'nkag').

qhe qhe mov To eat (impolite speech).

1. qheb (also 'qhib') To open, to open up (pronounced 'qhib' in Laos).
  Qheb qhov rooj. Open the door.
  qheb kev To open a road or trail, to proclaim or propagate a new doctrine or way of doing things.
  qheb lug Opened.
  qheb hlo To open up.

2. qheb A species of tree with a hard tough wood (tus). It is much sought after for house building because it is very hard and durable and splits readily into boards.

qhem qhuj qhem Clearing the throat.

qhev A slave, a servant, an employee (tus).
  tub qhe A male servant (tus) (t.c.)
  nkauj qhe A female servant (tus) (t.c.)
  ib tug qhev One servant, a slave.
  ua qhev To be enslaved.

1. qhib (cf. Definition No. 1 'qheb').

2. qhib
  (a) roob qhib The shin, the front of the lower leg.
  (b) roob hlaub The shin, the front of the lower leg.

qhia To teach, to instruct, to inform, to tell.
  qhia kev To teach the way, to teach a doctrine or way of doing things.
  Txhob qhia kuv. Don't tell me what to do!
  Thov koj qhia kuv. Will you please teach me.
  qhia ntawv To teach out of books.

qhiav Ginger.

1. qho T.c. from 'qhov' (cf. 'qhov').

2. qho Post verbal intensifier used with 'qhawv' (cf. 'qhawv').

qhob Unnaturally cold in body.
  qhob qhob Slightly cold in body as if on the verge of becoming ill.
  lub cev qhob laig dai Cold and shivering in illness.

1. qhov Place, location.
   qhov no Here.
   qhov twg Where?
   qhov ped Up there.
   qhov nrad Down there.
   ib qho One place (t.c.)
   Muab cia rau ib qho. Put it away in one place.
   Mob ob peb qho. Hurts in several places.
   qhov txhia qhov chaw Everywhere.
   (a) Mob qhov txhia qhov chaw. Hurts all over.
   (b) Mob qhovtxhiachaw. Hurts all over.

2. qhov Thing, article, points or divisions in a speech.
   qhov ib The first thing, the first point, in the
      first place (and similarly with other numerals).
   Kuv yuav hais ob peb qho xwb. I only want to speak
      of two or three things.
   qhovtxhiachaw Articles, things in general, things.

3. qhov Hole, a hole (lub).
   tho qhov To make a hole (cf. 'khawb' and 'tsheb').
   ib lub qhov One hole.

4. qhov Used as a part of many words where the idea of
      emptiness or the idea of a hole has some con-
      nection (clf. 'lub').
   qhov ncauj Mouth.
   qhov muag Eye, eyes.
   qhov ntsej The ear, the ear canal.
   qhov ntswg The nose, nostril.
   qhov rooj Door, gate (cf. 'rooj').
   qhov cub The cooking fire, fireplace.
   qhov txos The fireplace for cooking pig food.
   qhov tsos Armpit.
   qhov ntxa Grave.
   qhov qwb Depression at the back of the neck.
   qhov tsev A crack in the wall of the house.
   qhov rais Window.
   qhov tsua Cave in the solid rock.
   qhov av A hole in the ground.
   (a) qhov dej A spring of water.
   (b) qhov dej txhawv A spring of water.
   (a) qhov saus Place where water disappears into
      the ground.
   (b) qhov dej saus Place where water disappears
      into the ground.
   qhov ntwj A hole in the ground where the earth is
      sunken in of itself.
   qhov timthaj A well.
   qhov tuag The grave, death.

5. qhov Dimension, used in words describing dimensions.
   qhov ntev Length.
   qhov dav Breadth.
   qhov tob Depth.
   qhov siab Height.

1. qhoob To cradle in one's arms, to fondle an infant in
      one's arms.
   Note that 'ngee' is much the same in meaning but less
      used.

2. qhoob To call the young. Used of persons and of chickens
      only. (cf. 'cuab').

qhuj
   qhuj qhem Clearing the throat.

1. qhua Those not of the same surname or clan.
   ua qhua To visit those outside the clan.
   hnub ua qhua txws The day of preparation for the
      dead, day before burial, day when relatives
      bring rice, paper money, etc. as gifts for the
      deceased. (cf. 'tuag').
   cov ua hauv qhua Those relatives who bring rice and
      paper money, etc. as gifts for the deceased
      on the 'hnub ua qhua txws' (above) (cf. 'tuag').
   cov qhua tshoob Wedding guests (cf. 'tshoob').
   cov qhua vauv Bridegroom's party (cf. 'tshoob').

2. qhua Pertaining to diseases that produce a rash.
   qhua pias Measels.
   qhua maj Chickenpox.
   qhua taum Smallpox.

1. qhuab To discipline, to punish, to teach by discipline,
      train.
   qhuab menyuam To discipline or train children.
   qhuab qhia To teach by disciplining.

2. qhuab
   qhuab ke To teach the way, show the way (a specific
      term used in funerals) (cf. 'tuag').

qhuam
   lub tsho qhuam A singlet, a sleeveless shirt.

1. qhuas To praise, marvel at, admire, exult in.
   qhuas zoo To praise, to show appreciation for or to
      speak of the good of another.
   qhuas Vajtswv Ntuj To praise God, to glorify God.
   Nws rov qhuas nws. He praised himself. He boasted.

2. qhuas
   dab qhuas The objects pertaining to spirit worship
      in the home.

1. qhuav Dry, arid.
   liaj qhua Dry paddy field (t.c.)
   ntoo qhuav qhuav Dry tree or wood.

2. qhuav Alone, unembellished.
   noj mov qhuav xwb Eating just plain cooked rice without meat or vegetables.

3. qhuav Free, without payment.
   pub qhuav qhuav To give without payment or expectation of any return.

4. qhuav Of itself, having no condition or circumstance attached.
   tuaj qhuav qhuav xwb Just came with no special purpose or business.
   nyob qhuav qhuav xwb There with nothing to do, unoccupied, just living.
   taug kev khaws taw qhuav To obtain for nothing or without labor.
   qhuav nquas Dry, empty, having nothing.
   cev qhuav nquas Empty-handed.

5. qhuav
   nyuam qhuav Just now (cf. 'nyuam').
   ib nyuam qhuav A moment, a short time.
   nyuam qhuav tuaj Just came, arrived this moment or just a moment ago. (cf. 'los txog ntua').
   nyuam qhuav mob Just began to hurt.

6. qhuav
   qhuav plawv (cf. 'plawv' Definition No. 3).

7. qhuav
   siab tsis qhuav dej, ntsws tsis qhuav ntshav (cf. 'ntsws').

qhws qhws ntseg (lub) Type of long elaborate earring. (contr. 'poj co').

qhwv To wrap up.
   qhwv tshuaj To apply medicine and wrap with a bandage, apply a medical dressing.

R

1. rab Clf. for implements and tools, clf. for things with a handle and held in the hand.
   rab riam Knife.
   rab diav Spoon.
   rab taus Axe.
   rab rauj Hammer.

2. rab Clf. for a large area of fields (cf. 'daim' for single fields).

1. rag An alternative pronunciation sometimes heard for 'ras' (cf. 'ras').

2. rag
   mob ntsej rag (cf. 'ntsej').

1. raj A tube (lub), tube-like.
   lub raj kwv dej Bamboo water-carrying tube (lub).
   raj nplaim A type of flute (lub).
   raj pum liv A bamboo flute (lub).
   raj lev les Small reed flute made by children.
   raj plhe le A trumpet (lub).
   raj puab raj xyu Trumpets and horns, horns made of bamboo and buffalo horn.
   raj rawg Tube for holding chopsticks.
   tshiav raj To play the Chinese style violin.

2. raj
   raj ris laus (tus) Species of long-legged spider.

3. raj
   ua raj raj ncas (cf. 'pobkws').

ras Startled, suddenly surprised, stampeded, to stampede.
   npua ras The pigs suddenly scampered away.
   nyuj ras The cattle stampeded.
   nees ras The horse stampeded or suddenly galloped away, runaway horse.
   (a) ras dheev Startled.
   (b) ras pes dheev Startled.
   (c) ras pes hlo Startled.
   siab ras dheev Suddenly surprised or suddenly wakened to something.
   ras nroo ntws The sound of stampeding.

1. rais Window.
   qhov rais A window (lub).

2. rais
   rais los To come back (note that this expression is only used in calling the spirits.) (cf. 'rov los' for ordinary use.)

1. rau To place, to put.
   Rau qhov no Put it here.
   Yuav muab rau qhov twg? Where shall I put it?
   Muab rau rau hauv. Put it inside.

2. rau Toward, to.
   Pub rau kuv. Give it to me.
   Muab tso rau hauv. Put it inside.
   Nws hais rau kuv tias... He said to me...

3. rau The numeral six.
   rau lub tsev Six houses.
   rau caum Sixty.

4. rau Fingernail, toenail, hoof or claw.
   rau tes Fingernail.
   rau taw Toenail.

5. rau Gloves (but cf. 'looj tes').

6. rau Clf. for squares of embroidery.
   ib rau paj ntaub One square of embroidery work, one section of embroidery.

1. raub
   raub ris The crab (tus).
   raub ris teb The scorpion (tus).

2. raub Of a chicken scratching.
   qaib raub The chicken is scratching for food.
   qaib raub tsev Chicken scratching on the roof.

1. raug To encounter, to meet up with, to incur, to suffer or be afflicted with.
   raug mob To suffer pain or illness.
   raug dab To meet with an evil spirit, to suffer some calamity attributed to spirits.
   raug taubhau To hit the head on something.
   raug tes To bump and injure the hand or finger.
   raug plaub To meet with litigation, to be drawn into a court case.
   raug txim To be punished, to have met with punishment for crime or evil, convicted for crime.
   cov raug txim Criminals, prisoners.
   raug tswvyim To fall prey to their schemes.

2. raug To have fellowship, to be united in heart.
   raug nws zoo Friendly with him, on very good terms.
   sib raug zoo On very good terms, in good fellowship, united in heart.

3. raug According to, agreeing with.
   raug siab According to wish, pleasing, satisfying to the heart (cf. 'dhos' and 'hum').

4. raug To know, to understand.
   Koj yuav sij raug mentsis. You will know a little about it.

rauj A hammer (clf. 'rab').

raum The kidneys (clf. 'lub').

1. raus To immerse something in liquid for a period.
   raus dej To dip in water (cf. 'da,' 'tsau' and 'tsaug').

2. raus
   Muab xub raus lawm tshauv. (cf. 'laum' Definition No. 6).

3. raus
   kab raus (tus) A species of insect or bug.

rauv
   rauv taws To light a fire, to put wood on the fire (contr. 'cuam taws').

1. rawm To be in a hurry to do something.
   rawm noj In a hurry to eat.
   rawm rawm pw Sleepy, anxious to sleep.
   Txhob rawm mus. Don't be in a hurry to leave.
   Txhob rawm ua. Don't be in a hurry to do it.
   Txhob rawm tos kuv. Don't wait for me.

2. rawm To curse, to seal with misfortune.

3. rawm A species of bamboo.

rawg Chopsticks (clf. 'txwm').
   rawg noj mov Chopsticks for eating rice.
   raj rawg Tube for holding chopsticks.
   kais rawg To push food into the mouth with the use of chopsticks.

1. raws To pursue, to chase after, to follow after, according to.
   raws tau To overtake, to catch up with.
   sau raws txoj kab Write on the line.
   raws nraim To follow exactly, according to.
   Ua raws nraim nws txoj lus qhia. Do strictly according to what he taught.
   raws li no In this way.
   raws li nws hais As he has said.
   Muab nws raws khiav. Chase him out.

2. raws
    (a) raws plab Diarrhea.
    (b) lawv plab Diarrhea.
    (c) thoj plab Diarrhea.

rawv A restricted post verbal intensifier particularly
    adding the idea of firmness or steadiness to
    the action of the verb. (cf. Appendix 8).
    khi rawv Firmly tied.
    tuav rawv pas nrig Firmly held the stick.
    tuav qws rawv Held the club tightly.
    tuav tes rawv Held hands tightly.
    chim rawv Continued angry, very offended.
    tsev sw rawv A very messy house.
    kim rawv To continue kneeling (cf. 'txhos').
    nyob rawv ntawm phab ntsa Standing (or sitting)
    over by the wall.
    Also used similarly with the following verbs: (cf.
    the individual listings for meanings).
    npuav, puab, puag, nqa, cuam, coj

re T.c. from 'rev'

rev Clf. for a stem of flowers or leaves or fruit, etc.
    rev hnab The cluster of kernels in a head of rice.
    ib re paj ntoos A stem of flowers (t.c.)

1. ri A support or post stuck into the ground.

2. ri sua tag lawm To scatter (as of a group suddenly
    scattering when startled or afraid, also used
    of shot scattering from a shotgun).

3. ri txi txiv ri Bringing forth fruit and spreading.

rig To bind up by winding something around an article
    as a strength and a covering, e.g. binding a
    knife handle with rattan.

1. ris To carry on the back, to bear.
    ris lub kawm To carry a back-basket.
    ris dej To carry water in a bucket on the back.
    Yexu ris peb lub txim. Jesus has borne our sins.
    Kuv ris tsis tau. I cannot bear it. (scolding
    or criticism, etc.)
    ris hlo To carry on the back.

2. ris
    ris txiaj Grateful.
    Kuv ris nej txiaj. I am grateful to you.
    tsis ris nws txiaj To be ungrateful, to show lack
    of appreciation for another.

3. ris
    tsis ris siab Disobedient.
    ris siab hlo To repent, to turn away from.
    Dab txoj kev kuv twb yeejlos ris siab lawm. I have
    already turned away from spirit worship.

4. ris Trousers, pants (clf. 'lub' for a pair).
    ris tsho Clothing, trousers and jacket.
    rhais ris To tuck up the trousers.
    qaws ceg ris To roll up the trouser legs.
    hlws ris The crotch of the trousers.

5. ris
    raub ris The crab (tus).
    raub ris teb The scorpion (tus).

6. ris
    raj ris laus Species of long-legged spider (tus).

riab
    riab ntshau Small head lice (cf. 'ntshauv').

riam T.c. from 'riam' (cf. 'riam').

1. riam Knife (rab).
    nqa ib rab riam To carry a knife.
    knab riam Sheath for a knife.
    hniav riam Knife edge.
    roob riag Back of the knife (t.c.)
    npluav riam Side of the knife, face of the knife.
    hov riam To sharpen a knife on a stone.
    riam yeeb Knife for collecting opium.
    riam tw A blunt ended knife.
    riam ntse hau A sharp pointed knife.

2. riam Clf. for cuts with a knife.
    xuas ib riag rau... Made one cut with a knife...

1. rob To avenge, to revenge.
    rob caub To seek revenge, to avenge (cf. 'pauj tau'),
    to repay evil for evil.

2. rob To repay.
    rob nqe To seek payment, to seek repayment for a
    debt.

1. rog Obese, fat, stout, (of adults and of animals)
    (cf. 'roj')
    Note that this is not very polite when used of persons
    however. (cf. 'npag' and 'pham').
    npua rog rog A fat pig.
    rog nthaws Of an animal nice and fat.

2. rog War, pertaining to warfare.
   ntaus rog To war, to wage warfare, to fight a war.
   (a) ntaus rog To war, to wage warfare, to fight a war.
   (b) tua rog To war, to wage warfare, to fight a war.
   (c) ua rog To war, to wage warfare, to fight a war.
   tub rog (tus) A soldier.
   tsa rog To stage a mock "battle" as part of the animistic ritual at a funeral wherein the evil spirits are driven away.
   (a) tus tsa rog The one in charge of such a "battle" with the spirits. He leads a group in circling the house and shooting off guns in mock warfare.
   (b) tus hau rog The one in charge of such a "battle" with the spirits. He leads a group in circling the house and shooting off guns in mock warfare.

roj Oil, grease, fat, resin.
   roj npua Pork fat.
   thob roj The loose fat attached to a pig's intestines.
   roj av Kerosene.
   roj hmab Rubber.
   roj tsheb Gasoline, petrol.
   tsau roj A pitch torch.
   roj faiv fuaj Flashlight batteries (lub).
   roj ntoo Tree resin, coagulated tree sap (contr. 'txab').
   ntoo txiv roj (tus) Olive tree (as used among Catholic Christians in Laos).
   roj ntshav Flesh and blood.

ros tuaj dab ros Funny, laughable.
   lus tuaj dab ros A joke, a funny saying.

rov To return, to turn back upon.
   (a) rov los To return, to come back (cf. 'rais los').
   (b) rov qab los To return, to come back (cf. 'rais los').
   (a) rov hlo Returned.
   (b) rov ntsuj Returned.
   rov ntxiv To recompense, to make amends for.
   tshwm rov qub qab mus Went back the way he came.
   rov rooj The bench tipped up at one end.

1. roob Mountain (lub) (cf. 'toj').
   lub roob siab siab A high mountain.
   lub ncov roob A mountain peak.
   lub hauv roob The foot of the mountain.
   hauv lub qab roob At the bottom of the mountain.
   roob toj luag taw A mountain ridge which spreads out toward the valley like a foot.
   ntxee roob To cross the mountain ridge
   nto ncov roob To cross the mountain peak.
   tw roob The end of the mountain.

2. roob Mountain-like, having a ridge.
   (a) roob hlaub The shin, shinbone.
   (b) roob qhib The shin, shinbone.
   roob riag (t.c.) The back side of a knife, the thick or blunt edge of a knife.
   roob moj sab Wilderness, wild area of trees and mountains.

3. roob
   roob laj The pole laid down horizontally in the crossed ends of the saplings holding down the leaves on a roof.

1. roog
   dab roog T.c. from 'rooj' (cf. 'dab' Definition No. 1, p. 27).

2. roog
   (a) ib ntxees ntuj A far country, a distant place.
   (b) ib roog ntuj (t.c. from 'rooj'), a far country, a distant place.

3. roog
   hauv qab roog (cf. 'rooj').

1. rooj An article of furniture (lub).
   rooj noj mov (lub) A table for eating.
   rooj zaum (lub) A backless bench for sitting.
   rooj tiag taw (lub) A footstool.
   hauv lub qab rooj Under the table.
   hauv qab roog The downhill side of a table at a feast (contr. 'sam tsum').
   rov rooj The bench tipped up at one end.
   rooj vis zoo (lub) A throne (as used by Catholic Christians in Laos).

2. rooj Door, gate (lub).
   rooj ntug (t.c.) The "gate" of heaven.
   lub qhov rooj A door, a gate.
   qheb qhov rooj Open the door.
   kaw qhov rooj Shut the door.
   Note: See the entries under 'qhov' for various kinds of doors.

3. rooj Used as a classifier for various kinds of traps. Descriptions for the following are found under the various separate entries.
   rooj ntxiab   rooj nta npuj
   rooj yej   rooj qhaub
   rooj muj tim   rooj cuam koob
   rooj chav   rooj qws
   rooj nruab xaub

4. rooj Used as a classifier in other contexts.
   ib roog ntuj (t.c.) (Cf. 'roog').

5. rooj
   hnub rooj nteg thaum ub Previously, before.

roos To envelop, to surround as a cloud, to shield or
   cover from above as to shelter something from
   heat or rain.

roov A species of large bird (tus).

ru Tone change from 'ruv' (cf. 'ruv').

1. rub To grasp and pull with the hand.
   rub hlua To pull a rope.
   rub tes To grasp and pull the hand.
   rub rhe Pulled off.
   rub sawvdaws los ua ib ke zoo To unite all in one
      good fellowship, to bring everyone together.
   rub zog nws sawv tsees To raise him up by the hand.

2. rub
   rub sab neeb (cf. 'neeb' p. 137).

3. rub
   rub plig (cf. 'koom plig').

ruv The roof ridge.
   lub ruv tsev The roof, the roof ridge.
   duav ruv tsev To put on the roofing over the ridge
      of the roof.
   lub qab ru tsev Under the roof ridge (t.c.)
   nqaj ru (t.c.) The ridgepole (tus).
   ncej ru (t.c.) The center upright posts of a
      house (tus).

rua To open (eyes or mouth) (cf. 'qheb').
   rua muag To open the eyes.
   rua lo To yawn.
   rua qhov ncauj Open the mouth.
   rua qhov ncauj loj loj Open the mouth wide.

ruab khaub ruab (rab) A broom.
   Muab khaub ruab cheb tsev. Sweep the house with a
      broom.

1. ruaj Firm, enduring, durable, steady.
   Tuav ruaj ruaj li. Grasp it firmly.
   ruaj siab nyob To abide content, reside steadily.
   (a) ruaj nrees Very firmly, very steady.
   (b) ruaj qos nrees Very firmly, very steady.

2. ruaj
   (a) ruaj zog Surprised, amazed, apprehensive, wondering
   (b) ruaj zog tseg Surprised, amazed, apprehensive, wondering
      (cf. 'yoob zog' and other listings under 'zog').

1. ruam A step in walking. To go a step at a time.
   ib ruam ib ruam mus

2. ruam Dumb, unable to speak.

3. ruam Slow of understanding, foolish, stupid, unedu-
      cated.
   neeg ruam A foolish person, one slow of under-
      standing.
   hlwb ntag ruam Mentally dull, mentally retarded.

ruas Leprosy.
   mob ruas To have leprosy.
   mob uav mob ruas To have leprosy.

rwb Quilted.
   pam rwb (daim) A quilt.

1. rwg Pertaining to the small finger or toe.
   ntiv tes rwg qab The little finger.
   ntiv taw rwg qab The little toe.

2. rwg
   qhwb rwg Face downward.
   pw qhwb rwg To lie face downward, to lie flat on
      one's stomach.

rwj A boil (lub), an ulcer or an abcess.
   Kuv mob ib lub rwj. I have a boil. (or an abcess)

1. rwm A given name used for Hmong women.

2. rwm
   yuav luag tshwv rwm tib tiag Very close by.

rws To swoop.
   (a) rws sis To swoop, the swift downward flight of
      a bird.
   (b) rws ceev ceev To swoop, the swift downward flight
      of a bird.

RH

rhais To tuck in, to tuck up.
rhais ris To tuck up the trousers.
hmuv rhais plaubhau A hairpin.

rhau To drill.
rhau qhov To drill a hole (cf. 'qhov').

rhaub To heat up over the fire (cf. 'hau').
rhaub dej To heat up some water, to boil a kettle of water.
Rhaub cov zaub peb noj. Heat up the leftover vegetables for us to eat.

1. rhaus A slip knot (lub) (contr. 'pob caus').

2. rhaus To slip something out from a knot.

1. rhawv A large vessel or tub, especially one used for storing water or liquid (lub), a tank.

2. rhawv To persuade, to seek to persuade or to force a person to adopt one's point of view or one's way of doing things.

3. rhawv
rhawv kev To put through a road, to level a road.

rhe A restricted post verbal intensifier used particularly with verbs indicating breaking or tearing, etc. (cf. Appendix 8).
tawg rhe Broken.
rub rhe Pulled apart.
dua rhe Tear apart.
lub siab ntais rhe lawm My heart is broken.
ntais rhe Broken.
pob rhe Landslide.
ntuag rhe Torn apart.

1. rheeb Of a chicken scratching.
Qaib rheeb kab. The chicken is scratching for worms.

2. rheeb A kind of stinging vegetation.

rhees Restricted post verbal intensifier (cf. Appendix 8).
pov rhees To throw (into).
txawb rhees To throw.
laim rhees To cast away.

rhij Restricted post verbal intensifier used with 'nrov' (cf. Appendix 8) (cf. 'nrov' p. 178).

1. rhiab To tickle, ticklish sensation.

2. rhiab The feeling experienced in anticipation of pain or in places of danger, etc.
(a) rhiab rhiab neeg Of the feeling experienced when facing having a tooth pulled or something similar.
(b) rhiab siab Of the feeling experienced when facing having a tooth pulled or something similar.
rhiab qhov muag Dizzy eyes, of the feeling brought on by looking down from a great height, etc.

rhiam Perverse, deliberately obstinate and contrary.
rhiam niam rhiam txiv Of a child's perverse conduct toward mother and father.

rhiav A given name used for Hmong women.

rho To extract, to pull out.
rho hlo To pull out.
rho hniav To pull teeth.
Nws rho hlo riam los tua. He pulled out a knife to kill.
rho txheeb (cf. 'txheeb').

rhoob To cut or saw at something with a dull knife.
Hlais pheej tsis to lam rhoob mus li. No matter how I work at it it doesn't slice well but I'll just go ahead and cut it as best I can.

rhuv Restricted post verbal intensifier with 'daj'. (cf. Appendix 8, p. 474).
daj rhuv Very yellow, bright yellow.

rhuaj Restricted post verbal intensifier after 'nrov.' (cf. Appendix 8) (cf. 'nrov' p. 178).

rhuas
hais rhuas lawm Of one who in speaking fast or at length inevitably says something wrong.

1. rhuav To tear down, dismantle.
rhuav tsev To tear down a house.

2. rhuav Used figuratively of breaking a promise or a contract.

3. rhuav Restricted post verbal intensifier (cf. Appendix 8).
xuab taw rhuav (cf. 'xuab taws').

rhw To crush rice (especially used of the final pounding in the foot mill), to beat out the rice in the foot mill a second time after having sifted out the chaff once.

rhw txhuv To crush rice (especially used of the final pounding in the foot mill), to beat out the rice in the foot mill a second time after having sifted out the chaff once.

rhwb Restricted post verbal intensifier after 'dawb.' (cf. 'dawb') (cf. Appendix 8).
dawb rhwb Intensely white, very white.

S

1. sab A side, a direction.
sab xis Right side, the right, to the right.
(a) sab lauj The left side, to the left.
(b) sab laug The left side, to the left.
sab no This side.
sab nraud Behind, outside.

2. sab Thin (of liquids) (cf. 'nyeem'), of little density.

3. sab Intense, deep, serious (of illness, pain, injury, scolding, hard work, etc.)
neeg sab An injured person.
lawv sab They suffered, they were in real pain.
(a) hnov suab sab Heard a loud noise.
(b) hnov sab nrov Heard a loud noise.

4. sab A spider web.
kab laug sab A spider which makes a web (tus) (there are many varieties).

5. sab Of male wild animals which go about in pairs.
sab nyuj Wild oxen (pair of males).
sab tswb Wild boars.

6. sab choj To lay two small saplings across one another against a larger tree for a platform to use in felling the tree.

7. sab To discuss, confer.
sablaj To discuss, to confer, to talk over together.
Nws sab tsis tau laj. He hasn't talked the matter to a conclusion yet.
Nws tsis tau sablaj. He hasn't discussed it yet.

8. sab
tub sab (tus) A thief.

9. sab
sab foob To have a cold (C) (cf. 'khaub thuas').

10. sab
tsho tshaj sab (lub) A long gown.

11. sab
sam sab The day of burial (cf. 'tuag').

12. sab
rooj moj sab (cf. 'rooj' Definition No. 6).

13. sab
sabcib (lub) A basket-type rice strainer.

14. sab
rub sab neeb (cf. 'neeb' p. 137).

15. sab
ua sab ua sua Of one who has no certain dwelling but wanders here and there.

16. sab
thais sab (cf. 'thais').

1. saj To taste, to ascertain the flavor by tasting.
saj vimtom To taste the flavor.

2. saj
dawm saj A mountain gap, a mountain pass (cf. 'dawm').

3. saj zawg zog Flexible, to flex, to bend.

1. sam To castrate.
sam npua To castrate a pig.

2. sam
   sam qhab To put on the rafters of a house.

3. sam
   sam txhim To paint, to apply paint to (C).

4. sam
   sam sab The day of burial (cf. 'tuag').

5. sam
   samsim A preverbal indicating action that is still
   going on, "in the process of..."
   samsim noj mov (He) is still eating.
   samsim ua (He) is still doing it now.

6. sam
   (a) hujsam (tus) A Buddhist priest (C).
   (b) haujsam (tus) A Buddhist priest (C).

7. sam
   sam xyab To burn incense at the spirit shelf.

8. sam To add to (as adding oil to a lamp, etc.)
   (a) sam roj To add oil, to fill a lamp.
   (b) sam teeb To add oil, to fill a lamp.

9. sam
   sam hwm To correct, to admonish, to gently rebuke.

10. sam
    sam thiaj A high platform.

11. sam
    sam plaws Jumped upon.

12. sam
    (a) sam kiag An offensive word or term.
    (b) sam hlob An offensive word or term.

13. sam
    sam tsum The uphill side of a table at a feast, the
    honored place (contr. 'qab roog').

14. sam
    neeg zoo phij sam siab com viab Hypocrites (C)
    (persons with a good skin but a crooked heart).

1. sas Expletive and completive particle used at the end
   of sentences or utterances for emphasis.
   Kuv yog hmoob sas! I'm a Hmong.
   Tsis muaj sas! There is none!

2. sas
   khiav ib sas ib sas To move in fits and starts, to
   run a distance then stop and start again.

1. sav To wrench out of position, to sprain, to twist a
   member of the body and incur pain.
   sav duav A wrenched back.
   sav tes A twisted wrist or hand.

2. sav
   sav tsam To inconvenience, to hinder, to prevent or
   delay (cf. 'tabkaum').

1. sai Quickly, fast (cf. 'tsuag' and 'nrawm').
   Nws mus sai sai li. He went quickly.
   yem sai yem zoo The faster the better.
   ('yem' sometimes 'yim').

2. sai Mountain goat, wild goat (tus).

1. saib To look at, to look, to observe.
   sim saib To have a look at something to see or to
   determine something.
   Saib qhov no. Look here.
   saib ntsoov To look at steadily, to stare.
   ua neeb saib To do spirit worship to determine
   something.
   saib dheev Suddenly looked at.
   txus saib txus zoo The more (he) looked at it the
   better it seemed.
   yem saib los yem zoo The more you see of it the
   better it is. ('yem' also 'yim').
   saib tsis taus "Cannot look upon," i.e. to despise,
   to disrespect.
   (a) saib qaib To divine by observing the position of
   the feet, etc. of a slain chicken.
   (b) saib tshiav thawj To divine by observing the
   position of the feet, etc. of a slain chicken.

2. saib
   saib tsam It may be, perhaps.

sais
   sais nplaim qeej To cut brass to make the reeds for
   a set of Hmong musical pipes.

1. sau To write.
   sau ntawv To write, to write letters, write a book.

2. sau To gather together, to reap, to collect, to gather
   up, to harvest.
   sau nplej To harvest rice (bring it in).
   sau yeeb To gather in the opium.
   sau nqe To collect debts, collect payment.
   sau zog To gather things together.
   (a) sau lub siab To come to one mind, to come to a
   decision.
   (b) sau siab zog To come to one mind, to come to a
   decision.
   sau se To collect taxes.

Saub The legendary Hmong "creator."
  The Hmong universally attribute to "Saub" acts of
  creation and he is the one they look to as
  having taught them all the simple requirements of living such as firemaking, house-
  building, and the planting of crops. From
  the legends "Saub" has moral attributes different from the moral character of the Christian
  Creator-God. However, among the Hmong of
  Thailand the term "Saub" is used for "God"
  but prefaced by the qualifying term "Vajtswv"-
  King-Lord. Thus: "Vajtswv Saub" - God (the
  King-Lord Creator).

saud (cf. 'saum') (cf. Introduction p. xxii-xxiii).

saum Above, on top of, up.
  Nyob saum rooj. On the table.
  saum ntuj Above the sky, the heavens.
  nyob saum ntuj In the heavens.
  Nyob saud Up above (t.c.) (cf. Introduction p. xxii-xxiii).

1. saus To recede into, to recede and disappear.
  av saus The ground has slipped away leaving a hole
    (qhov saus) in the earth.
  qhov saus (lub) A hole in the earth where the
    ground has fallen in.
  qhov dej saus A place where the water disappears
    into the ground.

2. saus A small particle or foreign body such as might
    enter the eye and cause discomfort.
  Muaj ib lub saus tuaj hauv kuv qhov muag. Mas lub
    lub li. Koj nrog kuv saib. Something has
    gotten into my eye and is irritating it.
    Have a look, will you?

1. saw A chain, a necklace (clf. 'txoj').
  ib txog saw A necklace.
  saw hlau An iron chain.

2. saw
  cov saw pav Wrappings of cloth to bind the limbs
    of the dead.

1. sawb Clf. for one rib of meat.

2. sawb To shed.
  Ntoo sawb thawj lawm. The tree has shed its leaves.
  Note: This is not as common as 'zeeg nplooj.'

1. sawm To suffer or to bear (C).
  sawm khwv To bear pain or suffering (C).
  sawm txim To bear punishment, to suffer for sin (C).

2. sawm To perversely choose the wrong after being shown
    the right and the good.

saws To twist or spin thread.
  saws ntuag To spin or twist hemp thread.

1. sawv To arise, to get up.
  sawv tsees To arise, to stand up.
  sawv ntseg To stand erect, to stand upright.
  sawv ntsug Standing, standing upright, stand erect.
  sawv nrheev To stand straight up.
  sawv ntxov Early morning.
  sawv kev mus To start on a journey (also 'sawv
    taw mus').
  sawv hlwv To "raise" a blister.
  sawv hlo To arise.
  sawv nraim To stand in one place.
  tus hwj sawv The shaman's assistant who helps him
    in sessions of spirit worship.
  Koj lub ntsej muag sawv nraim hauv kuv lub siab. ("I
    have you in my heart.")
    Your face arises steadily in my heart. ("I
    have you in my heart.")

2. sawv
  neeg heev sawv (cf. 'heev').

3. sawv
  sawvdaws Everyone.
  Sawvdaws mus tsev lawm. Everyone has gone home.

4. sawv
  sawvhwm (daim) A towel (C).

1. se Taxes, tax.
  sau se To collect taxes.

2. se
  pojniam tub se Wife and children (t.c.) (cf. 'sev').

seb Hemp thread while in the process of bleaching and
    making ready for weaving (cf. 'xov') (clf.
    'ntshua' for hanks).
  hau seb To bleach the thread.
  ntxhua seb To wash the thread.
  laub zeb daus (clf. 'laub').

1. sej To keep putting off doing something.
  Note: When used in combination with 'sib' the resulting
    pronunciation is 'sev').
  sib sev To keep putting off some action.

2. sej
  nab hab sej A python (tus).

1. sem Of wood shrinking, to shrink.
   ntoo sem lawm The wood has shrunken.

2. sem A term used in bad language, an offensive word.

3. sem Of rice coming up poorly and not filled out.

4. sem To perish, to lose life.
   txoj siav tuav sem To perish, to lose life.

5. sem so (cf. 'sov').
   sem so (cf. 'sov').

1. sev Apron, the apron on a Hmong woman's garment. (clf. 'daim').
   sev sia The apron worn in front.
   sev npua The apron worn in back.
   plooj sev To sew an apron together.

2. sev Used to refer to a wife in certain combinations.
   koj poj koj sev Your wife.
   deev luag poj luag sev To commit adultery with another's wife.
   pojniam tub se (t.c.) Wife and children.

1. seeb Uncluttered.
   lub tsev khab seeb A roomy house, a house not cluttered up with things.

2. seeb Unencumbered.
   pojniam tab seeb seeb A childless woman.
   pojniam tab seeb lug A woman who does not easily become pregnant, a woman who is not encumbered with many children.
   tab seeb twj ham A single person, one who is "footloose and fancy free."

3. seeb "Be quiet!" (more polite than 'ua twjywm').
   Tswm seeb "Be quiet!" (more polite than 'ua twjywm').

4. seeb Time, occasion (cf. 'lub sijhawm').
   lub sim seeb Time, occasion (cf. 'lub sijhawm').

5. seeb Of one in authority sending persons on errands or business (similar to 'txib').

seej Tame, docile.
   nees seej seej li A tame horse.

1. seem Remaining, left over.
   ua seem To be left over, of a quantity remaining.
   seem li no There is this much left.

2. seem Handy, close at hand.
   seem tes Handy, close at hand.

sees Restricted post verbal intensifier (cf. Appendix 8).
   ua zam sees To dress up lavishly.
   tseev zam sees To dress in one's best (cf. 'ntxiag').

1. seev A large sack, especially a sack for carrying rice as used by the Hmong (lub).
   lub seev txhuv A rice sack.

2. seev To investigate, to inquire into, to spy out.
   seev mem tes To take the pulse.
   seev mob To investigate an illness. (cf. 'tuav tseev' and 'tshuaj').

3. seev To hum, to sigh or to moan.

4. seev To be lonely, to sigh for, to strongly wish for, long for.
   seev seev Lonely, homesick (cf. 'kho siab').
   Nws twb seev hais ib los tias... He said with a sigh longingly...

5. seev To hold a sustained note in singing, to speak with drawn out words, a prolonged tone.
   lus seev Drawn out words or speech.
   hais seev suab To speak or sing in sustained tones.
   neeg hais lus seev yees One who speaks with drawn out words.

1. si Play, playing (games and amusements).
   ua si To play (games, etc.)

2. si Weakness, physical weakening.
   (a) pheej si si To grow weaker and weaker physically (as of persons growing older).
   (b) nraus zus nraus zus To grow weaker and weaker physically (as of persons growing older).

3. si huv tibsi (cf. 'huv').

1. sib Preverbal indicating reciprocal action.
   Note: Used in this sense this word is often pronounced 'sis'; this is especially true as used among the Hmong in Laos.
   sib ceg To curse or to scold one another.
   (a) sib pab To help one another.
   (b) sib pab To help one another.
   sib tua To fight one another (to kill).
   sib ntaus To beat one another, to fight.
   sib ncaim To separate from one another.

```
   sib tib  Close to each other.
   sib xyaws  Mixed together.
   sib luag  Similar, like each other, equal.
   sib luag zos  Alike, the same, equal.

2. sib  Light in weight, not heavy.
   sib sib li  Quite light.

3. sib  Spaced far apart (contr. 'ti').
   sib sib  Spaced far apart, thinly spaced.

4. sib  Forcibly, energetically.
   sib zog  Forcibly, energetically.
   sib zog ua  To do energetically, do with a will.

5. sib
   hmoov zeb sib  Chalk.

6. sib
   (a) sib ziv  Just to sit idly without doing anything.
   (b) sib zoog  Just to sit idly without doing anything.
```

sid
```
   tamsid  From 'tamsim' (cf. Introduction p. xxii-xxiii).
           (cf. 'sim').
```

```
1. sij  Continually, repeatedly (cf. 'pheej').
   (a) sij ua  To do continually or to do repeatedly.
   (b) ib sij ua  To do continually or to do repeatedly.
   ib sij mus ib sij los  Continually coming and going.
   Kuv sij yuav vamkhom.  I will continue to trust.

2. sij raug  To understand, to know, to know about.
   Koj yuav sij raug mentsis.  You will know something.
   (about it).

3. sij
   yuamsij (lub)  A key (C).

4. sij
   sijhawm (lub)  A time, an occasion (C).  (cf. the
                  Hmong expression, 'sim seeb').
   lub sijhawm no  This time, on this occasion.
   lub puav sijhawm  Sometimes, occasionally.
   sijhawm dua lawm  The time is past, too late.

5. sij
   piamsij  Destroyed (cf. 'puas tsuaj').

6. sij
   (a) ib sij huam  Suddenly, quickly.
   (b) ib sij ib huam  Suddenly, quickly.
```

```
1. sim  To try, to test, to attempt.
   sim saib  Idiom for "try and see."
   Sim saib puas muaj zog ua.  Try and see if you have
                               strength to do it.
   sim lub siab  To test, to tempt, to try the heart.
   Koj sim qhia kuv saib...  Tell me and see...  (Try
                             telling me and see if I can understand.)

2. sim  A lifetime.
   sim no  This life.
   sim neej no  This life.
   sim neej  A lifetime.
   lwm sim  The next life.
   tas yus sim  Dead and finished.
   tshwm sim  To be born, to be manifested in living
              form.
   (a) ib sid  For a lifetime, "forever."
   (b) ib sim neej  For a lifetime, "forever.

3. sim  Concerning a time or occasion.
   lub sim seeb  A time or occasion (cf. 'sijhawm').
   samsim  (cf. 'sam')  A preverbal indicating that
                        action is still going on.
   tamsim  Immediately.
   Ua tamsim no.  Do it immediately.

4. sim
   hais sim suav lus  To speak so as to deceive or cheat.

5. sim
   liam sim  Ruined, destroyed (cf. 'puas tsuaj').

1. sis  To speak inaccurately or unclearly.
   hais lus sis  To speak with an accent.

2. sis  On the slant, slantwise.
   txiav sis  To cut on the slant.

3. sis  Sickly.
   pheej sis  Continually weak and sickly, not really
              well though not seriously ill.

4. sis  Often used as an alternative rendering of 'sib' in
        expressing reciprocal action (cf. 'sib').
   sis pab  To help one another (also 'sib pab').

5. sis
   txawm sis  Just so, as expected (C).
   Txawm sis maj!  Quite so!

6. sis
   lossis  An intensive particle, very (C).
   Koj ntaus kuv lossis mob heev.  It hurts terribly
                                   where you hit me.
   lossis zoo  Very good.
```

7. sis Used in connection with the interrogative particle 'los'. (cf. 'los' Definition No. 8, p. 116)

1. siv Sash, belt, band (clf. 'txoj') (cf. 'duav').
   sia siv To wrap a sash around one's waist, to put on a Hmong man's red sash.
   sivceeb The varigated headband worn by Hmong women (clf. 'thooj' for a set of them).
   hlab siv The red sash on a Hmong woman's apron.
   tw siv The embroidered ends on a Hmong woman's apron sash (cf. 'txwm' for a pair).

2. siv To use, to make use of.
   Yuav ua li cas siv? How do you use it?
   tsis txawj siv Don't know how to use.

3. siv To annoy, to bother, to cause trouble for (cf. 'txuv').
   siv siv siab To annoy, to cause trouble for.
   siv tom txwv To test or make trial of a person, as e.g. to try a person on food that he says he won't or shouldn't eat.

4. siv The transverse strands in basket weaving (contr. 'hlaub').
   cov siv The transverse strands.

5. siv twjsiv A utensil, an article of household use.

6. siv tus siv thawj The one who carries water at a funeral (cf. 'tuag').

7. siv Siv Yis The name of the head of the 'neeb' (cf. 'neeb') A given name for Hmong boys and men.

sia To wrap around the waist.
   sia siv To put on a sash, to wrap a sash around the waist (cf. 'siv').
   sev sia Hmong woman's apron worn in front.
   sia tawv A waist band, a girdle, a belt, leather belt.

1. siab The liver (lub) (physical organ) (clf. also 'nplooj').

2. siab The liver regarded as the seat of the affections much the same as "heart" in English. (clf. 'lub' or 'nplooj').
   siab coob siab ntau Of many minds, a heart going in every direction, undecided.
   siab dav Generous.
   siab fab Upset, heart in turmoil.

siab feeb pes tsia Confused.
siab heev Impatient, severe, harsh, stern.
siab hlob Covetous, gluttonous.
(a) siab kaj Refreshed, satisfied, pleased.
(b) kaj siab Refreshed, satisfied, pleased.
siab lim hiam (C) Cruel, ferocious, evil tempered.
siab luv Impatient, short-tempered.
siab maj In a hurry, rushed.
siab nka ncuv In despair.
siab nkiag Having a sharp memory.
(a) siab npau Angry.
(b) siab npau taws Angry.
siab nphau npog Very angry.
siab ntais rhe Heartbroken.
(a) siab ntaus yau Timid, fearful and afraid.
(b) siab ntaus yau ntshai Timid, fearful and pessimistic, timid and afraid.
siab ntev Patient, even tempered.
siab ntshiab A clear clean heart, open-hearted.
siab ntxhov Unsettled in mind, turbulent heart.
siab poob nthav Fearful (cf. 'nthav' and 'ntshai zog').
siab puab To be in earnest, to be concerned about.
siab puas ua To do with earnestness, do with a will.
siab puas tsus Completely discouraged (cf. 'poob tag').
siab ras dheev To suddenly awake to something.
(a) siab tus At peace, settled, quiet.
(b) siab tus yees At peace, settled, quiet.
siab tuab Courageous.
siab tuag nthi To be well satisfied, heart settled.
siab tuam tav Bold, courageous.
siab tuam yim Reckless, careless of danger.
siab vam To hope, hopeful.
siab xyov xeeb mentsis Careful, timid (C).
(a) siab zas Patient, meek, humble.
(b) zas xeeb Patient, meek, humble.
siab zam taus lus Meek, unresentful.
siab zoo A good heart, good-hearted.
siab xob pes vog Scared, fearful of punishment.
siab nruj siab heev Impetuous, impatient.
cia siab rau To constantly think of, continually bear in mind (cf. 'vam siab').
chob siab "Pierced" in heart, inwardly offended.
deev siab To comfort, to encourage the heart.
dhuav siab To dislike, to be tired of (cf. 'siab tsis nyiam').

kho siab Lonely, homesick, to miss (someone).
khuam siab Lonely, to be missing others.
mob siab Offended, "hurt" in heart.

npaj siab To prepare the heart.
ntxeev siab To turn against, to have a change of
   heart.

qab siab Peace, happiness, satisfaction (cf. 'kaj
   siab') (also 'siab qab').

ris siab hlo To repent, to turn away from.
tas siab Satisfactory.
tas siab tas ntsws Patient.
tu siab To be offended.
xeev siab Feeling of nausea.
xu siab Displeased, don't like it (cf. 'tsis nyiam').
zoo siab Pleased, happy.

Note: Below are a series of expressions all of which
   may be used to express action done—earnestly,
   from the heart, with a will, zealously, with
   dedication, with real interest. They are listed
   with the verb 'ua' (to do) but may be used
   similarly with other verbs. The particular
   connotation follows each phrase.

kub siab ua Hot hearted.
ib siab ua Single-hearted.
rau siab ua Putting the heart into it.
(a) mob siab ua Whole-heartedly.
(b) mob siab ntsuv ua Whole-heartedly.
tom siab ua From the heart.
ntxim siab ua From the heart.
muaj siab ua With a heart or with the will.
tshwv xeeb ua (C) With the heart.
(a) kub siab lug Earnestness, zeal, and dedication.
(b) mob siab ntsua Earnestness, zeal, and dedication.
(c) mob siab ntsuv Earnestness, zeal, and dedication.
(a) raug siab According to my desire, agreeing
   with the heart.
(b) dhos siab According to my desire, agreeing
   with the heart.
(c) hum lub siab According to my desire, agreeing
   with the heart.

siab tsis qhuav dej ntsws tsis qhuav ntshav Used of
   a person who makes much of a small matter and
   refuses to let it go at that.

3. siab High, tall.
   lub roob siab siab A high mountain.
   qhov siab Height.
   hais lus siab lawv To speak against others, to boast
      against others, to speak disparagingly (to
      speak words "higher" than others showing a
      low opinion of them).

4. siab
   hauv siab The chest, the chest region (cf. 'nrob').
   puag hauv siab To embrace, to hold to the breast.

5. siab A measure for rice or grain (one basin full).
   Ten 'siab' equal one 'tawv'
   Ten 'tawv' equal one 'tas'

sias A species of small black stinging insect (tus).

1. siav Life, existence (clf. 'txoj').
   txoj siav tu lawm Life cut off, life ended, died.
   tu siav nrho Died.
   ib txog siav (t.c.) One life.
   thooj siav thooj nqaij Of one flesh and blood.
   xauv siav "Life" neckring (one silver neckring put
      on a Hmong in childhood and always worn.
      Originally it is regarded as a protection to
      life) (cf. 'xauv').
   Note: 'txoj siav' is also frequently heard pronounced
      'txoj sia.'

2. siav Ripe.
   Txiv ntoo tsis tau siav, qaub qaub li. The fruit is
      unripe and very sour.
   dej siav Boiled water.

3. siav
   txog txog siav Winded, out of breath, panting.

4. siav
   siav ib kab Raised a welt (from a beating).

1. so To rest, to cease work.
   so dhuav To rest to full satisfaction.
   hnub so The Sabbath, day of rest.
   ib lub chib so One period of rest, one week.

2. so To wipe, to wipe dry, to wipe away.
   so tais To wipe dishes.
   so ntswg To wipe the nose.
   so kua muag To wipe away tears.

3. so
   (a) dej sem so Lukewarm water (cf. 'sov').
   (b) dej sov so Lukewarm water (cf. 'sov').

sob Of a weakening in bodily strength and energy, peaceable
   patient (as of persons and animals in middle
   age having passed youthful aggressiveness and
   energy).

1. soj To follow cautiously or stealthily.
   raws nws maj mam soj mus Followed him cautiously
      at a distance.

2. soj Completive and emphatic particle used at the end
   of utterances. You cheated
   Koj sim dag kuv ib pluag mov noj soj! You cheated
   me of a meal!

1. sov Warm.
   dej sov Warm water.
   (a) dej sov Lukewarm water.
   (b) dej sov so Lukewarm water.
   (c) dej sem so. Lukewarm water.
   (d) dej sov ntem ntauv Lukewarm water.

2. sov "warm" in the sense of bustling with activity.
   Koj lub tsev sov sov li. Your house is bustling with
   activity ("warm" with people and noise)
   (contr. 'dav').

soo To pull tight, to tighten a noose, to strangle
   (cf. 'zawm'). Especially used of a spring
   trap being set off to catch game in a noose.

1. soob Small of body (of persons).
   cev soob soob Small in body.

2. soob High in tone or pitch.

soov A kind of grain.

1. su Noon, the noon meal.
   (a) tav su Noon, the half day, noonday.
   (b) niag su Noon, the half day, noonday.
   noj su To eat the noonday meal.
   ntim su To take along food for the noonday meal.
   tav menyuam su About 10:30 A.M. (small noon).

2. su To swell, to rise (of bread, cakes, etc.) to
   increase in volume (contr. 'hnlos').

1. sub Interrogative and completive particle used to
   express probability with some doubt attached.
   Yog thiab sub? I think that's right, isn't it?
   Taskis yuav mus sub ne? We're going tomorrow,
   aren't we?
   Muaj thiab sub ne? I think there are some, aren't
   there? Probably there are some.

2. sub To put near the fire to dry (for a short period,
   as in drying one's feet, etc.) (contr. 'qha').
   sub yeeb To soften opium over a flame.

3. sub The blood or the influence of a person who has died
   by tragic accident. This is said to remain at
   the place of the death with the tendency to
   cause similar death to others in the clan.
   sub ntoo The influence of one killed by a tree.
   sub laum The influence of one killed by accidental
   shooting.
   sub pobzeb The influence of one killed by falling
   from a rock, etc.
   vij sub vij sw. (cf. 'vij').

suj An expletive particle used in chasing pigs.

suv suv tshuaj To put poison on arrow tips.

1. sua To converge.
   los sib sua tau ua ke To come together on the
   trail from converging paths.

2. sua To gather something together.
   sua lub vas los To gather in a fishnet (after it
   has been cast).
   rab sua teb A rake.

3. sua Of bees migrating or swarming.

4. sua ua sab ua sua (cf. 'sab').

5. sua ri sua tag lawm (cf. 'ri').

1. suab Voice, sound of the voice, tone, noise, sound.
   suab soob High in tone or pitch, high voice.
   suab laus Low in tone or pitch, low voice.
   hais seev suab To sustain a note or tone in speech or
   song.
   suab sab A loud noise.
   laug suab ntev A long tone, sustained note.
   cov suab The tones in Hmong spoken language.

2. suab Fern.
   nplooj suab Fern fronds.
   suab av Fern growing on the ground or rock.
   suab ntoo Tree fern.
   laug nplooj suab Cross stitch embroidery (fern
   frond pattern).
   tsov nplooj suab The bengal tiger (striped like
   fern fronds).

3. suab Pebbles, gravel.
   suab puam Pebble bank, gravel deposited by a stream.
   suab zeb Pebbles, small stones.
   tshav puam suab zeb A stony waste land.

4. suab Pregnant, having an unborn infant of several months (cf. 'xeeb tub') (contr. 'teeg').

5. suab tsev pheeb suab A temporary shelter (lub), leanto made of leaning branches.

6. suab fajsuab Haze.

suaj suaj kaum To finish.
txoj lus suaj kaum The last word, final word.

1. suam To scrape off (with an implement) (as scraping dry rice out of a pot, for instance).
rab suam An implement used for scraping.
Nws muab pobzeb suam new txhais tes. He took a stone and scraped his arm.

2. suam To cut with a slicing motion (cf. 'hlais').

1. suav The Chinese.
suav tuam tshoj The mainland Chinese, Yunnanese.
suav cev The overseas Chinese (also used for Chinese from the coastal provinces).
(a) suav daj Chinese Communists.
(b) suav liab Chinese communists.
suav thaj (C) (cf. 'thaj').

2. suav To count, to number.
Suav saib muaj pes tsawg. Count and see how many there are.
suav ntsoov hnub To count the days.

3. suav suav kwv ntas The constellation of Orion.

1. sw Disorderly, messy.
(a) tsev sw rawv A disorderly house, house in a mess.
(b) tsev sw sw A disorderly house, house in a mess.

2. sw vij sub vij sw (cf. 'vij') (contr. 'xyw').

1. swb To move something along a surface a little at a time.

2. swb To slip (as of a rope slipping down or along a pole, etc.)

3. swb To skid along (as a child moving along on the floor before it can crawl, as of a person pushing himself along on a log while sitting down).

4. swb To be defeated (in battle, in contest, in law cases) (cf. 'tais').
Nws tsis xav swb nej. He didn't want to give in to you.

1. swm To give hospitality to a guest.
swm swm To give hospitality to a guest, to let visitors sleep in one's house, etc.

2. swm Familiar (C).
muaj swm neeg To have acquaintances, to have friends or persons you are familiar with.

swv npua swv Of pigs digging in the ground to find food, pigs rooting (cf. 'tshom').

T

ta puag ta Just now, just a moment ago (sometimes 'puas ta').
puag ta no Just now, just this moment.
puag ta mus Went just a moment ago. (cf. 'nyuam qhuav'. 'puag ta' is a little less immediate than 'nyuam qhuav'). (also cf. 'tav').

1. tab Single, odd.
hnub tab Odd day of the month, the "male day." (contr. 'txooj').
ua tab To tie with a single rope (cf. 'ua txooj').
tab seeb (cf. 'seeb' Definition No. 2).

2. tab tabmeeg In front of, face to face, openly.
tabmeeg hais lus To speak face to face, speak openly.

3. tab

   hniav tabmeej The front teeth, incisors.

4. tab tom Just began to do.

   Kuv tab tom hais lus nws txawm khiav lawm. I had no sooner begun to speak than he ran off.

5. tab

   (a) tsuas tab... "If only..."
   (b) tab yog... "If only..."
   Tab yog yus ua li no yuav zoo xwb. If only one does this it will be all right.
   Tsuas tab yog yus ua li no yuav zoo xwb. If only one does this it will be all right.
   Tab yog kuv tuag mas kuv yuav tsis hais. Even if I should die I wouldn't tell.

6. tab

   Tab nimno mus... From now on....
   Tab nimno rov lawm yav tod... From now on and into the future....

7. tab To care for, to look after a person's needs.

   (a) tab tsis tau Can't care for him, can't look after him (Indicating the person's tastes are beyond my means to supply) (cf. 'hwj').
   (b) tab tsis yeej Can't care for him, can't look after him (Indicating the person's tastes are beyond my means to supply) (cf. 'hwj').
   (c) tab tsis nyog Can't care for him, can't look after him (indicating the person's tastes are beyond my means to supply) (cf. 'hwj').

8. tab

   tabkaum To hinder, to delay (C) (cf. 'tuav theem').
   (a) Tabkaum koj. "I have hindered you." i.e. I have interfered with your work. I have been a bother to you.
   (b) Tabkaum koj li haujlwm. "I have hindered you." i.e. I have interfered with your work. I have been a bother to you. (cf. 'sav tsam,' 'khwv koj').

9. tab

   pam tab A thin blanket (clf. 'daim').

10. tab

    tab pam The covering of a quilt.

11. tab

    tab tiab The lower portion of a skirt (cf. 'tiab').

12. tab

    tus tab choj The small wooden support set to hold a pole against a larger tree for felling (cf. 'choj').

tad

    cuabtad T.c. from 'cuabtam.' (cf. 'cuabtam' and Introduction p. xxii-xxiii).

tag This word is often heard in this tone when stressed but see the listings under 'tas.'

taj Late bearing, slow in bearing (contr. 'cauj').

    pobkws taj Late corn.
    hniav taj Teeth that come in late.
    hais lus taj tsawv Slow of speech (cf. 'nrho').

1. tam To sharpen, to bring to a keen edge (if it is only a little bit dull) (cf. 'hov').

    tam kom ntse To sharpen.

2. tam

    tamsim Immediately
    (a) Ua tamsid. Do it immediately (t.c.) (cf. Introduction p. xxii-xxiii).
    (b) Ua tamsim no. Do it immediately.

3. tam

    cuabtam Household utensils (cf. 'cuab').

4. tam

    tamfaj Probably (C) (cf. 'kwvlam').
    Tamfaj nws yuav tsis mus. Probably he won't go.
    Tsuav tamfaj ua li no peb kuj tsis txawj hais li cas. Seeing that is probably the way it is we cannot say anything. (cf. 'tsuav').

5. tam

    luj lam tam Poverty stricken.

1. tas Done, finished, completed (may be used as a verb by itself or as an auxiliary after another verb to indicate completed action).

    Note: This word is often pronounced 'tag' when stressed.
    ua tas Completed.
    tas lawm Finished.
    Noj tas lawm. Completely eaten, finished eating.
    tas nrho Completely (cf. 'tas zog'), intensely.
    zoo tas nrho Very very good.
    loj tas nrho Huge, very big.
    tas zog Completely, intensely (cf. 'tas nrho').
    qab tas zog Very very sweet.
    zoo nkauj tas zog Very beautiful.

Note: Although 'tas' is a verb in its own right it seems that the expressions 'tas nrho' and 'tas zog' may be classed with unrestricted post verbal intensifiers. See Appendix 8 and the page of additions at the end of the dictionary.

Note: The following are all expressions meaning finished or completed:
tas lawm, dawb lawm, hle lawm, khauv lawm

2. tas A measure for rice or grain (C).
ten 'siab' equal one 'tawv'
ten 'tawv' equal one 'tas'

3. tas An unrestricted post verbal intensifier commonly duplicated when used. It is probably a variation of 'tiag' which is more common (cf. 'tiag') (also cf. Appendix 8 and the page of additions at the end of the dictionary.)
(a) zoo tas tas Very very good.
(b) zoo tiag tiag Very very good.

4. tas taskis A morning, tomorrow (tomorrow morning).
taskis no This morning.
peb taskis Three mornings.

5. tas Tas tseeb! An expletive indicating annoyance.

6. tas siab Satisfied, satisfactorily.

7. tas siab tas ntsws Patient.

8. tas tas hnub tas hmo All day and all night, all the time.

1. tav Side, horizontal.
phab tav A person's side.
mob phab tav My side hurts.
tav toj The side of a hill.
tab hnub North or south (as distinct from where the sun rises or sets) (cf. 'hnub').
kev tav Path running along the side of a hill.

2. tav A period of time.
tav no Now. Until now.
txog tav no Until now.
tav ntej Previously, before.
Tav twg? When? Which period of time? (cf. 'thaum twg').
Tav twg kuj tau. Any time will be all right.

3. tav To prune, to snap off the young tendrils so as to produce more vigorous growth.

4. tav To restrain, to prevent, to oppose (cf. 'txwv').
Cua tuaj tav kev. A wind came and hindered progress.
(a) tav dej To dam up water.
(b) tauv dej To dam up water.
(c) xov dej To dam up water.

5. tav To drive animals by using a stick, etc. to keep them in the way, e.g. driving pigs to market.

6. tav siab tuam tav Bold, courageous (C).

7. tav tav ntxwv Courage, boldness (C).

8. tav tav su Noon, noonday (cf. 'su').

9. tav Rib, (of a person or animal) (clf. 'tus').

tai The name of the spirit who is supposed to have helped the Hmong when they came from China and crossed the sea.
ua npua tai To kill a pig in sacrifice to the 'Tai' spirit (also 'ua nyuj dab npua tai'). (cf. 'dab').

taig T.c. from 'tais' (cf. 'tais').

taij To implore, to beg or plead for something to beseech someone to do something for one with or without payment. (cf. 'thov').
Txhob taij taij! Stop begging me!

1. tais To fold, to fold over.

2. tais A cup, a basin (clf. 'lub').
tais phiab A shallow bowl, a basin.
tais phiab ntxuav muag A washbasin, basin in which to wash one's face.
ib taig dej (t.c.) A pan or basin of water.
so tais To wash the dishes.

3. tais To grasp with a pliers or pincers.
Muab rab ciaj tais ceev ceev. Grasp it firmly with the pliers.

4. tais To be defeated in a fight (cf. 'swb').
tais lawm Given in.

5. tais puab tais The groin.

6. tais
   niam tais (cf. 'niam').

1. tau Used before the verb as a sign that the action
        has been completed or that it has been done
        before.
        Kuv tsis tau ua. I didn't do it.
        Nws tau ua zoo xwb. He only did good.

2. tau Used after the verb as a sign of the potential
        mood indicating whether the action is permissible
        or not or whether it is prevented by some
        hindrance (contr. 'taus').
        noj tsis tau Inedible.
        ua tau May be done.
        tsis tau May not (Note: 'tsis taus' Cannot).
        pauj tau To avenge

3. tau Combined with 'yuav' and preceding a verb the
        combination indicates obligatory action.
        yuav tau ua Must do, must be done.
        (contrast 'yuav ua tau' Will be able to do).
   Note: The three usages listed above and the distinc-
          tion between 'tau' and 'taus' are not easy to
          grasp. Note the following illustrations:
        (a) Kuv yuav tsis tau. I cannot obtain it. (because
                of some hindrance).
        (b) Kuv yuav tsis yeej. I cannot obtain it. (because
                of some hindrance).
        (c) Kuv yuav tsis nyog. I cannot obtain it. (because
                of some hindrance).
        (a) Kuv yuav tsis tau yeej. I cannot obtain it yet.
        (b) Kuv yuav tsis tau tau. I cannot obtain it yet.
        (c) Kuv yuav tsis tau nyog. I cannot obtain it yet.
        Kuv tsis tau yuav. I haven't obtained it.
        Kuv tsis tau yuav tau. I haven't obtained it yet.
        Kuv yuav tsis taus. I cannot obtain it. (because
                it is physically impossible.)
        Kuv yuav tau yuav. I must obtain it.

4. tau A unit of measurement representing the width of
        one fist.

1. taub A gourd, a pumpkin (lub), pumpkin-like.
        plhuaj taub (lub) A gourd, empty gourd for carrying
                water, etc.
        taub dag Pumpkin (lub).
        taub maum (cf. 'maum').
        txiv taub ntoo Papaya (lub) (cf. 'txiv maum kuab').
        taub nkawj (lub) A wasp's nest.
        taub twg (lub) A whitish-green marrow squash, quite
                a large vegetable.
        taub hwb (lub) A gourd.

2. taub
        taubhau (lub) Head, the head.

3. taub
        taub teg Finger tip.

4. taub
        taub ntseg Ear lobe.

5. taub
        (a) taub ntswg The tip of the nose.
        (b) txiv taub ntswg The tip of the nose.

6. taub
        to taub (cf. 'to').

7. taub
        qeg taub Short in stature.
        neeg qeg taub A short person.

8. taub
        taub hnee The "head" or body of the crossbow.

9. taub
        ua dab taub dab qhev To be the slaves of the spirits.

1. taug To sag (contr. 'nruj').

2. taug To follow along, to follow the line or the path.
        taug kev To follow along the road, follow the path.
        taug laj To follow the ridge.
        taug qab To follow behind, follow another's footsteps.
        taug ceg faj khum To lie, to fabricate tales (to
                follow the vine tendrils going every direction).
        taug kev khaws taw qhuav To obtain without labor
                or payment (picking things up along the path).

3. taug Poison.
        muaj taug Poisonous.
        kua taug Snake poison.
        nab muaj taug A poisonous snake.

4. taug
        taug xaiv To tattle, gossip, spread rumors.

5. taug
        taug taug ntsej Hurts the ears (e.g. A loud noise).

6. taug
        quaj quaj taug li Continually crying (of children,
                etc.).

7. taug
        qab tsib taug Just below the house on downhill side.

tauj Descriptive of a variety of coarse grasses (cf. 'nyom').
hav tauj A grassy valley or expanse.
tauj dub "Black" grass (a pungent type of grass frequently used by Hmong as a flavoring particularly when cooking chicken).
tauj ntxhw Elephant grass.
tauj iab "Bitter" grass.

1. taum Beans or peas (clf. 'tus' or 'pluav').
taum qaib qua String beans.
taum lag Long beans.
taum puaj yem Very long type string beans (C).
taum suav Short beans.
taum mog Peas.
taum hwv Soybean curd (C).
taum pauv Soybeans.
phuas taum The curds in the making of bean curd.
kua si taum Brown bean curd cakes.

2. taum
(a) mob taum Smallpox.
(b) qhua taum Smallpox.
cog taum To vaccinate against smallpox.

3. taum
lus taum Old folks songs or ballads, stories told in song style (cf. 'kwv txhiaj' p. 92).

1. taus Axe (clf. 'rab').
Muab rab taus rau kuv. Hand me the axe.
hwv taus Hatchet (C).

2. taus Used after the verb as a sign of the potential mood indicating whether the action is physically possible or not. (contr. 'tau').
ris tsis taus Unable to carry it.
Kuv nyob tsis taus. I cannot live or remain. (cannot maintain physical existence.)
Kuv nyob tsis tau. I am not permitted to remain.
saib tsis taus To despise, to disrespect.
saib tsis taus To respect.
uv taus To bear with, to be patient under provocation.
zam taus lus Unresentful, able to forgive.
Note: Cf. 'tau' for further illustrations of the use of these two similar words.

3. taus
ib taus The width of one fist (t.c. from 'tau') (cf. 'tau' definition No. 4).

1. tauv Clf. for clouds and for clusters of fruit.
tauv huab A cloud.
ib tau huab One cloud (t.c.)

2. tauv To dam up, hold back.
tauv dej To dam up water (cf. 'tav dej').
tauv tsis taus Cannot hold back, can't help it.
tauv tsis taus lub kua muag Cannot hold back tears.

3. tauv
tauv las tshuaj tshuav To avoid doing work, to get out of doing things, to lie about idly.

1. taw To point, to indicate.
taw tes To point with the finger.

2. taw Foot, the foot (tus).
kotaw The foot (tus).
ntiv taw Toe.
ntiv taw xoo The big toe.
ntiv taw nta The three middle toes.
ntiv taw rwg qab The little toe.
rau taw Toe nail.
dab taws (t.c.) Ankle.
pob taws (t.c.) Ankle bone.
luj taws (t.c.) The heel.
yas taw Toe joint.
xib taws (t.c.) The sole of the foot.
mus nchias taw Go on tiptoe.
piav taw tes To dance.
plam taw Foot slipped.
ncav taw To stand on one's toes.
sawv taw mus To start on a journey.
xuab taw To drag the feet.
ntaug taw To stamp the feet.
taw phab ntsa The foot of the wall, wall foundation.

3. taw
taw npua Full-grown uncastrated boar.

4. taw
tus taw kev (cf. 'tuag').

1. tawb A basket (clf. 'lub') (There are various kinds of 'tawb', but a separate term 'kawm' is used for a back-basket).
tawb nees Basket for use on a horse pack saddle.
fam tawb A needlework basket.
tawb noog A birdcage.
tawb cuab ntses A woven basket-like fish trap.
tawb qhov muag Loosely woven basket for carrying meat or for storing utensils, etc.

2. tawb Clf. for a passing of feces or manure, a passing of urine, or an ejection of spittle.

3. tawb
dev tawb Of a dog scratching himself.

4. **tawb** To fool or play around.
   sib tawb Of two persons playing at fighting.
   tawb tau ntshav To get hurt in playing around.

1. **tawg** Breaks open, shatters, cracks open, cracks apart.
   tawg pleb Cracked open.
   tawg rhe Broken, broken apart.
   tawg rhe lawm Completely broken.
   ntaus kom lawv tawg To "break" them (in winning a
      fight or battle).
   tawg paj To flower, of flowers opening.
   Lub hwj tawg lawm. The bottle is broken.

2. **tawg** Clf. for slaps with the hand.
   ib tawg ncuav One slap on the face.

3. **tawg** In combination with 'ntho' a two-word restricted
   post verbal intensifier. (cf. Appendix 8)
   (cf. 'ntho' p. 196).

tawj Restricted post verbal intensifier after 'nrov'
(cf. 'nrov' p. 178).

1. **tawm** Out from, to come out.
   tawm lawm Came out from.
   tawm mus lawm Went out from.
   Muab tawm los. Take (it) out.
   xav tsis tawm Can't think of it (won't come out in
      my thoughts).
   tawm plaws Suddenly came out.
   tawm txhaws daws Of many fleeing out all at once.

2. **tawm**
   tawm hws Perspiration, to perspire.

3. **tawm** Used to express a remainder in counting.
   ib puas tawm More than one hundred.

4. **tawm**
   qhov ncauj tawm Canker sores, thrush mouth.

5. **tawm**
   tawm tsam To wage war (cf. 'tua rog').

6. **tawm**
   tawm thawj Just happened at the exact moment.

7. **tawm** Clf. for a length of things joined together.
   ib tawm tsheb One train (whole string of cars)
      (also 'ib ntus tsheb').
   ib tawm kev One stretch of road.

1. **taws** Firewood, fuel (clf. 'tsuam' for bunches).
   txiav taws To cut firewood (contr. 'txhib').
   rauv taws To light a fire, add wood to a fire.
   cav taws A log of firewood.
   cub hluavtaws A furnace, large fire.
   hluavtaws Fire.
   nplaim taws Flames
   txim taws Sparks.
   nplais taws Wood chips.
   nte taws To sit next to the fire.
   ib tsuag taws One bunch of firewood (t.c.)
   tsheb tawg (t.c.) A train (cf. 'tsheb').

2. **taws** To burn, to use as fuel.
   taws roj To burn oil.
   taws tsau To burn a torch, carry a burning torch.
   taws npoos To carry a pitch torch.

3. **taws** Used as a restricted post verbal intensifier with
      'npau.'
   npau taws To be angry (cf. Appendix 8).

4. **taws**
   taws tiab (cf. 'tiab').

1. **tawv** Hard, tough, stiff (contr. 'muag').
   ntoo tawv tawv Hard wood.
   lub siab tawv tawv Hard-hearted, firm in purpose.
   qhov muag tawv tawv Sleepy, heavy-eyed (eyes 'hard'
      and difficult to open).
   ceg tawv A lame leg (stiff leg), lame.
   yeem tawv Reluctant willingness, of one who obeys
      but only after dealt with severely.

2. **tawv** Skin, leather, bark (clf. 'daim' or 'phob').
   tawv ntoo Tree bark.
   (a) daim tawv A sheet of skin or leather.
   (b) phob tawv A sheet of skin or leather.
   laws tawv To skin, to strip off the skin.
   muab tshuaj lom daim tawv To tan leather.

3. **tawv** A measure for rice or grain.
   ten 'siab' equal one 'tawv'
   ten 'tawv' equal one 'tas'

4. **tawv**
   tawv tos Steadily.
   nrog tawv tos Dripped steadily.

1. **te** Frost.

2. **te**
   nyob pem te Over there in the village (nearby)
      (cf. 'pem').

1. teb Field, earth, ground (clf. 'daim') (cf. Appendix
        p. 487).
   poob pem teb Fell to the ground.
   teb npleg (t.c.) Dry rice field (contr. 'liaj').
   tebchaws Country, land, state (lub).
   ua teb To make or to cultivate dry fields, to do
           field work.
   nyob pem teb In the fields (cf. 'pem').
   teb peg Dry fields for farming on the flat plains.

2. teb To answer, to reply to.
   teb tias... Replied saying....
   zab teb To echo.

3. teb
   ua mob teb Birth pains, to be in labor giving birth.

teg T.c. from 'tes' (cf. 'tes').

1. tej A class, a group (cf. 'cov').
   (a) tej no These.
   (b) cov no These.
   hlob dua tej Greater than those or them.

2. tej
   (a) lawv tej Others, other persons, them.
   (b) luag tej Others, other persons, them.
   tej zaug Other occasion, on the other hand.

3. tej
   nyob pem tej hav zoov Over in the jungle.

4. tej
   ntuj fa tej lam A time of trouble and confusion
        (as of war and famine, etc.)

tem Senile, simple, forgetful.
   neeg tem toob A forgetful person, one simple-minded.
   ua tem toob ua hnem hnov Forgetful and absent-minded.

1. tes The lower arm and hand, pertaining to the lower arm,
        the hand or the fingers. (clf. 'txhais' for
        arm or hand; 'tus' for finger).
   txhais tes Lower arm, hand.
   kuv txhais tes xis My right hand (or arm) (cf. 'lauj').
   ntiv tes Finger.
   ntiv tes xoo Thumb.
   ntiv tes nta The three middle fingers.
   ntiv tes rwg qab The little finger.
   rau tes Finger nail.
   yas tes Knuckle, finger joint.
   dab teg (t.c.) Wrist.
   xib teg (t.c.) Palm of the hand.
   qaum tes Back of the hand.

   pob teg (t.c.) The wrist bone.
   taub teg (t.c.) Finger tip.
   nqws tes Missing one arm.
   cev tes To put out the hand.
   lauj tes To retract the hand.
   tsa tes To raise the hand.
   dauv tes To lower the hand to one's side.

2. tes Clf. for handfuls or for blows with the hand.
   ib teg nplej One sheaf of rice (t.c.)
   ntaus nws ib teg Hit him once (t.c.)

tev To peel (fruit, vegetables, etc.) (cf. 'laws'), to
     strip or peel off a layer.
   tev dos To peel onions.
   tev txiv To peel fruit.

1. tee A drop (of liquid, etc.)
   Dej nrog ib tee ib tee. The water drips one drop at
        a time. (or 'ib tees ib tees').

2. tee A spot, a freckle.

1. teeb A lamp, a light (clf. 'lub').
   zes teeb To light a lamp.
   teeb kublub Lamp used in opium smoking.
   teeb ntuj A storm lantern.
   teeb hnab tsog A pressure lamp.
   teeb xeeb Lamp wick (C).
   lub tsom teeb Lamp glass.
   nplaim teeb Lamp flame.

2. teeb
   khwb teeb Woven bamboo stool (clf. 'lub').

3. teeb
   mob sis teeb Small pimples exuding water.

4. teeb
   txhiaj teeb meem To speak in riddles, a riddle.

1. teeg
   av zoo zoo teeg A level place of good ground for use
        in planting a field.

2. teeg
   Npua teeg menyuam. The sow is carrying a litter.

teej
   teej qa teej num Household utensils (poetic).

1. teem To nail, to fix, to settle upon (C) (cf. 'ntsia').
   (a) teem caij To settle on a time to do something.
   (b) teem nyoog To settle on a time to do something.
   Lawv twb teem ib lub caij yuav mus. They have already settled a time to go.
   (a) teem txim To suffer punishment for sin or crime.
   (b) raug txim To suffer punishment for sin or crime.

2. teem
   lub teem qab koob (cf. 'koob').

3. teem To keep, store up, set aside.
   teem dej To store water.
   teem roj To store oil, set aside oil for use.

4. teem
   cuab xeeb puj teem (cf. 'cuab' Definition No. 8, p. 19).

5. teem Used as a name for Hmong men and boys.

tees A tone change from 'tee' sometimes used. (cf. 'tee').

1. teev A balance scale (clf. 'rab').
   luj teev To weigh in a balance scales.
   teev khaum Box for the balance scale.
   thauj teev The weight on the scales.
   phaj teev The plate on the scales.
   teev timtseeb Small balance scale.

2. teev
   teev keem (rab) A dibble, stick with a pointed end used for making holes for planting.
   lub teev keem The steel point put on such a stick.

3. teev
   teev dab (cf. 'dab' p. 28).

4. teev
   dej teev Standing water.

5. teev
   tsov pom teev A leopard (tus) (cf. 'tsov').

ti Close to, close together (cf. 'chwv') (contr. 'tib').
   (a) ti ntho Very close together.
   (b) ti nkaus Very close together.
   sib txuas ti Closely connected together.
   ti ti phoom phoom Crowded close together on top of one another.

1. tib Single, one only. There is only one.
   Muaj tib tug xwb.
   tib tug tug Only one son, only son.
   tib qho (t.c.) One place.
   tib ib lub siab Single-hearted.

2. tib of sudden sharp action.
   khiav tib plhaw Ran off in a sudden fright.
   tib qawg To startle.
   muab tib teg nws Hit him a sudden blow.

3. tib To pile up, piled one on top of another (contr. 'ti').
   sib tib Piled up.
   tib nkaus Piled close on top of one another.

4. tib
   tibneeg People, a person (clf. 'tus') (cf. 'neeg').

5. tib
   tibsi All, altogether (cf. 'huvsi').
   huv tibsi All, altogether, everything.
   Nws muab noj tas huv tibsi. He ate all of it.

6. tib
   ...tib tiag Very nearly.
   Yuav luag tas tib tiag. Just about finished.

7. tib
   (a) pob av luaj An anthill.
   (b) pob av muas yis tib An anthill.

tid Tone change from 'tim' (cf. 'tim' and Introduction p. xxii-xxiii).

tig To revolve, to turn around (cf. 'tsam').
   tig hlo To turn around, turn around and face the other way.
   tig cev Turn the body around.
   tig saib qab To turn and look backward.
   tig dua sab tod To turn the other way.

1. tij Elder brother (cf. kinship terms Appendix p. 484 and 493).
   kwvtij Younger and older brothers, brethren (see further explanation under 'kwv').
   tij laug Older brother.
   niam tij Wife of an older brother.

2. tij
   tij lim Having strength or effectiveness.
   khawvkoob tij lim Effective magic, wonderful magic.

3. tij
   tij yim poob (cf. 'poob').

1. tim Across the valley, over there (contr. 'tom').
   Note: This word is often heard 'tid' subject to tone change as outlined in the Introduction p. xxii-xxiii.
   nyob tid Located across the valley, over there (t.c.)
   Nws mus noj mov tim tsev. He went to eat in his house over there.
   tim ub Way over there.

2. tim Agreeing, alike, the same.
   tim nkaus The same, alike in all respects.
   muab tim ua ke To compare.

3. tim Because of, indicating that the cause or reason is
   attached to the subject following (similar to
   'vim') (cf. 'vim').
   (a) Tim li cas? Why? For what reason?
   (b) Vim li cas? Why? For what reason?
   Xyov puas yog tim kuv los tim nws. I don't know if
   it is because of me or because of him.

4. tim To witness.
   tim lus To witness.
   sib tim To witness one against another.
   tim ncauj ntsees tham To speak face to face.

5. tim ua timkhawv To witness, to bear testimony.
   (a) tus ua timkhawv A witness.
   (b) tus hais timkhawv A witness.

6. tim lub tsev timphooj A temporary house, a field shelter.

7. tim lub qhov timthaj A well.

8. tim teev timtseeb (cf. 'teev').

9. tim xov muj tim (cf. 'muj' and 'rooj').

10. tim timxyoob officers, sub-headmen, assistants to the
    leader.
    tuam timxyoob The head assistant.
    cov timxyoob saum ntuj "The heavenly assistants"
    (a term used for angels.)

11. tim cov tim tswv Officials (C).

12. tim
    (a) thob fab The foundation beams of a house (cf.
    'tsev').
    (b) tim cum The foundation beams of a house (cf.
    'tsev').

13. tim thwjtim Learner, disciple.

1. tis A wing (clf. phob' or 'sab').
   phob tis A wing.
   tis noog A bird wing.

2. tis A feather (from the wing or tail or body) (clf. 'tus').
   ib tug tis A feather.

3. tis To name.
   tis npe To name, to give a name to.

4. tis Used in certain kinship terms referring to women.
   tis dab hlob (cf. Kinship charts in Appendix p. 496-497).
   tis dab yau (cf. Kinship charts in Appendix p. 496-497).
   tis nyab (cf. Kinship charts in Appendix p. 496-497).

5. tis tis ntuag (cf. 'ntuag' p. 193).

6. tis peb txheej peb tis Great numbers, a great crowd.

7. tis cuaj txheej cuaj tis From the beginning of man's
   generations (C). (cf. 'puas txwv puaj tiam').

8. tis nrog lawv txuas tw tis Idiomatic expression for taking
   a wife from among their clan (cf. 'tshoob').

1. tiv To oppose, to resist, to meet or to endure opposition.
   tiv tseg To oppose, to resist.
   ua tiag tiv To resist, to bear with, to be patient
   under provocation. (cf. 'uv').
   Txhob ua phem rov tiv phem. Don't return evil for evil.
   tiv mob To bear pain.
   tiv nag To avoid or shelter from rain.
   tiv tshav To avoid or shelter from sunlight.
   Yus yuav tiv yus li nqe txim. One must bear his
   penalty for sin.

2. tiv tiv yam li Like, same as (cf. 'ib yam li').

3. tiv cuabtiv (cf. 'cuab').

4. tiv lub tiv qab koob Thimble (cf. 'koob').

5. tiv tiv txwv The bottom of (C).
   tiv txwv hiav txwv The bottom of the sea (C).

2. tiam
    tiamsis But, however (sometimes this is heard pro-
        nounced 'tibsis' especially in Laos).
    Kuv xav mus tiamsis tsis muaj nyiaj. I would like to
        go but haven't the money.

1. tias Restricted post verbal intensifier used after verbs
    involving speech, sound, or thought. (cf.
    Appendix 8).
        hais tias... Said, spoke saying...
        Kuv xav tias... I think that...
        piav tias... Explained that...
        nug tias... Asked that...
        teb tias... Answered that...
        nco tias... Remembered that...
        ntshai tias... Feared that...
    And similarly used with the following verbs:
        paub   yog   ntxhi   nloog
        qw   xam   hawv   cem
        ntxub   hu   quaj   hnov
        yws
    Note: The expression 'hais tias' is used to introduce
        quotations. Sometimes it is shortened so that
        'tias' is used alone after the subject without
        an intervening verb. In this case 'tias' may
        be understood as including the meaning of the
        verb 'hais' (to speak) Thus...
        (a) Nws tias... He said...
        (b) Nws hais tias... He said...
    Note also:
        (a) tias uas... That is to say...
        (b) yog tias... That is to say...

2. tias A birthmark on the face (lub) (cf. 'cos').

1. tiav Finished, sign of completed action. (cf. 'tas').
    ua tiav To finish.
    Yuav ua tiav huv huv li. It must be completely done.
        (You) must finish it.

2. tiav To come of age, come to a mature stage of growth.
    tiav hluas To attain young manhood.
    tiav nkauj To attain young womanhood.
    Zaub ntsuab twb tiav hauv lawm. The vegetable greens
        have formed clumps ready for picking.

1. to Having a hole, to be pierced with a hole. (contr.
        'thov').
    Lub hnab to qhov. The sack has a hole in it.
    to ntshua Having a big hole.
    Lawv tsoo phab ntsa to ntshua. They made a big hole
        in the wall.

tiab Skirt (clf. 'daim').
    nre tiab To pleat a skirt.
    tab tiab The lower portion of a skirt.
    taws tiab The lower border of a skirt.

1. tiag Really, truly, conforming to fact.
    This word is used as a final emphatic particle and also
    to modify the very which precedes it. In final
    position it is often duplicated for emphasis.
    Used in this way it is sometimes heard pro-
    nounced 'tas'.
        (a) Zoo tiag tiag! Excellent! Fine!
        (b) Zoo tas tas! Excellent! Fine!
    Xyov puas hais tiag los hais dag. I don't know if
        he spoke the truth or way lying.
    Yuav luag tag tib tiag. Almost finished. (cf.
        'tib').
    Tiag! Right! That's it! True! (also "Yog tiag!").

2. tiag A pad or cushion, to pad or to cushion, to lay a
        base for.
    tiag duav A pad worn at the waist in the back to
        serve as a rest when carrying a water bucket.
    lub rooj tiag taw A footstool.

3. tiag tiv (cf. 'tiv').
    ua tiag tiv (cf. 'tiv').

4. tiag
    tiag npab tiag tes To hit on the hands and arms.

5. tiag
    tiag ncauj To curse, to scold.

6. tiag
    lub tiag lub dawg Level places and gaps in a
        mountain ridge (cf. 'tiaj').
    Note: Here 'tiag' may be regarded as a tone change
        from 'tiaj' but if so it is a different pattern
        of change than otherwise observed. (cf.
        Appendix 1).

tiaj Even, level, smooth, a level place.
    tiaj lias Level.
    tiaj tiaj tus tus Flat and smooth.
    pw ntxeev tiaj To lie flat on one's back.

1. tiam A generation, a generation of persons who have
        died.
    ob peb tiam neeg Several generations of people.
    puas txwv puaj tiam (C) From the beginning of man's
        generations (cf. 'cuaj').

2. to Having a way through, "opened" to action.
   to kev ua Legitimate, all right to do, permissible.
   tsis to kev ua Not permitted, cannot do, not open
     to do, unlawful.

3. to Penetrating to the understanding.
   to taub To understand (same as 'nkag siab').
   to siab ntshua To understand.
   tsis to ntsej Can't understand (doesn't penetrate
     my ear).

4. to ntsiag to Silent, still, ineffective (of drugs, etc.)

1. tob Deep.
   lub niag qhov tob tob A huge deep hole.
   qhov tob Depth (cf. 'qhov').
   (a) Qhov tob yog li cas? How deep is it?
   (b) Tob li cas? How deep is it?

2. tob "Knife" as pronounced in Chinese (C).
   yeeb tob An opium knife, knife used in preparing
     opium.

3. tob txiv tob The large acorn-like seed used by Hmong
     children to make spinning tops.

4. tob lub kiv tob The small spinning top with bamboo shaft
     used as a plaything by Hmong boys.

tod T.c. from 'tom' (cf. Appendix 1).

1. tog To sink.
   (a) nkoj tog The boat sank.
   (b) nkoj dua hauv dej lawm The boat sank.

2. tog A low stool, a block, a chopping block (lub).
   lub tog rau ncoo A block used as a pillow.
   lub tog tsuav zaub npua Chopping-block for cutting
     up pig food.

3. tog Used to indicate density, heavy in proportion to
     bulk, e.g. of metals that will not float
     (cf. 'tog' Definition No. 1).
   hnyav tog Heavy in proportion to bulk (cf. 'hnyav')
     (cf. 'hnyav qes') (contr. 'ya').

4. tog A "side" in a conflict, etc., at the side, at the
     place.
   nyob tog tsev At the side of the house.
   tom tog hau knoj At the bow of the boat.
   Nws tuaj peb tog. He is on our side.
   ib tog nthuav ib tog kauv To open one roll and roll
     up the other (as in opening a scroll).

5. tog
   txog tog To the half-way point.
   Nws noj tsog tog xwb. He only ate half-way through
     (the feast).

6. tog More than.
   ob daig tog More than two bars (of silver, etc.)

7. tog
   ua ib tog cem All ganged together to curse (him).

8. tog sib tog (t.c.) (cf. 'tom').

9. tog
   ntos ib tog tuaj To weave one roll of cloth (cf.
     'tog' definition No. 4).

toj Hill, incline (contr. 'roob').
   nce toj To climb a hill, go uphill.
   toj kawg Bottom of a hill.
   tav toj To go along the side of a hill.
   toj pob Landslide.
   toj siab High hill.
   mem toj A crack in the hillside, a vein in the rock.

1. tom To bite, to sting (of animal and human bites and
     stings from vegetation but not of insect stings)
     (cf. 'plev').
   dev tom The dog bites, dog bite.
   dev sib tog The dogs are fighting (t.c.) (the term
     'sib tog' is commonly used of animals fighting since
     they do so by biting one another).
   Ob yam tshuaj sib tog. The two kinds of medicine
     don't agree with each other (cf. 'tsis sib hum').
   tom hniav qawv Biting and gnashing of teeth.

2. tom There (nearby), a term of location (contr. 'tim').
   Note: This word is often heard 'tod' subject to the tone
     changes outlined in the Introduction p. xxii-xxiii.
   nyob tod Over there.
   nyob tom ub Way over there.
   sab tom no Here, this side.
   sab tom ub Way over on that side.
   tom teb In the fields.
   tom qab Behind, afterward.
   tom ntej Before, ahead.
   tom thawj Through to the end, all the way through.
   Yuav ua tom thawj. You ought to carry it through.

3. tom Clf. for a time, a round or a turn, a section of
     road travelled, a pounding of rice, etc.
   loos dua ib tom Do it over again, fix it again.

toog

    ua yog toog To have a vision (contr. 'npau suav').
    yog toog A vision.

1. tooj Copper, brass, metal containing copper.
    tooj liab Copper.
    tooj daj Brass.
    tooj dawb Nickel, chromium.
    xov tooj Copper wire (also commonly used to refer
           to wire in general or to a metal spring) (clf.
           'txoj').
    tooj npab A bracelet (lub).

2. tooj To pull hand over hand.
    tooj mus To pull one's self along by a fixed rope.
    tooj xov To reel in thread hand over hand.

1. toom
    cuabyeej toomtxeem Household goods (cf. 'cuab').

2. toom
    ceebtoom To warn (cf. 'ceeb').

3. toom
    toom zaub toom mov To mix up vegetables and rice in
        disorder (as when a child stirs up the food
        unnecessarily when eating from a common dish).

1. toov To deceive, to lead astray (cf. 'haub').
    Leej twg haub toov koj? Who has led you astray?

2. toov
    ntoo toov laj (cf. 'ntoo').

1. tu To part, to break apart (as of a rope or thread or
      things that come in lengths).
    tu nrho lawm Tore apart.
    tu siab To be offended.
    tu siab nrho Highly offended, severed relations.

2. tu Of a flow stopping or being cut off.
    ntshav tu lawm Has stopped bleeding.
    (a) txoj siav tu lawm Has died, life cut off.
    (b) tu siav nrho Has died, life cut off.
    Kuv lub siab tu ib tw zawj qas zog. My heart skipped
        a beat.

3. tu To settle, to fix (cf. 'kiav').
    tu plaub To settle judgment, to make amiable settle-
        ment of a case of dispute (cf. 'plaub').

4. tom
    tom siab ua To do earnestly (cf. 'siab').

5. tom
    tab tom To initiate, to begin (cf. 'samsim').
    tab tom ua Just began to do.

6. tom
    siv tom txwv (cf. 'siv' Definition No. 3).

7. tom
    sib tom txheeb (cf. 'txheeb').

8. tom The following are terms used in playing with
      spinning tops.
    kaim tom The first top stands spinning.
    tsis tom The first top falls.

1. tos To wait for, to wait.
    tos ntsoov To wait.
    tos quj qees To continue to wait (not knowing the
        time is past).
    Tsis txhob rawm tos kuv. Don't wait for me.

2. tos To meet someone, to go to meet someone (wait for them).
    Nws mus tos nws txiv los tsev. He went to meet his
        father coming home.

3. tos Used at the beginning of sentences to refer to the
      cause or the reason why.
    Tos peb tsis pom nws yog vim li cas? What is the
        reason we cannot see him?

4. tos
    (a) kem tos Probably, it is most likely that.
    (b) kem tos li Probably, it is most likely that.
    Kem tos nws ntshai heev nws thiaj tsis kam. Probably
        because he is very afraid he won't do it.

tov To mix water into something else, to add water.
    Tov dej rau Mix some water into it. (contr. 'xyaw').

too nplej too (cf. 'nplej' p. 165-6).

1. toob Old and feeble-minded, senile (cf. 'tem').
    neeg tem toob Senile, forgetful, simple-minded.

2. toob
    zeb toob txuab A soft crumbly kind of rock.

3. toob
    toobxib Goods, articles, things (C).

4. tu To look after, to care for, to prepare.
   tu koom To pack up goods, to prepare for travel.
   tu cov menyuam To care for the children (cf. 'tu' Definition No. 5).
   tu tsiaj txhu To look after the animals.

5. tu
   (a) tu menyuam To give birth (cf. 'yug').
   (b) tu tub To give birth (cf. 'yug').
   Tu tub lawm tsis tau? Have you had your baby yet? (cf. 'daws cev').

6. tu To make an end of it, to do it once only and then no more, cease reports of it.
   tu zam (cf. 'tuag').

1. tub Son (clf. 'tus').
   tib tug tub Only son (t.c.)
   tub ki Sons and daughters, children.
   tseg tub tseg ki Bereft of children.
   pojniam tub so Wife and children.

2. tub Joined with various words following to indicate one who is engaged in the designated action (clf. 'tus').
   tub txib A messenger, one sent.
   tub qhe A slave, a servant (t.c.).
   tub sab A thief.
   tub luam A merchant, a trader.
   tub rog A soldier.
   tub dua kev A traveller, a stranger, passer-by.
   (a) cov tub txib tub qhe Messengers, servants.
   (b) cov tub txib tub txuas Messengers, servants.
   tub ntsuag Orphan.

3. tub To dip something into liquid.
   tub kua zaub To dip (something) into the vegetable broth or gravy.

4. tub
   tub nkeeg Lazy, listless (t.c.)
   ua dab tub nkeeg To have malaria (cf. 'nkees') (t.c.)

1. tug A part, a portion.
   kuv li tug My part (having been divided with me.)

2. tug T.c. from 'tus' (cf. 'tus').

tuj tuj lub (lub) A wooden spinning top (cf. 'lub').

tum To pile up in one straight pile.
   tum ua ib ke Piled up together, to pile.

1. tus Classifier for persons and living things, also clf. for long slender things like trees, pencils, pens, etc.
   Note: This clf. is often found as 'tug' subject to the tone changes outlined in the Appendix 1.
   ib tug One (article or person) (t.c.)
   kuv tus tub My son.
   Tus twg? Who? (also 'Leej twg?').
   tus uas The one which, whom.

2. tus Even, level, peaceful, still.
   tiaj tiaj tus tus Perfectly level.
   lub siab tus tus A heart at peace.
   tus yees Still, at peace, at rest.
   nyob lub siab tus yees With a heart at peace, settled and quiet attending to one's own business.
   Nws li hlwb tus tus. He has a good brain.

tuv liab Body lice (tus) (contr. 'ntshauv').
   tuv dub Bedbug (tus).
   ua tuv txias tom caj qwb As a bedbug bites the back of my neck without my seeing it. (idiomatic expression for "talking about me behind my back").

1. tua To kill (contr. 'tuag').
   tua npua To kill a pig.
   tua tibneeg To murder, to kill a person.

2. tua To fire a gun or a weapon.
   tua phom To fire a gun.
   tua hneev To fire a crossbow.
   tua rog To engage in warfare, to war (cf. 'rog').

1. tuab Thick (as of books, boards, etc.).

2. tuab
   siab tuab tuab A courageous heart, courage.

3. tuab
   neeg tuab Of a woman who easily becomes pregnant.

1. tuag To die, pertaining to death (contr. 'tua').
   Tua kom tuag. Kill it.
   tuag lawm Died.
   txhoj kev tuag Death.
   vij tuag As good as dead.
   qhov tuag Death, the grave.
   txhaws qhov tuag theej txhoj To die for another, to take another's place in death.
   tuag nthi Really dead, finalized, settled.
   ntees tuag (lub) Funeral rites, the time when all are gathered together at a funeral. (cf. 'ntees ploj ntees tuag').

(a) hnub ua qhua txws The day of preparation for the
    dead, the day before the burial.

hnub tshwm tshav The day of burial.

Terms Relating to Funeral Rites:
hais zaj qhuab ke (t.c.) The song sung at death to
    open the way for the deceased to travel on his
    way. (sung before the playing of the pipes).

(a) tus qhuab ke The one who sings the song as above.
(b) tus taw kev The one who sings the song as above.
tu zam To wash and clothe the body of the deceased.
tshov qeej tu siav To play the dirge on the Hmong
    musical pipes signifying that life has been cut
    off and ceased.

tshov qeej tsa nees To play the Hmong musical pipes
    when the deceased is raised on a stretcher
    between two poles and placed against the wall
    on the uphill side of the house for the rest
    of the funeral ceremonies.

cov ua hauv qhua Those relatives who bring rice,
    paper money, etc. as gifts on the day before
    the burial.(cf. 'qhua' and 'hnub ua qhua txws').

Terms for Those Helping in Funeral Rites:
cov nquam qauv The pallbearers.
tus txiv qeej The man who plays the pipes.
tus txiv nruas The man who beats the drum.
tus kav xwm The man in charge of ceremonies.
tus tshwj kab The man in charge of preparing the
    meat and vegetables for the feast.
tus tshaj thawj The man who cuts the firewood.
tus siv thawj The man who carries water.
tus cuab tsav The man in charge of offering food and
    offerings to the deceased.
(a) tus tsa rog The man who by himself or leading a
    group circles the house in mock battle. Some-
    times he carries the pipes or a crossbow or gun.
(b) tus hau rog The man who by himself or leading a
    group circles the house in mock battle. Some-
    times he carries the pipes or a crossbow or gun.
tus tsav phom One who shoots the gun in mock battle
    with the spirits.
tus txiv txiag The man who cuts boards for the
    coffin.
tus niam fam txam The woman in charge of making
    the rice (sometimes 'niam fam tsam' or 'txam
    fam').
(a) tus niam hauv paus cos The woman in charge of
    grinding corn and pounding rice.
(b) tus niam diaj zeb tuav cos The woman in charge
    of grinding corn and pounding rice.

2. tuag Used to indicate paralysis or loss of mobility and
    function.
    tuag tes tuag taw Paralysis (inability to use hands
    or feet).

3. tuag A restricted post verbal intensifier with 'nthi'
    siab tuag nthi To be well satisfied with (cf. 'siab')
    hais tuag nthi Finished discussing, settled.

4. tuag
    tuag ntxhai Of flesh that has softened and become
    whitened by being in the water a great deal.
    neeg tuag ntxhai Albino, without pigmentation (a
    person without normal skin color).

5. tuag
    dab tuag li Shoddy, poorly (cf. 'dab').

1. tuaj To come (to a place other than one's home, to come
    to a place where one does not reside or belong)
    (contr. 'los').
    Koj tuaj lawm. You have come. (you have arrived.)
    (this is the common greeting to a friend or
    visitor entering a home).
    tuaj quj qees Kept slowly coming.

2. tuaj To bear, to put forth (as of horns, hair, feathers,
    a tail, etc.)
    Nyuj tuaj kub. Cows have horns.
    Noog tuaj plaub. Birds have feathers.

3. tuaj To sprout, to come up out of the ground (of things
    planted).

4. tuaj
    tuaj dab ros Funny, to laugh.
    lus tuaj dab ros A joke, a funny saying.

5. tuaj
    mob tuaj leeg Of a skin infection spreading.

1. tuam To kick backward with the foot.
    nees tuam The horse kicks.
    Nees tuam neeg. The horse kicked a person.

2. tuam To build a structure between two points, to erect.
    tuam choj To build a bridge.
    tuam ciav dej To erect a water line of bamboo lengths.

3. tuam
    tuam txhob (rab) A digging implement for making holes
    for posts, etc.

4. tuam
    siab tuam tav Courageous, bold.

5. tuam
   siab tuam yim Reckless, careless of danger.
   Txhob tuam yim. Don't boast as if you know it all,
   Don't be rash.

6. tuam
   moj tuam Braids, hair braids.

7. tuam The Hmong pronunciation of the Chinese word for
   'large' or 'great' or 'chief' and therefore
   found in a number of expressions including
   these ideas.
   los tuam The eldest child.
   lus tuam mom Arrogant or threatening language.
   tuam cuab All people (C).
   tuam timxyoob Chief assistant (cf. 'timxyoob').
   lus tuam huam Very proud language, haughty speech.
   tuam tshawjchim A great enemy.
   los nag tuam tsam A heavy rain.
   tuam tshoj China.

8. tuam
   tuamham. (tus) Soldier (T).

1. tuav To grasp, to hold with the hand.
   tuav tes To hold the hand.
   tuav tes rawv To hold hands firmly.

2. tuav To beat or to pound out, especially to pound in
   the common footmill for hulling rice or grain
   (cf. 'cos').
   tuav cos To work the footmill.
   tuav txhuv To pound rice in the footmill.
   tuav ncuav To pound cooked rice to make it into
   consistency for rice cakes.

3. tuav
   hu tuav npe To call by name.
   tuav npe txog ntawm kwj tse No sooner said his
   name than he appeared.

4. tuav
   tuav theem To delay (cf. 'tabkaum').

5. tuav
   txoj siav tuav sem To lose life, to perish.

6. tuav
   ua tuav tseev To investigate, to inquire into
   (cf. 'seev').
   Ua thaj puav neeb ua tuav tseev. Hold a session or
   two of spirit worship to investigate (what
   the trouble is).

1. tw Tail, tail region, pertaining to the end (cf. 'tsw').
   tus tw The tail.
   kotw (tus) Tail, the tail.
   tuaj kotw Has a tail.
   nyob tom tw At the end.
   caj tw The buttocks.
   khiab tw (cf. 'khiab' and 'nees').
   tw siv (cf. 'siv' p. 295).
   tw roob The foot of the mountain.
   tw yaj pobkws Corn tassels.

2. tw Clf. for gusts of wind (also 'nthwv').

3. tw
   riam tw A blunt ended knife (cf. 'riam').

4. tw
   tw puam (cf. 'puam' and 'tsev').

5. tw The second-best, that left over or left to the end.
   cov tw cawv The left over whisky, second-best whisky.

1. twb Pre-verbal particle drawing attention to the state
   of affairs at the time. "indeed," "even,"
   "really."
   Kuv twb tsis paub. I really don't know.
   Kuv twb tsis tau hnov. I didn't even hear of it.
   Kuv twb muaj. I already have some.
   Thaum ntawd nws twb tsis tau mus ib zaug. At that
   time he hadn't even gone once.

2. twb
   ua twb zoo Be careful, take care.
   Ua twb zoo saib. Look carefully.

3. twb
   twb cwjmem To lower the pen to write.

4. twb
   ua twb cuab To live together as a single large family.

5. twb
   twb nkaus To connect (as in a switch, etc.) (contr.
   'nrug').

1. twg Which? Who?
   Leej twg? Tus twg? Who?
   Qhov twg? Where?
   Hnub twg? Which day?
   Thaum twg? When?
   (a) Mus qhov twg lawm? Where (has he) gone?
   (b) Dua twg lawm? Where (has he) gone?

2. twg
   taub twg (cf. 'taub').

3. twg T.c. from 'twm' (cf' twm').

1. twj
   twjywm Quiet.
   Nyob twjywm! Be quiet: (cf. 'tswm seeb').

2. twj kum (tus) A rhinocerous.

3. twj twjsiv A utensil, article of household use.

1. twm Water buffalo (clf. 'tus').
   kub twg (t.c.) Buffalo horn.
   dav noj twm (tus) A buzzard (cf. 'dav').

2. twm Single, lone, alone.
   twm tswb Single wild boar which keeps to itself.
   twm nyuj Single wild ox which keeps to itself.
   twm qaib A lone chicken, only one hatched in a brood.
   twm zeej Only one person, single person (C).
   ib lub twm qhov muag One-eyed, missing one eye.

3. twm xeeb Impatient, unrestrained temper.
   hais lus twm xeeb Impatient speaking, to speak before another is finished.

4. twm
   nas hoo twm (cf. 'nas' p. 136).

1. tws To carve, to hew.
   tws ntoo To hew a log smooth with an axe or knife.
   tws txiag To smooth a board with axe or knife, etc.

2. tws Short, coming short of (e.g. one line of writing shorter than another).
   tws tshwv Short, never quite reaches, never quite right.

3. tws To come to an end, the end (cf. 'tw').
   kev tws End of the road, road ends.
   lus tws Closing words, ending words.
   yivtws A pigtail (lub).
   (a) tws kev Don't know what to think or where to turn.
   (b) xav tws Don't know what to think or where to turn.

4. tws
   (a) Txhob tws koj roob qhib. Idiomatic expression meaning "Don't make trouble for those who are close to you." (lit. "Don't skin your own shinbone.")
   (b) Txhob tws yus cov. Idiomatic expression meaning "Don't make trouble for those who are close to you." (lit. "Don't skin or hew your own group")

1. twv To defy, to taunt, to guess, to compete.
   Twv saib Guess and see.
   twv txiaj To gamble, to wager.
   twv tsawm (cf. 'tsawm').

2. twv Clf. for clouds (also 'tauv').
   twv huab ntawd That cloud.
   ib tw huab One cloud (t.c.)

3. twv Large waves, swells in the ocean (contr. 'ntas').
   Dej nphau nphwv tej niag twv. The water rolled in great waves.

TH

1. thab To boast.

2. thab To make trouble or misfortune for another.
   thab plaub To raise a dispute or case at law.
   Lawv tuaj thab yus They come and make trouble for one.

3. thab To try to force a gift on someone.

4. thab To pound metal to increase its width.

5. thab To beg, to entreat for help (not commonly used)
   (cf. 'taij').

6. thab
   phim thabntxwv (cf. 'phim').

7. thab
   thab xib nyub (lub) An amplifier (T).

1. thaj Clf. for sessions of spirit worship (cf. 'neeb').
   ua ib thaj neeb Do one session of spirit worship.

2. thaj
   thaj neeb The spirit shelf (cf. 'neeb').

3. thaj Clf. for a patch or a grove of vegetation or for
   a field.

4. thaj Sugar (C).
   suav thaj Brown sugar syrup.
   piam thaj White sugar (C).

5. thaj
   kwvtij thaj kub Distant relatives.

6. thaj
   thim thaj To draw back, go part way and turn back.

tham To chat, to converse.
   sib tham To chat together.
   Nej tham dabtsi? What are you talking about together?
   tham pem To chat together about various subjects.
   tus txeev tham One who talks a lot.

1. thav A frame for making paper.
   thav ntawv Frame for making paper.

2. thav ntxwv (clf. 'daim') A loincloth, a mantle, a
   wrap-around garment without sleeves.

3. thav
   menyuam thav kauv Small half-grown barking deer.

thaib The Thai people (T).
   thaib ntsuab A Thai soldier.

1. thais To notch, to cut an indentation in wood or bamboo.
   thais ncej To cut a notch in the top of a post to
   hold a cross beam upon it.

2. thais
   thais plab To purge the bowels (cf. 'plab').

3. thais
   txiv thais liab A large male monkey (cf. 'liab').

4. thais
   thais sab Varicolored strips of material around the
   edge of a man's jacket.

5. thais
   thais huj (T) To take a photo (cf. 'yuam tibneeg').

1. thaiv To shelter, to stand between to shelter from attack,
   to protect, to come between and obscure the vision.

2. thaiv An anvil.
   thaiv ntaus hlau (lub) An anvil for forging metal.

3. thaiv
   ua tiag thaiv To bear with, to be patient under
   trial or provocation.

thau To withdraw something, to pull something out of.
   Muab thau los. Pull it out.
   Nws rov qab thau nws lo lus. He took back his word.
   He went back on his promise.

1. thaub
   thaub qab To go backward (of a vehicle, etc.)

2. thaub
   thaub ncho To walk backward, to go backward.

thaud (cf. 'thaum' and notes on tone variation in the
   Introduction p. xxii-xxiii).

1. thauj To transport (usually by animal but also of vehicles).
   (a) thauj khoom To transport goods by horse or animal.
   (b) thauj nra To transport goods by horse or animal.
   (cf. 'nra').

2. thauj
   thauj teev (cf. 'teev').

6. thawj
   thawj thiab To reincarnate, to transmigrate, of life reborn in another form.
   Nws tus plig mus thawj thiab lawm. His spirit was reincarnated.

7. thawj
   tshaj thawj Profit.
   noj tshaj thawj To make profit, to fix a price above the value to make profit.

8. thawj
   tus tshaj thawj The one who cuts firewood at a funeral (cf. 'tuag' p. 327).

9. thawj
   tus siv thawj The one who carries water at a funeral (cf. 'tuag' p. 327).

10. thawj
    tus povthawj An intermediary, a guarantor (cf. 'pov').

11. thawj
    tsam thawj (lub) A resting place along the way.

12. thawj
    hom thawj A seal, a mark of identification (cf. 'hom').
    ntaus hom thawj To mark for identification.

13. thawj
    ceebthawj Weight (in referring to children) (cf. 'ceeb').

14. thawj
    Ntoo sawb thawj lawm. The tree has shed its leaves. (not as commonly used as 'zeeg nplooj').

15. thawj
    Nws chwv chwv thawj. He won't talk. He refuses to answer.

16. thawj
    (a) saib tshiav thawj (cf. 'saib qaib' p. 288).
    (b) saib qaib (cf. 'saib qaib' p. 288).

17. thawj
    tawm thawj Just happened at that exact moment.

18. thawj
    dev thawj tswv (cf. 'dev' p. 35).

thawm
    dej thawm av The water soaks the soil.

thaum The time when.
   Thaum kuv nyob hauv tsev nws pheej tsis tuaj. He never comes when I am at home.
   thaum uas The time when.
   Thaum twg? When?
   thaum ub Long ago, of old, previously.
   thaum i Previously, just a short while ago.
   thaum hnub niaj hmo Every day and night.

thauv
   thauv vaiv Of something long and hanging down (as of long-eared animals, etc.)

1. thawb To shove, to push (cf. 'xyeeb' and 'xyob').
   Thawb qhov rooj: Push the door (open).

2. thawb (lub) Good name, reputation (C) (cf. 'meej').
   meej thawb

1. thawj The first, the head, the head of (C).
   chivthawj The beginning, the first.
   tus thawj zeej The headman.
   tus thawj zaug The first time.
   (a) thawj hom First class, first in quality.
   (b) thawj tom First class, first in quality.
   (c) thawj cov First class, first in quality.
   thawj txheej First in a series.
   cov ntaus thawj The elders, leaders or respected persons in the community.
   cam thawj lawm To argue against the leaders, to disrespect authority.

2. thawj To depend on someone. to follow others or do as they do.
   Txhob thawj lawv. Don't do as they do. Don't rely on their leadership.

3. thawj Through to the end, thoroughly.
   tom thawj
   Nws ua tsis tau thawj. He didn't complete the job.
   Yuav ntseeg tom thawj. You ought to believe through to the end.

4. thawj
   pamthawj (tus) A wooden mallet or maul especially one used for splitting logs.

5. thawj
   ham thawj To solder, to join metal by soldering.

thaws To rebound, to bounce back after hitting something.

thawv To jolt, to jar, to shake with short abrupt risings and fallings as with a vehicle upon rough ground (also 'tsuaj').
(a) thawv thawv li Of a vehicle jolting on rough ground.
(b) tsuaj tsuaj li Of a vehicle jolting on rough ground.

theb Restricted post verbal intensifier after 'nrov'. (cf. 'nrov' p. 178).

1. them To pay, to repay.
them nyiaj To pay money.
them nqe To pay a debt.

2. them
yaj them Tin.

3. them
them teb Alternative pronunciation of 'txhem teb.'

4. them
Nws lub plhu them xem lawm. His "face fell." (C)

thev To endure, to bear (as pain, etc.) (cf. 'nyiaj').
tsis thev Not long lasting, not durable.
(a) thev tsis taus Can't endure (pain, cold, etc.)
(b) nyiaj tsis taus Can't endure (pain, cold, etc.)

thee Charcoal.
hlawv thee To make charcoal.

1. theeb To swallow (C), (cf. 'nqo').
Theeb mentsis yeeb. Swallow a bit of opium.

2. theeb
lub siab khav theeb A proud heart.

3. theeb
maum theeb To talk or sing in one's sleep.

4. theeb
dab theeb kawg The name of a certain spirit.

5. theeb
thoob theeb plaws In all the world, completely, all over the world.

1. theej To take the place or position of another, to take something in place of another.
Note: This word is sometimes heard as 'thees' but i seems 'theej' is the Hmong word and 'thees' is nearer to the Thai pronunciation of a similar word.
Nws tuaj theej kuv chaw. He came to take my place.
Yexu theej peb lub txim. Jesus has taken our guilt upon himself.
Yexu theej peb qhov tuag. Jesus has taken our death penalty. (cf. 'this').
theej txhoj To offer offerings, etc. in the place of another to relieve sickness.
txhaws qhov tuag theej txhoj Of taking the place of death for another. When a person is seriously ill it is sometimes said that his spirit is stuck in the "death hole." An animal may then be killed to take the place of the spirit in the 'death hole' and thus release it for return.

2. theej
kavtheej (txoj) Rattan.

3. theej To put all the articles or the water from one vessel into another.
theej dej Pour all the water into another vessel (contr. 'hliv' and 'qee').
Muab theej kiag rau hauv kawm rau lawv ris. Put it all into their basket to carry.

1. theem Steps, levels of ascent, layer, story of a building.
Nyob theem tsev saum ub. On the upper story of the house. (cf. 'txheej' and 'qeb').

2. theem
tuav theem To delay (cf. 'tabkaum').

3. theem
hais lus theem To pause in conversation or speech, stop in the midst of a flow of speech.

theev To knock an object from side to side to loosen it, e.g. as in loosening a wedge to remove it.

thi A binding or a belt.
cov thi hneev The bamboo or rattan binding on a crossbow.
thi nyiaj Bound around with silver.
cov thi ntxaib A double binding.
thi tshuab The belt used to run a machine.

thib To pass off on someone else, e.g. as of an article of business passed off on someone else because the first individual does not want to deal with it.

thij Clf. for a whole stem of bananas (contr. 'kuam').

1. thim To bounce back, to go back on, to recant, of a
         gun kicking back when fired.
         phom thim The gun kicked back.
         Nws thim Yexu lawm. He gave up his faith in Jesus.
         thim thaj To draw back, to go part way and turn back.

2. thim Of colors fading or of cloth losing its color.

3. thim Of a temperature going down after rising.

this Instead of, on behalf of, in the place of another.
      (a) Yexu this peb tuag. Jesus died for us.
      (b) Yexu theej peb qhov tuag Jesus died for us.
      (c) Yexu txhaws peb qhov tuag Jesus died for us.
      (d) Yexu txauv peb qhov tuag Jesus died for us.

thiv To insert a piece of cloth when sewing.
      Thiv ib daig ntaub rau. Insert a piece of cloth in
      it. (e.g. when making a garment).

1. thiab And, also.
          Kuv yuav mus thiab. I'm going too.

2. thiab Sometimes used at the end of a sentence to indicate
          there is still something left unsaid.
          Koj puas nyiam kuv? Do you like me?
          Kuv nyiam koj thiab. Yes, I like you but...

3. thiab Pertaining to the fetus or unborn infant state of
          being.
          nruab thiab In the unborn state.
          ib txhis nruab thiab From before birth, from the
                                time of conception.
          tus thiab zeej The fetus or unborn infant.
          thawj thiab To reincarnate, to transmigrate and be
                       born in another state of life.
          hlawv thiab A particular spirit rite, (cf. 'hlawv').
          thiab qhauv A term used in spirit worship, e.g.
          If an older person dreams that he eats and
          can't be satisfied it is taken to signify that
          his spirit wants to be reborn and eat elsewhere.
          He therefore fears death and calls for the
          relatives to bring food, etc. They offer it
          to him pleading with his spirit not to leave
          and go to eat with others. A bit of cloth is
          then sewn on the person's jacket as a symbol.

1. thiaj Consequently, then, thereby (cf. 'txhiaj').
   Note: In this sense the word is usually found in
          combination with 'li' and said 'thiaj li.'
          However, in shortened speech the 'li' is
          sometimes omitted.
          (a) Kuv thiaj li hais tias... And so I said...
          (b) Kuv thiaj hais tias... And so I said...
          Kuv tsis muaj nyiaj kuv thiaj tsis mus. I have
          no money and consequently I did not go.
   Note: We list this word here because this is the
          pronunciation most commonly heard among
          Thailand White Hmong. However 'txhiaj' and
          'txhiaj li' is also heard and this pronunci-
          ation is more common in Laos and perhaps in
          other areas. This is closer to the Blue Hmong
          or Green Hmong pronunciation 'txha le.'

2. thiaj To hearken, to obey, to do as one says, to speak
          well of.
          Kuv xav thiaj koj. I want to do as you say.
          rov thiaj yus To be boastful, to speak well of
          oneself.
          pheej thiaj Continually speak well of another as in
          boasting of his ability to do things better
          than most, etc.

3. thiaj
   fab thiaj To fall backward.

4. thiaj
   sam thiaj A high platform.

tho To pierce, to make a hole or put through a path or
     road.
     tho kev To put through a road or cut a path.
     tho qhov To make a hole (cf. 'tsheb qhov', 'laum
     qhov,' 'tshau qhov' and 'lij qhov').

1. thob To spin around.
         thob log To spin (e.g. to spin a top).

2. thob
         thob roj The loose fat attached to the intestines.

3. thob
         (a) thob fab House foundation beams.
         (b) tim cum House foundation beams.

4. thob
         lus thob Hesitant speech (because of difficulty in
                   finding words, etc.)

1. thoj
         thoj plab Diarrhea (cf. 'plab').

2. thoj
   txiv cuab thoj The guava, fruit of the guava tree.

1. thom To fit logs together one on top of another as in making the corner of a log fence.

2. thom
   thomkhwm Socks (clf. 'nkawm' for pairs).

thos To peck, to strike at sharply (e.g. a chicken pecking or a snake striking) (cf. 'ncaws').

1. thov To beg or to ask for, to request something without payment (cf. 'taij').
   Thov pub mentsis txhuv rau kuv. (Please) give me a little rice.
   (a) thov qees To keep asking.
   (b) thov qos qees To keep asking.
   tus thov khawv A beggar, of one who begs or asks alms and especially one who won't work.

2. thov
   thov txhaum To go the wrong way in life, to do evil.

3. thov
   tus thov ntuj Of one who loves to move a lot (cf. 'tus tsiv taus').

4. thov
   thov xeem (cf. 'xeem').

1. thoob A bucket (clf. 'lub').
   thoob teg (lub) A hand pail or bucket.
   thoob ntsug (lub) A water bucket, tall wooden bucket.

2. thoob A bucketful, (clf. for buckets of water or other things).
   ib thoob dej A bucket of water.

3. thoob
   thoob puab (lub) A cloth bag slung from the shoulder to transport small articles.

4. thoob Whole, all, complete or completely.
   thoob zos The whole village.
   thoob plaws Completely, to the end.
   thoob theeb plaws Completely, all over the world.
   thoob zeej teb The whole earth, all people.
   thoob huvsi All of, the whole.
   hais thoob moos timfab To preach or tell everywhere.
   kev thoob txog... The road is through to...
   noob qe thoob tshaj Inguinal hernia.

1. thooj The same, equal or similar.
   zoo tsis thooj Not the same, not as good.
   thooj nkaus The same exactly.
   thooj peb cov The same as we are.
   (a) thooj siab Of one heart and mind.
   (b) thooj xeeb Of one heart and mind.
   (c) thooj siab hum hauv Of one heart and mind.
   thooj siav thooj nqaij Of one flesh and blood.
   thooj niam koom txiv, thooj pog koom yawg Of the same parentage.

2. thooj
   yeeb thooj (lub) A smoking pipe (either for smoking opium or tobacco).

3. thooj (clf. for sections of a log).

4. thooj (clf. for sets of headbands) (cf. 'siv ceeb').

thoov
   (a) khawb pas dej To dig out a pool of water.
   (b) thoov pas dej To dig out a pool of water.

1. thum To break off a habit.
   thum yeeb To break off taking opium.

2. thum
   tshwj thum Wasteful, extravagant (cf. 'phum lam').
   neeg tshwj thum A wasteful person, one who uses money and goods lavishly.

1. thuv Pine, the pine tree (tus).

2. thuv To walk around (cf. 'ncig').
   Yuav thuv lub ntuj pas dej no. Keep walking around the edge of this lake.

1. thuam To erase, to eliminate, to cross out, to reject (cf. 'phiv').
   (a) thuam tseg To reject and get rid of.
   (b) thuam kiag pov tseg To reject and get rid of.
   Lawv thuam thuam nws. They opposed him (refused to follow him, spoke against him).

2. thuam
   thuam yeem To mark something, to make a mark.
   (a) thuam yeem tes To make a fingerprint.
   (b) ntaus taub teg To make a fingerprint.

3. thuam
   pejthuam (tus) A tower or pagoda.

4. thuam
   luaj thuam Careless (cf. 'liam sim').
   neeg luaj thuam A person careless with belongings.

thuas   Khaub thuas The common cold, to have a cold (cf.
        'Khaub' and 'sab foob').

thuav   To unwind.

1. thwj (cf. 'Khav thwj' p. 93).

2. thwj
        thwjtim A learner, a disciple, an apprentice (C)
        (for 'thwjtid' cf. Introduction p. xxiii-xxiii).

3. thwj
        thwj txhiaj To covet another's wealth, to desire to
        harm another person for his money.

thws   To clear of weeds, to pull out (weeds, etc.)
        thws tau tsev To clear land for a house.

thwv   thwvcib (lub) Brick, a brick.

TS

1. tsa To set up, to set upright, to erect, to raise up,
        to lift up, to establish.
        tsa muag saib Lift up the eyes to look.
        tsa tes To raise the hand, raise the arm.
        tsa hlo To raise up.
        tsa cai "The case stands" (used to describe a
        successful law case).
        tsa ncej tsev To erect the posts of a house.
        tsa rog (cf. 'rog').
        tsa ncauj (cf. 'ncauj').

2. tsa To appoint to office.
        Lawv muab nws tsa ua nom. They made him an official.

3. tsa
        neejtsa (cf. 'neej').

1. tsab To pretend (cf. 'txuj').
        (a) tsab ua To pretend, to do something in pretense.
        (b) ua txuj tsab To pretend, to do something in
        pretense.

2. tsab Clf. for letters (written messages).
        Nws sau ib tsab ntawv rau kuv. He wrote me a letter.

3. tsab A given name for Hmong men.

4. tsab
        ntov pheej tsab (cf. 'ntov').

5. tsab
        txum tsab tos To wait quietly for game, to wait for
        a kill (when hunting).

6. tsab
        tsab ntxwv tsis vees Not steady on his feet, having
        a poor sense of balance (C).

7. tsab
        neeg tsab ntsuag Hypocrites.
        tsab ntsuag Hypocritical, pretending to be what it
        is not (as a stream that appears green and
        deep but instead is shallow).

1. tsag A cliff (lub) (cf. 'tsuas').

2. tsag
        qab tsag A porch (lower down than the 'qab khav').

3. tsag
        dej tsaws tsag A waterfall or rapids.

tsaj Burlap, Manila hemp.

1. tsam A period of time consisting of several hours.
        ib tsam In a little while, a little while.
        tsam no This period of time, now.
        nyob tsam In a while, in a short time.
        Note: This expression (or a shortened form 'tsam'
        by itself) is used idiomatically to mean
        "soon, shortly" (cf. 'nyob' p. 220).

2. tsam Bloated, expanded.
        lub plab tsam tsam Bloated stomach.

3. tsam
    tawm tsam To wage war (cf. 'tua rog').

4. tsam
    tsam thawj A resting place along the way.

5. tsam
    tsamphooj (lub) A tent (sometimes used for a 'mosquito net').

6. tsam
    vijtsam A mosquito net (lub) (C).

7. tsam To revolve (cf. 'tig').
    tsam mus tsam los Turning round and round (like the earth).

8. tsam
    sav tsam To inconvenience, to hinder, to delay or to prevent (cf. 'tabkaum').

9. tsam
    saib tsam Perhaps, it may be.
    Saib tsam nws yuav tuaj. I think he may come.

10. tsam
    zeem tsam To show appreciation for, to be grateful.
    Yuav zeem tsam tus Tswv mentsis. You ought to be grateful to the Lord.

11. tsam
    tsam pob (cf. 'pobkws').

12. tsam
    los nag tuam tsam A heavy rain, rained heavily.

13. tsam
    mob tsam chim (cf. 'mob' p. 129).

tsas A given name for Hmong men.

1. tsav To drive a vehicle.
    tsav tsheb To drive a vehicle.
    tus tsav tsheb A driver.

2. tsav To add to (cf. 'txhab').
    Tsav nws li ntshav rau. To give a blood transfusion.

3. tsav
    tus cuab tsav (cf. 'tuag' p. 327).

4. tsav
    tus tsav phom (cf. 'tuag' p. 327).

5. tsav
    tus tsav hauv One set up as leader, the head.

tsaib Pertaining to the year or years previous.
    tsaib no Last year.
    tsaib ub Year before last.
    puag tsaib ub Years ago.

tsaig Pertaining to the chin or jaw.
    puab tsaig The chin.
    tswb tsaig The red lobes on the side of a cock's head.

1. tsaim Of wood that tends to split or splinter.

2. tsaim
    tsiv tsaim (cf. 'tsiv').

1. tsau Full, satisfied (especially pertaining to eating).
    Kuv noj tsau lawm. I have eaten to the full.
    tsau npo Very full.

2. tsau A fire torch.
    (a) tsau roj A pitch torch.
    (b) taws npoos A pitch torch.
    tes tsau A hand torch.
    taws tsau To carry a lighted torch or stick.

3. tsau To leave an article in water to soak (cf. 'raus' and 'tsaug').
    tsau dej To soak in water.

tsaub Illegitimate, out of wedlock.
    menyuam tsaub An illegitimate child.

1. tsaug Thanks, used in expressions of gratitude and thanks.
    Kuv ua koj tsaug. I thank you.
    Us tsaug. Thanks!
    Note: At this point we are not clear whether this word expresses thanks in the way we ordinarily understand it without conveying obligation or whether it means "I am obligated to you because of your kindness."

2. tsaug
    tsaug zog To sleep (cf. 'ua dab ntub').
    tsaug tsaug zog li. Sleepy.
    pw tsaug zog To lie down in sleep.
    tsaug zog looj hlias Very sleepy.

3. tsaug Weak, feeble, sickly.
    tsaug tsaug leeg li Very weak, feeble.
    (a) tsaug tsaug li Very weak, feeble.
    (b) tsaug tsaug li Very weak, feeble.

4. tsaug The large long-quilled porcupine (clf. 'tus').
         (contr. 'nploos').
   txoj kab tsaug Porcupine trail.

5. tsaug En masse, all at once together.
   Lawv dhia ib tsaug nrov ntwg mus. The crowd ran
         off noisily together.
   ua ib tsaug ua To do all at once, to act en masse.

6. tsaug To briefly immerse an article in water, to rinse
         up and down in water (as e.g. in washing
         vegetables, etc.) (contr. 'tsau' and 'raus').

tsauj To cackle.
   qaib tsauj The chicken cackles.

tsaus Dark, darkness.
   tsaus tsaus li Very dark.
   tsaus ntuj Night, night time.
   tsaus zem zuag Dusk.
   tsaus ntuj ntais Nightfall.
   (a) ntuj tsaus nti A darkened sky.
   (b) tsaus ntuj nti A darkened sky.
   qhov muag tsaus ntais To faint or "blackout" (cf.
         'yeem').
   tsaus tsiav Phosphorescent.

tsawb The banana plant, the banana.
   txiv tsawb Banana fruit (clf. 'lub' for one single
         banana, 'thij' for a whole stem of fruit,
         'kuam' for a "hand" of bananas).
   Here we list some of the various types of bananas:
   txiv tsawb dub "Black" plants bearing large fruit
         that is green when ripe.
   txiv tsawb qab zib "Sweet" bananas.
   txiv tsawb qaub "Sour" bananas.
   txiv tsawb teem A type of very small banana.
   txiv tsawb pav A type of very small banana.

1. tsawg A little, few, not much, not many.
   tsawg mentsis A little less, a little too few.
   tsawg tsawg li Very few, very little.

2. tsawg How few? How many? How much?
   pes tsawg How few? How many? How much?
   Mob pes tsawg hnub? How many days has it hurt?
   Hais pes tsawg kuj tsis nloog. No matter how much
         you say (he) won't listen.

tsawj A word used in vile language.

tsawm To curse.
   ob leeg twv tsawm Of two persons who can't agree
         and who therefore each call on heaven to
         curse (cause death) the other party to
         see who is right.

1. tsaws To set down, to set aside, to lift off and set
         to one side.
   dav hlau tsaws The airplane lands.
   tsaws nees nra To lift off the horse pack baskets
         and set them to one side.
   tsaws mov los noj Set the rice pot off the fire in
         preparation for eating.
   Muab zaub tsaws cia. Take the vegetables off the fire
         and set them to one side.
   zaum tsaws To be sitting down.
   tsaws nqaij To let meat remain on the fire to cook
         for a long time until soft.

2. tsaws
   dej tsaws tsag A waterfall or rapids.
   dej tsaws ntxhee Swift turbulent water.

1. tsawv To grasp.
   (a) ntsiab nkaus To grasp the arm.
   (b) tsawv nkaus To grasp the arm.
   (c) nthos nkaus To grasp the arm.

2. tsawv
   tsawv neej To tell the fortune by use of a coin
         and egg determined by whether the coin will
         stand on the egg or not.

3. tsawv To ask of the spirits who is able to 'ua neeb'
         well.
         A term used in spirit worship (cf. 'neeb').

4. tsawv
   hais lus taj tsawv Slow of speech (cf. 'nrho').

5. tsawv
   huab ntsau tsawv A steady fog or cloudiness (cf.
         'huab').
   Note: It may be that 'tsawv' in definitions 4 and 5
         functions as a restricted post verbal intensi-
         fier but we have no other usage of 'tsawv' in
         this way.

1. tse Restricted post verbal intensifier (cf. 'quaj').
   quaj tse To make a loud noise (cf. Appendix 8).

2. tse Tone change from 'tsev' (cf. 'tsev').

tseb To sow seed by overhand broadcast sowing (contr.
         'txaws').
   tseb yeeb To sow opium seed by broadcast sowing.

tseg To cast away, to reject, to set aside, eliminate,
      to abandon, to leave.
pov tseg To throw away, cast aside.
Nws tseg lawv mus. He left them and went away.
tso tseg To put aside, to abandon, to give up.
tshwj tseg To reject, to cast out, to throw away.
Tseg koj. Excuse me if I go ahead to (eat, smoke,
      drink, etc.) without you.
tseg tub tseg ki Bereft of children.
tseg txij tseg nkawm Widowed, bereft of wife or
      husband.

tsej Restricted post verbal intensifier after 'nrov'
      (cf. 'nrov').

1. tsem To bark.
Dev tsom tsem. The dog is barking.

2. tsem Crooked (of roads, etc.)
kev tsem A crooked road.
kev tsem tov tsem tov The road winds from one side
      to the other, zigzag.

3. tsem Clf. for sections of a road. (cf. 'kev').

1. tsev House, home, building, a dwelling (clf. 'lub').
tsev teb A field house.
tsev pheeb suab A temporary shelter of branches.
tsev timphooj A temporary house or shelter.
vaj tsev House and grounds (house and garden).
ntxiv tsev To repair a house.
rhuav tsev To tear down a house.
qua tsev The site for a house.
khawb qua tsev To level a house site.
tsev loos lees A school (T).
tsev kawm ntawv A school.
tsev kho mob A hospital.
tsev xuas luas An open rest house or shelter (T).
lub tsev dav dav li An empty lonely house.
lub tsev sov sov House full of people and noise.
lub tsev khab seeb A roomy house, uncluttered house.
nruab tse In the house (t.c.)

2. tsev Clf. for households, a household.
ib tse neeg One household, one family.
Note: The names for the various parts of a house
      frame may be seen in the following diagram:
      (clf. 'tus' for all beams, posts and poles).

roob laj
nqaj ru
qhab
leem ceeb
nqaj tsuag (or) nqaj tsev
tw puam
ncej kaum (or) ncej tsev
ncej ru
nqaj nthab (or) yees tsev (or) yees nthab
thob fab (or) tim cum
thob fab (or) tim cum

1. tseeb True, pertaining to that which truly is in
      reality.
txoj kev tseeb Truth, the true way or doctrine.
lus tseeb tseeb True words, spoken truth.
tsis tseeb False, untrue (cf. 'cuav').
lus tseeb ntsiab True words, words concerning the
      essence of things.

2. tseeb A felt sleeping mat (clf. 'daim').

3. tseeb
lub tsho tseeb A wool jacket.

4. tseeb
yeeb tseeb The needle-like tool for rolling opium
      in preparation for smoking (C) (cf. 'yeeb').

5. tseeb
Tas tseeb! An expletive indicating annoyance.

1. tseem Pre-verbal indicating action still in progress.
Note: This word may be used singly or preceded by
      the syllable 'haj.'
Lawv haj tseem noj mov. They are still eating.
Nws tseem tsis tau mus. He still has not gone.
haj tseem ua Still in the process of doing something.

2. tseem
   ob hnub tseem Two full days.

3. tseem
   hais lus tseem ceeb To speak what is important and worthwhile.

tsees Restricted post verbal intensifier (cf. Appendix 8).
   sawv tsees To arise, to get up.
   plaubhau sawv tsees Hair "standing on end."

1. tseev To cause, to effect, to arrange.
   tseev kom zoo To make good, to fix.
   tseev kom tau To arrange so that it is brought about or so that a thing is obtained.
   Tsis tseev kom hle li. Don't allow it to slip off. You are not permitted to take it off.

2. tseev To prepare meat, to cut up meat after slaughter of an animal.
   tseev nqaij To prepare meat.
   tseev npua To cut up a slaughtered pig.

3. tseev To inquire into (cf. 'seev').
   ua tuav tseev To inquire into (cf. 'seev').

4. tseev Having power from the spirits to make people sick, etc.
   Nws txawj tseev tibneeg. He has the power to cause sickness.

5. tseev Species of chicken whose feathers curl and protrude.
   qaib tseev Species of chicken whose feathers curl and protrude.

6. tseev
   (a) tseev zam sees To dress up in one's best.
   (b) tseev zam ntxiag To dress up in one's best.

1. tsi To aim (cf. 'tsom').

2. tsi To pour the water off the rice after cooking and in preparation for steaming.
   (a) tsi kua To pour off the rice water.
   (b) muab kua ntxhais tsi To pour off the rice water.

1. tsib Five, the numeral five.
   tsib lub tsev Five houses.

2. tsib The gall-bladder (lub).

3. tsib The branch clusters at a bamboo joint.
   tsib xyoob The branch clusters at a bamboo joint.

4. tsib
   kab tsib Sugar cane.
   ib yag kab tsib A length of sugar cane.

5. tsib
   qab tsib taug Just below the house on the downhill side.

6. tsib
   zaub tsib A kind of sour vegetable.

7. tsib
   lub tsib faij A type of small bottle.

1. tsig A noose.
   ib phob tsig cuab noog A noose or snare to catch birds.

2. tsig Clf. for a cock crowing.
   qaib qua ib tsig The cock crows once.
   qaib qua thawj tsig The first crowing of the cock.

1. tsij To push by the end (as a saw, pole, piece of wood, etc.)
   tsij taws To shove a log farther into the fire.

2. tsij
   kov tsij To hasten, to do quickly (cf. 'kov').
   Kov tsij los tsev. Hurry home.

1. tsim To create.
   tsim ntuj tsim teb Created the heavens and the earth.

2. tsim Worth, value, honor.
   muaj muaj tsim Valuable, highly honored.
   tsim koob tsim hmoov Worthy of reward, of good fortune.

3. tsim
   tsim txiaj Worth money, worthwhile, worthy.
   neeg tsis tsim txiaj A worthless type of person.

4. tsim
   tsim nyog Valuable, to be worthy of, suitable, appropriate.
   tsim nyog ua Appropriate to do.
   tsim nyog haus (water) suitable to drink.
   Hnub no tsim nyog los txog. This is the day it would be suitable (or probable) for him to come.

5. tsim
   tsim txom To persecute, to cause to suffer.

6. tsim
   tsim dheev To wake up suddenly.

tsis   Negative particle.
  tsis ua   Will not do.
  tsis yog   No, is not.
  tsis yuav   Don't want.
  tsis kav   Nevertheless, no matter what.
  tsis tau   May not (something prevents).
  tsis taus   Cannot (physically impossible).

1. tsiv   To move oneself or one's place of abode.
  Nws tsiv mus nram moos.   He moved down to the plain.

2. tsiv
  tsiv nraim   To hide oneself.

3. tsiv
  tsiv tsaim   Of an animal prone to attack, of a
    person prone to scold or curse others.
  dev tsiv tsaim   A fierce dog.

4. tsiv
  tsiv siab   Somewhat angry and distressed.

5. tsiv
  tsiv tshuj tshuav   To avoid a person, to "steer
    clear of," won't listen to another.

tsia   Eyes momentarily "blacked out."
  siab feeb pes tsia   Confused, momentarily unable to
    see or think clearly.
  yeem tsia   To faint, to "black out." (cf. 'phov
    muag tsaus ntais').

tsiab
  noj tsiab   To eat the New Year feast
  This is the old and proper term and refers specifically
    to eating the meal when the pig is killed) (cf.
    'noj peb caug').

tsiag
  cwj tsiag   The trigger of a trap.

tsiaj   Animal, animals as a class.
  Note: The single word may be used but it often occurs
    in the expression 'tsiaj txhu' with the same
    meaning.
  tu tsiaj txhu   To care for animals, to raise livestock.
  tsiaj ncawg nkuaj   The animals enter the pen.

tsiam   To hit or bump against (cf. 'tsoo'), to purposely
    jump from a height (as e.g. of animals).
  Dais tsiam plob lawm.   The bear jumped from the tree.

tsias   A tantrum.
  menyuam ua tsias   The child has a tantrum.

1. tsiav
  khauj tsiav   To hit with the knuckle.

2. tsiav
  nab qa tsiav   A type of small lizard.

3. tsiav
  tsaus tsiav   Phosphorescent.

1. tso   To release, to free, to relinquish, to permit, to
    place.
  Tso nws mus.   Let him go.
  muab tso rau hauv   Place it in.
  tso tes   To relinquish, to let go with the hand.
  tso quav   To relieve the bowels, to defecate.
  tso zos   To urinate.
  tso plig   To free the spirit (cf. 'plig').
  tso ncauj   To permit.
  tso tseg   To give up, to abandon.
  tso paus   To pass gas.
  tso lus   To give permission.
  tso plhuav   To lay down, to put down.
  tso dag   To talk foolishly, to speak in jest.

2. tso   Used at the end of an expression to indicate that
    a pause or an interval of time must intervene
    before the succeeding action may take place.
  Tos ob peb hnub tso...   Wait a few days and then...

tsob   Clf. for a grove of trees or a clump of vegetation.
    Foliage or vegetation.
  tsob ntoo   Tree foliage.
  tsob nplej   A clump of rice stalks.
  tsob tshuaj   A bunch of medicinal vegetation.

1. tsog   The name given to a certain river spirit which is
    supposed to have a body with the appearance of
    being full of holes or depressions.

2. tsog
  hnab tsog (lub)   The mantle for a pressure lamp (so
    called because it is full of holes like the
    'tsog' spirit mentioned above).

1. tsom   To squint, to aim a gun, to sight through a tele-
    scope or a viewer of any kind. (cf. 'tsi').
  tsom phom   To aim a gun, to sight through a gunsight.
  tsom iav (daim)   A mirror, a looking-glass.
  tsom qhov muag (lub)   Eyeglasses, spectacles.
  tsom yeeb yaj   To sight through a telescope or a
    viewer.
  Tho tsom ncaj lawm nrad.   Make (the trail) straight
    down from here. ("aim" it straight).

2. tsom
   tsom teeb (lub) A lamp glass.

3. tsom To care for, to tend, to look after (cf. 'hwjxwm').
   (a) tsom kab tsom kwm To care for, nurture, look after.
   (b) tsom kwm To care for, nurture, look after.

1. tsos
   qhov tsos The armpit.

2. tsos Clf. for hairs.
   Ib tsos ob tsos plaub dob zuj zus. (He) pulled out one hair at a time.

3. tsos Restricted post-verbal intensifier. (cf. Appendix 8).
   nco dheev tsos Suddenly awoke to something, suddenly remembered.

1. tsov Tiger, tiger-like (clf. 'tus').
   tsov dub The black panther.
   tsov nplooj suab Bengal tiger.
   (a) tsov pom teev Leopard.
   (b) tsov txaij Leopard.
   tsov ntxhuav Lion.
   tsov cuam A legendary tiger, reportedly small, swift and with a human face.

2. tsov
   kab laug tsov (cf. 'kab').

tsoo To crush, to destroy, to ruin by crushing or collision.
   sib tsoo A collision.
   tsoo tes To crush a finger.
   tsoo nruab To crush bamboo and flatten it.
   tsoo nqaij To crush or beat up meat into a pulp.
   tsoo tawg ntsoog ntxaws. Smashed to pieces, completely crushed.
   tsoo kua txiv To crush fruit in a press to extract the juice.
   lub tsoo kua txiv A wine press, a press to extract fruit juice.
   tsoo taubhau To bump the head, to injure the head by forcible inpact (cf. 'nraus').

1. tsoob
   tus tsoob zeej A middleman, mediator, go-between (C).

2. tsoob Referring to sexual intercourse.
   (a) tsoob pim The act of sexual intercourse or coition between persons or animals (cf. 'pim' and 'qau').
   (b) sib tsoob The act of sexual intercourse or coition between persons or animals (cf. 'pim' and 'qau').
   (c) tsoob paum The act of sexual intercourse or coition between persons or animals (cf. 'pim' and 'qau').
   Note: The following words are all used to refer to the sex act and therefore should be avoided in ordinary conversation:
   'tsoob'   'nce'   'ntxi'
   'aim'   'phev'   'tshov'
   'txiag'

1. tsoom Quantity word for a portion or a part (cf. 'kwv' Definition No. 3).
   Koj yuav cuaj tsoom pub ib tsoom rau kuv. You keep nine portions and give one portion to me.

2. tsoom
   (a) tsoom zeej All people (C).
   (b) zeej tsoom All people (C).
   (c) luag zeej tsoom All people (C).

tsoos Clothing (mostly in reference to the dead).
   hnav tsoos To dress (especially to dress up for burial).
   tsoos hmoob Hmong costume.

1. tsoov To separate grain from chaff by bouncing the grain in a woven bamboo tray.
   tsoov txhuv To separate rice from chaff in the above manner (contr. 'zig').

2. tsoov
   txuam tsoov Of two varieties mixed together, half-breed.

tsu A tub-like vessel with woven bottom for steaming rice (lub), a rice-steamer.

tsub
   (a) sib tsub To press together one thing upon another, piled up.
   (b) sib nias To press together one thing upon another, piled up.

tsug A period of 13 days (cf. 'xi').
   ib tsug kaum peb hnub One period of 13 days, particularly the 13 days of waiting after a death before the release of the spirit.

1. tsuj To step on, to trample.
   tsuj nthi To trample underfoot.
   tsuj nthi ntawm taw tseg Put it under foot and get
      rid of it, i.e. to deliberately put a matter
      aside.

2. tsuj
   tshuaj tsuj yeeb Medicine or other foreign matter
      mixed with opium before smoking so as to make
      the opium go farther and last longer.

3. tsuj A kind of expensive cloth.
   ntaub tsuj ntaub npuag Fine expensive cloth.
   hnav tsuj hnav npuag To dress in finery.
   tsoos tsuj tsoos npuag Fine clothing.

1. tsum Sign of the imperative mood, indicating obligatory
      action, especially following 'yuav' and preceding
      the verb. (cf. 'tau' Definition No. 3, p. 307).
   yuav tsum noj mov Must eat.
   yuav tsum mus Must go.
   tsum nplua - shall be judged, shall receive punishment.

2. tsum Used after the verb to indicate action that can
      or cannot be done (cf. 'tau' Definition No. 2).
   nloog tsis tsum Cannot hear.
   Muab tsis tsum. (I) cannot get (reach) it.
   sau tsis tsum Cannot write.

3. tsum
   Tsum lawm! Enough! Stop!

4. tsum To be effective, to hit something when shooting.

tsus
   siab puas tsus Completely discouraged (cf. 'siab
      poob tag').

tsua Bedrock, solid rock mass.
   pobtsuas Cliff, rock mass (t.c.)
   qab tsuas Base of the cliff (t.c.)
   qhov tsua Cave in the rock.
   phab tsuas Rock surface (t.c.)

1. tsuab To grab with the hand.
   tsuab mov To grab a handful of cooked rice.

2. tsuab Dirty (cf. 'ceb muag' and 'txab').
   vuab tsuab Dirty (cf. 'sai' and 'nrawm').

1. tsuag Quickly (cf. 'sai' and 'nrawm').
   Tsuag tsuag los. Come back quickly.
   mob tsuag tsuag Quick successive pains.

2. tsuag Saltless, flat in taste, flavorless (contr. 'daw').

3. tsuag Vegetation.
   nroj tsuag Vegetation.
   hav xub tsuag A wilderness area.

4. tsuag
   nas tsuag (tus) A rat.

5. tsuag
   nqaj tsuag (tus) The side beams of a house (cf. 'tsev
      'tsev').

6. tsuag
   hais tsuag lus To speak unconvincingly, to speak
      softly, kindly, or without conviction (contr.
      'hais ceev nrooj').

7. tsuag To spray, to forcibly expell liquid from a small
      opeining or from the mouth.
   tsuag tshuaj To spray insecticide from a spray gun.

1. tsuaj To jolt, to jar, e.g. of a vehicle upon rough
      ground.
   (a) thawv thawv li Of a vehicle jolting on rough
       ground, also of a horse that keeps throwing
       its load (cf. 'thawv').
   (b) tsuaj tsuaj li Of a vehicle jolting on rough
       ground, also of a horse that keeps throwing
       its load (cf. 'thawv').

2. tsuaj
   puas tsuaj (cf. 'puas' Definition No. 2, p. 238).

1. tsuam To crush, to press, to smother, to block a trail,
      Of one thing pressing heavily upon another.
   tsuam qab tsib To crush sugar cane to extract juice.
   Ntoo vau tsuam kev. A tree has fallen and blocked
      the trail.
   ntoo tsuam tsev A tree has fallen on the house.
   ceg sib tsuam Legs crossed.
   tsuam hlab ntxhoo The embroidered ends on a Hmong
      woman's apron ties.

2. tsuam Clf. for bundles of firewood.
   ib tsuag taws One bundle of firewood (t.c.)

3. tsuam
   tsuam tubsab To investigate a case of theft.

1. tsuas A splitting wedge (tus).

2. tsuas To lose color, of colors "running" as when cloth
      is washed.
   tsuas ceg Of legs discolored from wearing cloth that
      runs.

3. tsuas A pre-verbal indicating the singularity of the action and thus translated by expressions such as 'simply' or 'only.'
Kuv tsuas hais txog kuv li. I can only speak of my own.

4. tsuas A pre-verbal indicating one action must precede before another can follow and thus translated by expressions such as 'if only,' 'unless,' 'except that,' 'only if.'
Note: In this sense 'tsuas' is used in the compound expressions 'tsuas yog' or 'tsuas tab yog.' Note also that the same sense is conveyed by the expressions 'tab yog' or 'tsuav' or 'tsuav yog.' (cf. 'tsuav').

Tsuas yog lawv qhia kuv mas kuv thiaj ntseeg. I believe simply because they taught me.
Tsuas yog lawv qhia kuv mas kuv yuav ntseeg. If only they teach me I will believe.
(a) Tsuas yog yus ua li no yuav zoo xwb. If only one does this it will be all right.
(b) Tab yog yus ua li no yuav zoo xwb. If only one does this it will be all right.
(c) Tsuas tab yog yus ua li no yuav zoo xwb. If only one does this it will be all right.
(cf. similar illustrations under 'tsuav').

5. tsuas
Tsuas xwv koj txawj ua. You can (are able to) do it.

1. tsuav A pre-verbal indicating one action must precede before another can follow and thus translated by expressions such as 'only if,' 'except that,' etc. (cf. 'tsuas' Definition No. 4).
(a) Nws tsuav tuaj mas kuv thiaj mus. Only if he comes will I go. Only because he came did I go. (I simply left because he came.)
(b) Tsuav yog nws tuaj mas kuv thiaj mus. Only if he comes will I go. Only because he came did I go. (I simply left because he came.)
Tsuav muaj neeg pab kuv thiaj kam ua. I will only do it if someone helps.
Tsuav yog lawv pab mas kuv thiaj mus. I'll only go if they help me.

2. tsuav tamfaj Probably (C) (cf. 'kwvlam').
Tsuav tamfaj ua li no peb kuj tsis txawj hais li cas. Seeing that probably is the way it is, we cannot say anything.
Tsuav tamfaj koj qheb nyog txoj kev rau kuv. Well then probably you can provide a suitable solution.

3. tsuav To chop up, to cut up fine (cf. 'txhoov').
tsuav zaub npua npuas To chop up pig food.
tsuav ngaij To chop up meat.
tsuav nruab To split and flatten bamboo.

4. tsuav A kind of pink colored fruit.
liab txiv tsuav Bright pink in color.

1. tsw To give off an odor, to smell.
tsw tsw li Of something smelling (usually evil-smelling).
tsw tsw qab Fragrant.
tsw nchauv To smell smoky.
tsw ntxhiab Of a sharp pungent odor.
tsw pos Of meat, etc. smelling slightly old but not really spoiled.

2. tsw
xyoob puaj tsw tsev (cf. 'xyoob').

3. tsw T.c. from 'tswv' (cf. 'tswv').

1. tswb A bell (lub).
tswb nyiaj Small silver bell (often worn as ornamental buttons).
tswb nees Horse bells.

2. tswb Chinese word for a pig, used in certain Hmong expressions.
twm tswb A wild pig which goes about alone.
sab tswb Wild boars which travel in pairs.
cheej tswb Wild pigs which go about in groups.

3. tswb
tswb choj (C) A legendary Hmong King. His father was reported to be a pig. As a boy king he was persecuted, killed and buried in a cave. He is expected to rise again and return as a Hmong Messiah King.

tswg A short post, post put into the ground to help hold the logs of a foundation in place (clf. 'tus').
txhos tswg To put such a post into the ground.

tswj
tswjhwm To control, subdue, restrain, govern, subject.

1. tswm To press down, to repress, to supress.
tswm kom ceev To press down tight (e.g. as grain in a basket, etc.).
Tswm seeb! Be quiet! (a more polite expression than 'ua twjywm').
tswm plab To supress diarrhea.

2. tswm To pound metal to make it shorter.

tsha   Restricted post verbal intensifier (cf. Appendix 8).
       qheb tsha lawm   Opened wide.
       Note: 'tsha' might be considered a tone change after
               'qheb' and thus be entered under 'tshav.'
               However, since we have just the one illustration
               we have entered it here.   (cf. 'tshav').

1. tshab   To pierce through.
       tshab lawm   Pierced, having been pierced through.
       tshab plaws   Suddenly pierced through.

2. tshab
       tshab xov (tus)   A go-between in arranging marriage.

3. tshab   An auxilliary verb after 'nloog' and other verbs.
       nloog tsis tshab   Didn't hear clearly.

4. tshab
       tsis muaj paj tshab mus   No money or food with which
       to make a journey.

1. tshaj   To add to.
       Muab roj tshaj rau lub teeb.   Add oil to the lamp.

2. tshaj   Surplus, profit, to be surplus or more than enough,
           better.
       tshaj thawj   Profit in business transactions.
       noj tshaj thawj   To make profit, to charge interest.
       tshaj mus lwm pwm   More than before.
       tshaj dua cov   Better than others, more than others.
       tsim txiaj tshaj   More valuable, better than.

3. tshaj   To save or put aside.
       Muab tshaj tseg.   Put it aside (to save it) (to
           particularly save some even though there is
           more remaining).

4. tshaj   Clf. for court cases, spasms, fits, etc.
       ib tshaj plaub   One case at law, one court case.
       huam ib tshaj ib tshaj   To have spasms or fits.

5. tshaj
       lub tsho tshaj sab   A long gown with sleeves.

6. tshaj
       tus tshaj thawj   (cf. 'thawj' Definition No. 8, p. 336).

7. tshaj
       tshaj cum   Tall and thin, slight in build.

8. tshaj
       noob qe thoob tshaj   Inguinal hernia.

3. tswm   To subdue or control (as a husband his wife, etc.)

4. tswm
       tswm ciab (tus)   A wax candle.

tsws
       ntoo ntshaub tsws (tus)   A species of small tree
       (cf. 'ntshaub').

1. tswv
       tswvyim   (clf. 'zaj')   Plan, scheme, cleverness,
           wisdom (C).
       kawg tswvyim   At the end of one's wits.
       raug lawv tswvyim   Fallen prey to their schemes.

2. tswv   Lord, owner, master (C)   (cf. 'los pav')   (clf.
          'tus').
       tus tswv tsev   The owner of the house, the head of
           the house.
       (a) nom tswv   Officials.
       (b) tim tswv   Officials.
       tus Tswv Yexu   The Lord Jesus.
       Tswv Ntuj   The Lord of heaven (Catholic term for
           God).
       Vajtswv   The King Lord (God).
       (a) Vajtswv Saub   The King Lord Creator or King
           Lord of Heaven (terms used for "God" by the
           Protestant Hmong in Thailand) (cf. 'Saub').
       (b) Vajtswv Ntuj   The King Lord Creator or King Lord
           of Heaven (terms used for "God" by the Protestant
           Hmong in Thailand) (cf. 'Saub').

3. tswv   Clf. for groups or classes belonging to separate
          owners.
       ob peb tsw nyuj   Several groups of cattle belonging
           to different owners (t.c.)
       ib tsw li   One owner's (t.c.)
       ib tsw nqe   A debt to one individual (t.c.)

9. tshaj
Khuam tshaj (cf. 'khuam' Definition No. 1, p. 101).

10. tshaj To spread abroad, to send out.
Noj tshaj koob meej. To eat for respect's sake.
(to spread abroad your good name).
Tshaj ib txog xov rau nej. (I) send a message to you.

tsham To visit, to have a look around.
Peb mus tsham xwb. We are just going for a visit.

1. tshav The light of the heavens, sunlight, moonlight.
tshav ntuj Daylight, sunlight, daytime.
Note: This expression is sometimes used figuratively of recovery from illness.
tshav ntuj lawm Recovered.
cov tshav Sunlight, the light and brightness of the sun.
pw las tshav To sleep under the open sky.
tshav tsis tau thawj The weather is not really clear and sunny yet.
tshav ntuj nrig Very bright all around.
Kuv nco koj tshav ntuj. I will remember and appreciate your kindness. (i.e. 'your brightness').
(a) tshav hli Moonlight, brightness of the moon.
(b) qaim hli Moonlight, brightness of the moon.

2. tshav A broad level area (clf. 'lub').
lub tshav puam A wide open level space, an expanse of bare ground.
lub tshav ua si A playground.
lub tshav dav hlau An airport.
tshav puam suab zeb A stony wasteland.

3. tshav To beat down grain stubble in the field in preparation for burning it off.
tshav quav nplej To beat down the rice straw for burning.

4. tshav To plane wood.
tshav ntoo To plane wood.
lub tshav A carpenter's plane.

5. tshav
tsheb sib tshav The cars sideswiped each other.

6. tshav
hnub tshwm tshav The day of burial (cf. 'tuag').

tshaib To be hungry.
tshaib plab To be hungry, a hungry stomach.
kev tshaib plab Hunger.

tshais Early morning, breakfast.
(a) tav tshais About 8-9 A.M.
(b) menyuam tshais About 8-9 A.M.
(a) tav niag tshais About 10 A.M.
(b) niag tshais About 10 A.M.
Note: For other terms for time cf. Appendix p. 491.
noj tshais To eat the morning meal, to eat breakfast.

1. tshau To sieve, to sift.
tshau xua To sift out the chaff.
lub vab tshaus A sifting tray (t.c.)
tshau hmoov To sift flour.
lub tshau hmoov A flour sieve.

2. tshau To pierce, to make a hole (cf. 'tho').
tshau qhov To make a hole.

tshaus T.c. from 'tshau' (cf. 'lub vab tshaus' under 'tshau').

1. tshauv Ashes, of things with the color or consistency of ashes.
cub tshauv The pile of ashes forming the fireplace in a Hmong home.
plua tshauv Fine dirt or dust (also 'plua tshauv av').
txho tshauv Ashy colored, having an ashy colored coating (e.g. some animals, vegetables, etc.)

2. tshauv
los nag tshauv A drizzling rain.

1. tshawb To hunt for, to search out, to go through a lot of things hunting for something (cf. 'fawb').
tshawb qhovtxhiachaw To turn things "upside down" in hunting for something.

2. tshawb
tshawb cuabtam To pillage or destroy, of a house and goods broken up by pillagers (contr. 'tshob').

3. tshawb To depart or disperse in anger.
tshawb lawm Dispersed in anger.

1. tshawj Silk (C).

2. tshawj
tshawjchim (tus) An enemy (cf. 'chim').

tshawm
(a) tshawm yuj A thick dark liquid medicine used in treating animals (C).
(b) tshawm sib A thick dark liquid medicine used in treating animals (C).

xeeb tsheej ua Khito To be born into Christ.
kawm tsheej kiag Learned it completely, really has learned it.
tsheej hnub tsheej hmo All day and all night, day and night (all the time).

2. tsheej
   tsheej haj Industrious, energetic (C).
   (a) neeg tsis tsheej haj A lazy person (cf. 'neeg tub nkeeg').
   (b) neeg tsis tsheej A lazy person (cf. 'neeg tub nkeeg').

3. tsheej
   tsis tsheej neeg About to die (i.e. not a 'whole' person).

4. tsheej
   pem ceeb tsheej The Hmong abode of the dead, mythical residence of 'huabtais' (cf. 'yeeb yaj kiag').

5. tsheej
   tsheej tsheej kiab kiab Of young people still pure and undefiled.

1. tshib To thin out growing vegetation to give room for better growth.
   tshib zaub To thin out the vegetables.
   tshib yeeb To thin out the growing opium poppies.

2. tshib
   luj tshib Elbow (cf. 'yas npab').

3. tshib Clf. for blows made with the elbow.

tshim One cubit, a measure of length being the distance between elbow and fingertip.

tshis The goat (tus) (cf. 'mes es' or 'mias ias').
   tus nwm tshis A young female goat not having had young.

tshia
   nag tshia Of rain blowing in, rain sprinkling in.

1. tshiab New, fresh and bright (of a face, etc.)
   lub tsev tshiab tshiab A new house.

2. tshiab Retainers, soldiers (poetical).

tshiam Of a child that is uncooperative and antagonistic to parents (cf. 'txuv').
   menyuam tshiam txiv The child is antagonistic to its father.

1. tshaws
   (a) paim tshaws lawm (cf. 'nplej').
   (b) ziab pag tshaws (cf. 'nplej').

2. tshaws
   (a) nplooj qoov tshaws (cf. 'pobkws').
   (b) npuav npaug tshaws (cf. 'pobkws').
   (c) tw yaj tshaws (cf. 'pobkws').

1. tshawv Sloppily, clumsily, carelessly.
   ua txab ua tshawv To do poorly, do carelessly.

2. tshawv Impolite or raucus language (contr. 'mos').
   lus tshawv

tshe The sound of the cry of a deer.

1. tsheb A vehicle (lub).
   tsav tsheb To drive a vehicle.
   tsheb vaubkib A passenger car.
   tsheb lubyoog Bus or truck (T).
   tsheb kauj vab A bicycle.
   tsheb pleg pleg A motorcycle.
   tsheb nqaj A railroad ('tsheb tawg' less commonly).
   tsheb cuab hlua A pulley.
   caij tsheb To ride in a vehicle (or on a vehicle).
   roj tsheb Gasoline.

2. tsheb
   tsheb qhov To drill a hole (cf. 'tho' and 'laum').

1. tshem To take away.
   Muab tshem rau saud. Raise the barrier.
   tshem mus Take (it) away, carry away.
   tshem cwjmem To raise the pen from writing.

2. tshem
   Nej ua tshem lawm. You have eaten it all.

3. tshem
   tshem tau khib To make provision of food, etc. for guests and strangers.

tshee To shiver (as with fever or in the cold).
   ua tshee tshee To shiver.

1. tsheej Complete, often used as an auxiliary verb to indicate completed action or to indicate action that can or cannot be completed.
   ua tsheej lawm Completed.
   ua tsis tsheej Can't complete it.
   mus tsheej Can go.
   tsheej ua ib cuab To become one family (to be completed into one family).

1. tshom Of animals rooting in the ground (cf. 'swv').
   npua tshom Pigs rooting. ('tshom' refers simply to digging; 'swv' implies digging for food).
2. huam tshom To jump in surprise or in being startled.

tshos T.c. from 'tsho' (cf. 'tsho').

1. tshov To blow or to play a musical instrument having reeds or fingerholes (contr. 'tshuab').
   tshov qeej To blow the Hmong musical pipes (cf. 'qeej').
   tshov raj pum liv To play a bamboo flute.

2. tshov Referring to sexual union in animals. (also 'sib nce, 'tsoob pim', 'tsoob paum') (cf. 'tsoob').

1. tshoob Referring to marriage or the marriage ceremonies.
   ua tshoob To marry.
   nrog lawv ua tshoob To take a wife from their family, to become related by marriage.
   noj tshoob haus kos To eat and drink the wedding feast.
   xaus tshoob The feast at the time of completing the wedding celebrations and obligations.
   zaj tshoob Wedding songs (cf. 'kwv txhiaj').
   Note: Below are terms referring to wedding participants:
   The Groom's party:
   (a) tus vauv The groom.
   (b) tus nraug vauv The groom.
   cov qhua vauv The groom's party (all men).
   tus phij laj The "best man."
   tus cev cawv The "toastmaster."
   tus tshwj kab The one in charge of the food.
   tus kav xwm The master of ceremonies.
   tus mej koob The middleman in arranging price (there are two 'mej koob') (also called 'mej zeeg').
   tus tshab xov Another term for a go-between in making marriage arrangements.
   The Bride's party: (party of her parents)
   (a) tus ntxhais The bride.
   (b) tus nyab The bride.
   cov qhua tshoob The bride's party, wedding guests (also referring to relatives and friends of the groom but not specifically of his official party).
   Note: Apart from these the bridal party is the same in name and number as the groom's party except for the absence of the 'phij laj.'

2. tshoob To be swept away as by wind or water.
   yog dej tshoob mus lawm Washed away by swift water.

3. tshoob
   tshoob nqaij To kill game at a great distance (cf. 'tshoov').

1. tshiav To chafe or to rub, to rub vigorously (contr. 'chwv').
   tshiav tshiav Of something that chafes or rubs.
   tshiav koob To clean the rust of a needle.
   tshiav phom To clean a gun.
   tshiav raj To play a violin.
   tshiav hlua tawv To soften up a leather rope by rubbing it.

2. tshiav (a) saib tshiav thawj (cf. 'saib qaib' p. 288).
   (b) saib qaib (cf. 'saib qaib' p. 288).

1. tsho Jacket, coat, upper garment with sleeves (clf. 'lub').
   lub tsho tseeb Woolen jacket.
   lub tsho tshaj sab Long gown with sleeves.
   hnab tsho tshaj sab A jacket pocket (t.c.)
   ntiag tsho Jacket front, front panel of a jacket.
   dab tshos The embroidered patch on the back of a Hmong woman's collar. There are various names according to the type of embroidery. (t.c.)
   Some of the types of embroidery are:
   dab tshos hneev nees One with small squares sewn on.
   dab tshos chev One with a pattern in coils.
   dab tshos ncai One with triangular pieces of embroidery sewn on.
   dab tshos kaus lev Another type of embroidery.

2. tsho The placenta, the after birth.
   tsho menyuam The placenta, the afterbirth.
   Note: That of a female child is buried in the bedroom. That of a male child is buried at the foot of the main center post of the house (cf. 'ncej dab' p. 147).

1. tshob A dipper (lub).

2. tshob To disrupt and scatter (cf. 'tshawb').
   tshob cuabtam Of a household breaking up and scattering.

3. tshob To follow in their ways.
   puab lawv qab tshob To follow in their ways.

1. tshoj Of moving a fallen log by pivoting it on one end and swinging the other end.

2. tshoj (C) China.
   tuam tshoj (C) China.
   suav tuam tshoj (C) The mainland Chinese.
   xov tshoj (C) Of a country or place outside China.

4. tshoob
   (a) neeg tsis tshoob hawb Of a wealthy person who
   purposely dresses poorly to disguise his wealth.
   (b) neeg tsis tshoob phiaj txwv Of a wealthy person
   who purposely dresses poorly to disguise his
   wealth.

1. tshooj Levels, stories (in height) (cf. 'txheej').
   sib tshooj One on top of another, overlapping.
   cuaj tshooj ntug Nine "heights" of heaven.

2. tshooj Clf. for a poetic couplet or verse in songs for
   the dead. One 'tshooj' consists of two 'nqes.'
   For ordinary songs the equivalent word is 'txwm.'

3. tshooj
   laum kib tshooj (tus) Centipede.

1. tshoom To forge a hole in metal, to pierce a hole in
   metal as in making place for a handle in an axe
   head, etc.
   tshoom nplos To forge a hole for a handle.
   tshoom qhov To forge a hole in metal.

2. tshoom
   tshoom ntseg ntseg li To fire straight up at something (cf. 'tshoob' and 'tshoov').

tshoov To fire at something very high and directly above
   one's head, e.g. firing from the base of a
   tree at something in the branches. (cf. 'tshoob'
   and 'tshoom').

tshuj In combination with 'tshuav' used as a two word
   restricted post verbal intensifier. (cf.
   Appendix 8).
   tsiv tshuj tshuav To avoid, to deliberately keep from
   someone's company.
   tauv las tshuj tshuav To avoid doing work, to get
   out of doing things.

1. tshum To push or knock one thing with another, to be
   pushed or knocked with something (cf. 'nplawm'
   and 'chob').
   tshum txiv To knock fruit down with a stick, etc.
   khaub tshum (or 'nplawm') qhov muag Hit in the eye
   with a stick.
   xyooj tshum (or 'chob') Struck with, or stuck with
   a piece of bamboo..
   tshum lub teeb To pump a pressure lamp.

2. tshum To urge, to seek to persuade to action, to "bring
   pressure upon."
   tshum kiav To seek to hinder from action.
   neeg tshum pum One who seeks to hinder another from
   action, etc.
   tshum lub siab To urge, to seek to persuade.

1. tshua To like, to greatly desire or long for.
   ob tug nyiam nyiam tshua tshua The two love each other.
   (a) tsis tshua nyiam Doesn't like very much.
   (b) nyiam tsis tshua heev Doesn't like very much.
   tsis tshua heev Not very much, not like much. (used
   after verbs to indicate moderation).
   Kuv paub tsis tshua heev. I don't know very well.

2. tshua
   tshua lam Reluctant, reluctantly, not very willing.
   Sawv ntxov tsaus ntuj nws tshua lam ua num li.
   Whether morning or night he is reluctant to
   work.

1. tshuab To blow.
   cua tshuab tuaj The wind is blowing this way.
   tshuab raj To blow a horn.

2. tshuab A machine (lub).
   (Used for machines of various kinds depending on the
   qualifying words following the noun 'tshuab').
   lub tshuab ntaus ntawv A typewriter (or 'sau ntawv').
   lub tshuab nias ntawv A printing press.
   tshuab ntuag A spinning wheel.

3. tshuab
   kooj tshuab (tus) Locust (cf. 'kooj').

4. tshuab
   Hmoob Yob Tshuab The Flowery Hmong as known in China.

tshuad Tone variation from 'tshuam' (cf. 'tshuam' and
   Introduction p. xxii-xxiii).

1. tshuaj Chemical, medicine, herbs.
   haus tshuaj To drink medicine.
   tshuaj lub Medicine pills.
   tshuaj kua Liquid medicine.
   tshuaj tua phom Gunpowder.
   xub tshuaj Poisoned arrows.
   tshuaj swm Tea leaves (C).
   kob sim tshuaj Tea leaves.

2. tshuaj
   tshuaj khib (lub) A mortar (for grinding peppers,
   etc.).

3. tshuaj To spy out, to investigate, to seek out information,
           (cf. 'seev').
   (a) tshuaj mem tes To take the pulse.
   (b) seev mem tes To take the pulse.

tshuam To meet together, to intercept, to join (as of
        roads, etc.)
   kev tshuam Crossroads, fork in the trail.
   ob txog kev sib tshuam The two roads join.
   ob tug dej sib tshuam The two streams join.

1. tshuav To come short of, lacking, remaining, less than.
   tshuav tsis ntev Not much lacking (in time), soon.
   Tshuav tsis ntev kuv yuav mus. I'll soon be going.
   tshuav tsis ntau Not much left, only missing a few
                     of being all gone.
   Mov noj tas lawm tsis yog? Tshuav thiab. The rice
      is all eaten isn't it? No, there is some
      left.
   Lawv tsis mus, tshuav kuv xwb. (They will not go,
      except me.) None will go except me.

2. tshuav In combination with 'tshuj' a two-word restricted
           post verbal intensifier. (cf. 'tshuj').

tshwb   tua tshwb nkauv To kill (game) very close by.

1. tshwj To reject, to throw out.
   tshwj tseg To reject, throw out, get rid of.
   tshwj cia To put aside for disposal.

2. tshwj thum Wasteful, extravagant (cf. 'phum lam').
   neeg tshwj thum A wasteful or extravagant person.

3. tshwj tus tshwj kab The man in charge of preparing meat
           and vegetables at a funeral or wedding feast
           (cf. 'tuag' and 'tshoob').

4. tshwj yog Excepting, except for.
   Tshwj yog tus ntawd, tsis muaj ib tug zoo li. There
      is no other as good as this one. (There is
      none as good, except for this one.)

1. tshwm To appear, to issue forth, to come out of (C).
   tshwm los Appeared, come forth.
   tshwm sim To appear, to be born, to appear in birth.

2. tshwm Of grain which has been worm-eaten leaving only
          the shell.

3. tshwm
   tshwm rov qub qab mus To go back the way one came.

4. tshwm
   hnub tshwm tshav The day of burial (cf. 'tuag').

1. tshwv
   tshwv xeeb ua (C) To "put your heart into it," to do
                      with a will (C) (cf. 'siab').

2. tshwv Restricted post verbal intensifier with 'qos' or
          without (cf. Appendix 8).
   lub siab chis qos tshwv Mildly angry, having a dark
                            face (cf. 'chim').
   tws tshwv Short of, never quite right.

3. tshwv
   yuav luag tshwv rwm tim tiag Very close by.

TX

1. txab Dirty, unclean, disgusting (cf. 'qias,' 'ceb muag').
   lus txab Disgusting language.
   qias qias txab txab Dirty and disgusting.
   npua txab txab Dirty pigs, pigs are dirty.
   txab ntsuav Dirty, soiled.
   ua txab ua tshawv To do carelessly and poorly.

2. txab Evidence (of crime, etc.)
   Koj muaj txab tsis muaj? Have you any evidence?

3. txab Milky secretion.
   txab ntoo Milky tree sap (contr. 'roj ntoo').
   txab yeeb The white milky secretion of the opium
              poppy pod.

txag T.c. from 'txaj' (cf. 'txaj').

1. txaj Ashamed, embarrassed.
    txaj muag Shame-faced, ashamed, embarrassed.
    neeg txawj txag li A person easily embarrassed.

2. txaj A room (clf. 'lub').
    txaj pw A bedroom.
    txaj tsev A room in a house.

3. txaj A sleeping platform, bed.
    hauv qab txag Under the sleeping platform (t.c.)

4. txaj ntseg A large fish trap built in a stream or
    river (non-portable).

1. txam To go through a narrow place, to wedge one's way
    through (e.g. as when forcing one's way through
    a crowd).
    txam mus To wedge one's way through (e.g. as when
    forcing one's way through a crowd) (cf. 'txiv').

2. txam txwm (C) A mark or imprint (as on a gun or a
    metal can).

3. txam niam fam txam (cf. 'tuag' p. 327).

txav To move, to shift, to change place or position.
    Txav mus tod. Move over a little bit.
    Txav tom ntej. Move back a little (away from the
    speaker).
    Txav rov los. Move this way (toward the speaker).
    Txav los ze ze. Come up close.
    txav zuj zuav To move slowly and dilatorily.

txaig T.c. from 'txaij' (cf. 'txaij').

txaij Varicolored, figured, striped or speckled and
    spotted.
    txaij vog Varicolored.
    txw txaij Freckled.
    tsov txaij The leopard (tus).
    qhov muag txaij Unable to see clearly.
    txaij ceg Tatoo on the legs.
    xyoob txaig A species of speckled bamboo (t.c.)

1. txais To borrow without interest (usually money or grain
    on a long-term basis with arrangement for gradual
    repayment) (cf. 'luab').

2. txais To receive something given, to accept, to catch
    something thrown.
    txais hlo Caught, received.
    (a) txais nkaus To receive, to catch.
    (b) txais nkuj nkaus To receive, to catch.

3. txais To ignite (of a flame, lamp, etc), to catch fire.

4. txais
    txais hais To interject, to interrupt in speaking.

5. txais
    txais siav npua To "receive" the life of the pig
    (in spirit rites) (cf. 'cob').

txau To squirt, to spray.
    txau dej To squirt water.
    txau tshuaj To spray insecticide with a spray gun.

txaug A chisel (rab), to chisel.
    txaug zeb To chisel a grindstone.
    txaug ntawv To pierce paper with a rounded chisel
    marking it as ceremonial paper money.

txauj
    nees txauj nkuaj Of a horse stamping or pawing in
    the stable.

1. txaum Clf. for a batch or brew of liquor.
    ua ib txaum cawv To make a batch of liquor.

2. txaum yim To entreat or to greet with outstretched
    cupped hands.

3. txaum
    xyuam txaum Of one who is impolite in asking for
    more than is offered, etc.

txaus Enough, sufficient.
    txaus lawm Enough.
    loj txaus lawm Sufficiently large, very large.
    txaus nkaus Enough, sufficient.
    txaus siab Satisfied.

txauv To replace with or to exchange for another (as
    officials are replaced in office, etc.) (cf.
    'theej,' 'this,' 'pauv').
    Yexu txauv peb qhov tuag. Jesus took the place of
    death for us.
    sib txauv kev To pass by one another on the road.

1. txawb To throw.
    xuas pobzeb txawb To pick up stones to throw.
    txawb rhees To throw.

2. txawb To support from underneath (contr. 'dai').
tsis muaj dabtsi dai, tsis muaj dabtsi txawb Not hanging from anything and not supported by any-thing underneath (e.g. the earth).
txawb teeb A lampstand (clf. 'lub').

txawg T.c. from 'txawj' (cf. 'txawj').

txawj Able (of learned or acquired ability) (cf. 'tau' and 'taus').
txawj ua Able to do it.
Kuv tsis txawj. I cannot (do it). I don't know how.
Koj puas txawj hais lus Hmoob? Can you speak Hmong?
tub txib tub txawg An able messenger (t.c.)

1. txawm Used to indicate a juncture in speech in a way similar to "and so" or "then" or "thereupon" in English.
Kuv txawm hais rau nws tias... And so I said to him...

2. txawm Consequently, therefore (cf. 'thiaj').
Koj tsis hais txawm tsis mus li. He won't go if he isn't told to. (lit. "If you don't tell him he therefore won't go.")
Lawv tsis pub nyiaj kuv txawm tsis mus. They wouldn't pay so I didn't go.
Lawv hais li cas nws txawm ua li cas thiab. He did whatever they said.

3. txawm Exactly, just so, just then (C).
Txawm sis maj. Quite so! Just as expected: (cf. 'ua ciav').
Kuv qheb qhov rooj nws txawm sis los txog. He arrived just as I opened the door. (in this sense sometimes said 'txawm siv').

4. txawm To arise of its own accord.
Cov zaub nws txawm nws xwb. The vegetable grew of itself without being planted.

5. txawm To put aside for use, to save.
Koj puas txawm lub puav txiaj? Have you any money put aside?

1. txaws To splash.
Dej ntas yuav txaws mus hauv lub nkoj. The waves were splashing into the boat.

2. txaws Of a group dividing up and scattering, to scatter.
txaws yeeb To scatter opium seed (contr. 'tseb').

3. txaws txheeb (to execute justice) In favor of relatives.

4. txaws txaws lis (to execute justice) According to principle.

txawv To differ, to deviate, different.
txawv mentsis A little different.
Txawv qhov twg? Where (or in what respect) is it different?
Ob yam no txawv qhov twg lawm? What difference is there in these two?
txawv suab lawm Off tone, different in tone.

txej Restricted post verbal intensifier after 'nrov.' (cf. 'nrov' p. 178 and Appendix 8).

txee A shelf (clf. 'lub').

1. txeeb To snatch away from, to attempt to seize something suddenly from someone else. (cf. 'txhav').
sib txeeb To contest possession of something, to seek to snatch something one from another.
txeeb tebchaws Rebellion, insurrection.

2. txeeb mob txeeb zig Bladder stones, difficult to urinate.

1. txeeg qub txeeg qub teg Old articles, old things, things left by parents to their children.

2. txeeg
(a) hav zoov nuj txeeg Wild virgin jungle (cf. 'xiab').
(b) hav zoov nuj xiab Wild virgin jungle.

1. txeej To fall (cf. 'poob').

2. txeej To unravel, to come apart (as of woven work, etc.)
Lub kawm txeej tas. The back basket is broken and coming apart.

3. txeej To spill over (because of being too full, etc.)
Lub mis txeej txeej. The breast is dripping milk.

1. txeem To penetrate, to force a way into, to carry through.
txeem txha To penetrate far into.
tus uas txeem One who carries through with an intended action.
mus tsis txeem Can't make any progress against (as against wind or waves, etc.)

2. txeem cuabyeej toomtxeem Household goods.

3. txeem
neeg xam txeem One who does some work and then
    passes the rest off onto others.

txees
  txees nees (archaic term for 'phab xyoob').

1. txeev To be split or cracked a little bit (of vessels, etc.).

2. txeev
  tus txeev tham Of one who talks a lot

3. txeev
  (a) lam hais (cf. 'lam').
  (b) txeev lam hais (cf. 'lam').

1. txi To bear fruit on the twig or branch (contr. 'txhawv').
  txi txiv To bear fruit.

2. txi To offer as a sacrifice, to sacrifice.
  txi dab To offer as a sacrifice to the spirits, to offer animal sacrifice to spirits.

txib To send someone on an errand or mission, to dispatch on a commission.
  tub txib A messenger, one sent on a mission.
  tub txib tub txawg An able messenger.

1. txig Pertaining to the cheek.
  xub txig The cheek bone.
  sawv ib txig To stand side by side, "cheek to cheek."
  kes txig To finger the cheek indicating shame toward someone.

2. txig Restricted post verbal intensifier after 'dub.' (cf. Appendix 8).
  dub txig Perfectly black (also 'dub nciab').

3. txig
  dub muag txig mus To go straight on without stopping (with black and determined face).

1. txij To reach to, up to the point of.
  txij no Up to this point.
  (a) txij nrho Reaching to.
  (b) txij nkaus Reaching to.
  txij no mus From this point on, from now on.
  txij thaum ntawd los txog nimno From that time until now.

2. txij
  txij nkawm An engaged person or couple.
  yog txij yog nkawm Are married.
  tseg txij tseg nkawm Bereft of husband or wife.

3. txij Restricted post verbal intensifier with 'txej' after 'nrov' (cf. 'nrov' p. 178 and Appendix 8).

1. txim Offense against law or custom, guilt, sin, crime.
  muab txim rau To hold as guilty, to accuse.
  sawm txim To bear punishment, to suffer for offense (C).
  nplua txim To fine, penalty for offense.
  (a) raug txim To suffer punishment for offense or sin.
  (b) teem txim To suffer punishment for offense or sin.
  txiav txim To decide the punishment for offense.
  nyob txim To be confined in prison for offense.

2. txim To bind tightly.
  Muab hlua txim ntiv tes. Bind the finger with a string.

3. txim Sparks, a spark.
  txim taws Sparks (of wood or metal, etc.)

txis To join in marriage.
  kev txis pojniam Marriage.
  (a) Muab ob tug txis ua niam txiv. To join a couple in marriage. To perform a wedding.
  (b) Muab ob tug sib txis ua niam txiv. To join a couple in marriage. To perform a wedding.

1. txiv Male, father, husband, male relative (clf. 'tus').
  kuv txiv My father.
  kuv tus txiv My husband.
  txivneej Male, a male individual, man.
  cov txivneej Men.
  txiv tshiab Foster father.
  txiv hlob Father's elder brother.
  txiv ntxawm Father's younger brother.
  Note: For other male relatives cf. Kinship Charts Appendix 11).
  tus txiv qeej The one who plays the pipes at a funeral.

2. txiv The male of animals.
  txiv nyuj A bull.
  txiv thais liab A large male monkey.

3. txiv Fruit (clf. 'lub' for one, 'tauv' for a cluster).
  txi txiv To bear fruit (on branch or twig).
  txhawv txiv To bear fruit (from the center stem as pineapples, bananas, etc.)

Various Kinds of Fruit
txiv cev nplaum The edible fig.
txiv cev txua Inedible figs.
txiv cuab thoj Guava.
txiv duaj Peach.
txiv kab ntxwv Orange, tangerine.
txiv lwj zoov Pomelo (T).
txiv mam auv Pomelo (T).
txiv lwvchi Leechee (C).
txiv lws suav Tomato.
(a) txiv maum kuab (T) Papaya.
(b) txiv taub ntoo Papaya.
txiv nyuj kub A sour wild fruit shaped like a horn.
txiv plab nyu Jackfruit.
txiv puv luj Pineapple (T).
txiv quav miv Tamarind.
txiv roj Term used for the olive.
txiv rau zaub Term used for limes.
txiv tsawb Banana (cf. 'tsawb').
txiv txhais Mango.
txiv mav poj Coconut (T).

4. txiv To interpret, to translate (cf. 'txhais'), speak
on behalf of.
txiv lus To interpret, speak on behalf of others.

5. txiv To press upon one (as a crowd, etc.), to wedge
one's way through as through a group or crowd.
sib txiv Crowded together. (cf. 'txam').

6. txiv
txiv caj ntswg The bridge of the nose.

7. txiv
(a) txiv ntswg The tip of the nose.
(b) txiv taub ntswg The tip of the nose.

8. txiv
txiv xaiv Funeral songs (cf. 'kwv txhiaj' p. 92).

9. txiv
Khav txiv To boast (cf. 'khav theeb'), proud.

10. txiv
lub txiv mis The nipple of the breast.

11. txiv
txiv kev To obstruct.
txiv nkaus Cut off, obstructed.

12. txiv
txiv txiag The covering board of a coffin.

1. txia Enlargement of the gullet, the crop of a bird,
goiter.
lub txia The crop of a bird.
mob txia Goiter.

2. txia To seep, of water oozing slowly in or out.
av txia dej Swampy ground.

3. txia To change form or nature.
rab qws txia ua nab The rod changed to a serpent.

4. txia The short cross strands in weaving, the woof (cf.
'hlaub').

1. txiab Scissors (clf. 'rab'), to cut with a scissors.

2. txiab
txiab neeb (cf. 'neeb' p. 137).

3. txiab
txiab xeeb Sick, sickness.

1. txiag A board, a slab.
txiag ntoo Wooden boards (daim).
txiag zeb A slab of rock (daim).
txiv txiag The covering board of a coffin.
txiag qhov rooj A door (boards on hinges).

2. txiag T.c. from 'txiaj' or 'txias.'
Note: When used in isolation 'txiag' has an evil connotation and should be avoided.

1. txiaj Money, wealth.
muaj muaj txiag Wealthy (t.c.)
nyiaj txiag Silver money, money (t.c.)
txiaj ntawv Paper money.
txiaj maj Silver coin, the French piastre.
twv txiaj To gamble for money, to gamble.
txiaj cub A kind of small Indo-Chinese coin used by
Hmong for decoration.
txiaj npliv A kind of small Indo-Chinese coin used
by Hmong for decoration.

2. txiaj
tsim txiaj Of value, worth money, worthy of respect.
neeg tsis tsim txiaj A worthless individual.

3. txiaj
ris lawv txiaj To be grateful to them.
Kuv tsis ris nws txiaj. I have been ungrateful to him.

4. txiaj
txiaj ntsim (lub) A kind or gracious act, a gracious gift, etc. (also 'txiaj ntsig').
pauj txiaj ntsim rau To make return for a favor or gift.

txiaj ntsha txiaj ntsim Gifts.
txuag txiaj txuag ntsig Gifts, acts of mercy.
txuag nws txiaj To care for, have mercy on a person.

5. txiaj A tenth of an ounce (cf. 'las').

txiam
(a) ywjtxiam As you please (cf. 'xij').
(b) xijpeem As you please (cf. 'xij').

1. txias Cold, unheated, uncooked.
dej txiag Cold water (t.c.)
txias txias rhiab rhiab "In a cold sweat" (as in facing a snake, etc.)

2. txias ua tuv txias tom caj qwb "Speaking evil of me behind my back" (cf. 'tuv').

1. txiav To chop, to cut off, to cut with a chopping motion (contr. 'hlais').
txiav taws To chop firewood (contr. 'txhib').

2. txiav To decide, to fix.
(a) txiav plaub To fix payment for an offense.
(b) txiav txim To fix payment for an offense.

3. txiav kev To explain, to set forth the way of doing things, to preach.

4. txiav The spleen.
mob txiav Enlargement and hardening of the spleen.

5. txiav muag Refusing to look at another person due to hatred.

1. txob To encounter or meet with trouble, especially court cases of dispute.
txob plaub To encounter litigation, be involved in a case at law, to give rise to dispute.
Kuv txob tau txoj kev phem... I have met with this evil way...

2. txob To trouble, to make trouble for.
Txhob txob xibhwb. Don't make trouble for the teacher.

3. txob Pepper.
kuatxob Red pepper.
hwjtxob Black pepper (C).

4. txob
(a) xeeb txob Worry, trouble, unsettled heart.
(b) txob siab Worry, trouble, unsettled heart.
(c) kev txob Worry, trouble, unsettled heart.

5. txob
txob puab Of a child that is fussy and troublesome.

1. txo To relinquish, to let down or turn over to another, release.
Muab lub kawm txo rau lawv. Give your back basket over to them.
txo faiv fuaj Put out the flashlight.
txo ceg ntoo To cut the branches off a fallen tree.
ntov txo ntswg To cut a leaning tree until it splits off and falls.

2. txo Of foreign matter found in water (contr. 'nro').
dej muaj txo Water with foreign matter in it.

1. txog To arrive at, arrived, to the point or to the limit of.
txog nimno Until now.
Nqa mus txog tsev. Carry it to the house.
Tsis tau txog. Hasn't arrived.

2. txog
hais txog... Idiom for "to speak of" or "to speak concerning..." (contr. 'hais rau...').

3. txog
txog txog siav Breathless, winded, heavy breathing.

txoj Clf. for lengths, of things that come in lengths.
txoj hlua A length of rope.
txoj kev A road, path, or way.
txoj lus A saying, a vocal expression.
txoj siav Life (sometimes heard 'txoj sia').
txoj kev... "The way of"
txoj kev dab The way of the spirits, spirit worship.
txoj kev Yexu Jesus' way, Christianity.
txoj kev nlom Idol worship, Buddhism.

1. txom
tsim txom To persecute, to cause to suffer.

2. txom
txomnyem Destitute, impoverished, suffering calamity.

3. txom
meem txom Irritating, irritated, provoked, provoking anger.

txos   qhov txos The fireplace for cooking pig food, etc.

1. txov To take life.
   txov txoj siav To take life, to kill.

2. txov
   nees txov lawj A brown horse.

1. txoob A mane, especially thick hair like a mane.
   txoob nees A horse's mane.

2. txoob A species of palm the heart of which is edible but not the fruit.
   txoob liab A kind of edible palm.
   xib txoob The fibres of this type of palm.

txoog
   kaj ntug txoog Early dawn.

1. txooj Clf. for a clump of bamboo.
   ib txoog xyoob One clump of bamboo (t.c.)
   Nej yog nqaij ib daig, tawv ib phob, xyoob ib txoog, ntoo ib tsob. You are very close relatives. (literally "one flesh, one skin, one clump of bamboo and one tree.")

2. txooj The "even" numbered days regarded as belonging to women. (cf. 'hnub tab').
   hnub txooj

3. txooj To tie with a double rope (cf. 'ua tab').
   ua txooj

txoom Wrinkled.
   txoom txoom li Of a person with many wrinkles.
   zaub txoom A kind of leafy vegetable with very wrinkled leaves.

txoov Pertaining to the spirits (cf. 'dab' and 'neeb').
   txoov neeb The leader or the greatest of the 'neeb'.
   txoov dab Great or powerful 'dab' (cf. 'dab').
   txoov dab nlom Idols, great idols.

1. txub Clf. for court cases.

2. txub
   hais cuaj txub kaum txub To speak of all kinds of things.

txug ua tsis muaj txug, tso tseg Couldn't do it despite trying hard and so quit (after having made repeated claim of ability, etc.)

1. txuj To pretend.
   (a) ua txuj To pretend (cf. 'tsab').
   (b) ua txuj tsab To pretend (cf. 'tsab').
   ua txuj mus To pretend to go.
   ua txuj tuag To pretend to die.

2. txuj
   txujci (clf. 'tus') (also 'tus txuj tus ci'), principle, method, way of doing things, science, rule, wisdom, skill or ability (cf. 'peevxwm').
   muaj txuj muaj ci Has a special method or rule of operation.
   Kuv tsis paub tus txujci. I don't know how it works. I don't know the plan.

3. txuj
   txuj lom Spices, condiments, food flavorings (other than onions, peppers, etc.)

4. txuj
   txujkum How, however, no matter how, no matter what (often in connection with 'tsis kav') (C).
   Txujkum tsis kav yuav tau ua xwb. It must be done no matter what happens.
   Yuav txujkum ua tau? How can it be done?

5. txuj Restricted post verbal intensifier after 'quaj.'
   quaj txuj txwv Sound as of a dog crying in pain (cf. Appendix 11).

1. txum Of a mattress or quilt.
   txum zooj (daim) A mattress.
   txum paj (daim) A cotton quilt, a quilt.

2. txum To take the place of another.
   txum nws chaw To replace him, take his position (C).

3. txum
   txum tsab tos To wait quietly to kill game, to wait for a kill.

4. txum
   txum tim Native (C), the inhabitant of a village as opposed to an outsider ('kum khej').

1. txus Sometimes used in the place of 'ntaus' (to hit) when speaking in anger against another.

2. txus Used in expressing 'the more the better,' etc. similar to the use of 'yim'. (cf. 'yim').
   txus saib txus zoo The more you see of it the better it is.

3. txuas
   ntshav txuas qos ntso Blood spurting, hemorrhage.

4. txuas A brush knife, a knife with a broad hooked end (clf. 'rab').

rab txuas

1. txw To seek to dissuade, to advise against an intended course of action.

2. txw
   txw txaij Freckles, freckled.

1. txwj
   (a) cov txwj laus The village elders, the leaders, old people, elders whose counsel is respected.
   (b) cov txwj cov laus The village elders, the leaders, old people, elders whose counsel is respected.

2. txwj
   kev txwj kev laus The traditions, teachings of the elders.

1. txwm A Meo poetic couplet (consisting of two 'nqes').
   Ob nqes ua ib txwg. Two halves make a couplet (t.c.)
   (cf. 'nqes', 'zaj', 'tshooj').

2. txwm Rhyme or correct poetic structure.
   Tsis muaj txwm tsis zoo nloog. If it doesn't rhyme it isn't nice to listen to.

3. txwm Clf. for pairs (cf. 'nkawm'). Used for pairs of chopsticks, horns, a married couple, etc.
   Ib txwg niam txiv mus. The parents went as a couple.

4. txwm Originally, from the beginning.
   Ib txwm ua li no lawm. It has always been this way.
   txwm keeb li Originally, from the beginning.

5. txwm
   txam txwm A mark or imprint, indented or raised markings as on a gun or a can (C).

6. txwm
   txhob txwm Purposefully, with intent.
   txhob txwm ua To do purposely, intentionally.

7. txwm
   tsis tau txwm xyoo Not yet a year old.

8. txwm Clf. for letters of the alphabet.
   ib txwm ntawv One letter.

3. txus
   ua ib siab txus tes ntxhias To go ahead with something even though very reluctant.

1. txuv Of adults or children that are petulant and peevishly fretful. (cf. 'tshiam' which is only used of children).

2. txuv To pester, to antagonize (cf. 'siv').
   txuv kov ywm loom li (C) Troublesome, pestering.

1. txua Non-glutinous (as contrasted with 'nplaum').
   mov txua Ordinary cooked rice as contrasted with glutinous rice ('mov nplaum').

2. txua To construct, to make.
   txua rooj To construct a table.
   txua nkoj To make a boat.
   txua hleb To make a coffin.

3. txua
   neeg ncauj txua A person who talks a lot, one who says whatever he thinks.

txuab
   pobzeb toob txuab A kind of soft stone.

txuag To care for, to preserve, to keep in good condition.
   (a) txuag nws To look after a person, to care for his welfare.
   (b) txuag nws txiaj To look after a person, to care for his welfare.
   txuag tau lub siab mentsis Be a little careful to do things the right way, etc.
   tsis txuag Doesn't observe custom or taboo, etc.

1. txuam To interfere in the affairs of others (cf. 'fim').

2. txuam
   txuam tsoov Mixed varieties, half-breed.

1. txuas To connect, to join together, to knot together.
   sib txuas Joined, connected.
   txuas lus To converse, to join words together.
   txuas quav To tell lies.
   sau sib txuas To write longhand, connected writing.
   sau tsis txuas To print, unconnected writing.
   nrog lawv txuas tw tis To take a wife from among their family, to be connected by marriage (cf. 'tshoob').

2. txuas
   qhov rooj txuas The side door of a house.

9. txwm   txwm kav (used before verbs to indicate action persevered regardless of advice or warning).
   Note: 'yej meem' is used similarly.
       mas txwm kav (or 'yej meem') thov nws pab Ask him to help regardless.
       txwm kav tso moo Kept telling everyone, kept spreading the news undaunted.

1. txws   A small can (clf. 'lub') (as for money, tobacco, opium, etc.)
       txws yeeb Can or box for keeping opium.

2. txws   ua qhua txws (cf. 'tuag' p. 327).

3. txws   kab txws Marbleworm (tus).

1. txwv   To rebuke, to forbid to do something (stronger than 'tav'), to prevent from action.

2. txwv   A nominalizing syllable added to many words, especially those taken from the Chinese. Compare the following words listed in their individual entries:

   ntxwv   cuamtxwv   kimtxwv   phuajtxwv
   hwjtxwv   zimtxwv   covtxwv   liam txwv
   lujtxwv   txhuam txwv   tiv txwv   phiaj txwv
   muastxwv   pomtxwv   hiav txwv   pobtxwv
   pivtxwv

3. txwv   puas txwv puaj tiam (cf. 'puaj' Definition No. 4).

4. txwv   kov txwv los (cf. 'kov' Definition No. 4).

5. txwv   txwvzeej txwvkoob Ancestors.

6. txwv   siv tom txwv (cf. 'siv' Definition No. 3).

7. txwv   Restricted post verbal intensifier with 'txuj' after 'quaj.' (cf. Appendix 11).
       quaj txuj txwv Sound as of a dog crying in pain.

txha   Bony, bone, pertaining to the hard core of an object.
       pobtxha (lub) A bone.
       pob qej txha A bone joint.
       pob qej txha txhauj lawm Dislocated joint.
       pobtxha qes lawm A sprained joint.
       txha ntoo The heartwood of a tree
       txha pobkws A corncob.

1. txhab   To add to, to increase (cf. 'tsav').
       txhab dej To add water (e.g. to meat or vegetables while cooking).
       muaj zog txhab mus To increase in strength.
       Yuav txhab ib lo lus thiaj txhua. You need to add a word to it so it will be complete.

2. txhab   A storehouse, a granary (clf. 'lub').
       txhab nplej A rice granary.
       txhab nyiaj A treasury.

3. txhab   kiav txhab (lub) An ulcer, an open sore.

4. txhab   hniav txhab (tus) A wisdom tooth.

5. txhab   txhab khaum (lub) The gunstock.

txhaj   To prick, to puncture (cf. 'hno').
       txhaj tshuaj To inject medicine.

txham   To sneeze, of sounds requiring aspiration.
       txham dej To sneeze because of water getting into the windpipe, etc.
       txham cuam Of animals getting water, etc. into the windpipe.

1. txhav   Stiff, hardened, paralyzed.
       txhav nrees Stiff, stiffened.
       lub siab txhav nrees Stiff-hearted, hard-hearted and disobedient.
       nplaig txhav Tongue-tied.

2. txhav   To rob, to seize forcibly, to snatch away (cf. 'lws', 'txeeb' and 'nyiag').
       txhav lawv nyiaj To steal their money, rob them.

3. txhav   txhav qaib The second joint in a chicken leg, the highest section of chicken leg.

1. txhais Clf. for arms, hands and feet.
   ib txhais tes One hand (or lower arm).

2. txhais To explain, to interpret (cf. 'piav' and 'txiv lus').
   txhais tsis tau Cannot explain it.

3. txhais
   ob cag peb txhais Outsiders, those of another clan.

4. txhais The mango fruit.
   txiv txhais The mango fruit.

5. txhais Of a trap springing, of a spring being released or of strands suddenly unravelling.
   txhais plhuav Of a trap springing.
   txhais dheev To suddenly unravel or spring open.

6. txhais
   txhais hwj A piece of broken glass.

7. txhais Something beyond the ordinary figure, used of fractions. Something over one "Baht," more than one piece of paper money.
   ib ntawv txhais

1. txhaub To add water to frying meat and vegetables so as to make a soup or gravy, etc.
   txhaub kua

2. txhaub To plunge metal into water after heating so as to prepare for forging and shaping.
   txhaub dej

3. txhaub To urge animals into fighting.
   txhaub dev To send a dog to attack someone.
   txhaub nyuj To incite bulls to fight each other.

txhauj To dislocate a joint.
   pob qej txha txhauj lawm Dislocated joint.

txhaum Wrong, wrongdoing, mistake.
   ua txhaum To do wrong, to make a mistake.
   qhov txhaum A wrong, a mistake (lub).

txhaus
   txhaus nees To force a horse to drink, to give a horse medicine via the nostrils.

txhauv A kind of grain similar to millet which is often used as a horse feed.

1. txhawb To raise and place horizontally, to erect in a horizontal position.
   txhawb yees To erect the horizontal crossbeams of a house (cf. 'tsev').
   txhawb txheej meej To put up the articles of spirit worship over the door.

2. txhawb
   txhawb nej lub siab To encourage you.

3. txhawb Of a vapor rising or of a fire approaching, to vaporize.
   txhawb tshuaj Of a medicinal vapor.

4. txhawb Pungent, descriptive of a sharp or pungent odor as e.g. of alcohol or of red pepper, etc. (cf. 'txhub').

txhawj To worry, to be concerned or distressed.
   kev txhawj Worry, distress, trouble.
   txhawj xeeb To be worried in heart, worrying.

txhawm To set aside, to save, to put aside for a purpose (cf. 'phaj').
   tsev txhawm nyiaj A bank (lub).
   txhawm kuv mentsis Lend me a little.
   txhawm cia them rau lawv Save to pay back the debt to them.

1. txhaws To stuff up, to block or plug an opening.
   txhaws ntswg A stuffed up nose.
   txhaws qa A sore and stuffed up throat.
   av txhawv lub qhov Dirt is blocking the hole.
   (a) txhaws qhov tuag To die for another, to take the place of another in death (cf. 'this').
   (b) txhaws qhov tuag theej txhoj To die for another, to take the place of another in death (cf. 'this').

2. txhawv Restricted post verbal intensifier with 'daws' (cf. 'daws').

1. txhawv To bubble up, to issue forth.
   qhov dej txhawv A spring.

2. txhawv Of fruit or grain which forms from the center of the stalk rather than on the branch, to bear (in the above sense) as e.g. rice, pineapples, bananas, etc.
   nplej txhawv txhij The rice has come to a head.

1. txhem
   txhem zaub To remove the strings, shoots and inedible leaves, etc. from vegetables.

2. txhem
   txhem teb To remove and pile up for burning the branches, vines, etc. after the trees have been felled in clearing a field for use (also said 'them teb.') (cf. 'them').

3. txhem
   xyeej txhem To despise.

4. txhem To divide off from.
   txhem hwb txhib To separate one from another and forbid to marry.

1. txheeb Closely related, close blood relatives.
   kwvtij txheeb txheeb Close blood relatives.

2. txheeb Gray in color, ashen.

3. txheeb To invite (C).

4. txheeb To pole a boat.
   txheeb nkoj To pole a boat (contr. 'nquam').

5. txheeb
   tebchaws txheeb tibneeg To take a census.

6. txheeb
   txheeb vam vam Thousands and tens of thousands (C) (sometimes used in expressing a great length of time, forever).

7. txheeb
   rho txheeb To divine or cast lots by selecting one from among a number of bamboo sticks.

8. txheeb Brother and sister marry brother and sister.
   sib tom txheeb

9. txheeb Complete, whole.
   txheeb hnub txheeb hmo All day and all night.
   suav tsis txheeb More than can be counted (cannot be counted to completion).

1. txheej Previous, preceding in time (C).
   txheej zaug The previous time or occasion.
   txheej thaum ub In the very beginning.
   cuaj txheej cuaj tis (C) From the beginning of the generations of man (cf. 'puas txwv puaj tiam').

2. txheej A tier, a story, a level or layer (cf. 'theem' and 'tshooj').

3. txheej
   txheej meej The articles of spirit worship put over the door (cf. 'txhawb').

4. txheej
   peev txheej Money to start business, capital (C).

5. txheej
   peb txheej peb tis A great crowd, great numbers.

6. txheej
   txheej txheem Basis, source of facts or information.

7. txheej
   Kuv tsis vwj nws txheej. I will not forget his kindness.

txheem To support (e.g. using a hand to support one from falling or using a pole to support a leaning tree or a heavy branch of a tree, etc.), to support or assist in a cause.
   txheej txheem (cf. 'txheej').
   (a) txheej nkaus To support with the hand to keep from falling, to hold up.
   (b) nres nkaus To support with the hand to keep from falling, to hold up.

txheev
   txheev dab To call the spirits to come, to invite the spirits (C).

1. txhib To split wood off lengthwise along the log.
   txhib taws To cut firewood in the above manner (contr. 'txiav taws').

2. txhib To constrain, to compel (cf. 'yuam').
   hais lus txhib To speak so as to cause to do quickly, to speak with alarm.

3. txhib
   txhem hwb txhib (cf. 'txhem').

4. txhib
   ntaus txhib ntawg (cf. 'ntawg').

1. txhij Complete, whole.
   txhij txhij txhua txhua Entirely complete, whole.
   Nws paub lus txhij. He knows the whole language.

2. txhij
   ib txhij At the same time, all together.
   ib txhij hais All talking at the same time, say it all together.

2. txhiaj Then, consequently (cf. 'thiaj').
   Yuav mus txhiaj zoo. You had better go.
   Kuv txhiaj (or 'txhiaj li') hais rau nws tias...
      Then (or "therefore") I said to him...
   Note: We have listed 'txhiaj' or 'txhiaj li' here and
         also under 'thiaj' or 'thiaj li.' We hear it
         more commonly said 'thiaj' or 'thiaj li' among
         Thailand Hmong but it is quite possible that the
         other rendering (which is also heard) is actually
         the original pronunciation. In Laos 'txhiaj'
         or 'txhiaj li' is more common and the Blue
         (or Green) Hmong for the same expression is
         'txha le.'

3. txhiaj To propound a riddle.
   txhiaj teeb meem To speak in riddles, riddles.
   txhiaj tau txhais tsis tau Able to speak riddles
      but not explain them.

4. txhiaj
   txhiaj khoov Conveying the idea "it would be better
      if..." (cf. 'yim').
   (a) txhiaj khoov ua li Done without knowledge, better
       if I hadn't done it.
   (b) yim leej ua li Done without knowledge, better
       if I hadn't done it.
   Txhiaj khoov txhob yug los. It would be better if
      (he) hadn't been born.

txhiam
   txhiam xwm Garden vegetables (as opposed to field
      crops).
   lais txhiam xwm To plant vegetables.
   txhiam laj txhiam xwm Vegetables.

txhiav
   txhiav dej A species of small wild palm similar to
      the areca palm. (tus).

1. txho
   xiav txho Light blue.

2. txho
   txho tshauv Having an ashy colored coating as some
      animals, some vegetables, etc.

3. txho
   mab txho The palm civet cat.

1. txhob Negative imperative (used before the verb either by
   itself or preceded by the negative 'tsis').
   (a) Txhob ua Don't do it!
   (b) Tsis txhob ua. Don't do it!
   Txhob hais lus. Don't talk!

3. txhij To smooth off the end of a piece of wood across
   the grain.
   txhij tuj lub To smooth the end of a spinning top.
   txhij qab xub To smooth off the butt end of an
      arrow.

4. txhij
   txhij txiv mim The Pleiades.

1. txhim To build with brick or stone (C).
   txhim tsev To build a brick or stone house.

2. txhim Flaky, not clinging together (e.g. pastry, etc.)

3. txhim
   sam txhim To paint, to apply paint to (C).

txhis
   ib txhis li Continually, forever (cf. 'ib sim').
   ib los ib txhis Continually, forever.
   ib txhis tsis kawg Continually without end, always
      forever.
   ib txhis nruab thiab los Continually from birth
      (This word is pronounced 'txhim' by some
      speakers).

txhiv To redeem an article by some payment in return.
   txhiv plig To offer the spirit of a slain animal
      in exchange for the return of the spirit of
      someone who is sick, etc.

1. txhia All, all kinds of.
   txhia yam All kinds of, all sorts.
   txhia leej All persons.
   qhovtxhiachaw Things, articles.
   txhia hnub txhua hmo Every day and night.

2 txhia Some.
   ib txhia paub ib txhia tsis paub Some (people)
      know and some do not.

1. txhiab One thousand (C).
   ib txhiab leej One thousand persons.
   txhiab niag tim puas xyoo Thousand of years (C).

2. txhiab To toast, to dry by the fire (cf. 'ci').
   txhiab maj To dry the hemp by the fire.

1. txhiaj A balad, a story song (cf. 'kwv' Definition No. 11).
   kwv txhiaj A serenade or ballad.
   hais kwv txhiaj To sing ballads, to serenade.

2. txhob
   tuam txhob (rab) A digging implement for making
      holes in the ground to insert posts, etc.

3. txhob
   txhob txwm Purposefully, with intent.
   txhob txwm ua To do intentionally.

1. txhoj
   txhoj ha (lub) A shallow valley (cf. 'hav') (t.c.).

2. txhoj
   theej txhoj (cf. 'theej').

3. txhoj
   txhoj pob Bothersome, mischievous.

4. txhoj
   txhoj khawv zoo Of a person or an animal that eats
      well.
   tibneeg txhoj khawv zoo A person who eats the tough
      with the tender alike.
   nees txhoj khawv zoo A horse that eats both tender
      and coarse grass without difficulty.

1. txhom To catch hold of, to seize and hold.
   txhom qaib To catch a chicken.
   txhom npua To catch a pig (especially in readiness
      for slaughter).

2. txhom
   cem txhom To scold or curse severely.

3. txhom
   siab txhom Flighty, not steady at one job, attempting
      many things but not getting far with anything.

1. txhos To set into the ground.
   txhos ncej tsev To put the upright posts of a house
      in place.

2. txhos To kneel.
   (a) txhos caug To kneel.
   (b) qhau hauvcaug To kneel.
   txhos caug rawv To remain kneeling.

txhoo
   ua txhuj txhoo To be weak in body.

1. noj txhooj Spoken of gathering for a meal called for
      by a leader wherein all who take part engage
      in a vow of silence concerning some event
      such as a murder or crime, etc.

2. txhooj
   Kuv txhooj xeeb cawv xwv xav pom nej (C) I want to
      see you very badly.

txhoov To cut up into bite size pieces for cooking and
      eating.
   txhoov nqaij To cut up meat (contr. 'tsuav').
   txhoov zaub To cut up vegetables.

txhu
   tsiaj txhu Animals.

1. txhub Of a sharp or pungent odor (as of red pepper, etc.)
   hnov kuatxob txhub To smell the pungent odor
      of peppers (cf. 'txhawb').

2. txhub A species of tree used for medicine.

3. txhub To fill in a hole, to cover over or fill up an
      opening or a low place (e.g. a landslide filling
      a valley, etc.)

txhuj
   ua txhuj txhoo To be weak in body.

txhuv Rice grains hulled but uncooked (cf. 'nplej' and
      'mov').
   txhuv txua Ordinary hulled rice.
   txhuv nplaum Glutinous hulled rice.
   tuav txhuv To hull the rice by pounding it in the
      footmill.
   tsoov txhuv To winnow the beaten rice by bouncing
      it in a bamboo winnowing tray.
   zig txhuv To separate out the light particles from
      the beaten rice by shaking it in the winnowing
      tray.
   luam txhuv To mill rice in a mechanical rice mill.

txhua Complete, whole, entire.
   txhua nrho All, completely.
   txhij txhij txhua txhua Whole, complete.
   nrhiav txhua ntxaws Searched everywhere.
   muaj txhij muaj txhua Has everything.

txhuam A brush (clf. 'rab'), to brush, to scrub with a
      brush.
   txhuam hniav To brush the teeth.
   txhuam pov tseg To erase, to scrub out.
   txhuam txwv A corn sheller.

txhuas Lead metal.

txhuav To suck, up, to pump with a suction pump, "cupping"
      done to relieve pain (placing an inverted heated
      cup on the skin).

1. txhwb Coarse or rough (C) (cf. 'ntxhib').

2. txhwb A leafy lettuce-like vegetable.
   zaub txhwb A leafy lettuce-like vegetable.

1. txhwj A hoe used for digging and cultivating.
   (a) pav txhwj A hoe (rab).
   (b) choj txhwj A hoe (rab).

2. txhwj
   zaub txhwj qaib Parsley.

3. txhwj To tell someone to quit talking or to quit
   scolding.

txhws To mash with the hands.
   txhws mov To mash the cooked rice with the hands
   to spread it out and loosen it.

V

1. vab A woven rattan or bamboo tray (clf. 'lub').
   lub vab tsoov txhuv A rice winnowing tray.
   lub vab tshaus A sieve, a sifter.
   lub nrog vab The inside area of the tray.
   ib nrog vab nqaij A trayful of meat.

2. vab nyuj vab (cf. 'nyuj' Definition No. 2).

3. vab
   (a) tsheb kauj vab A bicycle (lub).
   (b) tshuab kauj vab A bicycle (lub).

4. vab lom vab vab (cf. 'lom' Definition No. 5).

1. vag yeb vag To trouble or molest.

2. vag T.c. from 'vas' (cf. 'vas').

1. vaj A garden, an enclosure for planting vegetables,
   fruit, etc. (clf. 'lub').
   vaj tsev House and garden or gounds.
   lub rooj vag Garden gate (t.c.).

2. vaj A king, a ruler (clf. 'tus') (C), a Hmong surname.
   Nws yog ib tug vaj loj loj. He is a great king.
   ciaj ib nceeg vaj To establish a kingdom.
   nyuj vaj (cf. 'nyuj' Definition No. 2).

3. vaj
   hu vaj (tus) The great hornbill.
   hu vaj xyoob (tus) The small hornbill.

1. vam To rely upon, to trust in, to hope (cf. 'khom' (C).
   vam ntsoov To rely steadily upon.
   vam siab rau nws To trust in him, rely on him.
   Kuv lub siab vam... I hope that...
   vamkhom To rely upon, to trust in (C).
   chaw vamkhom A place of hope, something to rely on.

2. vam Ten thousand (C) (cf. 'meem').
   ib vam Ten thousand.
   ob vam Twenty thousand.

3. vam
   txheeb txheeb vam vam (cf. 'txheeb' Definition No. 6).

4. vam To flourish, to increase.
   vam coob coob To increase prolifically.
   huajvam To flourish, to increase.

5. vam
   muj vam lus Old fashioned language, archaic speech.

1. vas A net (clf. 'lub'), clf. for a casting of the net.
   sua lub vas los Gather in the net.
   ntaus ib vag One casting of the net (t.c.)

2. vas yeb vas (cf. 'yeb').

1. vaib Prone to bend and not to cut well (of a poor
   quality knife, etc.)

2. vaib Sometimes used with a meaning similar to 'lim
   hiam' (cf. 'lim hiam').

vaim A long flat worm-like parasite that exists in animal
   stomachs and in the human stomach.

vaiv thauv vaiv (cf. 'thauv').

vau To fall down from an upright position.
  vau hlo To fall down, fell down flat.
  ntoo vau lawm The tree fell down.

1. vaub
  ua lauj vaub To have lengths of badly knotted hair.

2. vaub
  (a) vaubkib (tus) A turtle.
  (b) vaubkib (tus) A turtle.
  vaubkib deg Water turtle.
  vaubkib nqhuab Land turtle.

vaum Hot and humid (of the weather).

vauv Son-in-law (cf. 'tshoob' and also the kinship charts
    Appendix 10).
  tus nraug vauv The bridegroom.
  cov qhua vauv The bridegroom's party.

vawj Restricted post verbal intensifier with 'vij'
    (cf. 'vij').

vees tsab ntxwv tsis vees Poor sense of balance, not
    steady on his feet (C).

1. vij To be close around, surrounding.
  vij lub zos huv huv All around the village.
  zaj vij hnub Rainbow around the sun.
  vij vog Surrounding, close, grouped close together.

2. vij To be troubled by the spirits of the departed.
  vij dab vij npog Evil omens, troubled by spirits
    and by evil omens.
  sub vij sw Troubled by the spirits of the
    dead (cf. 'sub' and 'sw').
  muaj vij To have trouble from the spirits of the
    dead (when a person dies of some accident
    the departed spirit sends an evil spirit to
    entice the living into similar calamity).

3. vij tuag As good as dead.
  vij tuag As good as dead.

4. vij
  (a) vijtsam A mosquito net (lub).
  (b) tsamphooj A mosquito net (lub).

5. vij
  (a) vij yog Because, for this reason.
  (b) vij yog li no Because, for this reason.
  Note: This is a variant rendering of 'vim' or 'vim
    yog' (cf. 'vim').

6. vij Restricted post verbal intensifier with 'vawj'.
  Dev tsem vij vawj. The dog whimpered and cried.
    (cf. Appendix 8).

1. vim Because, for this reason (C).
  Note: This word is found in various combinations with
    much the same meaning:
      yibvim Because (C)
      vim yog li no Because of this.
      vimchij Because.
  Sometimes the word is pronounced 'vij'. (cf. 'vij')
    Also compare the similar word 'tim.'
  Vim yog li no mas nws thiaj mob. For this reason he
    became sick.
  Vim li cas? Why?
  Yibvim kuv paub tas. Because I know all about it.

2. vim
  saj vimtom To taste the flavor (C).

vis To encircle or to make a circuit around game when
    stalking it in hunting.

viv vivncaus (tus) Sister (as called by her sisters)
      (contr. 'muam').
  kuv viv kuv ncaus My sisters (said by a woman).
  vivncaus (tus) Also used by a woman of her female
      cousins having a different surname (cf. Kinship
      Charts, Appendix 10).

viab com viab (cf. 'com').

1. vias
  vias li ub, vias li no To talk one way and another
      to no purpose.

2. vias
  viav vias (cf. 'viav').

3. vias
  kab nqos vias (tus) The locust.

4. vias
  phij vias On the surface, "skin deep," superficially.
  Nws ntseeg mentsis saum phij vias xwb. He only
      believes superficially.

viav To swing, to swing suspended from a point.
  ua viav vias To swing back and forth.
  ua ib viag One swing (t.c.).
  dai vias Hanging up, swinging suspended from a point.

vog Restricted post verbal intensifier (cf. Appendix 8). Used after colors it indicates that the color is predominantly the one indicated but speckled or mixed with others).
Also with the following verbs:
daj vog Speckled yellow (and so with other colors).
npau vog A burst of anger.
ci vog ci vog Flashing (as lightning, etc.)
vij vog Grouped close together, surrounding.
lub siab xob pes vog Very afraid.
Note: 'daj vog' is also sometimes used similarly to 'zom zaws' as a two-word restricted post verbal intensifier. (cf. 'zom zaws').

voj A circle, a cipher (clf. 'lub').
ib voj (t.c.) A circle, a circular slice or flat section.

1. vom To steam rice in a steamer after it has been cooked partly soft and had the cooking water poured away.
vom mov To steam rice in a steamer after it has been cooked partly soft and had the cooking water poured away.

2. vom vom vom hauv lub plab A churning in the stomach producing gradual weakness.

1. vos A metal tip fitted to an arrow.
xub vos An arrow with a metal tip (clf. 'xib').

2. vos To eat picking out one kind of food from the others in a common pot (e.g. eating only the meat from a stew).

3. vos lub vos hav A broad level valley.

4. vos A restricted post verbal intensifier (cf. Appendix 8).
caws vos Crouched together.
phom nrov nta vos Sound of a gunshot.

vov To cover, to cover over, to roof over.
vov tsev To put the roof on a house.
vov pam To cover with a blanket.
vov (or) kauv taubhau To cover the head.

voob muab av voob rau To cover over with earth.
Note: This word is uncommon (cf. 'faus').

voom A board fixed with a handle and used as a pusher for leveling ground or spreading earth (e.g. as when preparing the site for a house) (cf. 'rab').

voos Of a wound that festers again after having begun to heal.
mob voos The sore has festered again.

vub A refining pot or crucible (lub).
yeejvub Crucible for refining or melting silver.

vus Restricted post verbal intensifier after 'ci.' (cf. Appendix 8).
ci vus A great brightness in one place, a flash.

vuv Small crescent-shaped rice harvesting instrument that fits into the palm of the hand and having a short flat blade set in wood. (clf. 'rab').

1. vuab
(a) vuabkib Turtle (tus) (cf. 'vaub').
(b) vaubkib Turtle (tus) (cf. 'vaub').

2. vuab vuab tsuab Dirty (cf. 'txab' and 'ceb').

3. vuab vuab thawj Spatula used in opium smoking. (cf. 'yeeb').

4. vuab dej vuab The water flows around an obstruction.

1. vuag A very short time, an instant.
ua ib vuag dua Passed by in an instant.

2. vuag To grab in haste for something to prevent oneself from falling.
nws vuag hmab He quickly grabbed a vine.

vuas Shingles or tiles (clf. 'daim').
vuas ntoo Wooden shingles.
vuas luaj Tiles.

1. vwb nees vwb A black horse.

2. vwb vwb yeej Mercury, quicksilver.

1. vwj One of the Hmong clan surnames.

2. vwj Kuv tsis vwj nws txheej I won't forget his kindness.

vwm Insane, dispossessed of the senses.
neeg vwm An insane person, a crazy man.
vwm cawv "Crazy" drunk.
vwm loj vwm leg Reeling like a crazy man.

vws   A given name for Hmong men.

X

1. xa   To send (cf. 'fi').
Muab xa rau nws.   Send it to him.
(a) xa lus   To send a message.
(b) coj lus   To send a message.
xa nws mus   To send someone off on a journey.
peb hnub xa mov   Send food for three days (to the deceased.)

2. xa   To hit.

1. xab   Third, third in a series (C) (often used as a man's name).
los xab   The third child born in a family (C).

2. xab   phijxab   A large box for storage. (C) (cf. 'phij').

3. xab   Yeast, "mother" used for starting the fermentation in making wine and whisky, etc.

4. xab   raj xab   The bamboo tube leading from the windbox to the fire in a forge.

5. xab   hiab xab   A person's face (poetic).

6. xab   xabcuj   A tripod (C) (clf. 'lub').

xaj   lub tsev xaj   A courthouse, hall of judgment (T).

1. xam   To examine curiously, to scrutinize.
xam qhov xam qhov   Examined everywhere, looked all over curiously.

2. xam   To guess, to reckon, to figure out.
Kuv tsis txawj xam.   I can't figure it out. Can't guess.
xam hnub   To choose a lucky day (as for a burial or some special event).
xamphaj   To figure with numbers, to figure (C).
xam tsis pom   Can't see the future.
xam pom tom ntej   To see the future.
xam paub tom ntej   Foreknowledge, know the future.
(a) xam zoj   To reckon that...
(b) xam tias   To reckon that...

3. xam   neeg xam txeem   (cf. 'txeem' Definition No. 3).

4. xam   Coj nws mus xam.   Take him along to witness (the transaction or payment).

5. xam   tshuaj xam   Of medicine penetrating or circulating through the body.

1. xav   To think, to wish, to desire (cf. 'nyaj' and 'mem') (C).
Kuv xav mus teb.   I think I will go to the fields. (or) I want to go to the fields.
Kuv tsis xav mus.   I don't want to go.
Kuv xav tsis mus.   I think I will not go.
Kuv xav tias...   I think that...
xav tau lig   Too late, thought of it too late.
xav dheev   Suddenly thought of something.
xav tsis tawm   Can't think of it.

2. xav   An exclamatory particle, sometimes used with the idea of "No!"

xais   To pinch, to choke (not very commonly used) (cf. 'de').

1. xaiv   To select, to choose, to elect, to decide.
Xaiv cov zoo xwb.   Just pick out the good ones.
Yuav xaiv kiag.   You must decide.

2. xaiv   Gossip, rumors, idle tales.
lus xaiv   Gossip, idle talk.
taug xaiv   To gossip, to tattle, to spread rumors.
lis xaiv   Gossip.
neeg lis xaiv   A busybody, a gossip, rumor-monger.

3. xaiv   txiv xaiv   Funeral songs, songs of death.

xau To leak, to filter through.
    xau nag The rain leaks through.

1. xaub To slip down an incline.

2. xaub
    nruab xaub A pit trap. A bamboo covering is made
        over a pit near a game trail so that an animal
        coming along will slip into the pit onto
        sharpened bamboo spikes (clf. 'rooj').

xauj To peek at, to spy, to examine carefully, watch
        secretly.
    Nws xauj nkoos. He stooped to peek or examine.
    Tub sab nyas tuaj majmam xauj. The thief came and
        carefully spied (upon them).

1. xaus To finish off, to complete.
    (a) lus xaus Referring to particles, completives,
        etc. which are used to complete or round off
        the meaning of an expression.
    (b) lus tas Referring to particles, completives,
        etc. which are used to complete or round off
        the meaning of an expression.
    xaus tshoob The feast at the time of wedding festiv-
        ities thus finishing the wedding obligations
        (also 'noj tshoob') (cf. 'tshoob').
    lub pag lub xaus (cf. 'pag').

2. xaus
    koobxaus (lub) Gramaphone.
    phiaj koobxaus Gramaphone records.

1. xauv To lock, a lock (clf. 'lub') (cf. 'ntsuas phoo').
    xauv qhov rooj Lock the door (or gate).

2. xauv A neck-ring (clf. 'lub') (Worn by all Hmong and
        usually made of silver except for certain
        specified kinds as noted below).
    ib lub xauv One silver neck-ring.
    xauv siav The "life ring" This is the one ring worn
        by all Hmong since early youth and regarded as
        "locking" the life into the body ('xauv yus txoj
        siav').
    ib phiaj xauv A set of silver neck-rings.
    xauv keev Solid neck-ring.
    xauv khoob Hollow neck-ring.
    khawb xauv A clasp on the back of the neck-ring.
    (a) lub xauv hlau The twisted spirit ring made of
        steel, silver, and copper wire strands and
        worn to ward off evil spirits.
    (b) lub xauv dub The twisted spirit ring made of
        steel, silver, and copper wire strands and
        worn to ward off evil spirits.

3. xauv
    lub xauv nees The bit for a horse's mouth.

xawb To search through a lot of things to find something.
    npua xawb Pigs searching through rubbish to find food.

1. xaws To sew, to fasten by sewing, to sew clothing.

2. xaws
    cawv xaws Intoxicating liquor made half from 'nplej'
        and half from 'txhuv.'

3. xaws
    hau xaws The fontanelle on the head of a child.

xeb To rust, rust.
    xeb lawm Rusted.

1. xem Of a rough, coarse surface.

2. xem A class or a kind (cf. 'yam' and 'cov').

3. xem
    Nws plhu them xem. His "face fell." He lost
        color. (C).

4. xem
    hais lus plhov xem (cf. 'plhov').

1. xev To invent, to do without having learned or been
        taught.
    xev ua To do of oneself without having been taught.

2. xev To speak something merely thought up and not true,
        to lie.
    Nws lam xev xwb. He's just making it up.

1. xeeb To be born (C) (cf. 'yug').
    Yexu xeeb ua tibneeg. Jesus was born as a man.

2. xeeb To produce, to give rise to, beget (C).
    xeeb plaub To produce or give rise to litigation.
    xeeb menyuam To have a child in the womb, to be
        pregnant.
    Xeeb tub los tsis xeeb? Are you pregnant? (polite).

3. xeeb
    Note: 'xeeb' is the Hmong pronunciation of the Chinese
        word for 'heart,' regarded as the seat of the
        affections and in this sense equivalent of the
        Hmong 'siab.' It is found in many words involving
        the affections or mental activity and taken wholly
        or in part from the Chinese:

cimxeeb The memory.
fav xeeb To rebel, to turn against.
tshwv xeeb ua To "put your heart into it," to do
   with a will.
xov xeeb To thank, to offer gratitude (cf. 'xov').
yooj xeeb To try, to exert effort.
yuj xeeb "With all my heart" (especially in songs).
txhawj xeeb Worry, distress.
thooj xeeb Of one heart, in unity.
xeeb txob Worry, of unsettled mind.
mob xeeb txob Sickness and trouble.
xyov xeeb To be careful, timid.
neeg khoob xeeb "Hollow hearted," one ready to
   listen to others, teachable.
twm xeeb Impatient, short-tempered.
zam xeeb Patient, humble.
keev xeeb Pig-headed, heart closed to other ideas.

4. xeeb
   txiab xeeb Sickness

5. xeeb
   huabxeeb (lub) Peanut, the peanut(C).

6. xeeb
   teeb xeeb Lampwick (C).

7. xeeb
   phua kus xeeb (cf. 'phua').

8. xeeb
   cuab xeeb puj teem (cf. 'cuab' Definition No. 8).

9. xeeb
   xeeb poob Fell into (cf. 'poob').

10. xeeb
   xeeb ntxwv Grandchild (tus).
   xeeb lwj xeeb ntxwv Male descendents, grandchildren.
   xeeb mujmum Great grandchild.

xeem Clan, surname (cf. Appendix 3) (clf. 'lub') (C).
   Koj xeem dabtsi? What is your surname? What clan do
   you belong to?
kiav xeem To change one's surname, to change clans.
thov xeem The custom of asking a bit of cloth or
   silver, etc. of one from another clan so that
   the name of that clan will protect him. This
   is especially done for children after illness,
   etc. so as to gain better fortune. The child
   is then given a new name and a new surname.
   The silver is made into a neck ring or the
   cloth is sewed into a jacket.

1. xeev To wake up (cf. the Chinese) (cf. 'dheev').
   Nws xeev los. He woke up.

2. xeev
   xeev siab Nausea.

3. xeev
   xeev xwm To come of age.

xi
   puv ib tsug kaum peb hnub tos los xi To release
   the spirit thirteen days after death.

1. xib Palm, sole.
   xib teg Palm of the hand.
   xib taws Sole of the foot.
   xib khau Sole of the shoe.

2. xib Clf. for arrows (cf. 'xub').

3. xib To do according to the desires of another, to do
   as another likes (cf. 'xij').
   Xib koj. As you like.

4. xib To be pleased with, to approve of.
   Kuv tsis xib. I don't like it.
   xib rau nws Pleased with him.

5. xib
   daus xib daus npu Snow.

6. xib
   toobxib Goods, articles, things (C).

7. xib
   xibhwb A teacher (tus) (C).

8. xib
   xib txoob Palm fibre.

9. xib
   xib dub A species of bird (cf. 'dub').

10. xib
   cua moj lwg xib kaw A great wind (cf. 'cua').

1. xij According to the desire of another (cf. 'xib').
   Xij koj nyiam. As you like.
   xijpeem As you like (C), according to your wish,
   let it go at that (cf. 'ywj txiam' and 'dua'
   Definition No. 5).

2. xij
   Koj xij quaj tus dabtsi? Why are you still crying?

1. xim Small, fine (C).
   ua xim hum To do fine work (contr. 'moj hum').

2. xim
   khuvxim "What a pity!" "Too bad!" (C).

3. xim
   xyuam xim Careful (C).
   xyuam xim ua To do carefully (cf. 'twb zoo').

1. xis The right side, to the right, pertaining to the right.
   sab xis The right side (contr. 'lauj').
   sab tes xis The right hand, on the right hand.

2. xis To like, to enjoy (pertaining to taste, etc).
   Kuv tsis xis. I don't like it.

3. xis
   xisliv (daim) A straw mat, a sleeping mat (C) (cf. 'txum zooj').

4. xis
   xis zeej kib cuab (cf. 'kib').

xiv To simmer, to be on the point of boiling.
   Dej xiv. The water is simmering on the point of boiling.

xia A given name for Hmong girls.

1. xiab The waxing of the moon, used referring to dates in the first half of the month.
   hli xiab The new moon, the waxing of the moon.
   xiab ib The first day of the month.
   xiab ob The second of the month, and so 'xiab peb' etc. until the 15th.

2. xiab To elevate something by putting a block under it.

3. xiab Restricted post verbal intensifier after 'ntsuab.'
   ntsuab xiab Dark blue in color (cf. Appendix 8).

4. xiab
   xiab nyiaj xiab qhov ncauj To bribe.

5. xiab
   hav zoov nuj xiab Wild jungle.

xiam To spoil, to be ruined (T) (cf. the Hmong term 'puas').
   xiam lawm Spoiled, ruined (T).

xiav Purple, blue (cf. 'ntsuab').
   xiav tsaus Dark blue or dark purple.
   xiav txho Light blue or light purple.
   xiav lus Very purple, bright purple.
   Note: This expression is close to bad language and so 'xiav xiav' is used more commonly).

1. xo To bite, to bite down upon (of persons biting) (cf. 'tom' for animals biting).
   Txhob xo. Don't bit it.

2. xo
   xo nraim mus To go straight on (cf. 'ncaj').

1. xob A creature in the heavens supposedly responsible for thunder and lightning.
   xob quaj Thunder ('xob' cries out).
   xob laim Lightning ('xob' flashes).

2. xob
   (a) plaubhau xob vog Of hair "standing on end."
   (b) plaubhau sawv tsees Of hair "standing on end."

3. xob Unrefined gunpowder, saltpeter.

4. xob A full-grown uncastrated male animal.
   xob nyuj A bull.
   xob nees A stallion.

5. xob
   lub siab xob pes vog Scared, afraid of punishment.

6. xob
   nag xob nag cua A storm, a tempest.

7. xob
   pis pis qab xob Edible delicacies (e.g. cakes, etc.)
   Nej ua pis pis qab xob noj los? Are you preparing some delicacies to eat?

xom
   phojxom (cf. 'phoj').

1. xov Thread, string, wire (clf. 'txoj').
   xov hlau Wire (of iron or iron alloy).
   xov tooj Copper wire, a wire spring, the telegraph.
   ntaus xov tooj To send a telegram.
   lig xov Thread wound on a spool, sewing thread.

2. xov News, tidings, message.
   ntaus xov To send a message.
   fi xov To send a message (cf. 'xa').
   tus fi xov A messenger.
   coj xov To bear news, an intermediary.
   tshab xov (cf. 'tshab' and 'tshaj').

3. xov To fence, to enclose with a fence.
   xov ib lub vaj To fence in a garden.
   xov lajqab To erect a fence.

4. xov
   xovdawb A people, a populace (somewhat archaic
      language) (cf. 'pejxeem').

5. xov
   xov tshoj Country or place outside of China (C).

6. xov
   xov muj tim (cf. 'muj' Definition No. 5).

7. xov
   xov dej To dam up, a dam (cf. 'dej').

8. xov
   loj xov cem huvsi (cf. 'cem').

9. xov xeeb To thank, to offer gratitude (only used in
      being especially polite as when visiting those
      at some distance, etc.)

xoo Thumb or big toe.
   ntiv tes xoo Thumb (tus).
   ntiv taw xoo Big toe (tus).

1. xoob Loose, loose fitting, of something easing off
      (C) (contr. 'ceev').

2. xoob Not forcibly.
   hais xoob To speak not forcibly, restrained speech
      (contr. 'hais ceev').

xooj Surprised, startled (cf. 'ruaj zog' and 'yoob zog').
   xooj les Surprised, startled, amazed.

1. xoom A word used in vile language and therefore to be
      avoided.

2. xoom
   phom luvxoom (rab) A shotgun (T).

1. xu To miss the mark.
   xu siab Don't like it (cf. 'tsis nyiam').
   xu kev Off the road, not directly on the path.
   xu lawm Missed the mark.

2. xu
   (a) ua chov An evil omen, to be marked for evil.
   (b) ua npog An evil omen, to be marked for evil.
   (c) ua xu An evil omen, to be marked for evil.

1. xub Previous, before in order of time, first.
   Nws xub tuaj. He came first (before the others).
   Cia nws xub them nyiaj, kuv mam li muab rau nws.
      Let him pay first and then I will give it to him.

2. xub An arrow (clf. 'xib').
   xub vos An iron or steel tipped arrow.
   xub tshuaj A poisoned arrow.

3. xub An animal lair or den, a hive (in or on the ground
      or in a hollow tree, etc. Not a nest built of
      twigs, etc.) (cf. 'zes').

4. xub
   xub pwg Shoulder (lub).

5. xub
   xubntiag (lub) Chest, bosom, front surface.

6. xub
   xub txig Cheekbone (lub).

7. xub
   hav xub tsuag An uninhabited area of scrub vegetation.

xuj
   los nag xuj xuav A light rain.

1. xua Bran (contr. 'npluag').
   xua nplej Rice bran.
   lub vab tshaus xua A sieve to sift out the bran.

2. xua
   ua xua To have an itchy rash.

xuab To rub together, to rub along.
   xuab tes To rub the hands together.
   xuab hlua To twist string or rope (between the hands
      or with the hand against the leg, etc.)
   xuab taw To drag the feet.
   xuab taw rhuav To drag the feet slowly.
   xuab taw hluj hluav To drag the feet, to delay in
      taking action.

xuam Waste, garbage, refuse.

1. xuas To feel, to grope.
   xuas mem tes To take the pulse (cf. 'seev').

2. xuas To take hold of, to make use of.
   xuas phom tua To kill with a gun, take a gun and kill.
   xuas pobzeb txawb Pick up stones to throw.
   xuas tau keeb Got hold of the root of things.

3. xuas
   tsev xuas luas A shelter or rest house (T) (lub).

1. xuav Of loose or coarse ground.
   av xuav Loose ground with small stones.
   zeb xuav Coarse sand (cf. 'suab zeb').

2. xuav
   los nag xuj xuav A light rain.

3. xuav
   xuav kauv Whistling.

xw To scoop up, to scoop out (e.g. to scoop earth out of a pit or to scoop rice out of the bowl or a rice mill).

1. xwb Completive particle used at the end of an expression to indicate "singly," "only," "that is all," "simply that," etc.
   Kuv muaj ib tug xwb. I only have one.
   Kuv tsis paub xwb. I simply don't know.

2. xwb
   xwbfab To make a living, have a livelihood.
   tsis pom qab xwbfab Don't know how to make a living.
   ua nplej xwbfab To raise rice for a living.

3. xwb kuab (lub) (cf. 'kuab').

1. xwm
   (a) xwmkab (tus) The spirits of wealth and possessions that protect the household. They are represented by a paper on the wall of the uphill side of the house and between the 'qhov txos' and the spirit shelf. (cf. 'dab' p. 27) The paper on the wall is itself often called the 'xwmkab.' (also 'dab xwmkab').

2. xwm To come of age.
   xeeb xwm To come of age.

3. xwm To take care of, care for, to prepare, to get ready for (cf. 'tsomkwm').
   hwjxwm

4. xwm
   xwmfab Square, four-sided (C), a square (lub).
   xwbfab puajmeem In every direction (C).

5. xwm
   txhiam xwm Garden vegetables (as opposed to field crops).

6. xwm Matter, affairs, things (C).
   yam hauj yam xwm Things (C).
   muaj xwm To have business, to have affairs.
   Muaj xwm dabtsi? What's up? What's your business?

7. xwm
   kavxwm (tus) (cf. 'kav').

8. xwm
   Nws xwm tsis xyaj. He's gotten into trouble (round-about speech).

9. xwm
   cov noj xwm Leaders, elders, wisemen (C).

10. xwm A given name for Hmong men.

xws
   xws li As, like (cf. 'yam li').
   (a) Ib tug zoo xws ib tug. One is as good as another.
   (b) Ib tug zoo xws li ib tug. One is as good as another.

1. xwv To put (fruit, etc.) aside to ripen artificially as in rice chaff in a warm place.
   xwv txiv tsawb To ripen bananas in rice chaff.

2. xwv
   Kuv tias xwv koj hais. I respect what you say.
   Kuv tias xwv koj txawj. I respect your ability.

3. xwv To comfort or pacify a child.
   xwv menyuam To pacify the child, e.g. to cover the child so it will sleep.

4. xwv Used in combination with 'kom' ('kom xwv') to mean "to cause or to bring into effect. (cf. 'kom').

5. xwv
   xwv pov To put things aside.
   neeg xwv pov A thrifty person, one wise in the use or saving of money.

6. xwv
   neeg xwv khawv One who doesn't say much but whose words are worthwhile (cf. 'khawv').

7. xwv
   xwv xyem The waxy covering on a newborn infant.

XY

1. xya Seven, the number seven.
   xya tus Seven persons.

2. xya Of animals giving birth to their young (contr. 'yug') (C).

1. xyab Incense (C).
   hlawv xyab To burn incense (cf. 'sam').

2. xyab To expand, stretch out, extend.
   xyab tes To extend the hand.
   xyab nriav Stretched out flat.

xyaj Nws xwm tsis xyaj. He's gotten into trouble. (round-about speech).

1. xyav xyav moo To spread a report.

2. xyav xyem xyav (cf. 'xyem').

xyaum To follow, to imitate, to obey (e.g. laws, etc.) (cf. 'khws'), to study (C).
   Ua li cas koj tsis xyaum kev? Why don't you obey the law (or custom)?

xyaw To mix together, to mix ingredients (cf. 'tov' 'hauj').
   sib xyaws Mixed together (t.c.)
   xyaw keeb ncuav Cakes made with leaven or yeast, cakes with yeast mixed in.

1. xyem xyem xyav To know but be unable to think of how to say or express it.
   ua xyem xyav To hesitate between two decisions, to be uncertain what to say.

2. xyem xwv xyem (cf. 'xwv' Definition No. 7).

xyeeb To shove, to push (cf. 'thawb').
   xyeeb poob To shove and cause to fall.

1. xyeej Leisure, to have leisure time (cf. 'khoom') (In Laos the term 'xyeej' is not used).
   Kuv tsis xyeej siab. I have no time. I'm not free.

2. xyeej To despise, to slight or disparage, to disdain.
   hais lus xyeej lawv To speak disparagingly of them.
   Nej xyeej txhem peb. You despise us. You look down upon us.

1. xyeem To sacrifice, to offer as a sacrifice.
   xyeem rau dab To offer a sacrifice to the spirits.

2. xyeem khaws xyeem (cf. 'khaws').

xyiv xyivfab To be happy, to enjoy, happy (C).

xyo Given name for Hmong girls.

xyob To push, to put to flight (cf. 'thawb' and 'xyeeb').
   xyob pov tseg To push out, to chase out, get rid of.

xyom To reverence, to worship.
   Note: This is specifically used of the worship offered to deceased parents when male descendents bow and offer incense, etc. It may be used of reverence for living persons and of worship toward God.
   Xyom niam xyom txiv Xyom ntuj thiaj tau ntuj ntoo.
   thiaj tau zoo. Reverence heaven and heaven will provide trees. Reverence your parents and you will prosper.

1. xyov A particle indicating uncertainty. Used in answer to questions or before an expression indicating uncertainty and used either by itself or with a completive particle.
   (a) Xyov. I don't know.
   (b) Xyov as. I don't know.
   Xyov nws yuav mus tsis mus. I don't know whether he is going or not.

2. xyov xyov xeeb To be careful (C), to be timid or of a fearful heart.

xyoo A year.
   ib xyoos One year (t.c.)
   xyoo no This year.
   lwm xyoo Next year.
   ciaj no Last year.
   ciaj ub Two years ago.
   puag caib ub Several years ago.
   tsis tau txwm xyoo Not yet a year old.
   txhiab niag tim puas xyoo Hundreds and thousands of years (C).

1. xyoob Bamboo (clf. 'tus' for a single length) (there are many varieties of 'xyoob.' We list only a few.)
   ib txoog xyoob One clump of bamboo.
   xyoob iab A bitter and inedible type of bamboo.
   xyoob ntxhw Giant bamboo.

ntsuag xyoo Bamboo sprouts.
tsib xyoob The cluster of branches at a bamboo joint.
xyoob puaj tsw tsev Green split bamboo for the walls
    of a house, etc.

2. xyoob
    timxyoob (cf. 'tim' Definition No. 10).

3. xyoob
    phab xyoob (cf. 'phab').

xyooj Sexually active (whether of persons, animals or birds).
    Qaib tsis xyooj. The chicken is not sexually active.
    (The rooster does not approach the hens.)

xyoos T.c. from 'xyoo.' (cf. 'xyoo').

1. xyu To sigh or to give a whispered whistle.

2. xyu
    raj puab raj xyu Trumpets and horns (of bamboo and
        buffalo horn).

3. xyu T.c. from 'xyuv'. (cf. 'xyuv').

xyum Given name for Hmong men or boys.

xyuv A thick clump or area of leaves in a tree. Similar to
    'ntxhov.'
    ib xyu One clump of leaves (t.c.)

1. xyuam
    xyuam xim Carefully (cf. 'twb zoo').
    xyuam xim ua To do carefully.

2. xyuam
    xyuam txaum Impolite, seeking more than is offered,
        etc.

xyuas To visit, to pay a call.
    Nws mob. Mas koj puas mus xyuas? He's ill. Will you
        go to visit him?

xyw Ghost, the spirit of a deceased person which returns
    to the place of the death to trouble the living.

1. ya To fly.
    ya plaws To suddenly fly off.
    khiav ya ntxiag To suddenly depart.
    hnyav ya (cf. 'hnyav').
    hnub qub ya Meteor or falling star (cf. 'hnub'
        Definition No. 4).

2. ya Clf. for lengths of firewood, lengths of bamboo, etc.
    (contr. 'yas').

yab
    sib yab sib yaum To urge, to persuade, to try to get
        others to agree on action.
    siab ua yab ua yaum Of a double heart, to do something
        without putting the heart into it.
    Note: This is sometimes said 'saib ua yab ua yauv"

yag T.c. from 'yas' (cf. 'yas').

1. yaj To melt, melted.
    yaj lawm Melted.

2. yaj To disappear.
    yaj qas ntsuav Suddenly disappeared.

3. yaj To winnow.
    yaj nplej To winnow rice (by pouring the grain from
        a height for the wind to blow the chaff away).

4. yaj Sheep (clf. 'tus'). (C).
    tus yaj ntxwv The sheep (one sheep).
    tus menyuam yaj The lamb.

5. yaj Medicine (T).
    yaj yeeb Opium.

6. yaj
    yajhauv Matches (C).

7. yaj
    qos yaj ywv The white potato (C).

8. yaj
    yaj yuam (tus) The peacock.

9. yaj
    yeeb yaj (lub) A telescope or field glasses.

10. yaj
    yaj them Tin, galvanized iron.

11. yaj
    yeeb yaj kiab The abode of the dead.

12. yaj
    nuam yaj To bend the head backward and look around.

13. yaj
    nyob saum yaj Upon the earth, pertaining to this
        life (from the 'yang' and 'ying' concept
        in Chinese) (cf. 'yeeb' Definition No. 7).

14. yaj
    tw yaj pobkws Corn tassels.

yam Kind, sort, variety (C).
    (a) ib yam Of one kind, the same, one variety.
    (b) ib yam nkaus Of one kind, the same, one variety.
    Note: The expression "of one kind, the same" is often
        conveyed with the use of 'li.' Thus:
        (a) ib yam li Of one kind, the same.
        (b) ib yam nkaus li Of one kind, the same.
        (c) tiv yam li Of one kind, the same.

2. yam
    yam li no This kind, in this way, like this (cf.
        'xws li').

3. yam
    yam ntxwv A type, a likeness, an example, a symbol (C).

4. yam
    haj yam (cf. 'haj' Definition No. 2).

5. yam
    yam hauj yam xwm Things (C).

6. yam
    pej yam lus A foreign language, strange speech.

1. yas A joint, a section, a length.
    yas npab Elbow.
    yas tes Knuckle.
    yas taw Toe joint.

2. yas Clf. for sections or lengths (e.g. sugar cane,
        bamboo, etc.)
    ib yag kab tsib One length of sugar cane (t.c.) (cf.
        'ya').

3. yas (cf. 'nplej').

4. yas
    qhua tauj yas ob cag peb txhais Persons not of the
        same clan. (cf. 'qhua').

yav A time, a period of time.
    yav no This period of time, now (these few days).
    yav thaum ub Long ago.
    yav nram ntej Previously.
    yav tom qab Afterward.

1. yaig Smooth, of a surface worn smooth (e.g. a smooth
        rock or a smooth shoe sole, etc.)

2. yaig Pertaining to the spirits.
    ua neeb ua yaig To do spirit worship.
    cwj neeb cwj yaig The bell used in calling the
        spirits.

1. yaim To lick, to suck something in the mouth (e.g. a
        candy, etc.)

2. yaim Exclamatory particle.
    Yaim (or 'yaid'), ntshai kuv txiv sawv pauj. Gracious,
        I'm afraid my father has risen!

3. yaim
    mob kab yaim A skin disease of animals.

yau Small, younger in age (contr. 'hlob') (cf. 'yaus').
    Nws yau kuv. He's younger than I.
    yau yau li Quite young, quite small.
    siab ntaus yau Pessimistic, "small in heart," always
        expecting the worst.

yaug To rinse.
    yaug tes To rinse the hands.
    yaug qhovncauj To rinse out the mouth.

yauj Exclamatory particle.
    Au yauj! Gracious:

1. yaum To urge, to persuade, to try to get others to agree
        to act.
    Sib yab sib yaum To try to persuade one another.
    siab ua yab ua yaum (or 'yauv') (cf. 'yab').

2. yaum
    yaum dab Term used by a woman for her male cousins
        of a different surname (cf. 'yawm').

1. yaus Younger in age (cf. 'yau' which is the tone in
        which this word is most often found).
    menyuam yaus Young children.
    me yaus 'This humble person' (a polite term often
        used when referring to the speaker himself).

2. yaus
    tus yaus yeeb An opium smoker.

yauv
  siab ua yab ua yaum (or 'yauv') (cf. 'yab').

yawb A syllable used by young people as vile language.

1. yawg To menstruate (cf. 'coj').
   yawg cev To menstruate
   Note: This is not very polite. 'coj khaubncaws' or 'yawg khaubncaws' is the more polite term.

2. yawg Paternal grandfather or paternal grandfather's brother.

3. yawg A term used in combination to indicate certain family relationships (cf. Kinship Charts Appendix 10).
   yawg laus Father's sister's husband.
   yawg cuas Father of a son's wife or a daughter's husband (cf. 'yawm').

4. yawg
   yawg ntsuag Widower.

5. yawg
   niag yawg A familiar term of address in referring to men, especially older men.

6. yawg This word is often used as a roundabout way of referring to another person if you don't want to use his personal name.

1. yawm A term used in combination to indicate certain family relationships through the mother, sisters, or wife. (cf. 'yawg' and the Kinship Charts in Appendix 10).
   yawm txiv Maternal grandfather, maternal grandfather's brothers or mother's sister's husband.
   Note: The term 'yawm txiv' is also frequently used by a man in referring to his father-in-law. This is not strictly correct on his part but in doing so he follows the term used by his children for their maternal grandfather.
   yawm txiv yawg Maternal grandfather's father or maternal grandfather's brothers.
   yawm dab Wife's brothers.
   yawm yij Sister's husband.
   yawm vauv Husband's sister's husband.

2. yawm To scoop up, to scrape up, to gather up.
   yawm tsev To scoop up the refuse from sweeping a house.
   yawm ntses To scoop up fish into a basket.
   yawm pheej lias Gathered up a level basketful.

1. yaws To take down, to disassemble, to gather in (e.g. clothing from drying, etc).
   yaws hlua To bring in the snares after trapping.
   yaws khaubncaws los tsev To gather and bring into the house the washing that has dried.

2. yaws
   nplooj yaws Of roofing leaves blowing up in a wind.

1. yeb To straighten (cf. 'ncab').
   (a) yeb kom ncaj To straighten (e.g. a rod or an arrow).
   (b) yeb kom yiag To straighten (e.g. a rod or an arrow).

2. yeb
   yeb vas To do poorly or in pretence.
   Nws yeb vas xwb. He's just fooling. (e.g. making a fuss pretending to be hurt so as to escape work.)
   Lam yeb vas li no. Let it go at that. (i.e. It's not durable or well done but never mind.)

1. yej A type of deadfall trap especially used to trap rodents or small animals and consisting of a slab of wood or rock triggered to fall quickly. (clf. 'rooj') (cf. 'rooj').
   cuab yej A trap especially used to trap rodents or small animals and consisting of a slab of wood or rock triggered to fall quickly.
   tus quam yej caws A type of trigger for the 'cuab yej.'

2. yej
   yej meem This expression is used in a similar way to 'txwm kav' as a preverbal to indicate action persevered in regardless of advice or warning (cf. 'txwm kav').
   Nws yej meem thov xwb. He just keeps on begging.

1. yem Used before the verb and repeated after the verb before the modifier in expressions such as "the...the better."
   Note: This word is often heard pronounced 'yim' also.
   yem sai yem zoo The faster the better.
   yem saib los yem zoo The more you look at it the better it seems.

2. yem
   kujyem (cf. 'kuj').

3. yem
   taum puaj yem (cf. 'taum').

4. yeeb kab yeeb (cf. 'kab' Definition No. 11).

5. yeeb yeeb yaj (lub) A telescope or field glasses.

6. yeeb yeeb koob Reputation, glory, honor (cf. 'koob').

7. yeeb yeeb yaj kiab The abode of the dead, the abode of
   the spirits and particularly of 'nyuj vaj'
   (cf. 'dab').

   Note: 'yeeb' refers to the world of the spirits or of
   the immortals from the Chinese 'yang' and 'yin'
   concept. (cf. 'yaj' Definition No. 13):
   (a) nyob hauv nruab yeeb In the spirit world or the
       world of the immortals.
   (b) nyob hauv dab teb In the spirit world or the
       world of the immortals.

8. yeeb
   tsis thaj yeeb Non-productive.
   lub teb lub chaw nyob tsis thaj yeeb A non-productive
   area of land.

1. yeeg
   (a) mob yeeg A kind of venereal disease with pussy
       discharge.
   (b) mob cas A kind of venereal disease with pussy
       discharge.

2. yeeg qwj yeeg (lub) A snail.

1. yeej Victory, to overcome, to get the better of, to win
   in an encounter, to have success.
   kov yeej To win, to overcome.
   kov tsis yeej Defeated, cannot prevail, cannot handle
   the matter successfully.
   ntaus yeej To win in a fist fight.

2. yeej Used after the verb or the verb and the negative to
   indicate whether the action is possible or whether
   prevented because of inability to rise to it.
   (cf. 'tau' Definition No. 3).
   Kuv yuav tsis yeej. I cannot obtain it. (because of
   some hindrance, e.g. lack of money).
   Kuv yuav tsis tau yeej. I cannot obtain it yet.
   Kuv noj tsis yeej. I cannot eat it. (I've eaten too
   much already.)

1. yeeb Opium, opium poppies, pertaining to opium.
   (a) yeeb Opium.
   (b) yaj yeeb Opium.
   haus yeeb To smoke opium.
   (a) tus haus yeeb An opium smoker.
   (b) tus yaus yeeb An opium smoker.
   yoo yeeb The process of breaking off opium smoking.
   thum yeeb To break off taking opium.
   tshuaj tsuj yeeb Medicine or other foreign matter
   mixed with opium before smoking so as to make
   the more expensive opium go farther (typically
   aspirin).
   huam yeeb To crave opium.
   ib kab yeeb A swallow or a smoke of opium, the
   amount taken at one time.
   Opium Cultivation:
   tseb yeeb To plant opium seed (broadcast sowing).
   nthua yeeb To weed the opium.
   hlais yeeb To cut the opium, cut the poppy pods for
   the milk to secrete.
   sau yeeb To gather in the raw opium.
   dob yeeb To weed the opium the first time.
   las yeeb To weed the opium the second time around.
   txaws yeeb To scatter opium seed.
   riam yeeb (rab) The knife used for cutting the
   poppy pods.
   Implements of Opium Smoking:
   yeeb tob Knife used in preparing opium for smoking.
   yeeb phaj The plate for holding the articles used in
   smoking opium.
   vuab thawj The opium spatula.
   pliag deg The piece of shell on which the opium is
   rolled before smoking.
   yeeb tseeb The long wire or needle-like tool used to
   hold the wad of opium while preparing for
   smoking.
   txws yeeb The small box used to hold the raw opium.
   teeb kublub The opium-smoking lamp (lub).
   lub kublub The opium pipe.
   Process of Opium Smoking:
   ntaus yeeb To roll the wad of opium in preparation
   for smoking.
   ntsia yeeb To put the wad of opium into the pipe.
   sub yeeb To soften the wad of opium over a flame.

2. yeeb Tobacco, cigarette (tus).
   luam yeeb Tobacco, cigarette (tus).
   haus luam yeeb To smoke tobacco.
   lub yeeb thooj Pipe for smoking tobacco (typically
   a section of bamboo used as a water pipe).

3. yeeb
   (a) pob yeeb (lub) The Adam's apple.
   (b) pob qa (lub) The Adam's apple.

3. yeej Originally, previously, beforehand, of old.
Note: Sometimes 'yeej' is used alone in this sense.
Nws yeej los tsis muaj. He never had any.
Kuv yeej los qhia nej tsis txhob hais dabtsi. I had already told you not to say a word.

4. yeej Circular, round.
lub yeej A trench, a moat.

5. yeej (lub) A silver refining pot, crucible.
yeejvub (lub)

6. yeej kom (tus) The accuser, the person bringing a charge.

7. yeej Mercury.
vwb yeej

8. yeej (cf. 'cuab' Definition No. 2).
cuabyeej

1. yeem To agree to, to be willing, to admit (cf. 'kam' the Thai word 'nyoo' is also used).
Kuv tsis yeem li. I'm unwilling.
Nws yeem tias... He agreed that...
yeem lus A promise, to promise.
fiv yeem A promise of offerings to the spirits (cf. 'fiv').
pauj yeem To repay the promise to the spirits.

2. yeem A mark, a seal (clf. 'lub').
ntaus yeem To stamp, to mark with a seal.
(a) thuam yeem tes To take a fingerprint.
(b) ntaus taub teg To take a fingerprint.
thuam yeem To mark something, to make a mark.
lub yeem ntawv The official seal on letters.

3. yeem Unconscious
yeem tsia To faint, to "blackout."

4. yeem Clf. for layers of leaves in a roof.

5. yeem To measure (to measure quantity with a measuring vessel).

6. yeem tawv One who won't obey unless dealt with severely, obstinate.

7. yeem muag One who responds to patient instruction, pliable, teachable.

1. yees Pertaining to the main end beams of a house. (cf. 'tsev').
(a) yees tsev (tus) The main end beam of a house.
(b) yees nthab (tus) The main end beam of a house.
txhawb yees To erect the 'yees.'

2. yees P.v. intensifier after 'tus.' (cf. Appendix 8).
tus yees Settled, peaceful, at rest.

3. yees A craving, a habitual desire (as for drugs, etc.) (C).
Cov tshuaj no muaj yees tsis muaj? Is this drug habit-forming?

4. yees To quiver, to waver, move back and forth (cf. 'yoj').
ua yoj ua yees To quiver, to waver.

5. yees (cf. 'kwv' Definition No. 10).
kwvyees

6. yees ntxwv Tricks, magic (C).
(a) hwj huam yees ntxwv Magic, tricks (C).
(b) hwj huam yees siv Magic, tricks (C).
yees siv To do magic.

yeev Given name for Hmong girls and women.

yi Given name for Hmong girls and women.

1. yib Satisfied with payment or with the decision in settlement of a dispute, willing to accept settlement.
Yog nws tsis yib mas yuav ua li cas? What shall we do if he will not accept the settlement?

2. yib yibvim Because (C) (cf. details under 'vim').

1. yig To refrain out of politeness or to conform to custom.
Yig txoj kev txoj cai mam li noj. Only agree to eat after you have refused the invitation often enought to satisfy the requirements of custom.
Txhob yig yig. Don't keep on refusing out of politeness.

2. yig pheejyig Cheap, inexpensive (C).

3. yig T.c. from 'yim' (cf. 'yim').

1. yij A species of small wild bird similar to the quail. (tus).

2. yij yawm yij (tus) Sister's husband (cf. Kinship charts, Appendix 10).

1. yim The numeral eight.

2. yim To entreat with raised cupped hands, a gesture used in very formal greeting or in entreaty.
(a) ua yim To greet or to entreat with raised cupped hands.
(b) txaum yim To greet or to entreat with raised cupped hands.
txais yim To receive the greeting as above.

3. yim A household, a family (cf. 'tsev neeg').
(a) ib yig One household, one family (t.c.)
(b) ib tse neeg One household, one family (t.c.)
yim no This family.

4. yim To baste or to tack in sewing.

5. yim sai yim zoo (cf. 'yem' and 'txus').

6. yim (cf. 'tuam' Definition No. 5).
tuam yim

7. yim "The more," more so (cf. 'keem' and 'haj yam').
Yim tav lawv, mas lawv yimhuab qhia kev. The more they were hindered the more they preached.
yimhuab tsis zoo More evil, worse.
yimhuab zoo dua Much better.

8. yim yoojyim Easy (C).

9. yim leej An expression similar to 'txhiaj khoov' and conveying the idea "it would be better if..." (cf. 'txhiaj' Definition No. 4).
(a) Yim leej txhob yug los. It would be better if (he) hadn't been born.
(b) Txhiaj khoov txhob yug los. It would be better if (he) hadn't been born.
(a) Yim leej ua li Done without knowledge or forsight (i.e. If I had known I would not have done it.)
(b) txhiaj khoov ua li. Done without knowledge or forsight (i.e. If I had known I would not have done it.)

1. yis A given name for Hmong men and boys.

2. yis Siv Yis (cf. 'siv').

3. yis A cowlick, a tuft of hair turned up or growing out of pattern (clf. 'lub').
Note: A 'yis' on a horse is given a name according to the location and significance is attached accordingly.
lub yis tshaib plab 'yis' in abdominal region.
lub yis qheb qhov rooj 'yis' on the front legs (conveying fear of sickness or loss of money).
lub yis cwg kua muag 'yis' under the eye. (will bring death and tears).
lub yis txob plaub 'yis' on the navel (brings fear of court cases and disputes).
lub yis thoob khib 'yis' in the anal region. (brings fear of losing money).

4. yis
(a) pob av luaj An ant hill (lub).
(b) pob av muas yis tib An ant hill (lub).

yiv
yivtws A pigtail (lub).

yiag Erect, straight (of a tree or of a person's posture, etc.), straight-grained.
ntoo yiag A straight tree, tree with straight grain.
ntoo tsis yiag Tree with crooked grain that won't split easily.
yeb kom yiag To straighten (as a rod or arrow, etc.)

1. yias A round-bottomed, concave frying pan. This is the common type of cooking pan used in a Hmong home. A larger pan or cauldron of the same shape is used for cooking pig food, etc. (clf. 'lub').

2. yias To drive or to lead gently and patiently.

1. yob A given name for Hmong men or boys.

2. yob
Hmoob Yob Tshuab The flowery Hmong (or Miao) as known from China.

3. yob
dab yob tsov los tom Used of the spirits sending a tiger to bite someone.

1. yog The verb "to be," real, true, in conformity with the facts.
Yog. (in answer to a question) Yes. That is so.
Yog los maj. Common form of emphatic agreement. Yes!
yog tias... That is to say...
Yog kuv. It is I.

2. yog
  ua yog yoog toog To have a vision.

yoj To swing from side to side, to wave, to quiver.
  yoj hluavtaws To swing or wave a burning stick to light the way in the dark.
  ua yoj ua yees To waver or to swing from side to side (e.g. a branch shaking or swinging).

1. yom A completive particle used at the end of a sentence or expression when an affirmative answer is known or expected.
  Txujkum nyob taus yom? How can he stay?
  Nws yuav tsis mus yom? He's not going is he?

2. yom
  yom ceev Important (C).

yos To visit, to stroll or wander about (cf. 'cuav').
  yos zos To visit other villages.

yoo To fast, to abstain from taking something.
  yoo mov To fast, to abstain from rice or food.
  yoo yeeb To refrain from taking opium (so as to break the habit).

yoob Subdued, startled, dazed, confused (cf. 'ruaj zog' and 'hab nuv tseg').
  yoob zog Subdued, startled, dazed, confused.
  yoob hais tsis tau lus los Dazed into silence, subdued and silent.

yoog To follow, to imitate, to resemble, to be like.
  Peb yoog lawv ntseeg Yexu thiab. We followed them in believing Jesus.
  Nws rov mus yoog luag zeej tsoom. He went back and followed all the others.

1. yooj
  yoojyim Easy (C).

2. yooj
  yooj xeeb (C) To do with the heart, to do heartily.

yoov Insect (tus).
  yoov tshaj cum The mosquito (lit. "the thin insect").
  (a) yoov mos dab The horsefly.
  (b) yoov tom nyuj The horsefly.
  yoov mos ntsuab The housefly.
  yoov qaib The gnat.

yub A seedling, a sprout for transplanting (contr. 'kaus').
  yub nplej A rice seedling.
  ua yub To plant seedlings.

1. yug To give birth to a child, to bear (of persons) (contr. 'xya').
  Hnub twg yug los? When was he born?
  Nws yug menyuam ntxaib los tsis yog? She bore twins didn't she?
  yug zog los To be born.

2. yug To rear, to raise, to keep and care for (cf. 'tu').
  yug nqaij To care for and feed.
  yus xav yug yus txoj A person wants to look after himself.

1. yuj To hover, to fly in slow circles like a hawk.

2. yuj A species of tree especially valued for use in making water buckets, etc.

3. yuj
  kum yuj (cf. 'kum' Definition No. 5).

yum
  yumsiv Hard plastic.

yus Used in place of the first person pronoun 'kuv' when politely speaking of one's self (similar to the English use of "one").
  Dab pheej tom yus. The spirits are always biting one.
  Yog yus tsis mus mas lawv yuav cem. If a person (I) doesn't go they will scold him.

yuag Thin, emaciated (for persons or animals) (cf. 'nka').

1. yuaj
  chivkeeb huam yuaj In the very beginning.

2. yuaj
  duas yuaj xyoob Bamboo sheath, the thin tough sheath around a joint of bamboo.

3. yuaj
  los yuaj (tus) (cf. 'los' Definition No. 11).

1. yuam To go astray, to make a mistake.
  yuam kev To go astray, to take the wrong path, to make a mistake, to be wrong.

2. yuam To compel, to incite to action against the person's desire (cf. 'txhib').
  yuam noj To force to eat.

3. yuam To clamp, to retain in place with force.
  yuam phab ntsa To clamp the side walls of a house in place with poles bound together.

4. yuam To pay bail, to give guarantee for.
   muab nyiaj yuam lawv To give a money guarantee for.

5. yuam tibneeg To photograph a person, take a photo (cf. 'thais huj').

6. yuam
   yuamsij (lub) A key (C).

7. yuam
   yuam nyiaj To pawn silver.

8. yuam
   yaj yuam (tus) The peacock.

9. yuam Exclamatory completive particle. Let me first go
   Kuv mus xyuas kuv tsev tso yuam! look at my house!

1. yuas To practice (e.g. to practice music, singing, reading, etc.)

2. yuas
   mob yuas Coma coming on as an illness gets more severe.

1. yuav To want or desire.
   Kuv tsis yuav. I don't want (it).
   Kuv tsis xav yuav. I don't want (it). I have no desire for it.

2. yuav Used as an auxiliary before the main verb to indicate intended action or the future tense.
   Kuv yuav mus. I am going to go. (or) I intend to go.
   Note: 'Kuv xav mus.' I desire to go.
   Thaum twg koj yuav ua koj tsev? When are you going to build your house?

3. yuav Used with 'tsum' or 'tau' before the main verb to indicate obligatory action, the imperative mood. (cf. illustration under 'tsum' and 'tau').
   (a) Koj yuav tsum ua. You must do. (it)
   (b) Koj yuav tau ua. You must do. (it)

4. yuav To obtain (and "to buy" if money is involved) (cf. 'mua').
   yuav pojniam To obtain a wife, to get married.
   tsis tau yuav Haven't obtained it.
   Kuv yuav tsis tau. I can't obtain it.

yuax Completive particle (cf. Appendix 1).
   Koj xub saib kuv lub tso yuax. Better look at mine first.
   Nyias yuav mus nyias yuax. Each go his own way.

ywb
   zaum khooj ywb To sit squatting on the heels.

1. ywg To throw or to scatter by throwing.
   ywg dej To throw or scatter water over something.
   ywg tshauv To scatter or plaster ashes (as done over a person who has taken an overdose of opium).

2. ywg
   phoojywg A friend (C), (clf. 'tus').

1. ywj As you like, according to your wishes, (often combined with 'txiam' for a more complete expression with similar meaning. Very similar also to 'xijpeem').
   (a) ywj sau Write as you like.
   (b) ywjtxiam sau Write as you like.
   ywj ua Do it if or as you like.
   ywj nyob Constantly at home.
   ywj mob Always ill.

2. ywj
   pav ywj (cf. 'pav').

1. ywm
   twjywm Quiet (cf. 'twj').

2. ywm
   kav ywm A kind of vegetable with wide leaves.

yws To mutter, to continue talking angrily, to scold (but not as harsh as 'cem').

ywv
   qos yaj ywv The white potato (lub) (C).

Z

1. zab Echo.
   zab teb To echo, echo.

2. zab To lie ('Zab' being the name of a legendary figure who lied a great deal).

3. zab Unsettled, fidgeting, changing position.
   ua zab ua zuav Unsettled, fidgeting, changing position.
   zaum ua zab ua zuav Sitting and fidgeting.

1. zag (t.c. from 'zaj') (cf. 'zaj').

2. zag Donkey (as pronounced in Laos) (cf. 'luav').

1. zaj A dragon (clf. 'tus'), hence, the legendary dragon-power that controls the waters and the rain.
   (a) zaj kab The rainbow.
   (b) zaj sawv The rainbow.
   zaj vij hnub Rainbow around the sun.
   (a) lub pas zaj A lake.
   (b) lub pas dej A lake.

2. zaj Clf. for sayings, speeches, poems, hymns chapters, etc. Also clf. for times as of sorrow or grief, also for litters of young. (cf. 'nges' and 'tshooj').
   siab mob ib zag One time of grief (t.c.)
   hu zaj no Sing this verse.
   zaj npuas A litter of pigs (t.c.)

3. zaj muaj zaj To keep on talking so that a person cannot get away.

1. zam Dressed up colorfully.
   ua zam To dress in beautiful clothing.
   ua zam sees To dress lavishly.
   (a) tseev zam sees To dress up in lavish style or in one's best.
   (b) tseev zam ntxiag To dress up in lavish style or in one's best.
   tu zam To wash and clothe the deceased (cf. 'tuag').

2. zam To pass on the road going in opposite directions. To give way for an oncomer to pass on the trail or road.
   zam kev To give way for an oncomer to pass on the trail or road.
   tsis muaj chaw zam No way to get around it, no way out without meeting it.
   zam txim To escape punishment for sin, to "get around" sin.
   zam tsis tau li Can't get around it (can't escape punishment for sin).

3. zam
   (a) zam xeeb A patient heart (C).
   (b) siab zam A patient heart.
   siab zam taus lus Meek, unresentful.

1. zas To dye.

2. zas
   sib zas sib zas Of animals or fowl making as if to fight one another but before making contact.

zaig To wear down by rubbing or chafing (e.g. articles worn by a rope rubbing, also of wood turned in a lathe).

1. zais To conceal or hide something.
   zais siab To conceal one's feelings.
   lo lus zais A verbal secret.
   muab zais cia Hide it away.

2. zais The bladder (clf. 'lub').

3. zais
   zais plab Distended abdomen.

1. zaub Green leafy vegetation, especially edible vegetables.
   zaub ntsuab Leafy cabbage, mustard greens.
   zaub pob Head cabbage (lub).
   zaub kig Nettles, stinging vegetation.
   kim zaub To fry vegetables in a little fat.
   zaub looj pwm Radish.
   ua zaub To prepare or cook vegetables.
   zaub tsib Pickled green vegetables (mustard greens).
   zaub pos Sour pickled vegetables chopped up fine (mustard greens).
   zaub qaub Pickled cabbage.
   zaub paj Cauliflower.
   zaub txhwj qaib Parsley.
   zaub ntsuab dawb White leafy cabbage.
   zaub txoom A wrinkled leafy cabbage.
   zaub ceeb laug A slow growing type of leafy vegetable.
   zaub npluas roj A leafy cabbage with shiny leaves.
   (a) zaub ntsuab khaub hlab A variety of mustard greens with sawtooth leaves.
   (b) zaub ntsuab khaubncaws A variety of mustard greens with sawtooth leaves.

zaug T.c. from 'zaus' (cf. 'zaus').

1. zaum To sit.
   zaum ntua To sit down.
   rooj zaum (lub) A bench.
   zaum tsaws To be sitting down, sitting.
   zaum khooj ywb To squat on the heels.

2. zaum Sometimes a variant pronunciation for 'zaus,' a time. (cf. 'zaus').

zaus A time, a turn, an occasion.
  ntau zaus Many times.
  lwm zaus Next time.
  (a) qee zaus Sometimes.
  (b) zaus puav Sometimes.
  (a) txhia zaus Each time.
  (b) niaj zaus Each time.
  pes tsawg zaus How many times?
  zaus no This time (sometimes heard 'zaum no').
  zaus tom qab The time after.
  ib zaug Once, one occasion (t.c.)
  tej zaug On the other hand, other occasions, perhaps.

zaw
  mob plab zaw Cholera or dysentery.

zawg Together with 'ziag' a two-word restricted post verbal intensifier (cf. Appendix 8).
  los nag tshauv zawg ziag A drizzling rain.

1. zawj
  lub hav zawj An enclosed valley.
  lub qhov zawj A depression in the landscape with higher ground rising all around.

2. zawj
  Kuv lub siab tu ib tw zawj qos zog. "My heart skipped a beat." (cf. 'ntshai zog').

zawm To tightly wind around, to strangle (e.g. a parasitic vine strangling a tree, to tighten a rope on a tree or beam).

1. zaws To strip off.
  zaws nplooj To strip off the leaves.
  zaws ncau (cf. 'ncau').

2. zaws To massage.
  zaws plab To massage the stomach (cf. 'mos' and 'zom').

3. zaws Restricted post verbal intensifier combined with 'zom.' (cf. 'zom').

zawv To scrub, to rub, to rub with the hands in water (e.g. as in washing rice or washing clothes, etc.)
  zawv txhuv To wash the rice by rubbing it in water before cooking.

ze Near, nearby, close.
  Nws nyob ze ze. He is very nearby.
  Nyob ze kuv lub tsev. Close to my house.

1. zeb Rock, stone, stonelike.
  pobzeb (lub) A stone, rock.
  qhov zeb (lub) A cave in the rock.
  suab zeb Pebbles.
  lub zeb A grindstone.
  zom zeb To turn the grindstone.
  phiaj zeb A slate, a sheet of slate, sheet of stone.
  hmoov zeb Fine sand.
  hmoov zeb sib Chalk.
  txiag zeb A slab of rock.
  lag zeb A smooth surface of rock.
  ib ntxwg zeb A rock promontory, a jutting out of rock.
  zeb toob txuab A soft type of rock.
  txaug zeb To chisel stone, cut a grindstone.

2. zeb A restricted post verbal intensifier in combination with 'zuj'. (cf. 'zuj').

1. zeg Clf. for paddy fields. (cf. 'liaj').

2. zeg A litter while still unborn.
  tsis muaj zeg Not carrying a litter, of a female animal not pregnant.

zej
  zej zog Pertaining to the village (t.c.)
  yus zej yus zos One's own village.
  luag zej zog Other villages (t.c.)
  luag zej luag zos Other villages.

1. zem
  zem zuag Dim, dimly.
  tsaus zem zuag Dusk.

2. zem
  lom zem Noisy and crowded, commotion (C).

1. zes To light.
  zes lub teeb To light a lamp.

2. zes A nest (one built up of twigs, leaves, etc. and hanging separately. Not one in a hollow tree or in the ground. (contr. 'xub').
  zes noog A bird's nest.

3. zes Clf. for a nestful.
  ib zeg qe A nestful of eggs (t.c.)

4. zes To tease, to pester.
  Txhob zes zes. Don't tease (him).
  zes zes menyuam To pester a child.
  sib zeg To tease one another, to playfully fight (t.c.)
  Tsis txhob zes luag pojniam. Don't tease another's wife.

zev   A restricted post verbal intensifier used in combination
      with 'ziv'. (cf. 'ziv').

1. zeeg   To shed, of things shaken off by the wind, etc.
          Ntoo zeeg nplooj. The tree has shed its leaves.
          nplej zeeg Of rice shaken out of the hulls by the
          wind.

2. zeeg
   nraug zeeg muag Dizzy.

3. zeeg
   khauv zeeg cua A whirlwind.

4. zeeg   (cf. 'mej').
   tus mej zeeg

5. zeeg   A restricted post verbal intensifier used with
          'zoj.' (cf. 'zoj').

zeej   The Hmong pronunciation of the Chinese word for
       "man" and found in combinations derived from
       Chinese.

   thawj zeej (tus) Headman.
   tsoob zeej (tus) Middleman, intermediary.
   (a) tsoom zeej All people.
   (b) luag zeej tsoom All people.
   ib zeej tsoom neeg All persons.
   txwvzeej txwvkoob Ancestors.
   twm zeej Only person, one person alone.
   tus thiab zeej Child still in the womb.
   thoob zeej teb The whole earth, all men on earth.
   xis zeej kib cuab (cf. 'kib').

1. zeem   To admit, acknowledge, to give in (C).
          tsis zeem Won't admit, won't give in even after
          being caught and warned.

3. zeem
   zeem tsis tseeb neeg Can't clearly see people.

4. zeem
   zeem tsam   To show appreciation for, to be grateful
               (cf. 'tsam').

zib Honey.
   qab zib Very sweet, sweet as honey.
   zib muv Honey of the 'muv' (cf. 'zib me' and 'zib
   ntab').

1. zig
   khaub zig To encircle, to wind around (cf. 'khaub').
   Muab txoj hlua khaub zig. Wind up the string.

2. zig   A term used in winnowing rice in a winnowing tray.
         zig txhuv To shake all the rice together in the
         winnowing tray so as to bring the chaff to the
         surface. (contr. 'tsoov txhuv').

3. zig
   mob txeeb zig (cf. 'zis').

1. zij   Aslant, sloping, not vertical or straight.
         sau zij To write in a sloping script.

2. zij   To coerce, to drag someone into action against his
         will.
         Lawv zij nws mus ua nws pojniam. They dragged her
         away to make her his wife.

zim   zimtxwv (lub) A time, an hour (C).

1. zis   Urine ('pam' is clf. for a passage of urine).
         tso zis To urinate, to pass urine.
         mob txeeb zig (t.c.) Difficult to urinate, illness
                      characterized by difficult urination.

2. zis
   ruam zwb zis (cf. 'zwb').

ziv   Restricted post verbal intensifier combined with 'zev'
      and after 'quaj'. (cf. Appendix 8).
      quaj ziv zev The sound of pigs squealing.

zia   Sticky tree or vine sap, especially such as is used for
      trapping birds, etc.
      zia ntoo Sticky tree sap.
      zia hmab Sticky vine sap.
      txiv duaj zia Cling-stone peaches.

ziab   To dry in the sun.
       ziab pag tshaws (cf. 'nplej').

1. ziag   To tie, to bind.

2. ziag   Used by some persons in the same sense as 'tsam'
          Definition No. 1, a period of time consisting of
          several hours, a time.
   (a) zaus no On this occasion, now.
   (b) tsam no On this occasion, now.
   (c) ziag no On this occasion, now.
   Ziag no kuv nqhis dej. I'm thirsty (at this time).

3. ziag   Used in combination as a restricted post verbal
          intensifier.
          los nag tshauv zawg ziag Drizzling rain (cf. Appendix 8).
          quaj zuj ziag Sound of a cicada singing.

1. zias
   lauj haujlwm zias cia To put work deliberately aside.

2. zias
   sib zias Of animals fighting and biting one another.

ziav A bridge of branches used by tree climbing animals.
   ziav liab A place where two branches meet and used
      by monkeys as a bridge of communication.

zob
   zob xub To shave or smooth off arrows to make them
      round.

1. zog Strength, physical ability (clf. 'lub' for one's
      strength).
   nkim zog Fruitless, waste of strength and effort.
   poob zog To be discouraged, lose strength, lose
      heart.
   sib zog Energetically, to exert strength and effort.
   muaj zog txhab mus To increase in strength.
   muaj muaj zog Very strong.
   yoob zog Startled, amazed.
   nres zog To stand still.

2. zog Motion, movement.
   ua zog To move, to be in motion.
   Txhob ua zog. Don't move.

3. zog
   tsaug zog To sleep.

4. zog Unrestricted post verbal intensifier in the expression
      'tas zog,' similar to 'tas nrho' (cf. Appendix 8).
   zoo tas zog Excellent.
   Note: Used similarly following other verbs.

5. zog A restricted post verbal intensifier after 'qos.'
   Nws muaj siab qhia qos zog tiag. He really has a
      heart to teach (cf. Appendix 8).

1. zoj To tighten, to bind tightly, tight (as of clothing,
      etc.)
   Muab zoj cia. Bind it up and put it aside to keep.
   zoj nruas To put a skin head on a drum.
   zoj nees nra To tie up a horse load.

2. zoj Restricted post verbal intensifier with 'zeeg.'
      (cf. Appendix 8).
   ua zoj zeeg To do quickly or hurriedly.

3. zoj Restricted post verbal intensifier used after many
      verbs including the following:
   'xav,' 'saib,' 'hais,' 'nug,' 'fawb,' 'txhuam,' 'piav,'
   'teb,' 'nloog,' 'hu,' 'xam,' 'nco,' 'pam.'

1. zom To grind by rubbing two surfaces together.
   zom zeb To grind grain with a stone grindstone.
   zom hniav To grind the teeth together.

2. zom To chew the cud.

3. zom
   av zom zom Of deep sticky mud that clings to everything.

4. zom With 'zaws' a two word restricted post verbal intensi-
      fier (cf. Appendix 8).
   ua zom zaws Of many people doing something, each at
      the same time.
   hais zom zaws Everyone chattering.

1. zos A village (clf. 'lub').
   yus zej yus zos One's own village, of one's village.
   luag zej zos Pertaining to other villages.
   cuav zos To visit around the village (cf. 'yos').

2. zos Roundabout, not straight through, indirect.
   kev zos mentsis The road is a little roundabout.

3. zos
   (a) sib luag zos Similar, alike (cf. 'sib').
   (b) sib luag Similar, alike (cf. 'sib').

zov To watch, to tend, to care for, to look after.
   zov tsev To watch (look after) the house.
   Ua twb zoo zov. Keep careful watch.
   tus zov loog A jailor, a keeper.

1. zoo Good (contr. 'phem').
   zoo nkauj Beautiful, admirable.
   zoo dua Better, better than.
   zoo tsis cuag Not as good, inferior.
   zoo sib npaug Equally as good.
   zoo tas zog Excellent.
   ua zoo neeg To be a good person.
   zoo neej In good fortune, well-off.
   tsis zoo neej Not well off, poorly.

2. zoo
   twb zoo Careful.
   ua twb zoo Take care, be careful.

3. zoo T.c. from 'zoov' (cf. 'zoov').
   pcob zoo (t.c.) To be lost in the jungle.

zoog
   sib zoog Just sitting idle.

zooj Soft, malleable, capable of being moulded or formed (contr. 'nkig').
    zooj zooj li Soft, malleable.
    txum zooj (daim) A mattress.

zoov The jungle.
    hav zoov The jungle.
    poob zoo (t.c.) To get lost in the jungle.
    laj zoov The edge of the jungle.
    nruab zoo nruab tsuag In the jungle (t.c.)
    (a) hav zoov nuj txeeg Wild, virgin jungle.
    (b) hav zoov nuj xiab Wild, virgin jungle.

1. zuj Unrestricted post verbal intensifier (cf. Appendix 8).
    In combination with 'zus' indicating gradual action:
    deb zuj zus Gradually farther away.
    loj zuj zus Gradually becoming larger.
    In combination with 'zuav' indicating slow and delayed action:
    txav zuj zuav To move slowly and with delay.

2. zuj Restricted post verbal intensifier used in combina-tions indicating certain sounds (cf. Appendix 8).
    quaj zuj zeb The sound of pigs squealing.
    quaj zuj ziag The sound of a cicada singing.

zus Unrestricted post verbal intensifier used either singly or in combination to indicate gradual action (cf. Appendix 8).
    (a) loj zuj zus Gradually becoming larger (cf. 'zuj').
    (b) loj zus loj zus Gradually becoming larger (cf. 'zuj').
    ze zus ze zus Gradually coming nearer.
    siab zus siab zus Higher and higher.

1. zuag Pointed, to sharpen to a point.
    zuag cwjmem To sharpen a pencil.

2. zuag A comb (lub).

3. zuag Dim or dark.
    zem zuag Dim, dimly.
    tsaus ntuj zuag Dusk.
    tsaus zem zuag Dusk.

zuaj
    (a) zuaj plab To massage the stomach.
    (b) zaws plab To massage the stomach.
    (c) mos plab To massage the stomach.

zuam A tick (parasitic insect) (clf. 'tus').

1. zuav Dented, to dent, bent in, to have a depressed place. (cf. 'nluav' and 'hnlos').
    zuav lawm Dented.

2. zuav Post verbal intensifier together with 'zuj'. (cf. 'zuj').

3. zuav
    ua zab ua zuav Unsettled, fidgetting.

zwb Restricted post verbal intensifier with 'zis.' (cf. Appendix 8).
    ruam zwb zis Wide-mouthed, startled, amazed.

1. zwm To rely upon (as a populace relies or depends upon the king or ruler), to join in with, to belong to (as people belong to a political district for purposes of voting or taxation.)
    Peb zwm rau lawv, ua lawv pejxeem. We are of their political district.

2. zwm
    zwm rau hauv lub hleb To put into the coffin.

APPENDIX 1

PATTERNS OF TONE CHANGE IN WHITE HMONG

Tone change is a frequent occurance in Hmong speech
That is, whereas a word has a basic tone it may be said or
read in a different tone under certain circumstances. We
have attempted to describe this phenomenon below.

NOTE: The following analysis of tone change is presented
on the basis of all material available to date. There are
not a few exceptions to the patterns recorded. Very likely
further study will reveal a fuller and more adequate analysis.

A. Intonation and Stress

     Intonation and stress is superimposed upon the basic
tone pattern and may produce tone change. Illustrations
are many and varied. Change of intonation may be used to
convey surprise, anger, incredulity, etc.

     One very common illustration in this category is the
lengthened extremely high falsetto pitch often put on words
for very strong emphasis. This is especially found in
reduplicated words. Thus:

zoo <u>zoo</u> nkauj	very <u>very</u> beautiful
mob <u>mob</u> li	hurts <u>terri</u>bly
<u>puag</u> thaum ub	<u>long</u> ago
txom <u>txom</u> nyem	<u>terri</u>bly poor

B. Special Intonation - x

     We have lately discovered another intonation pattern
which we are indicating by the use of '-x' in the same way
as a tone mark. It may be compared with the other tones
in the tone chart of the Guide to Pronunciation. This
pattern indicates wonder or awe. As we have noted in the
section on orthography and pronunciation this is not a
tone phoneme in the same category as other tones but it
is symbolized in the same way as these tones for convenience. Illustrations follow.

444

Illustrations: (Special Intonation -x)

muaj ob lub diax	There are two!
koj xub saib kuv lub tso yuax	Better look at mine first!
yog li kuv hais ntag laux	Just as I said!
mus koj txog ntag laux	Went your way!
tsis dim li ntax	Won't escape!
tsis muaj li ntax	Haven't any at all!
kuv tsis ua kiag lix	I won't do it!
ciav mus tsis taus lix	How is it he cannot go?
ciav tsis muaj lix	How is it there are none?
koj tuaj lox	You've come!
koj ua lox	Did you do it?
koj hais lox	Did you tell?

If these sentences are said with the basic tones, they indicate a simple declaration or question and lack the element of surprise and wonder.

C. Conditions of Variation Between Tones -d and -m

As far as we can determine, the variation between tone -d and tone -m is governed by the following conditions:

1. A word with an -m tone precedes the word to which it is most closely tied grammatically.

```
Obtain  husband  from clan   Lee
 yuav     txiv   ntawm cov   Lis
```

Thus:

tamsim no	nram qab tsib taug
ib sim neej	nraum no
pem hauv dej	saum kuv taubhau
tim ntug dej	tom no
thaum ub	ntawm phab ntsa

2. A word with a -d tone follows the word to which it is most closely tied grammatically.

```
clf.  man  that   therefore   spoke  saying

tus  txiv  ntawd  thiaj  li    hais   tias
```

Thus:

  ob kwvtij ntawd   nyuam qhuav dua tod lawm
  hais li ntawd   mus sab nraud
  tamsim ntawd   nws nyob tid
  nyob ib sid   nws sawv tsees tamsid

In addition to the words listed under 5, Tone Chart:
Explanatory Notes (Guide to Pronunciation, p. xxiii
the '-d' tone also occurs on these words:

  pom, tshuam, lawm, cuabtam, menyuam, muam, niam

EXCEPTIONS:

    1. There are two classes of -m tone words.
        a. Those which sometimes take the -d tone
          (as above)
        b. Those which never take the -d tone. We
          have not yet been able to fully divide
          these two classes.

    2. There are a few cases where in parallel grammatical
constructions we find -d in one case and -m in the other
and which we cannot explain. For example:

let	the mother	with	you	go	also
cia	tus niad nrog	koj	mus	thiab

let	my mother	with	you	go	also
cia	kuv niam nrog	koj	mus	thiab

  Also cf.
    kev sib tshuam   lwm sim yuav pom
    nkawd luag zom zaws   nej twb paub lawm, mas...

3. There is one word ('nkawd') and perhaps a second word ('thwjtid') where the tone is almost always -d and only -m in special situations.

nkawd hais tias	the pair said
ua txij ua nkawm	to be married
cov thwjtid	the disciples
cov thwjtim ntawd	those disciples

D. Tone Change Brought About by the Proximity of Other Tones

A word or syllable with a high -b or a falling -j tone very often produces a change in the tone of the following word or syllable. This does not take place on every word and we have listed many exceptions below. Tone changes in this category are particularly noticeable in words preceded by one of the first five numerals all of which have a high tone.

Tones -b and -g may be regarded as dominant tones. They appear never to change, whereas all other tones may change according to the following patterns:

After a high tone -b or a falling tone -j

1. Tones: j, s, m   change to   g

2. Tone: v   changes to   ___(mid)

3. Tone: ___(mid)   changes to   s

4. No classifier (or noun used as a classifier) regardless of its own tone, affects a tone change in a following word.

Note: In addition to the exceptions listed after the illustrations, below we have found one other word that does not conform to the above rules. Thus:

zaum no	This time	qee zaus	Sometimes
ib zaug	Once	zaum puav	Sometimes
lwm zaus	Next time	txhia zaus	Each time
zaum tom qab	Afterward	niaj zaus	Each time
cuaj zaug	9 times	pes tsawg zaus	How many times

ILLUSTRATIONS AND EXCEPTIONS

ILLUSTRATIONS

Pattern 1. j - g

cuaj Nine.
xiab cuag Ninth lunar day.
daj 2 yard span.
ib dag One span of 2 yards.
  rau daj 6 spans of 2
     yards.
daj Yellow.
dej dag Yellow turbulent
       water.
taub dag Pumpkin.
dej Water.
nkoj deg Boat.
  qhov dej Spring.
kwj deg Gulley.
  dej hlob High water.
nruab deg In the water.
poob deg Fall in the water.
qab deg Downstream.
vuab kib deg Water turtle.
kaj (clf.) Batch.
ib kag zaub One batch of
  kaj zaub One batch
    of vegetables.
       vegetables.
leej Person.
ib leeg One person.
  leej twg Who.
cuaj leeg Nine persons.
  txhia leej Everyone.
tsib leeg Five persons.
lauj Left.
sab laug Left side.
  tes lauj Left hand.
liaj Paddy field.
laij liag Plow paddy field.
  ib lub liaj One paddy
yub liag Paddy rice sprout.
    field.
ncauj Mouth.
qaub ncaug Spittle.
  qhov ncauj Mouth.
ntxub ncaug To hate.
  lub ncauj Opening.
nkuaj Stable, pen.
rooj nkuag Door of the pen.
npoj Flock.
ib npog One flock.
nplej Rice (unthreshed).
teb npleg Rice field.
  ib teg nplej One hand-
noob npleg Seed rice.
    ful of rice.
paj npleg Puffed rice.
nplooj Clf. for liver.
ib nploog siab One liver.
nqaij Meat.
qab tsheej nqaig As tasty as
      meat.
ntuj Heavens.
kaj ntug Morning.
  saum ntuj In heaven.
rooj ntug Gate of heaven.
nruab ntug In the heavens.
ntiaj Strata.
ib ntiag ntuj One strata of the
  ntiaj teb The earth.
      heavens.
ntsej Ear.
pob ntseg The ear.
  qhov ntsej Ear canal.
ntsuj teb Portion of
ib ntsug teb One portion of
    field.
      field.
nyuj Cow.
nqaij nyug Beef.
roj nyug Beef fat.
xob nyug Mature bull.
nkuaj nyug Cow stable.
txiv plab nyug Jackfruit.

448

pluaj Clf. for split   ib pluag ncau One length of split
    rattan lengths.   rattan.
rooj Door, furniture.   ib roog mov One table of food.
                              dab roog Household spirit.
                              qab roog Lower side of table
                                  at feast.
txaj Bedroom.   rooj txag Bedroom door.
                              qab txag Under the bed.
txoj Clf. for road.   ib txog kev One road.
  txoj no This road.   cuaj txog kev Nine roads.
  txojkev The way.   tsib txog kev Five roads.
txaij Varicolored.   xyoob txaig Varicolored bamboo.
txawj Able.   tub txawg An able person.
txiaj Money.   nyiaj txiag Money.
txiaj 1/10 ounce.   ib txiag 1/10 ounce.
  rau txiaj 6/10 ounce.   cuaj txiag 9/10 ounce.
vaj Garden.   rooj vag Garden gate.
  lub vaj Garden.   qab vag Below the garden.
voj Circle.   ib vog One circle.
zaj Clf. for stanzas.   ib zag One stanza.
  zaj no This stanza.   cuaj zag Nine stanzas.

EXCEPTIONS

Pattern 1. j - g

yub nplej Rice shoot.   plab nyuj Cow stomach.
hnab nplej Rice hull.   hauv qab rooj Under the
qub nplej Old rice.   table. contr.'qab
ib leej A 'line' of houses.   roog' Lower side
ib lub qab ntuj no All under the of table.
    heavens.   ib phaj mov One plate
lub caij ntuj Season.   of rice.
ib kauj hlua One coil of rope. ib tshaj plaub A case at
ib ncauj hniav A set of teeth.   law.
pliag deg A small clam shell. ib thaj neeb A 'session'
mob faj Carbuncle.   of spirit worship.
ib ntxwj zeb An out-jutting rock. ib tshooj One chapter.
dob nroj To weed.

ILLUSTRATIONS

Pattern 1. s - g

ces (or ceg) Leg.   ib sab ceg One leg.
  ces npua Pigs leg.   ib ceg One leg.
  ces nees Horse leg.   ib txhais ceg One leg.
  ces no This leg.
cos Treadmill.   ncej cog Post of the treadmill.
  qhov cos The mortar   dauj cog Pestle of treadmill.
      of treadmill.
  cav cos Beam of tread-
      mill.
  taw cos Foot of tread-
      mill.

kaus   Fang, tusk.   tom ib kaug   Bitten once.
nkees   Lethargic.   ua dab tub nkeeg   To be lethargic.
ntses   Fish.   txaj ntseg   Fish trap.
                                  ntsaj ntseg   Basket fish trap.

las   Ounce.   cuaj lag   Nine ounces.
  kaum las   10 ounces.   ib lag   One ounce.
  xya las   7 ounces.   ob lag   Two ounces.
lus   Words.   paj lug   Proverb.
laus   Old.   nplej laug   Old rice.
                                  yeeb laug   Old opium.
                                  mob laug   Old illness.
                                  dab laug   Uncle.
                                  tij laug   Elder brother.
                                  kab laug sab   Spider.

plas   Clf. for an expanse.   ib plag teb   One large field.
  plas teb no This large
     field.
pluas   Clf. for a dose or   ib pluag mov   One meal.
     a meal.
tes   Hand.   xib teg   Hand.
  ntiv tes   Finger.   ib teg   One blow of the hand.
  txhais tes   Hand   dab teg   Wrist.
  co tes   Wave the hand.   npuaj teg   Clap hands.
                                  nkhib teg   Crotch of fingers.
                                  taub teg   Fingertip.
                                  ntxuaj teg   Wave the hand.
                                  thoob teg   Hand pail.

tus   Clf. for persons.   ib tug   One individual.
  tus no   This one.   cuaj tug   9 individuals.
  xya tus   7 individuals.   peb tug tub   Three sons.
tais   Cup.   ib taig   One cupful.
taws   Firewood.   tsheb tawg   Wood-burning engine.
txias   Cool.   dej txiag   Cold water.
vas   Net.   ib vag   One cast of the net.
vias   To swing.   ib viag   To swing once.
yas   Joint.   ib yag   One joint.
  yas tes   Knuckle.   cuaj yag   Nine joints.
zes   Nest.   ib zeg qe   One nest of eggs.
zes   Tease.   sib zeg   Tease one another.
zis   Urine.   mob txeeb zig   Difficulty in
                                        urinating.

zos   Village.   ib zog   One whole village.
  lub zos   Village.   zoj zog   Neighbors, villagers.

EXCEPTIONS

Pattern 1.   s - g

peb tus tub   Our son.   pobkws   Corn.
Saub tus tub   God's Son.   paj kws   Popcorn.
neb tus tub   Your son.   txoj qub lus   Old saying.

looj tes   Gloves.
ntiag tshos   Front edge of jacket.
nqaij nploos   Porcupine meat.
nqaij dais   Bear meat.

ib qais xov   1 skein of
   thread.
xyab tes   Extend the hand.
ib sab tes   One hand.
sib zas   Animals about
   to fight together.

ILLUSTRATIONS

Pattern 1. m - g

cem   To scold.
caum   10's in numeration.
  rau caum   60
  xya caum   70
daim   Clf. for flat ob-
     jects.
  daim teb   A field.
  xya daim   7 sheets.
kaum   Ten.
kawm   Back basket.

nkawm   Pair.
npaum   Same as, as much
     as.
nplawm   To beat.
ntim   Rice bowl.
     lub ntim   Rice bowl.
ntsawm   Forcibly strike
     with the hand or arm.
qawm   Friendly, show of
     affection.
riam   Knife.
  rab riam   Knife.

tom   To bite.
twm   Water buffalo.

yim   A household.
yim   Eight.
zaum   Occasion.
  zaum no   This occasion.

sib ceg   To scold one another.
peb caug   30.
plaub caug   40.
tsib caug   50.
ib daig teb   One field.
cuaj daig   9 sheets.

xiab kaug   10th of lunar month.
lub qab kawg   Under the basket.
ib kawg   One basketful.
ib nkawg   One pair.
sib npaug   Equal.

ib nplawg   One blow, struck once.
ib ntig   One rice bowl.

ib ntsawg   One such strike.

sib qawg   Show affection for each
     other.
roob riag   Back of knife.
ib riag   One stroke with knife.
tib riag   One stroke with knife.
sib tog   To fight, bite one another.
kub twg   Buffalo horn (this may
     just be poetic).
ib yig.   One household.
xiab yig   8th of lunar month.
ib zaug   One occasion.
cuaj zaug   9 times, 9 occasions.

EXCEPTIONS

Pattern 1. m - g

ncauj twm   Buffalo mouth.
nqaij twm   Buffalo meat.
ib pam quav   One passage of defecation.

ib ruam   One step.
mob ib phaum   One
     sickness.
ib phaum mob   One sick-
     ness.

ILLUSTRATIONS

Pattern 2. v - unmarked tone

cav Log.   qab ca Under the log.
  cav ntoo Log.
cev Body.   mob ib ce Hurts all over the body.
                               tawm ib ce hws Perspire all
                                   over the body.
cov Clf. for groups.   ib co One group.
  rau cov 6 groups.   cuaj co 9 groups.
chav tsev A room.   ib cha tsev One room.
diav Spoon.   ib dia One spoonful.
  rab diav Spoon.
hav Valley, expanse.   kwj ha Valley.
  lub hav Valley.   txhoj ha Shallow valley.
hov To sharpen.   zeb ho A sharpening stone.
hmuv Spear.   nkaug ib hmu To spear once.
  rab hmuv Spear.
hmoov Fortune.   txoj hmoo Fortune.
  hmoov zoo Good fortune.   muaj hmoo To have fortune.
hneev Crossbow.   tua ib hnee Shoot one bow.
  rab hneev Crossbow.   cuaj hnee 9 shots of the bow.
                               taub hnee Body of the cross-
                                   bow.
kev Way, road.   ncauj ke Mouth of the road.
                               kab ke Ceremony.
                               ua ib ke Together.
                               cab ke To lead.
                               qab ke Downhill side of road.
kwv Shoulder load.   ib kw One shoulder load.
  rau kwv 6 loads.   cuaj kw 9 loads.
kheev Clf. for small   ib khee One small bunch.
    bunches.   cuaj khee 9 bunches.
  xya kheev 7 bunches.
lev Bamboo mat.   ib le nplej One mat of rice.
ntav Half (vertically).   ib nta One half (vertically).
  ib nyuag ntav One half.
ntiv Finger.   ib nti nplhais One finger ring.
ntsiav pobkws Corn   ib ntsia pobkws One corn kernel.
    kernel.
ntshauv Head lice.   riab ntshau Small head lice.
phoov A handful.   ib phoo One handful.
plawv Heart.   plab plaw loj Clever, intelli-
  lub plawv Heart.   gent.
qhev Slave   tub qhe A slave.
  ib tug qhev One slave.
qhov Place.   ib qho One place.
  qhov no This place, here.
qhuav Dry.   liaj qhua Dry paddy field.
                               tebchaws mob sab qhua Dry area.
rev nplooj Flower stem.   ib re nplooj One flower stem.

ruv Ridge.   nqaj ru Ridge pole.
  ruv tsev **Roof.**   ncej ru Center poles holding up
                             the roof.

tauv huab A cloud.   ib tau huab One cloud.
tsev House.   ib tse neeg One household.
  lub tsev House.   kwj tse House drainage ditch.
                      nruab tse In the house.

tswv Master, owner.   ib tsw nqe Debt to the owner.
tshav Sunlight.   qheb tsha lawm Sky has cleared,
  tshav ntuj Sunlight.   sun has come out.
zoov Jungle.   nruab zoo In the jungle.
                    poob zoo To disappear in the
                         jungle.

EXCEPTIONS

Pattern 2. v - unmarked tone

nqaij tsov Tiger meat.   dej sov Warm water.
txoj siav Life.   dej sem so Warm water.
plev To sting.   ntuj tshav lawm Sunlight.
pub hmoov To give fortune. txoj kev Road.
ib txog sia One life.   ib ples One sting.

ILLUSTRATIONS

Pattern 3. unmarked tone - s

chaw Place.   tebchaws Country, land.
hlau Hoe.   ib hlaus One hoe (of earth).
  rab hlau A hoe.
hmo Night.   ib hmos One night.
  noj hmo To eat supper.
hno Rice.   noj hnos Eat rice.
  ua tau hno Make rice.
lo Clf. for words.   ib los lus One word.
  xya lo lus 7 words.
npua Pig.   zaub npuas Pig feed.
                    dab npuas Pig trough.
                    nqaij npuas Pork.
                    nkauj npuas Young female pig.
                    qaub npuas Small castrated boar.
nra Load, baggage.   ib nras One load.
nrau To butt.   nyuj sib nraus Cattle fighting
  nrau av To push up   together.
     earth.
  nyuj nrau Cows fighting.
ntu Clf. for period,   ib ntus One period.
     section.
  ntu no This period.

ntoo   Tree.

lub pob ntoos   Stump.
nreej ntoos   Flanging roots.
hleb ntoos   Coffin.
qab ntoos   Foot of tree.

ntxa   Grave.

rooj ntxas   Opening or door of
              grave.
toj ntxas   A hill with graves
             on it.

pa   Air.
  ua pa   To breathe.

hlab pas   Oesophagus.
caj pas   Throat.

pua   Hundred.
  rau pua   600.

ib puas   100.

ple   A sting.
  tus ple   A sting.

ib ples   A sting.

taw   Palm of hand or foot.
  kotaw   Foot.
  plam taw   Foot slipped.

xib taws   Sole of the foot.
pob taws   Ankle bone.
dab taws   Ankle.
luj taws   Heel.

tsua   Bedrock.

pob tsuas   Cliff, rock mass.
qab tsuas   Base of cliff.

tsho   Jacket.

hnab tshos   Jacket pocket.
dab tshos   Collar.
qab tshos   Low edge of jacket.

tshau   To sift.
xyaw   To mix.
xyoo   Year.

vab tshaus   Sieve, sifting tray.
sib xyaws   Mixed together.
ib xyoos   One year.

EXCEPTIONS

Pattern 3.   unmarked tone - s

xuab taw   Drag the feet.
xuab taw rhuav   Go slowly.
xiab rau   6th of lunar month.

kaj hli   Moonlight.
ntiag tshos   Front edge
              of jacket.
xiab xya   7th of lunar
           month.

ILLUSTRATIONS

Pattern 4. (No clf. or noun functioning as a clf. produces
           a tone change.)

ib lub liaj   ib tshaj plaub   lub ntim
lub ncaug   ib rab hmuv   ib thoob dej
ib lub zos   ib nkauj hlua   ib thoob roj
ntsuj teb   ib lub vaj   ib rab riam
ib phaj mov   lub kauj   ib ncauj hniav
                                             txoj kev

SUPPLEMENT TO APPENDIX 1

ADDITIONAL NOTES CONCERNING TONE CHANGE

We have described several patterns of tone change under heading D of Appendix 1. We have also noted that these tone changes do not necessarily occur on every word without exception. At this stage we have not discovered any rules which enable us to predict with certainty which words require tone change in the patterns described.

However, we do believe the evidence indicates that much depends on two factors: 1) the word class; 2) juncture. Thus the type of word in question and the closeness with which it is joined to the word preceeding or following appears to have bearing on whether or not a change in tone is required. Your attention is called to the following quotation:

> TONE SANDHI
> At the present stage of research, it would seem that sandhi changes occur when members of certain word-classes are joined syntactically, in what may be called "compounds." The following have so far been recorded: (Note that the first listed word-class of each group corresponds to the first element of each Meo compound given as an example.)
>
> 1. Numerals joined to classifiers: 'ob leeg' Two persons
> 2. Numerals joined to numerals: 'ib puas' One hundred
> 3. Nouns joined to modifying words (these latter being either Nouns or Verbs): 'teb npleg' Rice field
> 4. Autotelic Verbs joined to Nouns (as locative objects): 'poob deg' Fall in the water
>
> (The label "Noun" is here taken to include localizers, a subgroup of nouns which correspond to English prepositions, e.g. 'qab' Bottom or Under. The label "Verb" is here taken to include words corresponding to English adjectives, e.g. 'liab' To be red. An "Autotelic Verb" is a verb which may or may not take a noun object. In the latter case, the object modifies the verb.)

(The entire quotation above is taken from unpublished notes on a Phoneme tape made by Thomas Amis Lyman with the aid of the Green Hmong informant Cw Sa on May 21, 1963, in Kang Ho Village, Amphe Pua, Province Nan, Thailand and used by permission.)

While we believe this attempt by Mr. Lyman to describe Hmong tone change or tone sandhi is largely correct, we can hardly accept it as a fully adequate solution. In the material we have listed in Appendix 1, pp. 447-453 there are numerous illustrations of Mr. Lyman's four types of "compounds" but where tone change inexplicably does not occur.

Ernest E. Heimbach, 1964

APPENDIX 2

CLASSIFIERS

(followed by the words and classes
of words with which they occur)

cev   Suits of clothing.
cub   Fire.
cum   A group, a side.
cuam Lengths of leaves
      or thatch.
cha   Rooms of a house.
chib Periods of time.
chaw Lengths of cloth.
daj   Double arm's length,
      two yards.
diav Spoonsful.
* daim Flat things as
      fields, pages, etc.
fab   Divisions, sections.
hom   Kinds, sorts.
kab   Pipefuls of tobacco,
      opium, etc.
kob   Showers of rain.
kwv   Portion, part,
      shoulder loads.
kauj Coils.
kuam "Hand" of bananas.
khaw Mouthfuls.
* lo   Single words.
* lub Articles bulky or
      round.
lwj   Windbox bellows.
* leej Persons.
meem Layers of cloth.
maij Bolts of cloth.
* nkawm Pairs.
npaum Portions, times,
      fold.
nplooj Sometimes for
      liver, lungs.
nqes Verses, sentences.
nra   Packs (transport).
nrig Blows with the fist.
nrog Trayful.
ntiv Finger ring.
* ntu Time, period of few
      months, lengths of
      road.
ntwg Things carried on
      string or strip of
      bamboo.

nthwv Gusts of wind.
ntsuj Portions of a field,
      tract, lengths of road.
pab   Flock, group.
* pob Packets, lumps.
phoov Handful.
* phau Books, volumes.
phaum Season of rain, time
      of sickness, epidemic.
phiaj Sets.
plas Wide expanse.
* pluas Meals, doses.
qais Skeins of thread, rope.
* rab Scissors, knife, gun,
      spoon, chisel.
re   Stem of fruit, leaves,
      flowers.
rau   Squares of embroidery.
* tej Class, group.
tes   Blow, slap with the
      hand, sheaf of rice.
tom   A time, round, turn,
      section of road.
* tus People, animals, birds,
      things long or slender.
tw   Gusts of wind.
* tais Cupful, basinful.
tauv Clouds, clusters of
      fruit.
taus Unit of measurement.
tawb Piles of manure.
thaj Sessions of demon
      worship, groves, patches
      of vegetation.
thij Bunches of bananas.
thoob Bucketfuls.
thooj Sections of log, sets
      of headbands.
* tsab Letters.
tsig Number of times cock
      crows.
* tsob Plants, foliage.
tsw   Group, class.
tshaj Court cases, spasms of
      sickness.
tshooj Verses, especially of
      songs for the dead.

* txoj Series of words,   xem Kinds.
       thread, wire, rope,   xib Arrows.
       roads, arteries,   ya   Lengths of firewood,
       things that come in   bamboo, etc.
       lengths.   * yam Kinds, classes.
  txaum Brew or batch of   yeem Layers of leaves on
       whisky.   a roof.
* txhais Arms, hands, feet.   * zaj Paragraphs, speeches.

* Indicates the more commonly used classifiers.

APPENDIX 3

SOME HMONG SURNAMES

Yaj	Lis	Xyooj	Ham	Tsab	Muas
Vaj	Lauj	Thoj	Vwj	Hawj	Faj

APPENDIX 4

SOME USEFUL WORDS AND PHRASES

Personal Pronouns

	Singular		Dual	
1st Person	kuv	I	wb	We (two)
2nd Person	koj	You	neb	You (two)
3rd Person	nws	He, she, it	ob tug	Those two

Plural (three or more)

1st Person	peb	We
2nd Person	nej	You
3rd Person	lawv	Those few, them

Numerals

ib	- 1	kaum ib	-	11
ob	- 2	kaum ob	-	12
peb	- 3	nees nkaum	-	20
plaub	- 4	nees nkaum ib	-	21
tsib	- 5	peb caug	-	30
rau	- 6	peb caug ib	-	31
xya	- 7	tsib caug	-	50
yim	- 8	xya caum	-	70
cuaj	- 9	cuaj caum	-	90
kaum	- 10	ib puas	-	100

Words Describing Location

saum	Above	ntawm	There, nearby
hauv	Inside	tom	There, yonder
hauv qab	Underneath	tim	Across the valley
nraum	Outside	tom ntej	In front, before
nram	Down, down the hill	tom qab	Behind, after
pem	Up above, up the hill	sab xis	The right
qhov no	Here	sab laug	The left

Verbs

ua	To make, to do	hais	To speak
yog	To be	paub	To know
mus	To go	nyiam	To like
muaj	To have	yuav	To want
nyob	To reside	ntseeg	To believe
noj	To eat	mob	To be ill, hurt
nqa	To carry	ntxuav	To wash
tuaj	To come (to a place where one does not reside)	los	To come (to a place where one lives)

Descriptive Words

tsis Negative	luv Short	qes Low
zoo Good	hnyav Heavy	sai Fast
tseeb True	siab High	mam Slow
deb Far, distant	tiag Really	dawb White
ze Near	me Small	dub Black
ntev Long	loj Large	liab Red

Phrases

Koj lub npe hu li cas?	What is your name?
Koj mus qhov twg?	Where are you going?
Koj ua dabtsi?	What are you doing?
Koj hais li cas?	What did you say?
Ua li cas?	Why? How?
Kuv mus tsev.	I'm going home.
Mus ho tuaj.	Come again.
Koj tuaj los?	You've come. (polite greeting)
Kuv tsis paub.	I don't know.
noj mov	to eat
ua teb	to do field work
rov qab los	to return
Lus Hmoob hais li cas?	How do you say (this) in Meo?
Ua tsaug.	Thank you.

A Few Nouns

mov Cooked rice	ntxhais Daughter
nqaij Meat	pojniam Woman
zaub Vegetables	txivneej Man
teb Field	tibneeg Person
tsev House	ntiajteb World
lus Words	hluavtaws Fire
dev Dog	lub zos Village
qaib Chicken	npe Name
nees Horse	hnub Day, sun
npua Pig	ntoo Tree
ntawv Book, paper	roob Mountain
kev Road	riam Knife
tub Son	hluas nkauj Young woman
dej Water	hluas nraug Young man

APPENDIX 5

SOME USEFUL TERSE EXPRESSIONS

Cev nqaij daim tawv	This body, "the flesh," flesh and blood.
Cua daj cua dub	A high wind.
Cuaj txheej cuaj tis	Many generations.
Hav zoov nuj xiab	Dark wild jungle.
Hais cuaj txub kaum txub	To speak of all kinds of things.
Hauv roob hauv hav	On mountains and in valleys, everywhere.
Kev dab kev qhua	Ancestor worship.
Kev mob kev nkeeg	Sickness.
Kev neeb kev yaig	Spirit worship.
Kev ntsog kev ntsuag	Orphanhood, poverty, desolation.
Kev ploj kev tuag	Trouble and death.
Kev plaub kev ntug	Cases of justice, trouble with litigation.
Kev quaj kev nyiav	Sorrow, weeping, mourning.
Kev tshaib kev nqhis	Hunger and thirst.
Kev txhaum kev txim	Sin and guilt.
Khub khub dub dub	Dirty and mud encrusted
Khuam ntab khuam ntuv	Betwixt and between, caught between two uncertainties, can't really go either way.
Khuam xeeb khuam tshaj	Betwixt and between, caught between two uncertainties, can't really go either way.
Lam tau lam cem	Scold unreasonably.
Lam tau lam noj	Hang around and eat leftovers, etc. without a settled home life.
Lub siab tu ib tw zawj qas (or 'qos') zog	Scared.
Me nas me noog	Birds and small animals.
Nag xob nag cua	Bad rainstorm.
Noj dawb haus do	To be lazy, eat and drink without working.
Noj qab nyob zoo	Well off.
Neeg ciaj neeg tuag	The living and the dead.
Niaj tshaib yoo nqhis	Hungry and thirsty, cold and shivering.
Niaj no nkaug ntsim	Hungry and thirsty, cold and shivering.
Nplooj siab tsis qhuav dej	Discouraged, disheartened.
Nplooj ntsws tsis qhuav ntshav	Discouraged, disheartened.
Nram ntej nram ntxov	Previously.
Ntuj dub nciab teb tsaus nti	Sky and land all dark.
Ntuj txias teb tsaus	A place of cold and darkness.
Ntuj yuav fav teb yuav lam	Calamity is coming.

Ntshai ntshai ib ce tsaug tas	So afraid (he was) weak all over.
Nyob dawb nyob do	Doing no work.
Nyob dawb nyob huv	Well off.
Nyob tiaj nyob tus	Reside peacefully, live at peace.
Nyuj dab npua tai	Spirit ceremonies.
Ob pog peb yawg	Ancestors, predecessors.
Peb txheej peb tis	Great crowd on every side, great numbers.
Pojniam tub se	Wife and children.
Pw ntog noj, pw ntog haus	Lying around eating and drinking, expression for ease and luxury.
Puas txwv puas tiam	From the beginning of man's generations.
Plaub ceg kaum ntuj	The four corners of the heavens.
Qub txeeg qub teg	Old things, old articles.
Qheb siab qheb ntsws	Open the "heart."
Sawvdaws haiv neeg	All people, everybody.
Siab ua yab ua yauv	Do without heart.
Tas hnub tas hmo	All day and night.
Tas siab tas ntsws	Patient.
Tub txib tub qhe	Slaves, servants.
Tau koob tau hmoov	To be blessed, be of good fortune.
Tuav npe txog ntawm kwj tse	No sooner said his name than he appears.
Thoob zeej teb	All people, the whole earth.
Thooj siav thooj nqaij	One flesh and blood (idiomatic).
Thooj sia thooj nqaig	One flesh and blood (idiomatic).
Tseg txij tseg nkawm	Widowed or made widower, bereft of wife or husband.
Tsis deb tsis ze	Neither nearby or far away, not near and not remote.
Tsis ntev tsis luv	Sooner or later.
Txus saib los txus zoo	The more you see of it the better it is.
Txhiab nias tim puas xyoo	Hundreds and thousands of years, forever.
Txhia hnub txhua hmo	Every day and night.
Ua dab taub dab qhev	To be the slaves of the demons.
Ua dab ua tuag	To do poorly, carelessly.
Us dog ua dig	To do poorly, carelessly.
Ua lwj ua liam	To render useless, destroy.
Ua nkog ua nkig	To do poorly, carelessly.
Ua liam txwv qas ntsuav	To do poorly, carelessly.
Ua phis lis phais lais	To do poorly, carelessly.
Ua tus txias tom caj qwb	Speak evil of me behind my back.
Ua txab ua tshawv	To do poorly, carelessly.
Ua txij ua nkawm	To join in marriage.
Vij dab vij npog	Troubled by evil omens and spirits.
Vij sub vij sw	Troubled by the returning spirits of the departed.
Yim sai yim zoo	The faster the better.

APPENDIX 6

WHITE HMONG PROVERBS

In Hmong these sayings are called "flower language" ('paj lug'). These sayings are in set phraseology and they rhyme. In some cases they contain some Chinese words or Hmong adaptations of Chinese words. Some of the proverbs used are entirely Chinese, in which case we have marked them "(C)."

1. Nplooj tsis zeeg, zoov tsis kaj
   Ntiajteb tibneeg tsis tuag, ntiajteb ntim tsis tag.

   If the leaves don't fall the woods are dark;
   If people didn't die the world wouldn't contain
       them all.

2. Hla dej yuav hle khau,
   Tsiv teb tsaws chaw yuav hle hau.

   When you cross a stream you take off your shoes;
   When you move to a new place you ought to change
       headman.

3. Swm laus swm khoob,
   Zeej laus zeej tib toob. (C)

   Old trees are hollow;
   Old men are feeble-minded.

4. Pluag pluag ua plhu luag.
   Muaj muaj ua plhu quaj.

   The poor are happy.
   The rich weep.

5. Pobkws lig tawb lawv nqhis.
   Pobkws ntxov tawb lawv hmov.

   To covet the corn whether it is early or late.
   (i.e. You can't satisfy them no matter how you try.)

6. Noj zaub tsib hno tsuag qab tsheej nqaig,
   Haus dej qab tsheej caw.

   (with friends) To eat flavorless vegetables is as
   tasty as meat, and to drink water is as good as wine.

7. Dev laus tsis zov loog.
   Neeg laus tsis nquas plaub.

   Old dogs don't keep watch;
   And old men don't like to discuss court cases.

8. Noj tsis noj kuj tuav diav,
   Luag tsis luag kuj ntxi hniav.

   Whether you eat or not at least hold a spoon;
   Whether you laugh or not at least force a smile.
   (used in inviting persons to eat when they keep refusing)

9. Vwb txab vwb liam,
   Cawb txab kum hiam.

   (Not sure of the exact meaning but this seems to
   refer to accusing someone without evidence)

10. Ncauj kab zib nplaig kab ntse.
    Ntxias noj ntxias qhe.

    A mouth of sweetness and a tongue rightly salted;
    But only to deceive you so you will invite them to eat.

11. Foob laij foob tsheb tuam sab,
    Xwm laij nom tuam kus. (C)

    When the wind blows it is bound to hit the big
            mountains;
    When trouble comes (to the lesser) it is bound to
            hit the greater, too.

12. Ntuj dub ntuj txig li lub qhov kub twg.
    Xyov yus yuav tuag hnub twg.

    The heavens (concerning one's future) are as dark as
            the hole in a buffalo horn.
    Who knows when he will die?

13. Roob taus nkim puas tsuas.
    Laus nkim puas hluas.

    An axe ruins a wooden wedge.
    An old husband ruins a young wife!

14. Yeej kom tshij xas looj cib.
    pem kom puj yawb chib. (C)

    The accuser has eaten three baskets of chickens;
    But the defendant hasn't gotten up yet.
    (The guilty is in no hurry to go to his trial!)

15. Qhiav laus qhiav tsis ntsim.
    Neeg laus neeg tsis tij lim.

    Old ginger isn't peppery;
    Old people have no energy.

16. Ncauj hub ncauj rhaw txhaws tau,
    Ncauj tibneeg txhaws tsis tau.

    All kinds of vessels can be plugged,
    But you can't plug peoples' mouths.

17. Xyos tas qus xw.
    Tuam tas tsam xw. (C)

    The faint-hearted die of starvation;
    The brave die of over-eating.

18. Nceb yuav tuaj tsis tim coj mus tsau nruab deg.
    Neeg yuav muaj tsis tim mus nyob qhov zoo chaw.

    Mushrooms come up whether you put them in water or not;
    If one is rich it doesn't depend on where he lives.

19. Phua xyoob tim tsib.
    Qaib qua tim sijhawm.

    You split bamboo through the sides where the branches
        come forth;
    A cock crows in his time.
    (done according to time--a theif comes in the night, etc)

20. Nyuj tsis pom nyuj ntab.
    Neeg tsis pom hiab xab.

    A cow can't see the skin on its neck;
    A person can't see his face.

21. Txawj ntos tsis qeg (or 'qig') txias.
    Txawj hais tsis qeg (or 'qig') lus.

    An able weaver doesn't waste thread;
    An able speaker doesn't waste words.

22. Xyom ntuj thiaj tau ntuj ntoo.
    Xyom niam xyom txiv thiaj tau zoo.

    Reverence the heavens and they will give you good
        fortune;
    Reverence your parents and you will be well off.

23. Pub niag laus noj, niag laus nco tshav ntuj.
    Pub me yaus noj, me yaus zov nruj.

    Feed and care for the old folks and they will remember
        your kindness;
    Feed and care for the young and they will stay close
        by you.

24. Tsev nqeeg tsis yog koj chaws sim taws.
    Tsev vuas tsis yog koj chaws sim zeb.

    Don't try fire in a leaf covered house or stones
        in a shingled house. (don't try my patience!)

25. Hlau txias ntaus tsis tau.
    Lus txias hais tau.

    You can't forge cold iron;
    But you can repeat words once spoken.
    (You may not agree this time but I can speak to you
        about it again.)

26. Tsiaj txhu ua saum tswv txwv.
    Tub ki ua saum niam txiv.

    Animals are responsible to their masters;
    And children to their parents.

27. Noj tsis dua me yaus.
    Xav tsis dua tej laus.

    You can't surpass children for eating;
    And you can't surpass old folks for wisdom.

28. Koj yeejlos tes liag txais luag ncuav sov.

    "Did you borrow my money like taking a persons rice
        cake to devour." (Proverbial way of saying, 'But
        after all you really did borrow money from me
        but haven't yet paid it back.')

29. Tshav ntuj qab zeb qab ca qhuav.
    Los nag qab zeb qab ca ntub.

    If it is sunny it is dry under both stones and logs.
    If it is rainy it is wet under both stones and logs.

30. Hnub qub koj ntau pom dua ib lub,
    Plaub ntug koj ntau pom dua ib txub.

    You have seen more stars and more cases of justice
        than I have.*

    * Expression of politeness used in addressing elders
especially when asking advice or help in justice.

31. Hauv mis koj xub noj.
    Hauv tsoos koj xub hnav.

    You drank at the nipple and wore clothing before
        I did.*

32. Xyoob ib txoog ntoo ib tsob.
    Nqaij ib daig tawv ib phob.

    One clump of bamboo, one trunk of the tree.
    One flesh and one skin.

33. Nrab neeg hais nrab lus.
    Me neeg hais me lus.

    An ordinary person speaks so ordinary people can
        understand;
    A person of no status speaks words of no account.

34. Zaub tsib tsis yog ntxuag.
    Nciab tsis yog luag.

    Bitter vegetables are not suitable to eat with rice;
    Strangers are not good companions.

35. Qoob lig qoob npluag.
    Tub lig tub ntsuag.

    Grain planted late is mostly chaff;
    Late marriage leaves orphans.

36. Yog koj roj koj ntshav,
    Yog koj nqaij xeeb tawv hlav.

    "I am your offspring."

37. Thaum zoo mas nthee ib lub qe ob leeg twb noj tsis tas.
    Thaum phem mas tua ib tug ntxhw twb tsis txawj ob leeg
        noj.

    When things are going well even a single scrambled egg
        is more than enough for two people.
    When things are bad even an elephant won't satisfy one
        person.

38. Muab txab muab tsheej sab,
    Muab txim muab tsheej tim.

    You can rightly accuse me only if you have actual
        evidence of my sin.

* Expression of politeness used in addressing elders
especially when asking advice or help in justice.

39. Fajtim txaim pem cees,
    Txaws lis thiaj txaws thoos thees. (C)

        The lord is in heaven and so the whole world must be
            ruled according to principle.

40. Ntov ntoo saib ceg qhuav.
    Hais lus saib siab qeg.

        When you chop a tree you first look out for the dead
            branches;
        When you talk you better look high and low for who
            might be listening.

41. Hom txawm li muas txwv,
    Txiav txawm li thooj ntxwv.

        "When you cut off a bit of metal to make a bullet you
            don't add to it or take from it." It must be
            as we originally agreed. (Said to one who doesn't
            want to pay what was agreed.)

APPENDIX 7

THE WORK OF THE YEAR
(Approximate)

The first month beginning after the celebration of Hmong New Year which comes the first new moon after the rice harvest. Rice harvest is usually sometime in December or January.

Month		Activity
1	thauj nplej	haul home the rice
	thauj pobkws	haul home the corn
	hlais yeeb	collect opium
2	sau yeeb, hlais yeeb	collect opium
	luaj teb	prepare fields
	ntov ntoo	cut down trees
3	luaj teb	prepare fields
	ntov ntoo	cut down trees
	hlawv teb	burn off the fields
4	cog pobkws	plant corn
5	cog nplej	plant rice
	ua tsev teb	make field houses
	luaj pobkws	weed the corn
6	dob nroj teb npleg	pull weeds in rice fields
	luaj pobkws	weed the corn
7	las nplej	weed rice the second time
8	ua teb yeeb	prepare opium fields
	faus teb	hoe the fields
9	tseb yeeb	plant opium broadcast
	ntais pobkws	pluck the corn
	muab nplej	cut the rice
10	ntais pobkws	pluck the corn
	muab nplej	cut the rice
	thauj pobkws	haul in the corn
	pawv nplej	stack the rice
	dob yeeb	weed the opium
11	pawv nplej	stack the rice
	las yeeb	weed the opium second time
12	ntaus nplej	thresh rice
	yaj nplej	winnow rice
	thauj nplej	haul in the rice
	thauj pobkws	haul in the corn

APPENDIX 8

POST VERBAL INTENSIFIERS
(p.v. int.)

These are particles used immediately following the verb to intensify the action of the verb. In some cases they add a definable aspect to the action of the verb, in which case we have made note of it. We list below those that we have discovered. There may be more.

We have divided these particles into two major categories, each with subdivisions. Those categories are:

A. Unrestricted:
    Those that may occur with any verb.
B. Those that occur with only a certain group of
    verbs. We have listed with each intensifier
    those verbs with which it is used as far as we
    are aware at this stage. Refer to the main
    body of the dictionary for the full meaning
    of the verb.

A. Unrestricted Post Verbal Intensifiers

    1. Combination of two or more words

            ...kiag li (cf. 'kiag')
            ...li ub...li no
            ...ub...no

                ua li ub ua li no Do this and that
                ua ub ua no Do this and that
                hais li ub hais li no Say this and that
                hais ub hais no Say this and that

        (and so with many verbs, e.g. 'cem,' 'txawj,'
        'xyaum').

            ...phis lis phais lais (haphazardly)

                ua phis lis phais lais Do haphazardly
                hais phis lis phais lais Speak nonsense

            ...ua luaj (very, great)
                loj, coob, zoo, ntau, etc.

    2. Single word

            ...kiag (also '...kiag li') (decisiveness)

                mus, los, zoo, yuav, etc.

B. Restricted Post Verbal Intensifiers

   1. Combination of two or more words

      ...hlawv hlo (suddenly and efficiently)

         ntxeev hlawv hlo   tshem hlawv hlo
         ua hlawv hlo   tig hlawv hlo

      ...hlo li (cf. 'hlo')

      ...ncha nthi (loudly)

         ua ncha nthi   nrov ncha nthi   qw ncha nthi

      ...nplawg ntias (all doing together, all helping)

         ua nplawg ntias   cem nplawg ntias
         zaum nplawg ntias   los nplawg ntias

         (also) nyob, hais, ntaus, tuaj, txeeb,
         khiav, qw, nyiav, lawm

      ...nruj nris (nodding)

         tsaug zog nruj nris   ncaws nruj nris
         nyo nruj nris

      ...nrwb nraim (cf. 'tib nraim') (according to)

         ua nrwb nraim   ncaj nrwb nraim

      ...ntem ntauv

         sov ntem ntauv

      ...ntsuj ntsoov (or) ntsuj ntsees (or) ntsuj nrees
         (cf. 'ntsoov')

      ...pawg lug (of many things or persons together)

         nyob pawg lug   qw pawg lug
         zaum pawg lug   pov pawg lug
         ua pawg lug   txiav pawg lug
         cia pawg lug

      ...quj qees (slowly and steadily)

         tos quj qees   rov quj qees
         hais quj qees   mus quj qees
         los quj qees   chim quj qees

         (also) tuaj, ntaus, khiav, ua, etc.

...tawg ntho (sudden burst of action)

luag tawg ntho	nyiav tawg ntho
nthe tawg ntho	quaj tawg ntho
qw tawg ntho	nrov tawg ntho
cem tawg ntho	

...tib nraim (exactly according to) (cf. 'nraim')

ua tib nraim	piav tib nraim
hais tib nraim	qhia tib nraim
mus tib nraim	ncaj tib nraim
coj tib nraim	

...txiv tsuav (a quality of red color)

liab txiv tsuav

2. Single word p.v.int. only used in conjunction with another p.v.int.

...pes...

...pes nkaus (cf. 'nkaus')
...pes dheev (cf. 'dheev')
...pes hlo (cf. 'hlo')

...qos... (or) ...qas...

...qos ntsoov (cf. 'ntsoov')
...qos nrees (cf. 'nrees')
...qos qees (cf. 'qees')
...qos ntsuav (cf. 'ntsuav')
...qos nraim (cf. 'nraim')

Note: These particular words or syllables are more common in Blue Hmong speech but we have also heard them used sometimes by White Hmong and we therefore record them here. They may be only a carryover from Blue Hmong speech pattern.

3. Single word.

...diam (conveying the idea of greatness)

qab diam	paub diam
ua tau diam	muaj diam
ob tug diam	zoo ua luaj diam
zoo diam	kub hnyiab diam
hov ntev diam	hov deb diam
hov loj diam	hov siab diam

(also) tob, ntau, tsim, hluas, laus, nyias, tuab, nyiam, dav, etc.

...dheev (or) pes dheev (suddenness)

ras dheev	nco dheev
tsim dheev	saib dheev
pom dheev	hnov dheev
xav dheev	paub dheev

...dhoog (a quality of red)

liab dhoog

...hlo (or) hlo li (or) pes hlo (immediacy)

qheb hlo	zoo hlo
nqa hlo	ris hlo
rov hlo	keev hlo

(also) ntxeev, tig, tsa, rho, kwv, mus, los, sawv, hle, vau, poob, ua, kaw, muab, txias, hlawv, noj, haus

...lis (quality of yellow)

daj lis

...lug

du lug   qheb lug   tshab lug

...ncees (straightness)

ncaj ncees

...nkauj

zoo nkauj	hluas nkauj
ua nkauj	tiav nkauj
hu nkauj	hais nkauj

...nkaus (or) pes nkaus (completeness)

yam nkaus	puv nkaus
txais nkaus	hum nkaus
nres nkaus	txheem nkaus

(also) puas, ntsiab, tsawv, kawg, ceeb, tib, ti, nthos, puab, txaus, khaws, lo, npuaj, txiv, txij, cuag, zoo, thooj, tim, tsuam, nias, puag, kem.

...nkoos (stooped over)

laus nkoos	nraim nkoos
khoov nkoos	xauj nkoos

472

...npo

    puv npo

...nrees (or) qos nrees (the idea of having been
    so for some time) (contr. 'nkaus') (some-
    times said '...ntsees')

ruaj nrees	ruaj qos nrees
txhav nrees	txhav qos nrees
kaw nrees	kaw qos nrees

    (also) kem, chob, ntsia, nias, khaum, lo

...nraim (follow according to) (cf. 'tib nraim'
    and 'nrwb nraim')

ncaj nraim	raws nraim
sawv nraim	nrog nraim
xyuas nraim	mus nraim
lawv nraim	khaws nraim

...nraug

zoo nraug	hluas nraug

...nrho

tag nrho	tu nrho
txhua nrho	txij nrho
de nrho	

...ntws

ncha ntws	ntxhe hav ntws
poog ntws	nrov ntws

...ntais

ploj ntais	tsaus ntuj ntais
dua ntais	fos ntais

...ntias (cf. 'nplawg ntias')

    puv ntias   ua ntias   laim ntias

...nthi

tuaj nthi	tuag nthi
tsuj nthi	pw nthi
ploj nthi	ncha nthi

...ntho

lov ntho	tawg ntho

...nthwv

    hliv nthwv   nchuav nthwv

...ntso
  rau siab ntso

...ntsos

    ntseg ntsos   nrig nphau ntsos
    paj paws ntsos   caws qia ntsos
    dhia ntsos

...ntsoov (perception) (or 'ntsuj ntsoov'
    'qos ntsoov,' 'qas')

    ntsia ntsoov   paub ntsoov
    nco ntsoov   pom ntsoov
    vam ntsoov   xyuas ntsoov
    saib ntsoov   tos ntsuj ntsoov

...ntsees (or) nrees (sometimes used instead of
    ...ntsoov)

...ntsuav (or) qas ntsuav (or) qos ntsuav

    yaj ntsuav   qias ntsuav
    txab ntsuav   phum ntsuav
    dag ntsuav

...ntxias

    plos ntxias

...ntxhias

    nrov ntxhias   kam ntxhias
    plhaw ntxhias   kwm ntxhias
    plos ntxhias   pob ntxhias
    lav ntxhias   ntaus ntxhias
    hluas ntxhias

...paug

    dawb paug

...ploog

    liab ploog

...plaws (suddenness)

    dhau plaws   tshab plaws   thoob plaws
    dim plaws   cig plaws   tawm plaws
    ya plaws   phua plaws   kaj ntug plaws
    sam plaws

...plhuav

>   tso plhuav   txhias plhuav
>   plam plhuav   poob plhuav

...qees (constancy)   (or 'qos qees') (cf. 'quj
    qees')

>   qawj qees   qawj qos qees
>   hais qees   hais qos qees
>   thov qees   thov qos qees

>   (also) ua, noj, khawb, ntov, nkag, pab, cem

...qha

>   ncaj qha

...rawv   (tightly)

>   tuav rawv   khi rawv
>   sw rawv   npuav rawv
>   puab rawv   puag rawv
>   nqa rawv   cuam rawv
>   coj rawv

...rhe

>   rub rhe   tawg rhe
>   ntais rhe   dua rhe
>   pob rhe

...rhuv

>   daj rhuv

...rhees

>   pov rhees   txawb rhees   laim rhees

...rhuav

>   xuab taw rhuav

...tias

>   hais tias   paub tias   hnov tias
>   xav tias   yog tias   nco tias
>   hu tias   hawv tias   quaj tias

>   (also) ntxub, ntshai, cem, qw, yws, xam,
>   piav, nug, teb, nloog

...tseb

    liab tseb

...tsees

    sawv tsees

...txig

    dub txig

...txho

    dub txho

...vog

daj vog	ci vog	liab vog
dawb vog	dub vog	ntsuab vog

...zoj

xav zoj	fawb zoj
saib zoj	txhuam zoj
hais zoj	piav zoj
nug zoj	teb zoj

(also) nloog, hu, xam, nco, pam

4. With 'nrov'

This is a special class of words used after 'nrov' (sound) describing various sounds and noises. This category includes a great number of words varying according to the noise described or imitated. The list below is illustrative.

...nrov

nrov theb	...nrhawj	
nrov npawj	...nrhij nrhawj	
nrov tawj	...nkoos	
nrov pag	...nkhas	
nrov ntws	...nploj	
nrov tsej	...nplaj	
nrov poog	...nkuav	
nrov ploom	...nrawj	
nrov nreev	...nkhis nkhoos	
nrov ntsiaj	...quaj qee	
...ntxhias	...qis qawv	...nqag ntxhias
...lis loo	...nta vos	...nphiv nphav
...hnyev	...txij txej	...ntxhe hav ntws
...hlawv	...nplij	...rhij rhuaj
...nkuaj	...tawg ntho	

SUPPLEMENT TO APPENDIX 8

ADDITIONAL POST VERBAL INTENSIFIERS

Below are listed additional post verbal intensifiers gathered in the process of assembling material after Appendix 8 was completed. They are therefore not included in Appendix 8. Some do not appear in the main body of the dictionary. These are indicated by (*).

A. Unrestricted Post Verbal Intensifiers

```
...tiag   (or)  ...tiag tiag   (or)  ...tas tas
...tas nrho
...tas zog
...li ntag
...xuj xuav
...zuj zus
...zuj zuav
...zus
```

B. Restricted Post Verbal Intensifiers

  1. Combination of Two or More Words

...chos qos tshwv	lub siab chos qos tshwv
...dheev tsos	nco dheev tsos
...doj ...de	qaug doj qaug de
...hlawv hlias	looj hlawv hlias, tsis nco qab hlawv hlias
...hluj hluav	xuab taw hluj hluav
...looj hlias	tsaug zog looj hlias
...nco laws	puv nco laws
*... ncuj nco	ncaws hau ncuj nco (nodding in sleep)
...nkaug ntsim	no nkaug ntsim
*...nkuj nkaus	dhos nkuj nkaus (close fitting) txais nkuj nkaus (received)
*...nkuj nkis	noj nkuj nkis (of rats gnawing)
...nphoo ntxoj nphoo ntxuas	coob nphoo ntxoj nphoo ntxuas
...nplem nplav	nce nplem nplav
...npliag nplaws	ntub nag npliag nplaws
...nplhib nplhob	nti nplhib nplhob
...nrawg nroos	paub sib nrawg nroos
...nrawv nroos	tuaj nrawv nroos
*...nrhawv nrho	hlua tu nrhawv nrho (the rope broke)
...nrhuj nrhawv	hais lus nrhuj nrhawv
...nrhuj nrheev	sawv nrhuj nrheev

```
    ...ntsa iab              ci ntsa iab
    ...ntsoog ntxaws         tsoo tawg ntsoog ntxaws
    ...ntsuag ntseb          los nag tshauv ntsuag ntseb
    ...ntshaus ntshiv        to qhov ntshaus ntshiv
  *...pluj plaws             cig pluj plaws (flickering
                                 and going out)
                             tshwm pluj plaws (appearing
                                 and disappearing)
  *...pluj pliav             ntsais muag pluj pliav (eyes
                                 blinking)
    ...qog qees              ua qog qees, quaj qog qees
    ...qos zog               qhia qos zog
    ...qhawv qho             nqag qhawv qho lawv qab
    ...taj tsawv             hais lus taj tsawv
    ...tuag nthi             hais tuag nthi, siab tuag nthi,
                                 nyiam tuag nthi
    ...tshuj tshuav          tsiv tshuj tshuav, tauv las
                                 tshuj tshuav
    ...txhaws daws           tawm txhaws daws
    ...zawg zias             los nag tshauv zawg zias
    ...zom zaws              ua zom zaws, hais zom zaws (etc.)
    ...zoj zeeg              ua zoj zeeg
    ...zwb zis               ruam zwb zis
```

2. One word Restricted Post Verbal Intensifiers

```
    ...dhev (cf. 'dhuj dhev' after 'nrov')
                             sib xyaws dhev
    ...kawv                  suaj kaum kawv
    ...lees                  ntswj lees
    ...lias                  pheej lias, tiaj lias, dawb
                                 lias
    ...lus                   siav lus
    ...nciab                 dub nciab
    ...ncuv                  nka ncuv, dai npoo ncuv
    ...nkhawv                nqhis dej nkhawv
    ...npog                  nphau npog
    ...nphaws                ntaug nphaws
    ...npho                  cais npho
    ...nphoob                pham nphoob
    ...nphwv                 dej nphau nphwv
    ...nplas                 ci nplas
    ...nplho                 chaws nplho
    ...nquas                 qhuav nquas
    ...nqhos                 nthe sib nqhug nthe sib nqhos
    ...nqhug                 nthe sib nqhug nthe sib nqhos
    ...nrig                  tshav ntuj nrig, kaj nrig
    ...nrooj                 hais ceev nrooj
    ...nrheev                sawv nrheev
    ...nti                   ntuj tsaus nti, pos huab nti
    ...ntiag                 nias ntiag (cf. 'ntias')
    ...ntws                  poog ntws, ncha ntws
    ...nthav                 poob nthav
    ...nthaws                rog nthaws
```

...nthwb	lwj nthwb
...ntsees	taubhau ntsaub hau ntsees
...ntsug	sawv ntsug
...ntsuj	khiav ntsuj, rov ntsuj
...ntsuv	mob siab ntsuv
...ntsua	mob siab ntsua
...ntshov	ntshaus ntshov
...ntshua	to siab ntshua
...ntxaug	ntxub ntxaug
...ntxaws	nrhiav txhua ntxaws
...ntxiag	ya ntxiag, tseev zam ntxiag, ua noo ntxiag
...nyos	ua qaj qaug nyos
...pliag	ploj pliag
...ploog	liab ploog
...plhawv	phua plhawv, tawg plhawv, tsiv plhawv
...qawv	tom hniav qawv
...sees	ua zam sees
...taws	npau taws
...tsawv	huab ntsau tsawv
...tsha	qheb tsha lawm
...tshwv (or 'qos tshwv')	lub siab chis qos tshwv, tws tshwv
...vos	caws vos
...vus	ci vus
...xiab	ntsuab xiab
...yees	tus yees

3. Onomatopoetic Post Verbal Intensifiers (those used in imitation of natural sounds)

   a. Those used after 'nrov'

...dhev	quaj nrov dhev
...dhuj dheev	nrov dhuj dheev
...ncha ntws	nrov ncha ntws
*...nkhuj nkhoos	nrov nkhuj nkhoos (sound of chopping soft wood)
...nqag ntxhias	nrov nqag ntxhias
*...nqhawv	nrov tib nqhawv
*...nroo luj laws	nrov nroo luj laws
*...nroo rhuj rhev	nrov nroo rhuj rhev
...nroo ntws	nrov nroo ntws
*...nruj nreeb (or 'nruj nreev')	nrov nruj nreeb (sound of cutting wood)
*...ntuj ntiv	nrov ntuj ntiv (of rats eating)
...qis qawv	nrov qis qawv
*...rhuj rhuav	nrov rhuj rhuav (sound of cutting vegetation)

b. Those used after other verbs describing
   action which involves sound

...dhawv dhev	quaj dhawv dhev
...dhuj dhev	quaj dhuj dhev
*...hawv huav	ua hawv huav (of animals growling and ready to bite)
*...iv awv	quaj iv awv (of a dog crying)
*...nqhawv nqho	ua nqhawv nqho (of animals growling and panting)
*...nluj nlob	quaj nluj nlob (of a cat crying)
*...nphuj nphoos	quaj nphuj nphoos (of a tiger crying)
...nroo ntws	ua nroo ntws, ras nroo ntws, nrov nroo ntws
*...nroo ntuj ntws	xob nroo ntuj ntws (rolling thunder)
*...nruj nrawv	nrov (or) ua (or) khob nruj nrawv (the sound of chopping hard wood)
*...qig qag	quaj qig qag (of a frog croaking)
*...qog qees	quaj qog qees (of a large number of people or animals crying)
...tse	quaj tse, hais nrov tse
*...txuj txwv	quaj txuj txwv (of a dog crying in pain)
*...vij vawj	quaj vij vawj (of a dog crying)
*...zuj ziag	quaj zuj ziag (of a cicada singing)
*...zij zev	quaj zij zev (of a pig crying)
*...zuj zeb	quaj zuj zeb (of a pig squealing)
*...nuj neb	hais nuj neb (to speak in a whining voice)
*...tuj tes	hais tuj tes (to speak in a whining or whimpering voice)
*...luj laws	hais luj laws (to speak without expression)
*...nkig nkuav	hais nkig nkuav (of one who always speaks loudly)

APPENDIX 9

CLASSIFIED VOCABULARY

ANATOMY

adam's apple	pob yeeb	genitals	
ankle	yas taw	female	pim, paum
arm	txhais tes	male	qau, hnyuv
armpit	qhov tsos		hnyuv qau
upper arm	caj npab	glottis	nru
artery	leeg	groin	puab tais
back		gums	pos hniav
small of back	duav	hair	plaub hau
backbone	nqaj qaum	hand	tes
between	nraub qaum	back	qaum tes
shoulders		palm	xib teg
ridge at back	caj qwb	head	taub hau
of neck		heart	plawv
bladder	zais	heel	luj taw, dab
blood	ntshav		taw
body (main frame)	lub cev	intestine	hnyuv
bone	pobtxha	large	hnyuv dub
brain	hlwb	small	hnyuv dawb
breast	lub mis	jaw	puab tsaig
buttocks	ntsag, caj tw	joint	pob
cheek	plhu	kidney	raum
cheekbone	xub txig	knee	hauv caug
chest	hauv siab	leg	ceg
chin	puab tsaig	calf	plab hlaub
collar bone	qais	shin	hlaub, roob
ear	ntsej		qhib, roob
outer ear	pobntseg		hlaub
ear canal	qhov ntsej	thigh	ncej puab
ear lobe	taub ntseg	lips	di ncauj
elbow	luj tshib,	liver	siab
	yas npab	lungs	ntsws
eye	qhov muag	marrow	hlwb
pupil	ntsiab muag	mouth	ncauj
lashes	plaub muag		qhov ncauj
face	muag,	nail	rau
	ntsej muag	fingernail	rau tes
finger	tes, ntiv tes	toenail	rau taw
knuckle	yas tes	neck	caj dab
fingertip	taub teg	nose	ntswg
flesh	nqaij	bridge	caj ntswg
fontanelle	hau xaws	nostril	qhov ntswg
foot	kotaw	oesophagus	hlab pas
sole	xib taws	pulse	memtes
forehead	hau pliaj	rib	tav
gall bladder	tsib	side	phab tav

shoulder	xub pwg	toe	ntiv taw
shoulder blades	duav pus,	big toe	ntiv taw xoo
	nplooj pus	tongue	nplaig
spleen	po	tooth	hniav
stomach	plab	molar	hniav puas
testicles	noob qes	umbilicus	pij ntaws,
throat	caj pas		lub ntaws
inside and back	qa	vein	leeg
of mouth		wrist	dab teg
thumb	ntiv tes xoo		

ANIMALS, BIRDS, INSECTS

animals	tsiaj txhu	fly (noun)	yoov (T)
wild animals	tsiaj qus	horsefly	yoov mos dab
ant	ntsaum		yoov tom nyuj
bat (noun)	puav	housefly	yoov mos ntsuab
bear	dais	fox (red)	hma liab
honey bear	dais dev	frog	qav
black bear	dais nees	gibbon	cuam
bee (several	mes, muv,	gnat	yoov qaib
species)	ntab, daiv	goat	tshis
beetle	kab	wild mount-	sai
bird	noog	ain goat	
small chicken-	yij	goose	gus
like wild bird		hawk	dav
bull	nyuj	hen	poj qaib
full-grown un-	xob nyuj	hornbill	hu vaj xyoob
castrated bull		hornet	ntseeb
butterfly	npuj npaim	horse	nees
cat	miv	jackal	hma
caterpillar	kab ntsig	leech	hiab
centipede	laum kib tshooj	leopard	tsov txiaj
civet (Palm)	mab txho		tsov pom teev
cock	lau qaib	leopard cat	plis
cockroach	laum	lice (head)	ntshauv
cow	nyuj	body lice	tuv
cow bellows	nyuj nqov	lion	tsov ntxhuav
crab	raub ris	lizard	nab qa
crocodile	khej (T)	Iquana	nab qa nqhuab
crow (noun)	uab, uab lag	another	kawv
deer (barking)	kauv	species	
Sambar	muas lwj	lobster	cw
dog	dev	locust	kooj tshuab
donkey	luav	monkey (large	
dove	nquab	male, short-	
duck	os	tailed)	txiv thais liab
eel	ntses nab	leafmonkey	nyaj
elephant	ntxhw	Rhesus	liab
fish	ntses	mosquito	yoov (T),
flea	dev mub		yoov tshaj cum

moth	npauj		snail	qwj, quj yeeg
mule	luj txwv		snake	nab
otter	ntshuab		python	nab hab sej
owl	plas		poisonous	
brown fish			snake	nab muaj taug
owl	lib nyug		spider	kab
another	plhaub hwb		spider which	
species			makes a	
panther (black)			web	kab laug sab
	tsov dub,		spider which	
	pom txwv		makes no	
parakeet	leeb nkaub		web	kab laug tsov
parrot	iam		long-	
peacock	yaj yuam		legged	raj ris laus
pheasant	nraj		squirrel	nas ncuav
pig	npua		red-bellied	nas hoo twm
boar	taw npua		Zebra	nas ciav
cas. hog	las npua		tick (noun)	zuam
sow	maum npua		tiger	tsov
wild pig	npua teb		Bengal	tsov nplooj suab
porcupine	tsaug		toad	qav kaws
(long quilled)			turtle	vaub kib
small por-	nploos		water	
cupine			turtle	vaub kib deg
quail	noog w		land	
rabbit	luav		turtle	vaub kib nqhuab,
rat	nas			vuab kib
house rat	nas tsuag		water buffalo	twm
rhinocerous	twj kum		wasp	nkawj
scorpion	raub ris teb		worm	kab
sheep	yaj		earthworn	cua nab
skunk	luj		marble-	
sloth	liab npog muag		worm	kab txws

BUILDING

beam			depth	qhov tob
horizontal	nqaj		erect (verb)	
long side	nqaj tsuag		erect the upright	
foundation	thob fab,		poles of house	
	tim cum			txhos ncej
main crossbeam	yees tsev,		place hori-	
	yees nthab		zontally	txhawb
breadth	qhov dav		horizontal	
build (verb)			beams	txhawb yees
build a bridge	tuam choj		height	qhov siab
build a water-			house	tsev
line	tuam ciav dej		back of	
with brick or			house	qaum tsev
stone	txhim		length	qhov ntev
construct (verb)	txua		level (verb)	qua
demolish	rhuav			

notch (to notch a post to fit crossbeams)	thais ncej	shingles	vuas ntoo
post (a post in the ground to help hold in place the logs of a foundation)	tswg	split (boards or tree)	phua ntoo
		steep (of a vertical roof)	ntseg
rafters (small lengthwise) narrow poles fixed from sides to ridge pole to which roofing is tied	puam qhab	support (as a pole to a leaning house)	txheem
		tiles	vuas luaj
		upright (to set upright)	tsa
		wall (side)	ntsa, phab ntsa
to put on these roof poles	sam qab	to clamp together with poles	yuam phab ntsa
repair (verb)	ntxiv	separation between wall boards	qiag
ridgepole	nqaj ru		
roof (ridge)	ruv	wood	ntoo
of a house	ruv tsev	hard, durable wood for house building	ntoo qheb
to roof house	vov tsev		
roofing (grass) make roofing lengths of leaves	nqeeb cuam nplooj		

CLOTHING AND SEWING

apron	sev	loincloth	thav ntxwv
front	sev sia	measure (verb)	ntsuas
back	sev npua	mend (clothing)	ntxiv khaub ncaws
to sew edging on apron	plooj sev		
button	khawm	pleat (top of skirt)	nre tiab
cloth	ntaub	pocket	hnab tshos
clothing	hkaub ncaws, tsoos tsho	puttees	nrhoob
cotton	paj	rags (old clothing)	khaub hlab
cut (verb)	txiav	sash (belt)	
cut on the slant	txiav sis	men's	siv
dress (verb)	hnav tsoos	leather	siv tawv
embroidery	paj ntaub	to put on	sia siv
gown (long)	tsho tshaj sab	embroidered ends	hlab ntxhoo
hat (cap)	kaumom	seam	leej leeg
headband	siv ceeb	sew (verb)	xaws
insert (to insert in garment)	thiv	shoes	khau
jacket (garment with sleeves)	tsho	silk	tshawj
		skirt	tiab
lining	meem hauv	socks	thom khwm
		thread	xov
		trousers	ris
		crotch	hlws ris
		turban (black)	phuam

COLORS

Black	dub	red	liab
perfectly black	dub txig	bright red	liab ploog
blue	ntsuab, xiav	light red	liab tseb
light blue or purple	txho, xiav txho	dark red	liab dhoog
		speckled red	liab vog
		striped	txaij
dark blue or purple	xiav tsaus	varicolored	huab
		white	dawb
very blue	ntsuab xiab	perfectly white	dawb paug
green	ntsuab	speckled white	dawb vog
lavender (or pink)	paj yeeb	yellow	daj
pink	liab txiv ruav, paj yeeb	very yellow	daj lis, daj rhuv
purple	xiav	speckled yellow	daj vog
light purple or blue	xiav, xiav txho		
dark purple or blue	xiav tsaus		

FAMILY AND KINSHIP

(cf. Kinship Charts Appendix 10)

aunt	
father's sister (older or younger)	phauj
mother's older sister	niam tais hlob
mother's younger sister	niam tais yau
mother's brothers' wives (older or younger)	niam dab laug
father's older brother's wife	niam hlob
father's younger brother's wife	niam ntxawm
great aunt (paternal grandfather's sisters)	phauj pog
brother	
older brother as called by brothers	tijlaug
younger brother as called by brothers	kwv
as called by sisters	nus
brother-in-law	
husband's older brother	txiv laus
husband's younger brother	called by given name
wife's older brother	yawm dab hlob
wife's younger brother	yawm dab yau
sister's husband	yawm yij
wife's older sister's husband	txiv laus
wife's younger sister's husband	txiv hluas
children	menyuam
daughter	ntxhais, mentxhais
daughter-in-law	nyab

father	txiv
father-in-law	txiv
grandchild	xeeb txwv
grandfather (Paternal)	yawg
(Maternal)	yawm txiv
grandmother (paternal)	pog
(maternal)	niam tais
great grandchild	xeeb mujmum
great grandparents (on father's side)	yawg suab, pog koob
great grandparents (on mother's side)	yawm txiv yawg, niam tais pog
great great grandparents (on father's side)	yawg suab, pog suab
husband	tus txiv
mother	niam
mother-in-law	niam
nephew	
son of older brother	tij tub
son of younger brother	kwv tub
parents (or parents-in-law)	niam txiv
sister (older or younger)	
as called by brother	muam
as called by sister	vivncaus
sister-in-law	
husband's sisters	(called by given name)
wife's older sister	niam laus
wife's younger sister	niam hluas
older brother's wife (as called by man)	niam tij
older brother's wife (as called by woman)	tis nyab
younger brother's wife (as called by man)	niam ncaus
younger brother's wife (as called by woman)	tis nyab
son	tub, metub
son-in-law	vauv
uncle	
father's older brother	txiv hlob
father's younger brother	txiv ntxawm
mother's brother (older or younger)	dab laug
wife	pojniam

FOODS AND COOKING

bamboo sprouts	ntsuag xyoob	boil (to boil in water, cook)	hau
banana	txiv tsawb		
beans	taum	to boil over	phwj
long beans	taum lag	cabbage	zaub pob
short beans	taum suav	variety of mustard greens	zaub ntsuab
soybean	taum pauv		
string beans	taum qaib qua	cakes (steamed)	ncuav
bean curd	taum hwv	cauliflower	zaub paj
		choko	taub maum

chop (to chop up fine)	tsuav	peppers	kua txob
		peppery	ntxim
cocoanut	txiv mav poj (T)	pomelo	txiv lwj zoov
cook (to cook for a long time as meat to soften it)	tsaws	potato (sweet) white	qos liab qos yaj ywv
		pound (to pound rice in treadmill	tuav txhuv
corn	pobkws		
cornmeal (steamed)	mov kuam	puckery	pluas
cucumber	dib	pumpkin	taub dag
cut (to cut in pieces for cooking)	txhoov	radish	zaub looj pwm
		rice (cooked)	mov
egg	qe	rice gruel	kua dis
white	hli	rice water	kua ntxhais
yolk	nkaub	uncooked rice	txhuv txua
eggplant	lws	uncooked glutinous rice	txhuv nplaum
fat	roj		
ferment	phwj	rice cakes	ncuav
fry (to fry with or without fat)	kib	to eat other things with rice	ntxuag mov
to add water to frying vegetable	txhaub kua	to pour the water off rice	tsi
garlic	qej	washing rice (rubbing with hands)	zawv
ginger	qhiav		
guava	txiv cuab thoj	dip out rice to eat	hais mov
jackfruit	txiv plab nyug		
leechee	txiv lwv chi	rise (of bread, cakes)	su
leek	dos	roast (over or beside fire)	ci
lettuce	zaub ntsuab	salt	ntsev
lime	txiv rau zaub, txiv qaub uas rau zaub	saltless	tsuag
		salty	daw
mango	txiv txhais	sausage	hnyuv ntxwm
meat	nqaij	scramble (beat up and fry in fat as eggs)	nthee qe
meat cracklings	kiav nqaij		
fatty meat	nqaij rog	simmer (verb)	xiv
lean meat	nqaij ntshiv	slice (verb)	hlais
melon	dib pag	sour	qaub
millet	pias	spice (herbs)	txujlom
mince (verb)	tsuav	steam (as of rice at the side of the fire)	ncu
mix (to mix together)	xyaw		
mushroom	nceb		
noodles (rice)	peev choj		
orange	txiv kab ntxwv	sugar (white)	piam thaj (C)
papaya	txiv maum kuab, txiv taub ntoo	sugarcane	qab tsib
		brown syrup	suav thaj
parsley	zaub txhwj qaib	tamarind	txiv quav miv
pea	taum mog	tea (or tea leaves)	kob sim tshuaj, tshuaj swm(C)
peach	txiv duaj		
peanut	huab xeeb		
pineapple	txiv puv luj (T)		
pepper (black or white)	hwj txob		

toast (verb)	txhiab	to add water	txhaub kua
over or beside		to frying	
fire	ci	vegetables	
tomato	txiv lws suav	to break into	npaws
tuber	looj pum	pieces for	
uncooked (raw)	nyoos	cooking	
vegetable	zaub	water (to heat)	rhaub dej
garden vegetable	txhiam xwm	wheat (flour)	hmoov mog
to remove strings,		winnow (to winnow	
inedible leaves		after pounding)	tsoov txhuv
from vegetable	txhem zaub	yeast	keeb
		for wine, whisky	xab

FIELD WORK

burn (off trees		mark (to make	hom teb
and brush)	hlawv	ground intended	
clear (to clear		for making field)	
off weeds)	thws	overgrown (weedy)	fab
clear the un-		pick (break	
burned branches		off corn)	ntais pobkws
when making a		plant (verb)	cog
new field	txhem, them	plant rice	cog nplej
corn	pobkws	plant in bare	
early	pobkws cauj	patches of	
late	pobkws taj	rice	ntxiv nplej
crops (grain)	qoob loo	plow (verb)	laij
cultivate (verb)	faus	plow paddy	
cut (down weeds	luaj teb,	fields	laij liag
and brush in	luaj nroj	prune (verb)	tav
making new fields)		reap (to reap	
cut vegetation	luaj	with a small	
dig (up ground)	khawb av	half-moon shaped	
to dig out	nthua	knife ('vuv')	
fell (to fell		held in palm	
trees)	ntov ntoo	of hand)	nruam
field	teb	seedling (not	
rice field	teb npleg	when on the	
paddy	liaj	plant)	yub
ground (noun)	teb	rice seedling	yub nplej
grow (of crops		separate (to	
coming up)	tuaj	separate off	
harvest (to harvest		fields)	kem teb
by hand)	muab, hlais	sow (broadcast)	tseb
harvest opium	sau yeeb	sow opium	tseb yeeb
haul (transport by		stack (to stack	
animal or vehicle)	thauj	harvested rice)	pawv nplej
hoe (verb)	khawb, ncaws	stubble	quav nplej
to hoe out	nthua	to beat down	
		stubble for	
winnow (verb)	yaj nplej	burning	tshav quav nplej
(rice)		weed (verb)	dob nroj
		weed second time	las

HOUSEHOLD AND FURNISHINGS

basin	tais phiab	porch	qab khav
basket (rattan for storing clothes)	miaj loos	covered area below porch	qab tsag
plaited bamboo for storage	phawv	quilt	rwb, pam rwb
bench	rooj zaum	rack (back rack for carrying wood)	khib
blanket	pam	room (noun)	cha tsev
bowl (rice)	ntim	sack (large rice sack)	seev
box (for storage)	phij xab	shelf	txee
broom	khaub ruab	shelf over fire for drying things	tsuav ntxaij
chopping block	log cam		
corner	kaum tsev	spirit shelf	thaj neeb
cup (wine or small teacup)	pib txwv	shell (to shell corn)	dhas pobkws
demon (articles over a door)	txheej meej	sifter (noun)	vab tshaus
dipper	tshob	smoke (to smoke of a fire)	ncho pa, pob pob li
door	qhov rooj		
side door	qhov rooj txuas	soot	nkhawb
front (downhill side)	qhov rooj tag	spirit	dab
		bedroom spirit	dab roog
fence (noun)	laj kab	spirit paper (on wall of a Meo house)	xwm kab
fire (cooking)	qhov cub		
firewood	taws		
frame (for making paper)	thav ntawv	sweep (verb)	cheb
gourd	plhauj taub	table	rooj noj mov
granary	txhab	thatch (long grass used in thatching)	nqeeb
hook (noun)	nqe lauj		
house	tsev	tray	vab
back (uphill)	qaum tsev	treadmill (for pounding rice)	cos
front (downhill)	qab tsib taug	tripod	xabcuj
ladder	ntaiv	trough	lub dab
light (to light a fire)	rauv taws	tube (bamboo tube for carrying water)	raj
loom (weaving)	ntos		
mat (plaited bamboo)	lev	wall (side)	phab ntsa
felt sleeping mat	tseeb	warm (to get warm by the fire)	nte taws
mattress	txum zooj		
net (mosquito)	vij tsam, tsam phooj	waterline	ciav dej
		window	qhov rais
pillow (and region where head is placed)	hauv ncoo	work (noun) (esp. domestic)	haujlwm, num
to place things as a pillow	rau ncoo		
platform			
bamboo guest	lawj		
sleeping platform	chaw pw		
storage platform over fire	nthab		

MEDICAL

anesthetic	loog	indigestion	kem plab
bandage (verb)	qhwv	infectious	mob txawj kis
bitter	iab	inject	hno, txhaj
blister (noun)	hlwv	injury	raug mob
(verb)	sawv hlwv	itch (verb)	khaus
blood poisoning	mob npuag	kidney	raum
boil (noun)	rwj	kidneystone	mob tees zis
breathless	txog txog siav	laxative	tshuaj thais plab
bruise	dhoog ntshav		
callous	kaub puab	leprosy	mob ruas
carbuncle	mob fab	lethargic	nkees nkees li
chew	xo	lie (verb)	pw
chickenpox	qhua maj	on the back	pw ntxeev tiaj
cold (noun)	khaub thuas, sab foob khaub thuas	on the side	pw ua ntsais
		on stomach	pw khwb rwg
		malaria	dab tub nkeeg, mob npaws
constipation	cem quav		
convulsion	huam ib tshaj	massage	zaws
cool (as fever going down)	laj	measles	qhua pias
		menstruate	coj khaubncaws, yawg cev
cotton wool	paj		
cough	hnoos	miscarriage	nchuav menyuam
cupping	txhuav	mouthful	ib khaws
diarrhea	lawv plab, raws plab, thoj plab	nausea	xeev siab
		paint (medicine)	pleev tshuaj
		perspire (verb)	tawm hws
dislocation	txhauj	phlegm	qeev
dizzy	qhov muag kiv	blood-stained phlegm	qeev ntshav
effective (of medicine)	ntxim	pierce	chob
epidemic	mob teb hlob	placenta	tsho menyuam
eye	qhov muag	powder (medicine)	tshuaj hmoov
open the eye	rua qhov muag	pregnant (noun)	xeeb tub
close the eye	qe qhov muag	pulse	mem tes
rub the eye	mos qhov muag	take the pulse	seev mem tes, tshuaj mem tes
fever	lub cev kub, kub cev		
flatulence	nchi plab, tsam plab	pulseless	mem tes tsis dhia
foam (at the mouth)	ua npuas ncauj	can't feel pulse	mem tes nkaum lawm
force (as a child medicine)	yuam	pus	paug
fracture	lov pobtxha	recover (verb)	nquag
goiter	mob txia	rinse (the mouth)	yaug qhov
gonorrhea	mob cas, mob yeeg (T)	scab	kaub puab
groan (verb)	ntsaj	scar (noun)	caws pliav
hemorrhage	los los ntshav	scratch (verb)	khawb
heal (verb)	kho mob zoo	shiver (verb)	tshee
hiccough	ntsos	smallpox	qhua taum
hurt (verb)	mob	sneeze (verb)	txham

490

soak (as a foot in water) raus dej
sore (ulcer) kiav txhab
sour qaub
spasm (muscular) ceeb nkaus
spit (verb) nti ncauj
  spit forcibly nto qaub ncaug
spleen po
  enlarged spleen txiav loj, mob txiav
splinter ntshiv ntoo
sprain qes
stiff txhav
  stiff neck txhav caj dab
sting (verb) plev
swallow (verb) nqos
  swallow whole nqos kiag
sweet qab
swelling o
thin (of persons) yuag

thrush (mouth) qhov ncauj tawm
tooth hniav
  pull tooth rho hniav
  tooth root hauv paus hniav
  broken tooth hniav khis, hniav ntais
toss (in sleep) nti, da, phov
tumor lub mob
urine zis
  to urinate tso zis
  difficulty in urinating mob txeeb zig
vernix (waxy covering of a new baby) xwv xyem
vomit (verb) ntuav
weak (feel weak in body) tsaug, qaug zog, nluas
worms (intestinal) cab
worry mob xeeb txob, siab txhawj

RELIGIOUS AND MORAL

angels cov tub txib saum ntuj
angry (verb) chim, npau siab
apostle (messenger) tub txib
archangels timxyoob saum ntuj
ashamed txaj muag
authority hwjchim
baptism txoj kabke ntxuav
believe (verb) ntseeg
Bible Vajtswv phau ntawv
bless foom zoo
church (people) cov xovdawb
  (temple) lub tsev pe Vajtswv
confess (verb) lees txim
covet (lust after) kev ntshaw
create (verb) tsim
Cross (noun) khaublig ntoo, ntoo khaublig, ntoo ntsia tes
crucify teem saum khaub lig ntoo
curse foom tsis zoo

death kev tuag
deceive (verb) dag
demon king dab ntxwg nyoog, nyuj vaj
disciple thwjtim
disobedient (obstinate) tawv ncauj
doctrine (teaching) txojlus qhia
evil (noun) kev phem
evil spirit dab
fear (verb) ntshai
fellowship sib raug zoo (united in heart)
forever ib txhis tsis kawg
glory hwjchim kaj
God Vajtswv ntuj, Vajtswv Saub, Huabtais ntuj
gospel (good news) txojlus zoo xov zoo, moo zoo
grace (gener- osity) siab dav
guilty muaj txim

heaven (in)	(saum) ntuj ceeb tsheej	recant	thim Yexu
(used by Hmong in Laos but refers to abode of dead)		repent	ntxeev siab tshiab
		resurrection	sawv tsees
hope	lub siab vam	sabbath	hnub so
just (true)	ncaj ncees	sacrifice (verb)	xyeem
kneel (bow the knee)	txhos caug, qhau hauv caug	salvation (escape)	kev dim
		Satan	dab Xata, dab ntxwg nyoog
		save (verb)	cawm
lie (verb)	dag	Savior	tus Cawmseej
life	txojsiav	seek	nrhiav
long suffering	siab ntev	sin (wrong and guilt)	kev txhaum, kev txim
love	nyiam, hlub		
lust	siab hlob		
mercy (verb)	hlub	spirit (human)	ntsuj, ntsuj plig
obey (listen)	nloog lus		
parable	lus piv txwv, piv lus	steadfast (enduring)	ruaj nrees
patience	siab ntev	Sunday	Vajtswv Hnub
peace	siab tus tus	teach	qhia
persecute (verb)	tsim txom	thank (verb)	ua tsaug
pity (verb)	khuvleej	true (really)	tiag
praise (verb)	qhuas Vajtswv	trust	vamkhom, muab siab rau,
pray (supplicate)	thov		
pride	siab khav theeb	truth	txojkev tseeb
priest (Buddhist)	hujsam, haujsam	witness (verb)	ua timkhawv
		worship (bow down to)	pe
promise (noun)	lus yeem		
protect	povhwm		
punish (sin)	teem txim		

TIME

qaib qua thawj tsig	first cock crow
hauv ntuj ntsa, hauv ntuj ntsa iab	first light
kaj ntuj txoog	early dawn
kaj ntug huv (or) kaj ntug plaws	daybreak
hnub tawm	sun appears
tav tshais (or) menyuam tshais	about 8-9 A.M.
tav menyuam su (or) menyuam su]	about 11 A.M.
tav niag su (or) tav su	noon
tav su dua mentsis	just after noon
hnub qaij	early afternoon
hnub liab ploog (or) hnub dai npoo ncuv	Sunset time
hnub poob, hnub poob qhov	sun disappears
tsaus ntuj zuag, tsaus zem zuag	dusk
tsaus ntuj ntais	nightfall
tu ntuj sia	full darkness
tav caij neeg nce chaw pw	bedtime
tav caij neeg ntub ntsiag zog	folk fully asleep
ib tag hmo	midnight
ib tag hmo dua	after midnight
qaib qua thawj tsig	first cock crow

hmo ntuj	night-time	ib tsam	a period of
nruab hnub	day-time		several hours
ib hmos	one night	puag hnub hnub	2 days before
ib hnub	one day		yesterday
ib lub hlis	one month	hnub hnub	day before
ib xyoos	one year		yesterday
ib chua moo	one hour (Thai)	nag	yesterday
ib pliag	an instant	nag hmo	last night
ib mentsis	a very short time	hnub no	today
ib chim	a short period	taskis	morning,
kaj ntuj	tomorrow morning		tomorrow
nagkis	day after tomorrow		(morning)
nag nrauv	2 days after		
	tomorrow		

UTENSILS, TOOLS AND IMPLEMENTS

adze	piab	hoe (curved)	hlau
anvil	thaiv	Thai style	pav txhwj,
axe	taus		choj txhwj
axle (swivel)	qag	kettle	hwj
basin	tais	teakettle	hwj kais
shallow basin	tais phiab	knife	riam
basket (open for		brush knife	
carrying earth)	ciblaug	(hooked end)	txuas
bellows (black-		half-moon rice-	
smiths)	lwj	cutting knife	vuv
bottle	hwj	ladder	ntaiv
bowl (shallow)	tais phiab	lamp	teeb
rice bowl	ntim	lock	ntsuas phoo
broom	khaub ruab	loom (weaving)	ntos
brush (verb)	txhuam	mallet	pam thawj
tooth brush	txhuam hniav	mattock	pav txhwj,
bucket	thoob		choj txhwj
chisel (noun		nail (iron or	
and verb)	txaug	steel)	ntsia hlau
chopping block	log cam, tog	paddle (spatula)	duav
chopsticks	rawg	pliars	ciaj
corn sheller	txhuam txwv	plow (noun)	khais
crossbow	hneev	pole (for carrying	
cup	tais	on shoulder)	ntas
digger (stick		pot (clay)	hub
for making		pusher (wooden,	
holes)	tuam txhob	used for level-	
drill (noun)	lig koob txam	ing the ground)	voom
(verb)	lij	rack (back rack for	
forceps	ncais	carrying fire wood)	khib
frying pan	yias	rake	rab sua teb
(round bottomed)		scale (balance)	teev
gun	phom	scissors	txiab
hammer	rauj	shovel	duav
hatchet	hwvtaus	sickle (rice)	liag

spear	hmuv	tray (bamboo or	
spoon	diav	rattan)	vab
steamer (rice)	tsu	treadmill	cos
stool (low)	tog	tripod	xabcuj
woven bamboo	khwb teeb	trough	lub dab
strainer (basket		utensils	
rice strainer)	sab cib	household utensils	twj siv,
sword	ntaj		cuabtam
tongs	ciaj	(tools)	cuabyeej,
			cuabxwm

APPENDIX 10

KINSHIP CHARTS

KEY:

 male

female

 or all relationships are as called by the individual thus marked

Elder siblings are put to the right of the individual.

Younger siblings are put to the left of the individual.

Siblings put only on the right are called by the same name whether older or younger than the individual.

All those on the same line are of the same generation.

══ married

KINSHIP CHART 1

PATERNAL
ANCESTRY
(as called by a man or
a woman except where
otherwise indicated.)

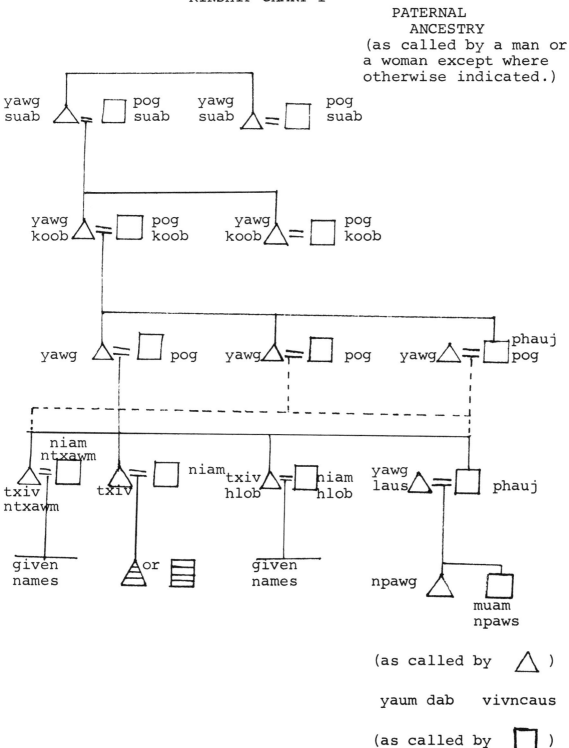

(as called by △)

yaum dab   vivncaus

(as called by ☐)

KINSHIP CHART 2

MATERNAL ANCESTRY
(as called by a man or
a woman except where
otherwise indicated.)

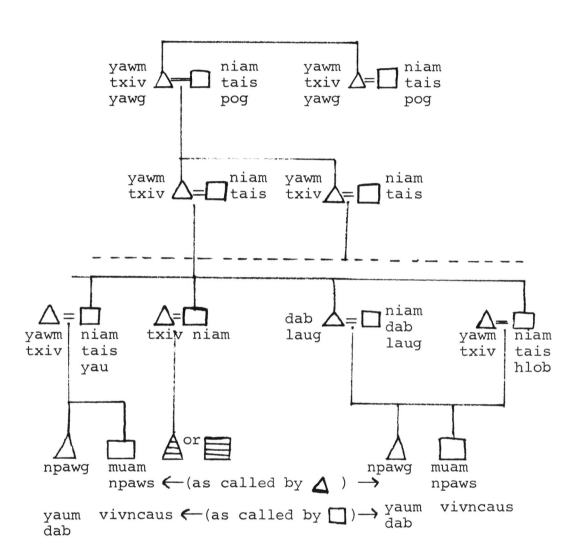

KINSHIP CHART 3

SIBLINGS and POSTERITY

of a MAN

(kwvtij)

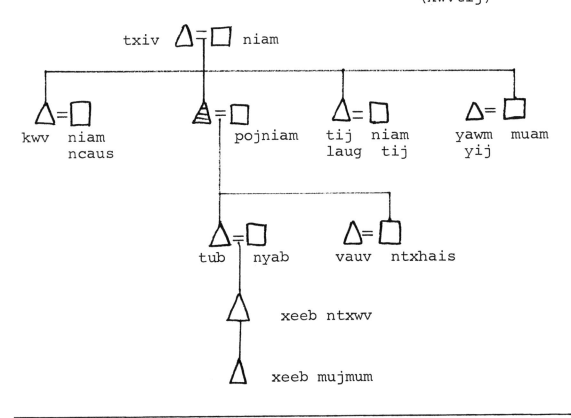

KINSHIP CHART 4

FAMILY of WIFE

(neejtsa)

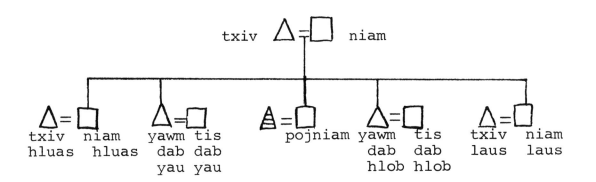

KINSHIP CHART 5

SIBLINGS and POSTERITY

of a WOMAN

(kwvtij - until marriage)
(neejtsa - after marriage)

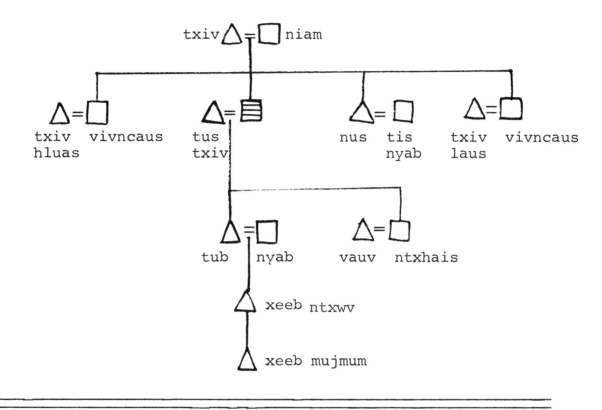

txiv △＝□ niam

txiv   vivncaus   tus   nus   tis   txiv   vivncaus
hluas   txiv   nyab   laus

tub   nyab   vauv   ntxhais

xeeb ntxwv

xeeb mujmum

KINSHIP CHART 6

FAMILY of HUSBAND

(kwvtij)

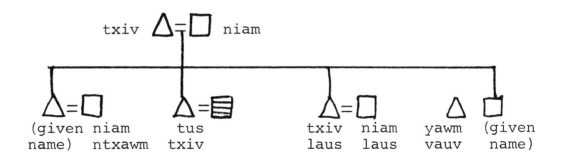

txiv △＝□ niam

(given niam   tus   txiv   niam   yawm   (given
name)   ntxawm   txiv   laus   laus   vauv   name)

SOUTHEAST ASIA PROGRAM PUBLICATIONS
Cornell University

Studies on Southeast Asia

Number 16   *Cutting across the Lands: An Annotated Bibliography on Natural Resource Management and Community Development in Indonesia, the Philippines, and Malaysia,* ed. Eveline Ferretti. 1997. 329 pp. ISBN 0-87727-133-X.

Number 15   *The Revolution Falters: The Left in Philippine Politics after 1986,* ed. Patricio N. Abinales. 1996. Second printing, 2002. 182 pp. ISBN 0-87727-132-1.

Number 14   *Being Kammu: My Village, My Life,* Damrong Tayanin. 1994. 138 pp., 22 tables, illus., maps. ISBN 0-87727-130-5.

Number 13   *The American War in Vietnam,* ed. Jayne Werner, David Hunt. 1993. 132 pp. ISBN 0-87727-131-3.

Number 12   *The Political Legacy of Aung San,* ed. Josef Silverstein. Revised edition 1993. 169 pp. ISBN 0-87727-128-3.

Number 10   *Studies on Vietnamese Language and Literature: A Preliminary Bibliography,* Nguyen Dinh Tham. 1992. 227 pp. ISBN 0-87727-127-5.

Number 9   *A Secret Past,* Dokmaisot, trans. Ted Strehlow. 1992. 2nd printing 1997. 72 pp. ISBN 0-87727-126-7.

Number 8   *From PKI to the Comintern, 1924–1941: The Apprenticeship of the Malayan Communist Party,* Cheah Boon Kheng. 1992. 147 pp. ISBN 0-87727-125-9.

Number 7   *Intellectual Property and US Relations with Indonesia, Malaysia, Singapore, and Thailand,* Elisabeth Uphoff. 1991. 67 pp. ISBN 0-87727-124-0.

Number 6   *The Rise and Fall of the Communist Party of Burma (CPB),* Bertil Lintner. 1990. 124 pp. 26 illus., 14 maps. ISBN 0-87727-123-2.

Number 5   *Japanese Relations with Vietnam: 1951–1987,* Masaya Shiraishi. 1990. 174 pp. ISBN 0-87727-122-4.

Number 3   *Postwar Vietnam: Dilemmas in Socialist Development,* ed. Christine White, David Marr. 1988. 2nd printing 1993. 260 pp. ISBN 0-87727-120-8.

Number 2   *The Dobama Movement in Burma (1930–1938),* Khin Yi. 1988. 160 pp. ISBN 0-87727-118-6.

Cornell Modern Indonesia Project Publications

Number 75   *A Tour of Duty: Changing Patterns of Military Politics in Indonesia in the 1990s.* Douglas Kammen and Siddharth Chandra. 1999. 99 pp. ISBN 0-87763-049-6.

Number 74   *The Roots of Acehnese Rebellion 1989–1992,* Tim Kell. 1995. 103 pp. ISBN 0-87763-040-2.

Number 73   *"White Book" on the 1992 General Election in Indonesia,* trans. Dwight King. 1994. 72 pp. ISBN 0-87763-039-9.

Number 72   *Popular Indonesian Literature of the Qur'an,* Howard M. Federspiel. 1994. 170 pp. ISBN 0-87763-038-0.

Number 71   *A Javanese Memoir of Sumatra, 1945–1946: Love and Hatred in the Liberation War,* Takao Fusayama. 1993. 150 pp. ISBN 0-87763-037-2.

Number 70   *East Kalimantan: The Decline of a Commercial Aristocracy,* Burhan Magenda. 1991. 120 pp. ISBN 0-87763-036-4.

Number 69 *The Road to Madiun: The Indonesian Communist Uprising of 1948,* Elizabeth Ann Swift. 1989. 120 pp. ISBN 0-87763-035-6.

Number 68 *Intellectuals and Nationalism in Indonesia: A Study of the Following Recruited by Sutan Sjahrir in Occupation Jakarta,* J. D. Legge. 1988. 159 pp. ISBN 0-87763-034-8.

Number 67 *Indonesia Free: A Biography of Mohammad Hatta,* Mavis Rose. 1987. 252 pp. ISBN 0-87763-033-X.

Number 66 *Prisoners at Kota Cane,* Leon Salim, trans. Audrey Kahin. 1986. 112 pp. ISBN 0-87763-032-1.

Number 65 *The Kenpeitai in Java and Sumatra,* trans. Barbara G. Shimer, Guy Hobbs, intro. Theodore Friend. 1986. 80 pp. ISBN 0-87763-031-3.

Number 64 *Suharto and His Generals: Indonesia's Military Politics, 1975–1983,* David Jenkins. 1984. 4th printing 1997. 300 pp. ISBN 0-87763-030-5.

Number 62 *Interpreting Indonesian Politics: Thirteen Contributions to the Debate, 1964–1981,* ed. Benedict Anderson, Audrey Kahin, intro. Daniel S. Lev. 1982. 3rd printing 1991. 172 pp. ISBN 0-87763-028-3.

Number 60 *The Minangkabau Response to Dutch Colonial Rule in the Nineteenth Century,* Elizabeth E. Graves. 1981. 157 pp. ISBN 0-87763-000-3.

Number 59 *Breaking the Chains of Oppression of the Indonesian People: Defense Statement at His Trial on Charges of Insulting the Head of State, Bandung, June 7–10, 1979,* Heri Akhmadi. 1981. 201 pp. ISBN 0-87763-001-1.

Number 57 *Permesta: Half a Rebellion,* Barbara S. Harvey. 1977. 174 pp. ISBN 0-87763-003-8.

Number 55 *Report from Banaran: The Story of the Experiences of a Soldier during the War of Independence,* Maj. Gen. T. B. Simatupang. 1972. 186 pp. ISBN 0-87763-005-4.

Number 52 *A Preliminary Analysis of the October 1 1965, Coup in Indonesia (Prepared in January 1966),* Benedict R. Anderson, Ruth T. McVey, assist. Frederick P. Bunnell. 1971. 3rd printing 1990. 174 pp. ISBN 0-87763-008-9.

Number 51 *The Putera Reports: Problems in Indonesian-Japanese War-Time Cooperation,* Mohammad Hatta, trans., intro. William H. Frederick. 1971. 114 pp. ISBN 0-87763-009-7.

Number 50 *Schools and Politics: The Kaum Muda Movement in West Sumatra (1927–1933),* Taufik Abdullah. 1971. 257 pp. ISBN 0-87763-010-0.

Number 49 *The Foundation of the Partai Muslimin Indonesia,* K. E. Ward. 1970. 75 pp. ISBN 0-87763-011-9.

Number 48 *Nationalism, Islam and Marxism,* Soekarno, intro. Ruth T. McVey. 1970. 2nd printing 1984. 62 pp. ISBN 0-87763-012-7.

Number 43 *State and Statecraft in Old Java: A Study of the Later Mataram Period, 16th to 19th Century,* Soemarsaid Moertono. Revised edition 1981. 180 pp. ISBN 0-87763-017-8.

Number 39 Preliminary Checklist of Indonesian Imprints (1945-1949), John M. Echols. 186 pp. ISBN 0-87763-025-9.

Number 37 *Mythology and the Tolerance of the Javanese,* Benedict R. O'G. Anderson. 2nd edition 1997. 104 pp., 65 illus. ISBN 0-87763-041-0.

Number 25   *The Communist Uprisings of 1926–1927 in Indonesia: Key Documents*, ed.,
             intro. Harry J. Benda, Ruth T. McVey. 1960. 2nd printing 1969. 177 pp.
             ISBN 0-87763-024-0.

Number 7   *The Soviet View of the Indonesian Revolution*, Ruth T. McVey. 1957. 3rd
             printing 1969. 90 pp. ISBN 0-87763-018-6.

Number 6   *The Indonesian Elections of 1955*, Herbert Feith. 1957. 2nd printing 1971.
             91 pp. ISBN 0-87763-020-8.

Translation Series

Volume 4   *Approaching Suharto's Indonesia from the Margins*, ed. Takashi Shiraishi.
             1994. 153 pp. ISBN 0-87727-403-7.

Volume 3   *The Japanese in Colonial Southeast Asia*, ed. Saya Shiraishi, Takashi
             Shiraishi. 1993. 172 pp. ISBN 0-87727-402-9.

Volume 2   *Indochina in the 1940s and 1950s*, ed. Takashi Shiraishi, Motoo Furuta.
             1992. 196 pp. ISBN 0-87727-401-0.

Volume 1   *Reading Southeast Asia*, ed. Takashi Shiraishi. 1990. 188 pp.

             ISBN 0-87727-400-2.

Language Texts

INDONESIAN

Beginning Indonesian through Self-Instruction, John U. Wolff, Dédé Oetomo, Daniel
     Fietkiewicz. 3rd revised edition 1992. Vol. 1. 115 pp. ISBN 0-87727-529-7. Vol.
     2. 434 pp. ISBN 0-87727-530-0. Vol. 3. 473 pp. ISBN 0-87727-531-9.

Indonesian Readings, John U. Wolff. 1978. 4th printing 1992. 480 pp.
     ISBN 0-87727-517-3

Indonesian Conversations, John U. Wolff. 1978. 3rd printing 1991. 297 pp.
     ISBN 0-87727-516-5

Formal Indonesian, John U. Wolff. 2nd revised edition 1986. 446 pp.
     ISBN 0-87727-515-7

TAGALOG

Pilipino through Self-Instruction, John U. Wolff, Maria Theresa C. Centeno, Der-Hwa
     V. Rau. 1991. Vol. 1. 342 pp. ISBN 0-87727—525-4. Vol. 2. 378 pp. ISBN 0-87727-
     526-2. Vol 3. 431 pp. ISBN 0-87727-527-0. Vol. 4. 306 pp. ISBN 0-87727-528-9.

THAI

A. U. A. Language Center Thai Course, J. Marvin Brown. Originally published by the
     American University Alumni Association Language Center, 1974. Reissued by
     Cornell Southeast Asia Program, 1991, 1992. Book 1. 267 pp. ISBN 0-87727-506-
     8. Book 2. 288 pp. ISBN 0-87727-507-6. Book 3. 247 pp. ISBN 0-87727-508-4.

A. U. A. Language Center Thai Course, Reading and Writing Text (mostly reading), 1979.
     Reissued 1997. 164 pp. ISBN 0-87727-511-4.

A. U. A. Language Center Thai Course, Reading and Writing Workbook (mostly writing),
     1979. Reissued 1997. 99 pp. ISBN 0-87727-512-2.

KHMER

Cambodian System of Writing and Beginning Reader, Franklin E. Huffman. Originally published by Yale University Press, 1970. Reissued by Cornell Southeast Asia Program, 4th printing 2002. 365 pp. ISBN 0-300-01314-0.

Modern Spoken Cambodian, Franklin E. Huffman, assist. Charan Promchan, Chhom-Rak Thong Lambert. Originally published by Yale University Press, 1970. Reissued by Cornell Southeast Asia Program, 3rd printing 1991. 451 pp. ISBN 0-300-01316-7.

Intermediate Cambodian Reader, ed. Franklin E. Huffman, assist. Im Proum. Originally published by Yale University Press, 1972. Reissued by Cornell Southeast Asia Program, 1988. 499 pp. ISBN 0-300-01552-6.

Cambodian Literary Reader and Glossary, Franklin E. Huffman, Im Proum. Originally published by Yale University Press, 1977. Reissued by Cornell Southeast Asia Program, 1988. 494 pp. ISBN 0-300-02069-4.

HMONG

White Hmong-English Dictionary, Ernest E. Heimbach. 1969. 8th printing, 2002. 523 pp. ISBN 0-87727-075-9.

VIETNAMESE

Intermediate Spoken Vietnamese, Franklin E. Huffman, Tran Trong Hai. 1980. 3rd printing 1994. ISBN 0-87727-500-9.

* * *

Southeast Asian Studies: Reorientations. Craig J. Reynolds and Ruth McVey. Frank H. Golay Lectures 2 & 3. 70 pp. ISBN 0-87727-301-4.

Javanese Literature in Surakarta Manuscripts, Nancy K. Florida. Vol. 1, *Introduction and Manuscripts of the Karaton Surakarta.* 1993. 410 pp. Frontispiece, illustrations. Hard cover, ISBN 0-87727-602-1, Paperback, ISBN 0-87727-603-X. Vol. 2, *Manuscripts of the Mangkunagaran Palace.* 2000. 576 pp. Frontispiece, illustrations. Paperback, ISBN 0-87727-604-8.

Sbek Thom: Khmer Shadow Theater. Pech Tum Kravel, trans. Sos Kem, ed. Thavro Phim, Sos Kem, Martin Hatch. 1996. 363 pp., 153 photographs. ISBN 0-87727-620-X.

In the Mirror: Literature and Politics in Siam in the American Era, ed. Benedict R. O'G. Anderson, trans. Benedict R. O'G. Anderson, Ruchira Mendiones. 1985. 2nd printing 1991. 303 pp. Paperback. ISBN 974-210-380-1.

To order, please contact:

Cornell University
SEAP Distribution Center
369 Pine Tree Rd.
Ithaca, NY 14850-2819 USA

Online: http://www.einaudi.cornell.edu/southeastasia/publications
Tel: 1-877-865-2432 (Toll free – U.S.)
Fax: (607) 255-7534

E-mail: SEAP-Pubs@cornell.edu
Orders must be prepaid by check or credit card (VISA, MasterCard, Discover).